"Assembling urgent conversations in decolonial, transnational, and intersectional feminist research from a rich array of geopolitical perspectives, the editors of *Pluriversal Conversations on Transnational Feminisms* compellingly argue for the need to transgress methodological nationalism. The book will be a vital resource for scholars interested in genre- and border-crossing knowledge production."

Prof. Neda Atanasoski, *Dept. of Women, Gender and Sexuality Studies, University of Maryland College Park, USA; Author of* Humanitarian Violence: the U.S. Deployment of Diversity *(2013)*

"This volume of outstanding essays contributes to current conversations on pluriversality, by bringing together transnational, intersectional and decolonial feminist methods and perspectives. It draws on a multiplicity of locations and modes of knowing – and forms of writing – to radically rethink key questions around justice and solidarity, for feminists across the Global North and South."

Prof. Srila Roy, *University of Witwaterstrand, South Africa; Author of* Changing the Subject. Feminist and Queer Politics in Neoliberal India *(2022)*

"This edited collection is, as Marisol de Cadena and Mario Blaser (2018) express it "*A world of many worlds*", capaciously conversing across South/East/North/ West disparate contexts, using a smorgasbord of academic and creative genres to transgress methodological nationalism. It is an experimental and adventurous text, which includes both emerging and seasoned academic voices. One gets the feeling that the process of pluriversal conversing and writing the book was as significant as the book product for the authors."

Vivienne Bozalek, *Emerita Professor, Department of Women's and Gender Studies, University of the Western Cape, South Africa; Co-editor of* Higher Education Hauntologies. Living with Ghosts for a Justice-to-come *(2021)*

Pluriversal Conversations on Transnational Feminisms

This edited volume brings transnational feminisms in conversation with intersectional and decolonial approaches. The conversation is pluriversal; it voices and reflects upon a plurality of geo- and corpopolitical as well as epistemic locations in specific Global South/East/North/West contexts. The aim is to explore analytical modes that encourage transgressing methodological nationalisms which sustain unequal global power relations and which are still ingrained in the disciplinary perspectives that define much social science and humanities research.

A main focus of the volume is methodological. It asks how an engagement with transnational, intersectional, and decolonial feminisms can stimulate border crossings. Boundaries in academic knowledge-building, shaped by the limitations imposed by methodological nationalisms, are challenged in the book. The same applies to boundaries of conventional – disembodied and ethically unaffected – academic writing modes. The transgressive methodological aims are also pursued through mixing genres and shifting boundaries between academic and creative writing.

Pluriversal Conversations on Transnational Feminisms is intended for broad global audiences of researchers, teachers, professionals, students (from undergraduate to postgraduate levels), activists, and NGOs, interested in questions about decoloniality, intersectionality, and transnational feminisms, as well as in methodologies for boundary transgressing knowledge-building.

Nina Lykke is Professor Emerita, Gender Studies, Linköping University, Sweden, and Adjunct Professor, Aarhus University, Denmark.

Redi Koobak is Chancellor's Fellow and Senior Lecturer in Interdisciplinary Gender Studies, University of Strathclyde, UK.

Petra Bakos is a literary scholar with a PhD in comparative gender studies from the Central European University (CEU), Hungary/Austria.

Swati Arora is Lecturer in Performance and Global South Studies at Queen Mary University of London, UK.

Kharnita Mohamed is Lecturer in Anthropology at the University of Cape Town (UCT), South Africa.

Routledge Advances in Feminist Studies and Intersectionality

Routledge Advances in Feminist Studies and Intersectionality is committed to the development of new feminist and pro-feminist perspectives on changing gender relations, with special attention to:

- Intersections between gender and power differentials based on age, class, dis/abilities, ethnicity, nationality, racialisation, sexuality, violence, and other social divisions.
- Intersections of societal dimensions and processes of continuity and change: culture, economy, generativity, polity, sexuality, science and technology;
- Embodiment: Intersections of discourse and materiality, and of sex and gender.
- Transdisciplinarity: intersections of humanities, social sciences, medical, technical and natural sciences.
- Intersections of different branches of feminist theorizing, including: historical materialist feminisms, postcolonial and anti-racist feminisms, radical feminisms, sexual difference feminisms, queer feminisms, cyber feminisms, posthuman feminisms, critical studies on men and masculinities.
- A critical analysis of the travelling of ideas, theories and concepts.
- A politics of location, reflexivity and transnational contextualising that reflects the basis of the Series framed within European diversity and transnational power relations.

Managing Editors:
Prof. Jeff Hearn, Örebro University, Sweden
Prof. Nina Lykke, Linköping University, Sweden

Editorial Board Members:
Dr. Kathy Davis, Institute for History and Culture, Utrecht, The Netherlands
Prof. Anna G. Jónasdóttir, Örebro University, Sweden
Prof. Elżbieta H. Oleksy, University of Łódź, Poland
Dr. Andrea Petö, Central European University, Hungary
Prof. Ann Phoenix, University of London, UK
Prof. Chandra Talpade Mohanty, Syracuse University, USA

Narratives of Unsettlement
Being Out-of-joint as a Generative Human Condition
Madina Tlostanova

Pluriversal Conversations on Transnational Feminisms
And Words Collide from a Place
Edited by Nina Lykke, Redi Koobak, Petra Bakos, Swati Arora and Kharnita Mohamed

Voices from Gender Studies
Negotiating the Terms of Academic Production, Epistemology, and the Logics and Contents of Identity
Edited by Edyta Just, Maria Udén, Vera Weetzel, and Cecilia Åsberg

For more information about the series, please visit https://www.routledge.com/ Routledge-Advances-in-Feminist-Studies-and-Intersectionality/book-series/RAIFSAI

Pluriversal Conversations on Transnational Feminisms

And Words Collide from a Place

Edited by Nina Lykke, Redi Koobak,
Petra Bakos, Swati Arora
and Kharnita Mohamed

LONDON AND NEW YORK

First published 2024
by Routledge
4 Park Square, Milton Park, Abingdon, Oxon OX14 4RN

and by Routledge
605 Third Avenue, New York, NY 10158

Routledge is an imprint of the Taylor & Francis Group, an informa business

© 2024 selection and editorial matter, Nina Lykke, Redi Koobak, Petra Bakos, Swati Arora and Kharnita Mohamed; individual chapters, the contributors

The right of Nina Lykke, Redi Koobak, Petra Bakos, Swati Arora and Kharnita Mohamed to be identified as the authors of the editorial material, and of the authors for their individual chapters, has been asserted in accordance with sections 77 and 78 of the Copyright, Designs and Patents Act 1988.

All rights reserved. No part of this book may be reprinted or reproduced or utilised in any form or by any electronic, mechanical, or other means, now known or hereafter invented, including photocopying and recording, or in any information storage or retrieval system, without permission in writing from the publishers.

Trademark notice: Product or corporate names may be trademarks or registered trademarks, and are used only for identification and explanation without intent to infringe.

British Library Cataloguing-in-Publication Data
A catalogue record for this book is available from the British Library

Library of Congress Cataloging-in-Publication Data
Names: Lykke, Nina, editor.
Title: Pluriversal conversations on transnational feminisms : and words collide from a place / edited by Nina Lykke, Redi Koobak, Petra Bakos, Swati Arora, Kharnita Mohamed.
Description: Abingdon, Oxon ; New York, NY : Routledge, 2024. | Series: Routledge advances in feminist studies and intersectionality | Includes bibliographical references and index.
Identifiers: LCCN 2023020028 (print) | LCCN 2023020029 (ebook) | ISBN 9781032457994 (hbk) | ISBN 9781032458014 (pbk) | ISBN 9781003378761 (ebk)
Subjects: LCSH: Feminism. | Intersectionality (Sociology)
Classification: LCC HQ1155 .P585 2024 (print) | LCC HQ1155 (ebook) | DDC 305.42—dc23/eng/20230724
LC record available at https://lccn.loc.gov/2023020028
LC ebook record available at https://lccn.loc.gov/2023020029

ISBN: 978-1-032-45799-4 (hbk)
ISBN: 978-1-032-45801-4 (pbk)
ISBN: 978-1-003-37876-1 (ebk)

DOI: 10.4324/9781003378761

Typeset in Times New Roman
by Apex Covantage

Contents

List of Figures	*xii*
List of Contributors	*xiii*
Acknowledgements	*xx*
Epigraph: Sister Ode	*xxiii*
PRALINI NAIDOO	

1 Colliding Words and Worlds: Pluriversal Conversations on Transnational Feminisms 1

NINA LYKKE, REDI KOOBAK, PETRA BAKOS, SWATI ARORA, AND
KHARNITA MOHAMED

PART I
Myriad Tongues and Multiple Emotions (On Affected Writing and Ethics) 27

PETRA BAKOS, REDI KOOBAK, AND KHARNITA MOHAMED

2 A Black Woman Died at the Intersection(ality) Today 33

WANELISA A. XABA

3 Pedagogies of Precarity 37

KHARNITA MOHAMED

4 Scenes of Precarity: Where Is the Exit? 41

REDI KOOBAK

5 Affected Writing: A Decolonial, Intersectional Feminist Engagement With Narratives of Sexual Violence 46

REBECCA HELMAN

6 Notes From My Field Diary: Revisiting Emotions in the Field 60

SUSHEELA MCWATTS

x   *Contents*

7   **Whiteness as Friction: Vulnerability as a Method in Transnational Research**   72

HEATHER TUCKER

8   **From Affective Pedagogies to Affected Pedagogues: A Conversation**   77

PETRA BAKOS, REDI KOOBAK, AND KHARNITA MOHAMED

9   **"I Will Meet You at Twilight": On Subjectivity, Identity, and Transnational Intersectional Feminist Research**   89

EDYTA JUST

10   **Living an African Feminist Life – Decolonial Perspectives: A Conversation**   103

VICTORIA KAWESA, REDI KOOBAK, AND NINA LYKKE

PART II
Portals of Possibility (On Methodologies)   121

SWATI ARORA, PETRA BAKOS, AND NINA LYKKE

11   **Can Methodologies Be Decolonial? Towards a Relational Experiential Epistemic Togetherness**   125

MADINA TLOSTANOVA

12   **Reading Transnationally: Literary Transduction as a Feminist Tool**   139

JASMINA LUKIĆ

13   **Writing Love Letters Across Borders: A Conversation on Indigenous-Centred Methodologies**   155

HEMA'NY MOLINA VARGAS, FERNANDA OLIVARES MOLINA, CAMILA MARAMBIO, NINA LYKKE, AND KHARNITA MOHAMED

PART III
Intrepid Journeys (On the Epistemic Implications of Geopolitical Situatedness)   173

SWATI ARORA, NINA LYKKE, AND KHARNITA MOHAMED

14   **#MeToo Through a Decolonial Feminist Lens: Critical Reflections on Transnational Online Activism Against Sexual Violence**   181

TIGIST SHEWAREGA HUSSEN, AND TAMARA SHEFER

Contents xi

15 **Translocality: A Decolonial Take on Feminist Strategies** 196
CAROLINE BETEMPS

16 **Re-Routing the Sexual: A Regional and Relational Lens in
Theorizing Sexuality in the Middle East (West Asia)** 203
ADRIANA QUBAIOVA

17 **Beautiful Diversity? Diversity Rhetoric, Ethnicized Visions,
and Nesting Post-Soviet Hegemonies in the Multimedia
Project *The Ethnic Origins of Beauty*** 215
DINARA YANGELDINA

18 **Reducing Costs While Optimizing Health? A Transnational
Feminist Engagement With Personalized Medicine** 232
MARIA TEMMES

19 **The Meanings of Chronopolitics and Temporal Awareness in
Feminist Ethnographic Research** 246
CHRISTINE M. JACOBSEN, AND MARRY-ANNE KARLSEN

20 **Disrupting the Colonial Gaze: Towards Alternative Sexual
Justice Engagements With Young People in South Africa** 259
TAMARA SHEFER

21 **Studying Happiness in Postcolonial and Post-Apartheid
South Africa: Theoretical and Methodological Considerations** 274
CARMINE RUSTIN

22 **Decolonization, the University, and Transnational
Solidarities: A Conversation** 287
SWATI ARORA, REDI KOOBAK, AND NINA LYKKE

Index *302*

Figures

17.1 Mosaic from the project "The Ethnic Origins Of Beauty",
© Natalia Ivanova. Reprinted with permission from
Natalia Ivanova. 218

17.2 Art collage from the project "The Ethnic Origins Of Beauty"
© Natalia Ivanova. Reprinted with permission from
Natalia Ivanova. 220

20.1 An example of billboards placed in predominantly
poor Black communities as part of HIV public education
in South Africa, © Guy Harling 2012. Reprinted with
permission from Guy Harling. 264

Contributors

Swati Arora is Lecturer in Performance and Global South Studies at Queen Mary University of London. Her work exists at the convergence of performance and visual culture, feminist theory, Black Studies, and dramaturgies of urban space in the Global South. Her writing has been published in *Contemporary Theatre Review*, *New Theatre Quarterly*, *Wasafiri*, *Studies in Theatre and Performance*, *South African Theatre Journal*, and *Injury and Intimacy: In the Wake of #MeToo in India and South Africa* (MUP). She is part of the executive committee of Theatre and Performance Research Association, UK.

Petra Bakos is a literary scholar with a PhD in comparative gender studies from the Central European University (CEU), Vienna (formerly Budapest). In her thesis, she explored Pannonian borderlands consciousness through literary works conceived as sites and sources of decolonial and feminist resistance against coercive state-sanctioned identity categories. Parallelly with her doctoral research, she has been working as a gender studies tutor and creative writing instructor at CEU's Romani Graduate Preparation Program. She is also an art critic and essay writer, and her first novel is cued to be published in 2024.

Caroline Betemps is a PhD candidate in Postcolonial Feminisms, Gender Studies, at Linköping University. Their doctoral research on "Decolonial feminisms: dialogues and frictions between the Global South and Global North" explores the possibilities of an equitable debate between different North-South feminisms that does not reproduce colonial violence. Their publications include the book *Acá soy la que se fue* (2019), a compilation of stories made by and for migrants from Abya Yala and the Caribbean in Europe; and the article "Decolonial transnational feminisms". Born and raised in Brazil and migrated to Uruguay, Spain, Germany, and Sweden, Betemps has been an activist in social ecology and independent communication before concentrating on anti-racist and anti-colonial feminisms. They identify as a white immigrant and gender non-conforming person. Their current academic interests focus on decolonial and transnational feminisms, anti-racist and LGBTQIA* movements, whiteness, and critical European studies.

xiv *Contributors*

Rebecca Helman holds a PhD from the University of South Africa (UNISA). She is a Research Fellow at the University of Edinburgh, working on the *Suicide Cultures: Reimagining Suicide Research* project. Rebecca previously worked as a researcher at UNISA's Institute for Social and Health Sciences and the South African Medical Research Council-UNISA's Violence, Injury and Peace Research Unit. Her research interests include gender, violence, and sexualities within "postcolonial" contexts, as well as decolonial, feminist approaches to research and writing.

Tigist Shewarega Hussen, PhD, is a post doc researcher at the Hub for Decolonial Feminist Psychologies in Africa at the Department of Psychology, the University of Cape Town. Her research interest focuses on the exploration of a digital Pan-African constellation of feminist activism for social justice across the continent. She also works in the Women's Right Program (WRP) at Association for Progressive Communication (APC). She is the Project Coordinator and Research Lead for the Feminist Internet Research Network (FIRN) project.

Christine M. Jacobsen is Professor at the Department of Social Anthropology, the University of Bergen (UiB), working with questions related to gender, migration, and diversity. She previously directed the Centre for Women's and Gender Researcher at the UiB. Her most recent book is the edited volume (with Marry-Anne Karlsen and Shahram Khosravi) *Waiting and the Temporalities of Irregular Migration* (2020). Jacobsen's current research uses temporality as an analytical lens to examine power relations and experiences in irregular migration.

Edyta Just is an associate professor and senior lecturer in the Unit of Gender Studies at Linköping University. She is also a director and coordinator of InterGender International Consortium. Her field of expertise includes Gender Studies, Pedagogy (founding member of Teaching and Learning Differently Network), and Medical Humanities (affiliate of Centre for Medical Humanities and Bioethics, Linköping University).

Marry-Anne Karlsen is a researcher at the Centre for Women's and Gender Research at the University of Bergen. Her most recent books are *Migration Control and Access to Welfare. The Precarious Inclusion of Irregular Migrants in Norway*, and the edited volume (with Christine M. Jacobsen and Shahram Khosravi) *Waiting and the Temporalities of Irregular Migration.*

Victoria Kawesa is a PhD student in Gender Studies at Tema Genus, Linköping University, Sweden. She is an anti-racist, feminist activist, writer, and scholar, and currently finishing her doctoral thesis "Black Mask/White Sins: Becoming a Black Obuntu Bulamu African Feminist". The thesis is based on autophenomenology as a methodological approach to account for her bodily lived

Contributors xv

experiences of resistance in a white Western context, Sweden, while also having the experience of growing up in a black normative context, Uganda. Her theoretical lens is Feminist New Materialism of subjectivity, Critical Race and Whiteness studies, Postcoloniality/Decoloniality, Phenomenology of Whiteness and Blackness as well as African Feminism and African Philosophies of Ubuntu. She is the co-author of the *Afrophobia report* (2014) about discrimination and racism against Afro-Swedes, and *Colored by Sweden: Experiences of Discrimination and Racism Against Youth With an African Background* (2007).

Redi Koobak is Chancellor's Fellow and Senior Lecturer in Interdisciplinary Gender Studies, University of Strathclyde, UK. Prior to this, she was based at the Centre for Women's and Gender Research, University of Bergen, Norway, as a Postdoctoral Researcher 2019–2022. Current research interests are intersections of postcolonialism and postsocialism, decolonial perspectives in Eastern Europe, transnational and local feminisms, and creative writing. She is the author of *Whirling Stories: Postsocialist Feminist Imaginaries and the Visual Arts* (2013) and co-editor of *Postcolonial and Postsocialist Dialogues: Intersections, Opacities, Challenges in Feminist Theorizing and Practice* (2021). She serves as the co-editor of *European Journal of Women's Studies*.

Jasmina Lukić is Professor in the Department of Gender Studies, Central European University (CEU), Vienna; PI of EUTERPE: European Literatures and Gender from a Transnational Perspective (2022–2026); and CEU coordinator for GEMMA Erasmus Mundus in Women's Studies and Gender Studies (2006–2023). She has served on several editorial boards, including *European Journal of Women's Studies*, and *Aspasia, International Yearbook on Interdisciplinary Women's and Gender History*, and published two monographs on contemporary Serbian literature: Metafiction: Reading the Genre (*Metaproza: čitanje žanra*) and The Other Face: Inputs to Reading Serbian Poetry (*Drugo lice, prilozi čitanju novijeg srpskog pesništva*), and numerous articles and book chapters in literary studies, women's studies, and Slavic studies. An edited volume *Women and Citizenship in Central and Eastern Europe*, with J. Regulska and D. Zavirsek, was published in 2006. Her most recent publication is *Times of Mobility: Transnational Literature and Gender in Translation*, edited with S. Forrester and B. Faragó (2019).

Nina Lykke is Professor Emerita, Gender Studies, Linköping University, Sweden, and Adjunct Professor, Aarhus University, Denmark. She participated in the building of Feminist Studies in Scandinavia and Europe more broadly for many years. She is also a poet and writer and has recently co-founded an international network for Queer Death Studies. Current research interests are feminist theory; intersectional methodologies; queering of cancer, death, and mourning in posthuman, queerfeminist, materialist, decolonial, eco-critical and spiritual-material perspectives; autophenomenography; and poetic writing. She is an author of xvi *Contributors*

numerous books such as *Cosmodolphins* (2000), *Feminist Studies* (2010), and *Vibrant Death* (2022).

Camila Marambio is a curator, a nomadic researcher-artist, a permaculture enthusiast, an amateur dancer, and a collaborative writer. She curated the National Pavilion of Chile at the Venice Art Biennale 2022. In 2021, she held a postdoc position at the Royal Institute of Art, Stockholm. She has a PhD in Curatorial Practice from Monash University, Australia (2019). She is the founder of the nomadic research practice *Ensayos* on the archipelago of Karokynka/Tierra del Fuego, at the southernmost tip of Abya Yala (The Americas); since 2010 *Ensayos* has brought together artists, scientists, activists, policy makers, and local community to exercise speculative and emergent forms of eco-cultural ethics at the world's end. Her writings have been published in *Third Text, Australian Feminist Studies, Discipline, The River Rail*, and *Kerb Journal*, among others. She is a co-author of the book *Slow Down Fast, A Toda Raja* with Cecilia Vicuña (2019).

Susheela Mcwatts has a PhD in Women's and Gender Studies and master's degree in Industrial Psychology. She is the manager of the Arts and Humanities Faculty at the University of the Western Cape (UWC) in Cape Town, South Africa. Prior to her joining UWC, she was the Director of the Verifications Project at the South African Qualifications Authority (SAQA) and the project manager of the Ethical Leadership Project in Cape Town, which was a joint research and teaching project of the tertiary institutions in Cape Town, the Independent Electoral Commission, the Moral Regeneration Movement, and the Premier's Office. She also worked as the Operations and Research Project Manager for the Centre for the Study of Higher Education, previously the Education Policy Unit, a specialist research unit which focused on policy research and analysis and was attached to the Faculty of Education at UWC.

Kharnita Mohamed is Lecturer in Anthropology at the University of Cape Town (UCT). Her research is focused on epistemology, death, disability and debility, race, and gender towards developing conceptual tools for thinking about settler colonialism in and for the Global South. She is a novelist, and her 2018 debut novel, *Called to Song*, received the 2020 University of Cape Town's Meritorious Book Award, was shortlisted for the 2020 National Institute for the Humanities and Social Sciences Fiction Award, and long listed for the 2019 Sunday Times Barry Ronge Fiction Prize.

Fernanda Olivares Molina is a 32-year-old Selk'nam woman. She studied hospitality management in Santiago (Chile) and is currently CEO at Fundación Hach Saye, a foundation created to protect both Selk'nam culture and biodiversity of Isla Grande de Tierra del Fuego. She moved definitively to Tierra del Fuego in 2021 after 8 years of travelling and moving inside Chile. She had three favourite

Contributors xvii

places to live in (San Pedro de Atacama, Torres del Paine, and Rapa Nui) and moved between them from time to time until she decided to return to her ancestral homeland, where she has been improving her skills and connection with the territory.

Pralini Naidoo is a PhD candidate at the Department of Women's and Gender Studies, University of the Western Cape, South Africa. Her work is focused on tracing narratives of (food) seed through women who have descended from indenture in South Africa. As an activist, poet, gardener, designer, mother, and eternal student, she is passionate about the intersections of the social, political, environmental, and creative. She is the author of *Wild has Roots*, a collection of poems, reflections, and short stories.

Adriana Qubaiova is a visiting professor at the Central European University (CEU) in Vienna. She holds a PhD in Comparative Gender Studies from CEU. Placing herself between the fields of Gender and Sexuality Studies, Middle Eastern Studies, and Queer Anthropology, she has been building a new conceptual framework for the study of "the sexual" in the West Asia region. She is currently working on a book project tentatively titled "Hedging Sexualities in Beirut" based on her ethnographic fieldwork in Lebanon.

Carmine Rustin is a feminist scholar who is former Chief Researcher in the Parliament of South Africa and now a lecturer in the Department of Women's and Gender Studies at the University of the Western Cap-e. She has more than 20 years of research and research management experience. She is interested in gender justice, gender-related legislation, and happiness. She teaches Gender in South African politics and culture as well as feminist research methodologies.

Tamara Shefer is Professor of Women's and Gender Studies in the Faculty of Arts and Humanities at the University of the Western Cape, Cape Town. Her scholarship has been directed at intersectional gender and sexual justice, with particular emphasis on young people. She is currently engaged with re-conceptualizing academic knowledge with emphasis on embodied, affective, feminist, decolonial pedagogies and research, and thinking with art and activism. Most recent books include *Knowledge, Power and Young Sexualities: A Transnational Feminist Engagement* (co-authored with J. Hearn, 2022, Routledge) and *Routledge International Handbook of Masculinity Studies* (co-edited with L. Gottzén & U. Mellström, 2020).

Maria Temmes is a postdoctoral research fellow at Tampere University. Her research is on feminist science studies, focusing on sociological and historical aspects of biomedicine. Her PhD (Central European University, 2018) examined the relation between individual patients and broader medical data in systems medicine research and demonstrated how categories such as gender appear

xviii *Contributors*

in molecular medicine research. She previously worked as an assistant professor of comparative gender studies at the Asian University for Women in Bangladesh, where she broadened her research with global perspectives to biomedical research. Currently, she works as a postdoctoral researcher in the project Gendered Chronic Disease, Embodied Difference and Biomedical Knowledge.

Madina Tlostanova is a decolonial thinker, fiction writer and professor of postcolonial feminisms at Linköping University, Sweden. Her research interests include decolonial thought, particularly in its aesthetic, existential and epistemic manifestations, feminisms of the Global South, postsocialist human condition, fiction and art, critical future inquiries and critical interventions into complexity, crisis, and change. Her most recent books include *What Does It Mean to Be Post-Soviet? Decolonial Art From the Ruins of the Soviet Empire* (2018), *A New Political Imagination, Making the Case* (co-authored with Tony Fry, 2020), *Decoloniality of Knowledge, Being and Sensing* (2020), the co-edited volume *Postcolonial and Postsocialist Dialogues. Intersections, Opacities, Challenges in Feminist Theorizing and Practice* (co-edited with Redi Koobak and Suruchi Thapar-Björkert, 2021), and the experimental *Narratives of Unsettlement. Being Out-of-joint as a Generative Human Condition* (2023).

Heather Tucker (she/they) is a feminist anthropologist, researcher, and gender specialist with a strong interest in public health and social equity and over a decade of experience conducting research. She has carried out feminist ethnographic research with LBQ women in Ghana and is currently a post-doctoral research fellow working on a study with the Western Kenya LBQT+ Feminist Forum to measure empowerment and implement mental health programmes among LBQT women and transgender and non-binary people assigned female sex at birth in Western Kenya. Her current position is with the Center for Global Health Equity and the School of Public Health at the University of Michigan.

Hema'ny Molina Vargas is a writer, poet, and craftswoman with four children and three grandchildren. Above all, she is Selk'nam. As an exiled Indigenous woman from her country, Tierra del Fuego, she is one of the three generations that grew up without land, expatriates from Tierra del Fuego when the genocide began, and that have been discriminated against to this day. She is the president of The Selk'nam Corporation Chile and strives to remove her community from the perception of its "extinction", a stigma that, in 2019, finally ended when the Selk'nam Corporation requested the Chilean state to recognize the existence of Selk'nam, in a bill. As an activist, she works to give visibility to her community. The Indigenous community of Covadonga Ona brings together families of Selk'nam descendants who have maintained their oral memory through the transmission of their ancestral knowledge and connection throughout generations. The Selk'nam Corporation, formed in 2015 to guarantee the repair, safeguard, and strengthening of Selk'nam cultural identity, and to allow Selk'nam people to participate in civil matters, is the vehicle through which the Selk'nam present their legal status as an existing organization. As a writer, she has published on numerous online platforms in Chile and Argentina and also a collection of poems *Madre Tierra* [Mother Earth], 2010.

Wanelisa A. Xaba is a decolonial thinker, storyteller, and researcher from Cape Town. She obtained a Bachelor's degree in Social Sciences, Honours in African Studies, and master's degree in Social Development at the University of Cape Town. She obtained her PhD in the Women and Gender Studies Department at the University of the Western Cape. She is interested in merging decolonial thought and ancestral wisdom for Black liberation.

Dinara Yangeldina is a lecturer at the Centre for Women's and Gender Research (SKOK), University of Bergen, Norway. Her main research interests include post-soviet feminist activism, popular culture and media, translation, racialization, and postcoloniality. Her PhD, awarded 2023, and titled, *The politics of Racial Translation: Negotiating Foreignness and Authenticity in Russophone Online Intersectional Feminism and Timati's Hip-hop (2012–2018)*, is dedicated to the travel and translation of the idiom "race as resistance" via Russian-language intersectional feminism and hip-hop.

Acknowledgements

The coming into being of this volume was funded by a four-year grant from STINT, the Swedish Foundation for International Cooperation in Research and Higher Education, project title "New Tools for Transnational Analysis in Postgraduate Intersectional Gender Research – Towards Long-Term International Collaborations in Doctoral and Postdoctoral Training" (IG 2012–5160). The research residencies for doctoral students and postdocs, the conferences, and workshop gatherings at the four partner universities (University of the Western Cape, South Africa; Central European University, Budapest, Hungary/Vienna, Austria; Bergen University, Norway; Linköping University, Sweden), which led to this book, were all funded by STINT, and so was the language editing. We want to warmly thank STINT for the grant that made the project possible, as well as for allowing very generous extensions, when the project was delayed due to personal circumstances (death of the PI's life partner) as well as the COVID-19 pandemic. A special thanks to STINT Senior Programme Manager Mattias Löwhagen for handling our requests for these extensions with care and understanding.

We would like to thank Andrew W. Mellon Foundation for supporting "New Imaginaries for an Intersectional Critical Humanities Project on Gender and Sexual Justice" project (Grant no. G-31700714) at Women's and Gender Studies Department, University of the Western Cape, and thereby strengthening the South African participation in the project.

Moreover, we would like to thank the Centre for Women's and Gender Research at Bergen University, Norway, acknowledging the centre's support to Redi Koobak's postdoctoral work, which – together with the postdoctoral affiliation to Gender Studies, Linköping University, funded by the STINT grant – enabled her to commit to this project.

We also want to very warmly thank all the participants in the STINT project who took part in one or more project events (residencies, conferences, meetings, and workshops) at the four partner universities in Linköping, Sweden (2016); in Bergen, Norway (2017); in Budapest, Hungary (2018); and in Cape Town, South Africa (2019.) Without your commitment to the debates and the book project, this volume would not have materialized. Special thanks *to the University of Western Cape-affiliated participants*: Caili Forrest, Carmine Rustin, Janine Lange, Pralini Naidoo, Rebecca Helman, Susan M. Gredley, Susheela Mcwatts, Swati Arora,

Acknowledgements xxi

Tamara Shefer, Tigist Shewarega Hussen, and Wanelisa A. Xaba; *to Central European University-affiliated participants*: Adriana Qubaiova, Elissa Helms, Heather Tucker, Ida Hillerup Hansen, Jasmina Lukić, Lieke Hettinga, Maria Temmes, Masha Semashyna, Noemi Anna Kovacs, Petra Bakos, Stanimir Panayotov, and Tegiye Birey; *to Bergen University-affiliated participants:* Christine M. Jacobsen, Dinara Yangeldina, Marry-Anne Karlsen, Redi Koobak, and Tone Lund-Olsen; *to Linköping University-affiliated participants*: Björn Pernrud, Caroline Betemps, Edyta Just, Madina Tlostanova, Marianna Szczygielska, Marietta Radomska, Nina Lykke, Vera Weetzel, and Victoria Kawesa.

We also want to thank specially invited guest lecturers and panelists who contributed to the STINT events at the four universities next to the aforementioned participants: Professor Neda Atanasoski, University of California, Santa Cruz, USA; Professor Kalindi Vora, University of California, San Diego, USA; Professor Kari Jegerstedt, Bergen University, Norway; Professor Libora Oates-Indruchova, University of Graz, Austria; from the University of Western Cape, South Africa: Professor Floretta Boonzaier; Professor Desiree Lewis; Professor Zethu Matebeni; PhD student Landa Mabenge; Research Fellow Kealeboga Ramuru, African Gender Institute; and Director Elsbeth Engelbrecht, Triangle Project.

Warm thanks go also to the local project co-coordinators and administrative organizers of the annual residencies, conferences, meetings, and workshops. We are grateful for all the work you did to make these events happen at the four universities: Professor Jasmina Lukić and Administrator Noemi Kovacs, Central European University; Professor Tamara Shefer and Administrator Dr. Susheela Mcwatts, University of the Western Cape; Professor Christine M. Jacobsen and Administrator Tone Lund-Olsen, Bergen University; and Professor Nina Lykke and Administrator Björn Pernrud, Linköping University.

A special thanks to Dr. Björn Pernrud for your invaluable, always very inventive, meticulous, and loyal administrative support as part of the main Linköping project coordination. You, Björn, have shown that administrative work can be an art, and not just an instrumental task, and that its mastery as a sophisticated art is crucial for making a political difference within academic institutions. Thank you very much also for the collaboration on the writing of the application to STINT.

A warm thanks to Dr. Elizabeth Sourbut, who did the language and style editing of the chapters by contributors whose first language is not English, as well as the general copy editing of the manuscript before submission. Thanks for your always so precise and wonderful work with the nitty-gritty, but so crucial language details.

We also want to thank Routledge Commissioning Editor Emily Briggs and Senior Editorial Assistant Lakshita Joshi for support and collaboration on the editing process, as well as the anonymous reviewers for useful comments on the manuscript.

Moreover, we would like to thank series co-editor, Senior Professor Jeff Hearn, Örebro University, for his valuable comments in the final manuscript preparation phase.

xxii *Acknowledgements*

Thanks also to Professor Madina Tlostanova, Linköping University, who – next to authoring a chapter for the book – also took part in the first round of book editing and commenting on contributions in their early stages.

Thanks to Dr. Redi Koobak, Dr. Petra Bakos, and Prof. Nina Lykke for organizing and teaching the creative writing seminars which were an integrated part of the project.

We – the five editors – would also like to thank each other for the editorial collaboration which, in the final and crucial rounds of editing, had to take place only online due to the COVID-19 pandemic. Some things would have been easier had we not had to cancel a planned editorial seminar in the spring of 2020. But we did, indeed, manage to organize very productive editorial online meetings, and met regularly for the whole period of the pandemic; this meant that we also came to share and relate to the different experiences of precarity that the pandemic generated or reinforced for several members of the editorial team.

Finally, we want to mention that the order of co-editors' names on the cover of the book does not reflect a hierarchy in academic positions, but the actual workloads put into the nitty-gritty details of the editing work. We decided collectively to opt for this principle as the most fair solution to a problem that we all feel is tricky to handle in the neoliberal academy.

February 2023
Nina Lykke
Redi Koobak
Petra Bakos
Swati Arora
Kharnita Mohamed

Postscript

We (Kharnita, Petra, Redi, and Swati) would like to express our sincere gratitude to Nina for all her care and patience that steered this book to life. She has been a steady influence and kept the project moving forward from the initial funding application idea through the multitude of the project's events to the minutest finishing touches to the manuscript. She has done all of this through multiple challenges over the years, including the COVID-19 pandemic which required all of us to work with extreme degrees of flexibility, amid anxiety, changed life circumstances and plans, illness, and grief. Her commitment to this book never wavered and she ensured that we stayed the course with grace and integrity, honouring the project's and its participants' processes. A heartfelt thank you, dear Nina!

February 2023
Kharnita Mohamed
Petra Bakos
Redi Koobak
Swati Arora

Epigraph: Sister Ode

Pralini Naidoo

1.
When Lorde said "Poetry is not a luxury"[1]
she wasn't kidding
How often, while struggling to surface,
I have found myself here
in the belonging of a poem,
a language I did not know that I knew

When the world bears down
with its stifling labels
trying to iron me out – flatten my creases,
Poetry, like an errant thread,
dances through me,
unravelling even, my own acquiescence

And words collide from a place
where the deep inside meets the far beyond
creating textures, rhythms and images
from the palette of love's noticing

Here I am free

A friend once confided
"I can only write poetry in Amharic"
This made me smile and sad at the same time
I mused on my mother's tongue, now erased from mine,
and on why it was that Tamil is not the language which forms
on my lips in moments of deep communion

At times like these, Poetry rolls her eyes
she skips, somersaults

xxiv *Epigraph: Sister Ode*

and flips a middle finger at the
"should", "musts" and "have tos"
of my adopted colonial language

This tongue through which you speak,
says Poetry, transcends
the language of the mind, of the oppressor,
of deeply buried silences,
and of things deliberately blacked out
this is spirit's whisper!

2.
Once I sat with you
under the ochre smile of a South African mountain
on the lawns of Montfleur[2]
sharing these words which had surged through me

You – an unlikely sisterhood –
asked questions of these strangely assembled words
and read your lives through
my deck of poems

I believe that you tapped into
your own deeply embedded knowing,
perhaps translating those words with your own spirit
weaving them into your unique trajectories

With and through the cards you shared secret and sacred places
longings deep in your marrow
that not everyone would understand
Secrets, which, even you did not fully understand

It occurred to me just how many we were
disrupting, sharing, reclaiming,
writing, loving and dreaming
These were acts of justice

And through so many intrepid journeys
You were finding ways to honour
the buried murmurs of those who came before us
and creating portals of possibility for those to come

3.
These words have never really been mine
It seems that Poetry speaks in myriad tongues

Epigraph: Sister Ode xxv

and multiple emotions
I realize how fluid she is
and how foolish to believe that her meanings
are stuck in time and place

On days when my clarity drowns in murky pools
I reach for my love poems
in their Tarot deck –
Poems inspired by lovers,
and oceans, and ancestors, and dreams

Then as my heart asks its question
I realize that these old words have new answers,
alchemized by the passions, wounds, wisdoms and visions
of so many sisters

Postscript

A poem about my relationship with poetry, this contribution honours how I have come to know so many of the people who have been a part of the project from which this volume emerged. In 2019, I collated many of the poems which I had begun writing parallel to my PhD process. Perhaps it was my way of resisting the cerebral takeover. I developed the poems into a set of tarot cards which now accompanies me on all my academic ventures. I have had the absolute privilege of having my poems read (as tarot cards) by many of the colleagues who have contributed to this volume. In this rather organic sharing, I have learnt so much about their realities, journeys and what lights their fire. While Sister Ode only mentions the lawns of Montfleur, my fellow voyagers in the project have had poetry/tarot readings in conference rooms, bars, restaurants, on my deck at home and in my lounge. What an honour!! As such, I really believe that the poems have become imbued with their spirit. I am deeply touched and overwhelmed by the trust and intimacy that we have shared.

Pralini Naidoo

Notes

1 Lorde (1993: 37).
2 A venue in the Western Cape, South Africa, where contributors to this volume held a writing retreat in 2019.

Reference

Lorde, Audre. 1993. *Zami; Sister Outsider; Undersong.* New York: Quality Paperback Book Club.

1 Colliding Words and Worlds

Pluriversal Conversations on Transnational Feminisms

Nina Lykke, Redi Koobak, Petra Bakos, Swati Arora, and Kharnita Mohamed

"And words collide from a place" – these words, which form part of the title of this volume, are borrowed from the epigraph, the poem *Sister Ode*, written by South African scholar and poet Pralini Naidoo. She is one of the participants in the international research project that led to this book. The four-year project was funded by STINT, the Swedish Foundation for International Cooperation in Research and Higher Education,[1] and gathered researchers from different parts of the world. The contributors to the book are first of all doctoral students, postdocs, and professors with academic affiliations to universities in South Africa, Hungary/Austria,[2] and Scandinavia, that is, located along Global South/Global North and East/West axes. Several authors also have backgrounds in activism, including arts activism. Between 2016 and 2019, we met through a pre-planned series of conference events and short-term residencies at each other's universities. These events and residencies were organized with the purpose of facilitating continuing conversations across borders and differences. We wanted these conversations to become *pluri*versal instead of *uni*versal, that is, voicing a plurality of geo- and corpopolitical as well as epistemic locations instead of taking a point of departure in a normative, hegemonic, unitary academic mode. The overall aim was to produce a joint volume on transformatory – transnational, intersectional, and decolonial – feminist methodologies and conceptual frameworks. The gatherings gave rise to multiple collisions – of words, worlds, and bodies. Our different geo- and corpopolitical points of departure, the multiple languages involved, different theoretical and/or activist-political belongings, and our privileged or precarious positions in academia created outspoken, and sometimes not-so-clearly spoken, collisions. But, just as *Sister Ode* gives voice to experiences from the project, "unlikely sisterhood[s]" emerged as well. When we – the five co-editors, who, like the group of contributors as a whole, differ in terms of geopolitical locations, academic positionalities, racializations, sexual identities, and other differences – look back on these collisions, they appear frustrating, but also generative. Collectively exposing ourselves to collisions within the project created new knowledges and valuable opportunities for radical worldmaking through vulnerability. Along these lines, we understand generative collisions to be moments that critical researchers, such as the contributors to this volume, inevitably encounter when trying to collaborate across differences in order to make a difference in the world.

DOI: 10.4324/9781003378761-1

2 Nina Lykke et al.

As we are taking collisions of words, worlds, and bodies as our starting point, we hope that this volume will contribute to ongoing efforts to recalibrate academia, helping it to become attuned to radically decolonizing, transnational, and inter-sectionally situated feminist knowledge-building. Moreover, we locate ourselves within a critical-affirmative tradition of undoing boundaries between academic and creative, conceptual and affective, writing. Contributors to the volume share the belief that academic writing and knowledge-building need to step down from the conventional god's-eye position and universalizing outlook, and instead seek embodied and situated points of departure in messy, pluriversal landscapes, where colliding words, worlds, and bodies are the order of the day. Academic writing has conventionally been understood as a disembodied, third-person form of writing that speaks with a universalizing and unifying voice. In contrast, in recent decades, knowledge production that is ethically committed to struggles for social and environmental justice worldwide has often been linked to writing differently (Stacey and Wolff 2013; Lykke 2014; Pandian and McLean 2017) – writing in the first-person, writing with the body, affect and emotions, writing from critically self-reflective positions and situatednesses. In resonance with these kinds of alternative writing commitments, the volume begins from the belief that engagements with transnational, intersectional, and decolonial feminisms require a radical rethinking of speaking positions, voices, and writing modes.

Askew Arrivals in Places Where Words Collide

(Excerpt from an editorial meeting[3])

Kharnita: We should definitely write something about the life of the project in the introduction. It's so fascinating, but you have to be inside it to know, and in some ways, perhaps, some of us were insiders, but still not quite so inside in terms of having a sense of power over the conceptual terrain through which the project travelled, if that makes sense?

Redi: When talking to different participants over the course of the years, it's often struck me that people have been unsure what this project is about. The official title of the project was "New Tools for Transnational Analysis in Postgraduate Intersectional Gender Research", while this book, which has been on our agenda from the very start, was given the working title "New Tools in Transnational Feminisms". But we've spent so much time discussing: What are these "new tools"? What is "transnationalism"? What are "transnational feminisms"? What is it that we're doing? I feel it was running through as a constant theme in all the gatherings, and also outside of them. So many project participants have asked me such questions over the years. There's been a lot of uncertainty. I've been wondering why that is. Is there an ambiguity in the topic? In the conceptual framework? Why this confusion? I don't know if others have perceived it in a similar way, but I've perceived some kind of uncertainty around what the project is about and also what it is that we hope to achieve with the book.

Colliding Words and Worlds 3

Swati: Yeah, I came in towards the end of the project, so I always felt like an outsider, at the periphery. I felt that there was a pre-existing, overarching plan, and that you all knew each other. I attended the very last project event in South Africa in 2019, a two-day seminar, and then somehow ended up as part of the editorial team. I think the working title of the project "New Tools in Transnational Feminisms" was a source of confusion for me. It sounded as though we're delving into new territory, inventing something new. Again, I wasn't really sure what the book intends to achieve. Now, having read all the contributions, I think what's happening is very exciting. So, I think it was the working title itself that was deceptive.

Kharnita: At the same time, if you look at the breadth of what emerged in the process, I think the ambivalence around the working title provided such a broad scope for our work. There's something very productive and fertile about this breadth. So, maybe having a working title that people aren't sure of and don't agree on allows something.

Petra: To connect back to the questions that Redi just raised. I participated from the second gathering in Sweden in 2016, which also included the first residence period of the project. I also took part in the ensuing three annual gatherings in Bergen (2017), Budapest (2018), and Cape Town (2019). All these events were very different, and therefore people who entered the project, or came back to it, at different points in time, got a different general sense of what the project is about. I think this is one of the reasons why people have different perceptions of it. Like you, Redi, I also received inquiries from various project participants. During the past few months, I've been asked questions like: Are we still on? Is this still happening? Sometimes I also wondered myself. I partly attribute these ponderings to the general sense of uncertainty that came with the COVID-19 pandemic, which has made people less busy, but at the same time more busy, or busy in a different way. Also, people are hungrier for certainties. At the same time, when I think about the whole length of the project, I would say that those participants who enjoyed the process most are the ones who actually allowed themselves the space for experimentation within it. I think this is how we ended up with such a versatile, and at the same time really exciting, body of texts, that more and more project participants embraced the idea that we're searching for something emerging, rather than representing something already given . . .

Kharnita: So, the idea of "new tools" allowed us to think that we're searching for something, maybe searching for the new, but not really finding the new, and instead (laughs) returning to the old, right?

Swati: The title should perhaps be "Searching for dot dot dot"?

Kharnita: Yeah, it was this open space that was so productive.

Nina: Going back to what you just said, Swati, about the working title "New Tools in Transnational Feminisms" as deceptive . . . I think, in my capacity as project leader, I've so many times emphasized that this

4 *Nina Lykke et al.*

was just a working title and not an endpoint, that is, that this was the neoliberal-sounding title that actually brought us the grant to fund the project, and funding is, as you know, such a bloody important thing in academia these days. Without it, the gatherings we organized to think collectively about transnational, intersectional, and decolonial feminisms couldn't have materialized. I do agree with all the participants who didn't like the working title or felt ambivalent about it. I never really liked it either. But I wanted a grant to enable us to gather together as junior and senior scholars from different global locations in order to conduct a collective project and help each other rethink our research from transnational, intersectional, and decolonial feminist perspectives. My point here is that the critique of the neoliberal focus on "new tools" needs to be articulated in conversation with, and not detached from, the ambivalences embedded in the conditions for obtaining funding for such collective gatherings and thinking processes as those we've gone through in this project. Thinking through the economic foundations is also a question of situating knowledges.

Kharnita: We can say we're tricksters, reworking neoliberal conditions.

Petra: Yeah, exactly. Maybe this is one of our tools.

Nina: Using trickster tools to change neoliberal academia, and neoliberal conditions more broadly. I really like that way of looking at these complex issues.

Petra: You reminded me about something that those of us coming from the Central European University in Budapest have talked about often, namely that one of the greatest gifts of this project was exactly to convene in various places with people from very different geopolitical realities. I remember our first gatherings in Sweden and Norway where, actually, people who came from South Africa took it for granted that, for those of us who came from Hungary, the Swedish and Norwegian reality would be familiar, close to home, while the South African one was different. But, actually, Scandinavia represented as much of a cultural shock in the positive sense, with all its richness, as later South Africa did with all its richness, while, from another angle, the South African reality was much closer to our everyday experiences in Eastern European countries, for example, than the Scandinavian reality. For instance, I've never before been in a country where everything works. So, I also felt that our conversations in the project have turned us more and more towards the lateral relations between Eastern Europe and South Africa. We actually started to feel in our own skin what it means to be placed . . . what's the word . . . gosh, now I'm thinking in two languages . . . I'm sorry I can't find the word . . .

Kharnita: Just describe the word you're searching for . . .

Petra (showing the different moves with her hands): When you come in not parallel, not horizontally, and not vertically, but askew . . .

Redi: Yeah. I know what you mean. I felt that the South African project team, especially when coming to Sweden, but also to Norway, thought that they were the askew arrivals into Europe. At the same time, those of us coming from Eastern Europe felt that we're also the askew arrivals to this clear-looking North/South polarity that was being drawn between Scandinavia and South Africa. Moreover, I'm also certain that those of us who were coming from Eastern Europe, but also from Africa or Latin America, but now having become part of Scandinavian academia as postdocs or PhD students, had our own sense of being the askew arrivals, when taken as the representatives of the "Western world" or the "Northern hemisphere". We were, all of us, all the time, repositioning ourselves within this project. For me, that was a very enriching experience, as a scholar and also personally. So, askew and queer arrivals to the seemingly clear-cut axes of Global North/Global South, and East/West, is that what the project perhaps, first of all, is about?

Kharnita: The breaking down of nationalisms, and nationalist as well as geopolitical stereotypes in an embodied way. . . . I think this is a profound insight and a profound ontological and epistemic shift, which came out of this process.

Between Politics of Location and the Traps of Methodological Nationalisms

The issue of locatedness, of naming the place from which one speaks (Koobak and Thapar-Björkert 2014), has become one of the epistemological foundations of feminist theory and gender scholarship during the past decades. Since its inception, the concept of a "politics of location" (Rich 1986) has aimed to encourage reflection upon, and responsibility for, how feminists know and act within the locations they inhabit, reproduce, and transform. In her oft-cited piece, *Notes Toward a Politics of Location*, feminist scholar Adrienne Rich argues for the importance of "recognizing our location, having to name the ground we're coming from, the conditions we have taken for granted", and in particular taking her own "whiteness as a point of location", for which she "needed to take responsibility" (Rich 1986: 219). For postcolonial feminist theorist Chandra Talpade Mohanty, the term "politics of location" refers "to the historical, geographical, cultural, psychic and imaginative boundaries which provide the ground for political definition and self-definition for contemporary US feminists" (Mohanty 1995: 68). She articulates the importance of recognizing the multiplicity of locations and modes of knowing, and the knowledges that arise from them. For many feminists, the struggle for accountability is embodied and material and thus has to begin with the body, with its specificities, while also emphasizing diversity and multiple locations of power. This involves a privileged focus on the embodied self, which serves as the anchoring point and ground of validation for feminist writing.

In this volume, thinking about the embodied self and the politics of location is taken to also involve a geopolitical level. This gesture, however, evokes questions about spatiality and territoriality, as well as drawing attention to what have come to be termed problems with methodological nationalism. Particularly common across

6 *Nina Lykke et al.*

the social sciences and humanities, methodological nationalism assumes that the nation/state/society is the natural social and political form of the modern world; hence, the nation-state often ends up being taken as a "natural" unit of analysis, while geopolitical inequalities, including the historical effects of imperialism and colonialism, are erased. However, the taken-for-granted nature of the nation-state as a standard analytical frame has been strongly criticized by many scholars in recent decades. Anthropologists Wimmer and Schiller, for example, argued that it "reflects and reinforces the identification that many scholars maintain with their own nation-states" (2003: 576). Problematically, then, treating national contexts as given and allowing the nation to stand as an unproblematized entity will lead to knowledge that mirrors a specific national context but is presented in general or universalist terms (cf. Chernilo 2006; Nowicka and Cieslik 2013).

With an even more radically critical gesture, feminist philosopher Rosi Braidotti equates methodological nationalism with a Eurocentric subjectivity, which takes "Europe's alleged universal civilizing mission and its self-proclaimed monopoly over scientific rationality" as an undisputed point of departure for science and philosophy (2011: 215). To avoid these traps, and at the same time remain attentive to the politics of location and situatedness in a geopolitical sense, we need to retain awareness of the context without "going national". This means having qualified insider knowledge without keeping our analysis within the limited frame of a national imaginary and its truths. Different frames have been mobilized to perform as alternatives to methodological nationalism. In this volume, we focus on three interconnected approaches: transnational, intersectional, and decolonial feminisms, which are brought into pluriversal conversations with each other, rather than handled as competing conceptualizations.

Pluriversal Conversations Between Transnational, Intersectional, and Decolonial Feminisms

When we define the book's conversations between transnational, intersectional, and decolonial frameworks as pluriversal, it is, as underlined in the beginning of this chapter, because we want to critically distance our approach from the monologic, universalizing speaking modes of conventional disciplinary scholarship. Our aim is to delink from the scholarship that feminist theorist Donna Haraway, in her classical reflection on "situated knowledges", described as articulations of the "God-Trick" of "Man, the One God, whose Eye produces, appropriates, and orders all difference" (Haraway 1991: 193). With the figure of "Man, the One God", Haraway refers to the positivist knower, whose vantage point is normatively embodied as white Western upper/middle class, heteropatriarchal privilege that gets hidden through the academic conventions of allegedly "neutral" and disembodied modes of analysis and language. This volume aims to disrupt this "God-Trick" by gathering texts from pluriversally situated perspectives that have been formerly erased and/or mis/appropriated by "Man, the One God".

Furthermore, stressing geo-political and decolonial aspects, we chose the term "pluriversal", because it emerged out of decolonial scholarship, and is linked to critiques of what decolonial scholar Santiago Castro-Gómez has framed as "zero-point hubris" (Castro-Gómez 2021). According to Castro-Gómez, zero-point hubris is the colonial episteme of Western modernity that implies an epistemic knowledge hierarchy, which casts its top layer as the "self-evident" peak of history. The notions of pluriverse and pluriversal(ility) (Mignolo 2013: 351–53), pluriversal politics (Escobar 2020) and pluriversal hermeneutics (Tlostanova and Mignolo 2009) work as a critical-affirmative cluster of concepts, apt for addressing and making visible other epistemes, emerging from alternative, subjugated or "submerged" (Gómez-Barris 2017: 1) perspectives. As decolonial scholar Arturo Escobar (2020: xvii) notes, such perspectives can be put to work to decolonize and depatriarchalize universalizing speaking modes. Working pluriversality is a way of building an analytical platform for what decolonial scholars Marisol de la Cadena and Mario Blaser have reflected as "a world of many worlds" (2018).

Claiming the concept of pluriversality in our main title, we want to emphasize the diversity of geo- and corpolitically situated perspectives through which the contributors to this book try to transgress methodological nationalisms and the disciplinary boundaries that make nation-bound approaches appear as if they were indisputably given. Moreover, we want to foreground a shared commitment to engage in such transgressions without regressing to cultural relativism. Committing to pluriversal conversations is not a way of promoting cultural relativism; but rather, as decolonial scholars Madina Tlostanova and Walter Mignolo argue, an attempt to take seriously the need "to (re)construct, more specifically, the difference in the loci of enunciation and the politics of knowing beyond cultural relativism" (2009: 18). It is a way of stressing "that other truths also exist and have the right to exist, but [that] their visibility is reduced by the continuing power asymmetry, which is based on coloniality of knowledge, power, being and gender" (Ibid.: 18).

The transnational, intersectional, and decolonial frameworks that the contributors to the volume call forth from their differently located positions offer points of exit from methodological nationalism. But it is important to note that these three approaches have different genealogies and their applicability is always dependent on the specific geo- and corpopolitical contexts in which they are put to use. Our efforts to bring these three frameworks' differences into conversation have made it clear to us that they should be neither collapsed into one another nor profiled as simply opposing. To contextualize this claim, this chapter provides a brief overview of the genealogies of transnational, intersectional, and decolonial frameworks. The aim of the overview is to offer an entrance point to the further discussions and theoretical framings of the three frameworks, taking place in the volume.

We are aware that genealogical overviews often tend to foreground US-based sources, and especially this chapter's accounts for the concepts of transnational feminisms and intersectionality offer no exception. However, the rest of the book's chapters principally foreground otherwise located voices, while the volume as a whole critically affirmatively challenges the geopolitical power asymmetries, involved in international academic publishing. It does so, first, through the composition of the group of authors, embodying locations in the Global South, East, North, and West, as well as through their commitment to take these locations into

8   *Nina Lykke et al.*

account as their geo- and corpopolitically situated positions of enunciation. Second, the chapters of the book can also be considered as geopolitically distributed interventions into the debates on transnational, intersectional and decolonial feminisms insofar as they cumulatively draw on a wide range of theorizations that emerge not only from the Global North and West but from the Global South and East as well. In these ways, our book not only speaks about but is also making an effort to embody pluriversal conversations.

Transnational Feminisms

Let us start this introductory overview of the conceptual frameworks involved in our pluriversal conversations, by focusing on the concept of transnational feminisms. This is an analytical approach that developed as a critical alternative to different post-World War II takes on internationalism. During the second half of the 20th century, Cold War and development discourses transcended "the national", but in politically problematic ways. In the wake of the Cold War, so-called area studies, for example, emerged in academia as research focusing on regions of the world that, seen from a Western (predominantly US) vantage point, were of political and/or economic "interest" (Eastern Europe and the Soviet Union, the Middle East, Africa, etc.). Area studies have been heavily problematized by critical leftist scholars (e.g. Chow 2006), but, recently, they have also been revisited in a more positive vein. A special issue of the journal *GLQ: A Journal of Lesbian and Gay Studies* suggests that area studies could enter into potentially fruitful conversations with queer studies, tracing new cross-border solidarities and non-US-dominated epistemologies (Arondekar and Patel 2016). Another important rethinking of area studies is embodied by the branch of postsocialist studies, which unmoors the notion of "postsocialist" from the spatiotemporalities of Soviet imperialism, and instead brings postsocialist and critical postcolonial and decolonial approaches into conversation (Atanasoski and Vora 2017; Koobak et al. 2021). These kinds of radical queer and critical postsocialist rethinkings of area studies are touched upon in some contributions to this volume. Among the conceptual frameworks that have emerged to facilitate a transcending of the national level in a political, epistemological, and methodological sense are also the concepts of "translocalities/translocalidades" (Alvarez et al. 2014) and "translocational" (Anthias 2020). In contrast to the notion of "transnational", the terms "translocal" ("translocalities/translocalidades") and "translocational" encourage a focus on interconnections between different locations whose specific national circumscriptions are of less importance for cross-border social relations than other aspects of belonging and identification. This alternative is also addressed in this book. But even though some chapters of the volume thus engage with other conceptualizations, the overarching framework is the conversation between transnational, intersectional, and decolonial feminisms.

   Transnational feminism was introduced in the late 20th century (Mohanty 1988; Grewal and Kaplan 1994; Alexander and Mohanty 1997) and has been further developed in recent decades (Lock Swarr and Nagar 2010; Tambe and Thayer

Colliding Words and Worlds 9

2021). Like area studies, it emerged as an alternative framework for addressing issues of internationalism, but, politically, these two conceptualizations have very different genealogies. Transnational feminism developed as a critical alternative to the discourses on internationalism in the UN system and among internationally committed NGOs. The latter discourses constructed the world as a multitude of separate, but equal, nation-states, while remaining blind to the intertwined colonial, imperialist, and capitalist histories that have shaped contemporary landscapes of worldwide geopolitical inequalities. Against these backdrops, transnational feminism emerged as an analytical approach that aims to facilitate critical understandings of hegemonic, social power structures, and to prompt modes of transcending methodological nationalism, while disrupting epistemologies of ignorance regarding geopolitical histories of colonial and capitalist oppression. Transnational feminism was also launched as an analytical approach that was intended to facilitate the nurturing of alliances and coalitions that, seen from below, can challenge and change these hegemonies, as well as take into account a world of cross-border mobility and forced migration.

In a recent volume on transnational feminism (Tambe and Thayer 2021), postcolonial feminist scholar Inderpal Grewal, who, together with Caren Kaplan, initiated the seminal volume on the topic, *Scattered Hegemonies* (1994), reflects retrospectively on the concept. She argues that transnational feminism is a conceptual framework that has aimed from the outset to cut across methodological nationalism and "to think about how histories of colonialism, feminism, racism, and modernity linked gender constructs across nations and nationalisms" (Grewal 2021: 56–7).

According to Grewal (2021: 59), transnational feminism still holds analytical power today. It is a way to approach social power structures, which now more than ever can only be politically resisted and counteracted from below, with a starting point in understandings that transcend the national without losing their foundations in a politics of location. Even though "transnational feminism" has "shared its key term with transnational corporations", Grewal recommends its continued usefulness as "a descriptive category whose political project is recognizing the power of the global and the national that is made through relation and boundary-making and boundary-transgressing projects" (2021: 59). Grewal considers that identifying and analysing acts of making, as well as transgressing, borders can be used as a way to "puncture universalisms" and "Eurocentric normative ideas" (2021: 60).

Throughout this book, transnational feminism is used in this way, that is, as an analytical approach that open-endedly and with different variations, but still with a firm emphasis, insists on the dual need to transcend methodological nationalism and transgress a blind ontologizing of the world into dichotomized and ahistorically conceived, large-scale entities, such as "developed/developing countries", "first/third world", "Global North/Global South", and "East/West". This volume demonstrates that, applied in this way, transnational feminisms constitute an analytical framework which is appropriate for addressing important geopolitical collisions, that is, collisions of worlds and worlding practices, from critical feminist perspectives.

10   *Nina Lykke et al.*

Intersectionality

Intersectionality is another lens that the collective of contributors to this volume has found to be of key importance in the conversation about ways to address colliding words, worlds, and bodies. When Black Feminist scholar Kimberlé Crenshaw (1989) first coined the concept, she emphasized the violent aspect of the metaphor: intersections are spaces where collisions, violent traffic accidents, occur. Whether it is taken as a framework for understanding social power structures, or dimensions of subject formation, intersectionality refers to collisions – to crossroads that become arenas for the violently clashing effects of racist, sexist, homophobic, and classist power formations. As emphasized by Black Feminist scholar Jennifer Nash (2019, 2021), transnational and intersectional feminisms have been considered different, complementary, and sometimes even conflicting; transnational feminisms look at transgressions of national borders, whereas intersectional feminisms consider the border-crossing effects of social structures along the lines of gender, race, class, and sexuality, and embodied subjectivities. The contributors to this volume agree with Nash when she underlines that the transnational and the intersectional should be seen as productively intra-acting approaches, rather than as competing frameworks. Accordingly, this is the way in which intersectionality is used in this volume. This implies that transnational power relations, geopolitical structures, and specific locations are scrutinized as part of the intersections to be analytically taken into account.

However, intersectionality is not only a conceptual framework that deals with collisions of bodies and social power structures but also a notion that has triggered passionate political debates and clashes within feminism. Nash approaches these debates under the heading "intersectionality wars" (2019: 35ff.), referring to the ways in which the concept of intersectionality emerged out of intersections of Black US feminism and critical race theory (Crenshaw 1989, 1991; Matsuda 1991; Collins 1998), while also becoming field-defining for Gender Studies in forms that have been accused of whitening and neoliberalizing the notion (Bilge 2013). Nash's focus is the United States. However, the conflicts about intersectionality have spilled over into other parts of the world as well and have become a nodal point for critiques of white feminism. These collisions are also thematized in different ways in this volume.

Decoloniality

A third framework that is useful for cutting across delimiting, nation-bound outlooks, while positioning an embodied politics of location at the centre, is decoloniality. Together with transnational feminisms and intersectional approaches, decolonial perspectives also figure prominently in many contributions to this volume. As pointed out by some decolonial scholars, decolonization should not be used as a mere metaphor but rather taken seriously as a demand for undoing settler colonial distributions of land (Tuck and Yang 2012). Moreover, a decolonial approach is a lens through which to understand contemporary geopolitical landscapes as the outcome of a colonial matrix of power and knowledge which continues to produce systematically racialized hierarchies and global inequalities today (Mignolo and Escobar 2013).

Decolonial analysis dismantles the long-term effects of the entangled histories of empires, imperialism, colonial expansionism, and capitalist extractivism. Decolonial feminist scholars (Lugones 2003; Tlostanova 2010) have described how gendered and sexualized dimensions and oppressions are inextricably involved in these histories. Decolonial approaches show how knowledge production continues to be steeped in epistemologies of ignorance that make it necessary to engage in processes of unlearning Western universalisms and relearning pluriversal approaches, located in geopolitical and corpopolitical difference (Tlostanova and Mignolo 2012). At the centre of such approaches are the perspectives of social and environmental justice activists and Indigenous communities, who are vitally engaged in alternative worlding practices, but whose transformatory efforts to resist colonial and racial capitalist extractivism are frequently invisible, "submerged" (Gómez-Barris 2017) and not taken into account from macropolitical vantage points.

However, as Swati Arora emphasizes in her discussion of the "Decolonize the University" movement (Arora 2021), which has been active in many countries around the world over the last few years, it is, perhaps, useful to not define decolonization as "*one* action" which can stand in for all kinds of decolonizing practices at the university. Decolonization, in the sense used by Fanon (1963), is in fact impossible because questions of land redress require the abolition of the university as we know it. We could, instead, use this moment to consider decolonization as a pluriversal activity that "requires a continuous commitment" (Arora 2021: 8) to social and epistemic justice and embodied challenges to the hegemonic colonial, racist, casteist, and ableist knowledge-building practices that are embedded within university systems.

In this volume, decolonial perspectives are approached along similar lines, and linked to carefully (self-)reflexive and situated considerations of both disruptions and complicities in epistemic positions, shaped by racialized and colonial hierarchies. Contributors engaging in decolonial critique are committed to the work of "bridging the gaps between the extremes of decolonial academism and decolonial activism" (Tlostanova 2023: 147), which, as pointed out by Madina Tlostanova, have become an issue insofar as "decoloniality", like before it the concept of intersectionality has turned into a "buzzword" in certain academic circles (ibid.: 145).

Overall, transnational, intersectional, and decolonial feminist approaches remain in conversation throughout the book. Yet we want to emphasize what this brief summary of the three frameworks has also demonstrated: that none of them are to be considered fixed terms with final definitions. The point that transnational feminist scholars Amanda Lock Swarr and Richa Nagar stress in the introduction to their seminal work *Critical Transnational Feminist Praxis* (2010) applies very much to both intersectional and decolonial approaches:

> We work within a crisis of representation that relies on critical transnational feminism as inherently unstable praxis whose survival and evolution hinge

12 *Nina Lykke et al.*

on a continuous commitment to produce self-reflexive and dialogic critiques of its own practices rather than search for resolutions and closures – not to reproduce exercises in narrow "navel-gazing", but always in relation to overlapping hegemonic power structures at multiple and temporal and geographic scales.

(Lock Swarr and Nagar 2010: 9)

Hence, the ways in which the three frameworks are entangled in this volume should be seen as contributions to this collective rethinking and to a continuous and committed unfolding of embodied, praxis-related conceptual work.

Postdisciplinarity and Emergent Methodologies

"Discipline is empire", writes Canadian Black Studies scholar Katherine McKittrick (2021: 38). A rigid separation of academic disciplines reduces knowledge into easily classifiable boxes, and methodologies that produce such disciplinary knowledge create canons. The story of Black liberation and Black embodied knowledge is, as foregrounded by McKittrick, a case in point. It cannot be reduced to commodifiable knowledge categories because it is a story of struggle that was fought with flesh and blood. To undo the harm of colonial knowledge systems, McKittrick asks us to become undisciplined and refuse disciplinary loyalties. "Methodology as an act of disobedience and rebellion" can resist the organizational impetus of academic logics, she writes (2021: 35). A disobedient relationality means crossing disciplinary borders and doing the work with the materiality of your whole body, when "theory in the flesh means one where the physical realities of our lives – our skin colour, the land or concrete we grew up on, our sexual longings – all fuse to create a politic born out of necessity", as Cherry Moraga and Gloria Anzaldúa have said (1981: 23).

There is a gap between such calls to undisciplining and mainstream research traditions of many humanities and social science disciplines that are firmly embedded in methodological nationalism and eagerly engaged in disembodied Western-centric God tricks. Critical scholars who want to pose research questions from different, geo- and corpopolitically grounded perspectives run easily into problems, because it is difficult to bridge the gap, among others due to a lack of transgressive methodologies. This state of the art poses heavy obstacles for the unfolding of pluriversal research that wants to undo the universalistic approaches of Western-centric scholarship and disciplinary divides, and it is also detrimental for doctoral students and junior scholars in precarious positions, whose careers are most dependent on institutional acknowledgement. To counteract this situation, the four-year project on which this book is based aimed to establish frameworks for posing transgressive questions, while collectively reflecting upon the processes of doing so. This was the rationale for the conference events and short-term residencies, by means of which the project participants from Gender Studies Centres at universities in South Africa, Hungary, and Scandinavia were given the opportunity to take part in each other's university lives. The events and residencies, and the preparations for this volume, invited contributors to help and inspire each other across different corpo-political, geopolitical, and disciplinary locations, in order to reflect upon transgressive and discipline-disruptive methodologies and modes of integrating them into their own research. The aim was to collectively consider if and how research can be critically as well as affirmatively transformed through reflections on transnational, intersectional, and decolonial feminist perspectives, which take politics of location and embodiment seriously, and open up opportunities for engagement with more personal, poetic, and narrative writing modes.

It was a precondition for the project gatherings that disciplinary boundaries, including those between academic and creative modes of working, should not be policed, but rather questioned, challenged, and, if possible, transgressed. In this sense, the project was grounded in long-standing feminist critiques of the disciplinary boundaries, which formed the basis for interdisciplinary Gender Studies Centres such as the ones from which the project emerged. Some feminists have over the years defined Gender Studies as a successor discipline (Harding 1986: 142), considered as an authoritative corrective to narrowly defined disciplinary knowledges. Others, however, have argued for radical postdisciplinarity (Case 2001; Lykke 2010, 2011) in so far as intersectional phenomena and research questions articulated against the background of social and ecological justice activism require approaches which fundamentally cross-cut and disrupt disciplinary boundaries. As Nina's academic trajectory has been characterized by active onto-epistemological and practical–political work to sustain the latter position (Lykke 2010, 2011), she used her position as a project leader to ensure that the project platform was from the start opened to experiments with post-disciplinary boundary transgressions. At the same time, it was also underlined that ongoing research commitments of participants should be respected, since it is not realistic to think that people, for example, can completely change the direction of their PhD project, when they are in the middle of it! But boundary transgressions were encouraged, among other ways, through creative writing workshops that were organized as an integrated part of the work throughout the project period. (An in-depth reflection on these workshops by Petra Bakos, Redi Koobak, and Kharnita Mohamed can be found in Chapter 8 of this volume.)

An entangled line of inspirations to challenge disciplinary boundaries came from the decolonial perspective which, through decolonial feminist scholar Madina Tlostanova's commitment to the project as a member of the coordinating Linköping team, set the agenda from the start. Tlostanova's chapter (this volume) was the first to be written for this book and has figured on the reading list for the annual gatherings since the first project year. Disruptions of disciplinary doxa and outlooks are central to decolonial scholarship, and along such lines Tlostanova foregrounds, among others, the classic reflections on methodology by decolonial scholars such as Chicana queerfeminist Chela Sandoval's *Methodology of the Oppressed* (2000), and Indigenous (Aotearoan) scholar Linda Tuhiwai Smith's *Decolonizing Methodologies. Research and Indigenous Peoples* (1999). Tlostanova argues for a shift of perspectives away from the Western "geography of reason" (Gordon and Tlostanova 2021), the reason defined by a Euro-US-centric

14   *Nina Lykke et al.*

colonial logics, towards decolonial and decentring approaches. She also suggests a range of alter-methodologies such as defamiliarization, pluriversal hermeneutics, horizontal relationality, and love – that is, methodologies which radically challenge and transgress conventional understandings of that concept.

The invitations to experiment with methodological transgressions have triggered a focus on reflexivity and a curiosity for decolonial and other kinds of emergent, postqualitative methodologies (St. Pierre 2018; Lykke 2022). This includes alternative writing strategies (Lykke 2014) and decolonial alter-methodologies, that is, methodologies that are put to work not as fixed and static tools or analytical models, but as approaches growing out of the researchers' ongoing efforts to engage creatively with transformatory research aimed at critical and affirmative shaping of alter-ontologies and alter-epistemes. This engagement with transgressions is reflected throughout the book via experimental approaches to the three main conceptual frameworks of transnational feminisms, intersectionality, and decoloniality, which in turn were enriched with new dimensions. The strivings towards transgressive approaches manifest themselves through Part I's reflexive focus on the ways in which affected and embodied writing experiments that work with fiction, creative non-fiction, and mixed-genre (academic and creative) texts can challenge hegemonic power. The efforts to critically disrupt but also to affirmatively recalibrate ways of thinking about methodologies are also reflected in Part II, which offers examples of decolonial, intersectional, transnational, and Indigenous-centred alter-methodologies. Finally, endeavours to shape transgressive approaches are further present in Part III, considered in tandem with investigations of global power asymmetries, approached from a multiplicity of different, geopolitically located positions of enunciation.

To give readers an introductory overview of the diversity of methodological approaches emerging out of the experimental and open-ended processes, which shaped the book, we will provide one more glimpse of the editorial team's pluriversal conversations. In another snapshot from an editorial meeting, the five co-editors each emphasize what they found most methodologically important when reading the contributions.

Kharnita: For me, what was interesting and striking when reading through the final manuscript was the different kinds of reflexivity that emerged across the contributions. Different people used multiple kinds of reflexivity to rethink themselves and their own epistemic approaches. I find that very interesting. The multiplicity of forms of reflexivity and how it becomes possible to think of reflexivity in very complicated, complex, and interesting ways beyond very narrow framings. I think that the ways in which the contributors rethought their projects, many of them over a long period of time, was fascinating, and it was interesting to see how the projects were enriched by the critiques people made of their own approaches. I really appreciated seeing that. I think it would be great to teach with a set of those chapters to show students that, actually, your project doesn't end. Your project is constantly under revision, as you incorporate new modes of knowledge. So, for example, Rebecca Helman's and Susheela Mcwatts' chapters, which both involve strong engagements with affect, were very interesting to me. One assumes that situated knowledge and affect is so widely dispersed across feminist thinking that it is almost an orthodoxy for some, and yet to see how both of these authors use the opening that affect provides them to reengage with their research projects was just lovely. The reflexivity and situated knowledge involved here is really lovely to think about. A multiplicity of potential is opened up in these pieces . . .

Swati: I found it striking that there is a strong focus on decolonization in many contributions, and this made me think about the question, for us as editors and for the contributors: What do we really understand by decolonialization? What I have in mind is that Fanon (1963), for instance, writes about decolonization in a very specific manner: the sovereignty of people, and freedom, and ownership of land, resources, and infrastructure. But what does decolonization mean for us as teachers, writers, and researchers? Are we, this mix of people across disciplines and across situations, using the terms as a metaphor, for instance? And what kinds of changes are we referring to when we use it? What does it mean to do decolonial feminist writing? What is our relationship to the university? We all have very different positionalities at the moment – only two of us have any kind of professional stability, although we all know that no one is really permanent, at least going by the recent developments in the UK and USA. So, what does it mean to embody feminist solidarity when we collaborate across geopolitical divides and differing relationships to institutions?

Redi: What I also find important in the contributions is that there is such a strong focus on writing strategies – on how to write for different purposes. I wrote down a list: writing to explore, writing to question, writing to challenge, writing to provoke, writing to dream, writing to love, writing to repair, writing to build, writing to conceal, writing to reveal, writing to obscure – all different functions of writing. But still, they exemplify a focus on self-reflexivity and rethinking of one's own epistemological positions. And there are also more experimental forms of writing, and different aims for these writings as well. I personally found a lot of strength and inspiration in our conversations in the meetings that really urged me to carve out a different kind of space for my own writing, a different kind of voice, strengthened by a newly found sense of belonging and togetherness that really resonates with Pralini's beautiful poem, the epigraph of our book: "How often, while struggling to surface, I have found myself here in the belonging of a poem, a language I did not know that I knew".

Swati: I have been thinking a lot about how the form and content of the contributions relate to the time during which the editing of the book took place – a time of pandemic and immense grief. Everyone has been

16 *Nina Lykke et al.*

mourning and hurting for different reasons. What does it mean to do feminist scholarship during this time of protracted grief? At the start of 2022, we lost bell hooks, who wrote that "I came to theory because I was hurting" (1994: 59). Her theoretical style remains very accessible, being rooted in her lived experience of growing up as a Black, queer, feminist poet and academic in the USA. I love the fact that this book includes creative non-fiction as a way of doing theory in a different manner. It is a powerful mode of challenging, and exposing, disciplinary thinking as colonial. The contributions also highlight that each one of us has a varied and embodied relationship to theory, reminding us how bell hooks paved the way for doing embodied and affected feminist scholarship.

Petra: I have tried to group the tools that we used while shaping the book: tools of writing, reading, approaching, collaborating, and convening. At the moment, for example, we are using the tool of convening. I think it also influenced the editorial process that we, in the editorial team, regularly convened online throughout this past pandemic year, when, with some people very close to us, we could not meet up at all. What kind of space did this create? Kharnita spoke about reflexivity, and I found that, throughout this process of working with the contributors, reading their texts, as well as reading my own comments from before, and reflecting upon certain changes now, we have generated, or maybe not generated, but reestablished quite important tools of relating to ourselves as well. I'm thinking of tools of reflection, but also tools of boundary-setting – of thinking about feminist solidarity, also with oneself, with myself, with ourselves, within a collaborative process. I am thinking here, for example, of Susheela Mcwatts' chapter, which Kharnita also mentioned. Susheela was very reflexive and at the same time very self-critical in her chapter, so for her the challenge was to be empathetic with herself, with her past endeavours. I feel that practising feminist solidarity with ourselves, with our past selves, with ourselves who were perhaps not aware of all those things that we are aware of today, can be a very strong tool as well.

The other track I took in my reflections on the contributions to this volume was the title of this project, which was initially about "new" tools. But many of the tools that we have been using and deploying are actually ancient: empathy is an ancient tool; collaborative work is an ancient tool; thinking holistically instead of thinking in compartments is ancient; engaging with sensory aspects, which comes back in Edyta Just's chapter, and many other chapters as well, is ancient. So, many of these so-called "new" tools are, actually, rediscovering pre-existing toolkits. Therefore, decolonization is not only happening in space, but it happens through time, too.

Kharnita: I would say that it is a reclaiming of toolkits after patriarchy and after Anglocentric work, and that it creates this sort of return. I love the idea of reclaiming after having had to confront the sort of violence that was imposed on a particular mode of scholarship. . . . I love the idea that feminist scholarship is about reclaiming those older. . . . I don't want to call them tools or technologies. Rather, I would talk about a reclaiming of all the modes of being in the world that still have relevance but have been erased. However, the problem with this framing is that it creates a sense of temporality, where the others to be reclaimed are located in the past and, hence, are primitive. . . . So how do we frame this issue properly? We have to be very careful. . . . But the idea is lovely.

Nina: I want to address the question about the new-ancient methodologies emerging through the reflexive processes the project participants have engaged in, by highlighting the radical transformation which the project's original title has undergone as a consequence of our collective reflections. From the early stages, we used the working title "New Tools in Transnational Feminisms" for the book. However, in my capacity as a project leader, I have underlined all the way through that this was not meant to be the final book title. Looking back now, I would like to make this emphasis even stronger; throughout the process, the terms in the working title: "New", "tools", "transnational feminisms", have all been critically scrutinized, revisited, and rethought.

Petra and Kharnita have just nailed the problems adhering to the term "new". "Tools", too, is a problematic concept because it suggests a positivist methodology, which claims that it is possible to separate method, context, and the task at hand. We've discussed this, among others, in relation to Madina Tlostanova's chapter, and her critique of the concept of methodology. She stresses that methodologies are contextual and develop as part of specific research projects. I agree very much, and use the terms "postqualitative methodologies" (St. Pierre 2018) and "emergent methodologies" (Lykke 2022), to describe methodologies which evolve in resonance with the project and not separated from it.

"Transnational" is also a concept that can create problems. If used in isolation, it may slide towards associations with transnational capital and neoliberalism, which implies an erasure of geopolitically and corpopolitically anchored locationality and situatedness. However, linking the concept firmly to feminist perspectives, as we have done it throughout the STINT project, as reflected in the short title "New Tools in Transnational Feminisms", gives it an important critical edge. As we have elaborately accounted for the concept of "transnational" earlier in this introductory chapter, this implies that it is in our context connected to a genealogy of feminist analyses that are critically concerned with geopolitical power inequalities, and coalition building from below to challenge these hegemonies. Still, as the development of our discussions during the project period have shown, the concept of "transnational feminisms" needs to be brought into continued conversation with intersectionality, and decoloniality.

18 *Nina Lykke et al.*

When we inserted "transnational" in the title of the project application to the STINT Foundation, we were aiming to gather a group of doctoral students, postdocs, and professors from locations in a transnational space – crudely defined through the axes of Global South/East/North/West – who were interested in feminist perspectives, to see if we could, collectively, help each other to generate approaches for transgressing the methodological nationalisms and limitations in the research that each of us was doing. But the idea was not simply to develop "new tools" to be applied within an abstractly defined transnational feminist framework. Instead, we wanted to take the collective, interrelational, always emergent and processual aspects of methodological work into account in a transnationally composed group of feminist scholars, while also taking seriously the different corpopolitical and geopolitical starting points of each participant's research. It was a prerequisite for the activities organized within the framework of the project that participating PhD students, for example, could not jump, from one moment to the next, into applying new key approaches, totally different from the ones in which they were already engaged. An important methodology, therefore, was to see how, in this particular transnational and feminist group of junior and more senior scholars, we could help each other to revisit and rethink – but not totally rework – ongoing research projects, from entangled intersectional, decolonial, and transnational feminist perspectives.

Petra: Before we end this discussion of methodological approaches, I want to highlight the open-ended and experimental character of the volume. It has also been of key importance that its open-ended search calls for experimentation and creative approaches.

Shaping the Volume

To be true to the pluriversal approach, contributors were, as mentioned, encouraged to use different formats and writing styles, and, against this background, the book has developed into a mixed-genre book. More conventionally written academic chapters are (in particular, in Part I) juxtaposed with ones that make their arguments through the telling of personal non-fiction stories and poetic narratives. Furthermore, several chapters are in themselves based on combinations of academic and creative writing formats, while others are formed as interview conversations. With the format, we want to pay tribute to the multiple and long intersectional feminist traditions of disrupting the monologue formats of universalizing academic speech acts through personalized forms of writing – disruptions that were famously claimed by, among others, classic women-of-colour multi-genre texts such as *This Bridge Called My Back* (Moraga and Anzaldua 1981).

Pluriversality has also characterized the composition of the group of authors, contributors, and co-editors. The foundations for the group were first created when

Colliding Words and Worlds   19

Nina, a queerfeminist professor at the Gender Studies Centre of Linköping University in Sweden, initiated a project application for a four-year exchange programme for doctoral students and postdocs through an application to the Swedish Foundation for International Cooperation in Research and Higher Education (STINT). To do so, she invited feminist professors and leaders of the Gender Studies Centres at the Universities of Bergen and Western Cape, and at the Central European University in Budapest, to join the application. These were all centres with well-established feminist doctoral programmes, recognized for their international outreach, and their infrastructural and theoretical ability to attract transnationally committed doctoral students from several countries and disciplinary backgrounds. A large network was already in place from Nina's many years of European and more global feminist networking, collaboration, and relationship-building.

The successful application secured a financial infrastructure that could link the four Gender Studies Centres. It also created the necessary institutional infrastructure for transforming this into a project that actually allowed the exchange of a larger group of feminist doctoral students and postdocs across the borders of the Global North/Global South and East/West axes of geopolitical power. The original idea that the doctoral students and postdocs would remain in the project for several years. Some of the participating doctoral students returned one or more times to project events. However, due to different situations at the four participating Gender Studies Centres, the composition of the group of doctoral students changed a lot over the four-year period, whereas the group of coordinating professors and postdocs stayed the same. This created some collisions, because feedback loops between the events did not work in an ideal way. Still, the shifting composition has also had generative aspects; it allowed for an even larger, more multiple, and pluriversally located group of contributors to the book than originally foreseen.

However, even with this larger transnational group of committed authors and co-editors from many locations and backgrounds, it was clear from the start that the book would have gaps in terms of geopolitical situations and epistemic points of departure. We have worked from the current research engagements and situated positions of the involved doctoral students, postdocs, and professors at the four partner universities. This means that there are topics that we would have liked to see covered in the book, but which we have had to leave as gaps, because we all agree that tokenistic representation does not work. For example, at an editorial meeting, Swati pointed out that there is no engagement with the question of caste in the book. She emphasized that we should be open about gaps such as this and acknowledge them, but not necessarily rush to superficial tokenistic representations. Along similar lines, Nina brought up the issue of Indigenous feminisms. She argued that Indigenous feminisms are key to two chapters in the book – Chapter 10's interview conversation with Black Feminist scholar Victoria Kawesa, and her take on African and decolonial feminism, and Chapter 13, which deals with a project in which Nina has been involved together with Indigenous women in Chile. Still, Indigenous feminisms is a topic which is far broader and more diverse than anything that can be "covered" by two single chapters. Kharnita concluded this discussion, underlining with Mohanty (1988) that one is never representative

20   Nina Lykke et al.

of a culture; intersectional differences are at work in so many specific ways that representativity will always build on highly hegemonic abstractions and erasures of difference.

As the main aim of the project was to generate co-learning, the idea was also to engage PhD students and postdocs in the editing of this volume. The book process was initiated from the start by Nina, in her capacity as project leader. Redi, an Estonian, Scandinavia-based feminist who completed her PhD in Gender Studies at Linköping University, was hired to conduct postdoctoral research within the framework of the project. She was also involved in co-editing the book and organizing creative writing workshops at the partner universities to sustain the book-shaping process. At the first residency in Linköping in 2016, Petra, pursuing her doctoral studies at the Central European University in Budapest, entered the editorial team, and became engaged in the organizing and teaching of the writing workshops as well. Later, at the residency in South Africa in 2019, where the final pulling together and editing of the book was to be launched, the editorial team was further expanded. Kharnita, who back then was preparing her doctoral dissertation at the University of Western Cape in South Africa and had partaken in the very first project kick-off meeting in Linköping but not at subsequent residencies, entered the editorial team, as did Swati, who was finishing her postdoctoral research at the same university at the time. In addition to encompassing different positions within the academic system, the composition of the editorial team also mirrors the project's ambitions to both embody and cross-cut Global North/South and East/West divides.

A Book With Three Parts

The three parts, which constitute the volume, are each given a title that refers to poetic wordings from the Epigraph, the poem *Sister Ode*, in which Pralini Naidoo lovingly celebrates the conversations, she has had with other participants in the project which led to this book. We will end this introductory chapter with an overview of the volume's three parts but leave the more detailed chapter-by-chapter presentations to the opening sections of each part.

In Part I, *Myriad Tongues and Multiple Emotions (On Affected Writing and Ethics)*, we have clustered ten chapters which focus on affected writing and the ethical issues implied when researchers write *with* their interlocutors disrupting conventional reductions of research participants to objects of study. In different ways, the contributions to Part I explore how the becoming attuned to affective appeals by interlocutors engenders emergent methodologies and epistemic changes for the authors. The chapters investigate how the mobilizing of affect as embodied and geo-corporeal opens up avenues for feeling/sensing/thinking transnationalism otherwise and reflects upon what the role affect as a mode of knowing offers for the making of methodologies and methods. Part II, *Portals of Possibility (on Methodologies),* gathers together three chapters, which reflect explicitly upon the question of methodologies and methods. Since the overall focus of the book is to explore ways to disrupt methodological nationalisms, questions of methodologies and

Colliding Words and Worlds 21

transgressive modes of doing research cross-cut all three parts of the volume. Still, to emphasize the book's theoretical take on methodologies, we decided to devote its middle part to explicit discussions of methodologies, which, with Naidoo's poetic phrasing, are considered as portals of possibility, that is, malleable guides to knowledge-shaping processes, grounded in transformative practices paving the way for social and environmental justice-to-come. It is not coincidental that this part is composed as a smaller section in the middle of the book. This is a symbolic gesture, with which we want to stress that methodologies should make up neither beginnings nor ends of research; they are always intertwined in research practices and happening in the messy middle of ongoing relations between researchers and interlocutors (Tiainen et al. 2020). In Part III, *Intrepid Journeys (On epistemic Implications of Geopolitical Situatedness)*, eight chapters come together to take readers on a journey through shifting geopolitical locations in the Global South, North, East, and West, asking how askew angles and intrepid (self-)critical reflections upon epistemic entrance points are necessary for border- and boundary-crossing conversations between transnational, decolonial, and intersectional feminisms, and for coalition buildings in times and spaces of colliding words and worlds.

Notes

1 STINT, The Swedish Foundation for International Cooperation in Research and Higher Education, is a funding agency, set up by the Swedish Government in 1994 in order to further and strengthen internationalization of Swedish higher education. An important aim of the agency is to enable international collaboration for younger researchers (doctoral students and postdocs) with a strong focus on new forms of knowledge shaping and partnerships beyond (Western) Europe. The original title of the project application to STINT – "New Tools for Transnational Analysis in Postgraduate Intersectional Gender Research: Towards Long-Term International Collaborations in Doctoral and Postdoctoral Training" – and the explicit focus on university partnerships along Global South/East/North/West axes were conceptualized along the lines of the overall priorities of the funding agency. A short working title "New tools in transnational feminisms" was adopted shortly after the start of the four-year project in 2016. However, certain tensions around the conceptual framework, implied in the original project title, as well as, to some extent, also in the short-title, came up along the road. Project participants pinpointed that "new tools" might sustain the problematic understanding that the issue of "methods and methodologies" can be treated in the abstract and delinked from geopolitical and corpopolitical situatedness of the research and the researchers. Moreover, participants emphasized that the term "transnational analysis" needs to be firmly connected to feminist perspectives, and brought in conversation not only with intersectionality as stipulated in the original title but also with decolonial thinking. These discussions characterized the joint efforts of the participants and shaped the collective development of the project, which eventually resulted in this volume and its focus on emergent methodologies and pluriversal conversations between transnational, intersectional, and decolonial feminist approaches.

2 The academic year 2018/2019, when the Department of Gender Studies at the Central European University hosted its part of the STINT project events, was the university's final academic year in Budapest. From 2017, when the infamous Lex CEU targeting the Central European University took effect, the university's situation in Hungary became increasingly untenable, and during the next two years CEU gradually left Hungary, its home for 28 years. Although the European Court of Justice ruled in 2020 that Lex CEU

22 *Nina Lykke et al.*

violated European law, by that time the university had committed itself to its new campus in Vienna, Austria. It should be noted that Lex CEU is only one of numerous tools being deployed by the current right-wing Hungarian government to hinder critical pedagogical and research commitments in general and gender studies in particular.

3 The volume's editorial team of five scholars with backgrounds at the four partner universities of the STINT project, University of Western Cape (South Africa), Central European University (Hungary/Austria), Bergen University (Norway) and Linköping University (Sweden) met regularly online over a period of three years (2020–2022) to edit the volume. The process was organized as a collective learning process and worked as such, but became more protracted than planned due to the COVID-19 pandemic. We decided to record meetings where important editorial discussions and decisions were taken, and the recordings were afterwards shared digitally among the co-editors, as well as transcribed so that all members of the editorial team had access to all materials and full overview of the process. The excerpts from the editorial discussions which we include in the introductory chapter are collectively edited versions of selected parts of the transcriptions.

References

Alexander, M. Jacqui, and Chandra Mohanty (eds.). 1997. *Feminist Genealogies, Colonial Legacies, Democratic Futures*. New York, NY: Routledge.

Alvarez, Sonia E., Claudia de Lima Costa, Norma Klahn, and Millie Thayer (eds.). 2014. *Translocalities/Translocalidades: Feminist Politics of Translation in the Latin/a Américas*. Durham, NC: Duke University Press.

Anthias, Floya. 2020. *Translocational Belongings: Intersectional Dilemmas and Social Inequalities*. New York, NY and London: Routledge.

Arondekar, Anjali, and Greta Patel. 2016. "Area Impossible: Notes Toward an Introduction." *GLQ: A Journal of Lesbian and Gay Studies* 22 (2): 151–71.

Arora, Swati. 2021. "A Manifesto to Decentre Theatre and Performance Studies." *Studies in Theatre and Performance* 41 (1): 12–20.

Atanasoski, Neda, and Kalindi Vora. 2017. "Introduction: Postsocialist Politics and the End of Revolution" (Special Issue). *Social Identities* 24 (2): 139–54.

Bilge, Sirma. 2013. "Intersectionality Undone: Saving Intersectionality From Feminist Intersectionality Studies." *Du Bois Review* 10 (2): 405–24.

Braidotti, Rosi. 2011. *Nomadic Theory: The Portable Rosi Braidotti*. New York, NY: Columbia University Press.

Case, Sue-Ellen. 2001. "Feminism and Performance: A Postdisciplinary Couple." *Theatre Research International* 26 (2): 145–52.

Castro-Gómez, Santiago. 2021. *Zero-Point Hubris. Science, Race and Enlightenment in Eighteenth Century Latin America*. Trans. George Ciccariello-Maher and Don T. Deere. Lanham, MD: Rowman & Littlefield.

Chernilo, Daniel. 2006. "Social Theory's Methodological Nationalism: Myth and Reality." *European Journal of Social Theory* 9 (1): 5–22.

Chow, Rey. 2006. *The Age of the World as Target: Self-Referentiality in War, Theory, and Comparative Work*. Durham, NC, and London: Duke University Press.

Collins, Patricia Hill. 1998. "It's All in the Family: Intersections of Gender, Race and Nation." *Hypatia* 13 (3): 62–82.

Crenshaw, Kimberlé W. 1989. "Demarginalizing the Intersection of Race and Sex: A Black Feminist Critique of Antidiscrimination Doctrine, Feminist Theory and Antiracist Politics." *University of Chicago Legal Forum* 1989: 139–67.

Crenshaw, Kimberlé W. 1991. "Mapping the Margins: Intersectionality, Identity Politics, and Violence Against Women of Color." *Stanford Law Review* 43: 1241–99.

de la Cadena, Marisol, and Mario Blaser. 2018. "Introduction. Pluriverse". In *A World of Many Worlds*, edited by Marisol de la Cadena and Mario Blaser, 1–23. Durham, NC and London: Duke University Press.

Escobar, Arturo. 2020. *Pluriversal Politics. The Real and the Possible.* Durham, NC and London: Duke University Press.

Fanon, Frantz. 1963. *The Wretched of the Earth.* New York, NY: Grove Press.

Gómez-Barris, Marcarena. 2017. *The Extractive Zone: Social Ecologies and Decolonial Perspectives.* Durham, NC: Duke University Press.

Gordon, Lewis, and Madina Tlostanova. 2021. "Epilogue: Conversation With Decolonial Philosopher Madina Tlostanova on Shifting the Geography of Reason." In *Freedom, Justice and Decolonization*, edited by Lewis Gordon, 127–35. London: Routledge.

Grewal, Inderpal. 2021. "Rethinking Patriarchy and Corruption: Itineraries of US Academic Feminism and Transnational Analysis." In *Transnational Feminist Itineraries: Situating Theory and Activist Practices*, edited by Ashwini Tambe and Millie Thayer, 52–71. Durham, NC and London: Duke University Press.

Grewal, Inderpal, and Caren Kaplan. 1994. *Scattered Hegemonies: Postmodernity and Transnational Feminist Practices.* Minneapolis, MN: University of Minnesota Press.

Haraway, Donna. 1991. "Situated Knowledges: The Science Question in Feminism and the Privilege of Partial Perspective." In *Simians, Cyborgs and Women: The Reinvention of Nature*, edited by Donna Haraway, 183–201. London: Free Association Books.

Harding, Sandra. 1986. *The Science Question in Feminism.* Ithaca, NY: Cornell University Press.

hooks, bell. 1994. *Teaching to Transgress: Education as the Practice of Freedom.* New York, NY and London: Routledge.

Koobak, Redi, and Suruchi Thapar-Björkert. 2014. "Writing the Place From Which One Speaks." In *Writing Academic Texts Differently: Intersectional Feminist Methodologies and the Playful Art of Writing*, edited by Nina Lykke, 47–62. New York, NY and London: Routledge.

Koobak, Redi, Madina Tlostanova, and Suruchi Thapar-Björkert (eds.). 2021. *Postcolonial and Postsocialist Dialogues: Intersections, Opacities, Challenges in Feminist Theorizing and Practice.* New York, NY and London: Routledge.

Lock Swarr, Amanda, and Richa Nagar (eds.). 2010. *Critical Transnational Feminist Praxis.* New York, NY: SUNY Press.

Lugones, María. 2003. *Peregrinajes/Pilgrimages: Theorizing Coalition Against Multiple Oppressions.* New York, NY: Rowman & Littlefield.

Lykke, Nina. 2010. *Feminist Studies. A Guide to Intersectional Theory, Methodology and Writing.* New York, NY and London: Routledge.

Lykke, Nina. 2011. "This Discipline Which Is Not One." In *Theories and Methodologies in Postgraduate Feminist Research. Researching Differently*, edited by Rosemarie Buikema, Gabriele Griffin, and Nina Lykke, 137–50. New York, NY and London: Routledge.

Lykke, Nina (ed.). 2014. *Writing Academic Texts Differently: Intersectional Feminist Methodologies and the Playful Art of Writing.* New York, NY and London: Routledge.

Lykke, Nina. 2022. *Vibrant Death: A Posthuman Phenomenology of Mourning.* London: Bloomsbury.

Matsuda, Maria. 1991. "Beside My Sister, Facing the Enemy: Legal Theory Out of Coalition." *Stanford Law Review* 43 (6): 1183–92.

McKittrick, Katherine. 2021. *Dear Science and Other Stories.* Durham, NC: Duke University Press.

24 *Nina Lykke et al.*

Mignolo, Walter. 2013. "Delinking. The Rhetoric of Modernity, the Logic of Coloniality and the Grammar of De-coloniality." In *Globalization and the Decolonial Option*, edited by Walter Mignolo and Arturo Escobar, 303–68. New York, NY and London: Routledge.

Mignolo, Walter, and Arturo Escobar (eds.) 2013. *Globalization and the Decolonial Option*. New York, NY and London: Routledge.

Mohanty, Chandra T. 1988. "Under Western Eyes: Feminist Scholarship and Colonial Discourses." *Feminist Review* 30: 49–74.

Mohanty, Chandra T. 1995. "Feminist Encounters: Locating the Politics of Experience." In *Social Postmodernism: Beyond Identity Politics*, edited by Linda Nicholson and Steven Seidman, 68–86. Cambridge: Cambridge University Press.

Moraga, Cherríe, and Gloria Anzaldua (eds.). 1981. *This Bridge Called My Back: Writings by Radical Women of Color*. New York, NY: Kitchen Table, Women of Color Press.

Nash, Jennifer. 2019. *Black Feminism Reimagined: After Intersectionality*. Durham, NC and London: Duke University Press.

Nash, Jennifer. 2021. "Beyond Antagonism: Rethinking Intersectionality, Transnationalism, and the Women's Studies Academic Job Market." In *Transnational Feminist Itineraries: Situating Theory and Activist Practices*, edited by Ashwini Tambe and Millie Thayer, 37–52. Durham, NC and London: Duke University Press.

Nowicka, Magdalena, and Anna Cieslik. 2013. "Beyond Methodological Nationalism in Insider Research With Migrants." *Migration Studies* 2 (1): 1–15.

Pandian, Anand, and Stuart J. McLean. 2017. *Crumpled Paper Boat: Experiments in Ethnographic Writing*. Durham, NC: Duke University Press.

Rich, Adrienne. 1986. "Notes Toward a Politics of Location." In *Blood, Bread and Poetry: Selected Prose 1978–1985*, edited by Adrienne Rich, 210–33. London and New York, NY: Virago and Norton.

Sandoval, Chela. 2000. *Methodology of the Oppressed*. Minneapolis, MN: University of Minnesota Press.

Smith, Linda Tuhiwai. 1999. *Decolonizing Methodologies: Research and Indigenous Peoples*. London and New York, NY: Zed Books.

Stacey, Jackie, and Janet Wolff (eds.). 2013. *Writing Otherwise: Experiments in Cultural Criticism*. Manchester: Manchester University Press.

St. Pierre, Elizabeth Adams. 2018. "Writing Post Qualitative Inquiry." *Qualitative Inquiry* 24 (9): 603–8.

Tambe, Ashwini, and Millie Thayer (eds.). 2021. *Transnational Feminist Itineraries: Situating Theory and Activist Practices*. Durham, NC and London: Duke University Press.

Tiainen, Milla, Taru Leppänen, Katve Kontturi, and Tara Mehrabi. 2020. "Making Middles Matter: Intersecting Intersectionality With New Materialism." *NORA: Nordic Journal of Feminist and Gender Research* 28 (3): 211–23.

Tlostanova, Madina. 2010. *Gender Epistemologies and Eurasian Borderlands*. New York, NY: Palgrave.

Tlostanova, Madina. 2023. "Decoloniality. Between a Travelling Concept and a Relational Onto-Epistemic Political Stance." In *Coloniality and Decolonisation in the Nordic Region*, edited by Adrián Groglopo and Julia Suárez-Krabbe, 145–63. London and New York, NY: Routledge.

Tlostanova, Madina, and Walter Mignolo. 2009. "On Pluritopic Hermeneutics, Trans-Modern Thinking, and Decolonial Philosophy." *Encounters* 1 (1): 11–27.

Tlostanova, Madina, and Walter Mignolo. 2012. *Learning to Unlearn: Decolonial Reflections From Eurasia and the Americas*. Columbus, OH: Ohio State University Press.

Tuck, Eve, and K. Wayne Yang. 2012. "Decolonization Is Not a Metaphor. Decolonization: Indigeneity." *Education & Society* 1 (1): 1–40.

Wimmer, Andreas, and Nina Glick Schiller. 2003. "Methodological Nationalism, the Social Sciences, and the Study of Migration: An Essay in Historical Epistemology." *International Migration Review* 37 (3): 576–610.

Part I

Myriad Tongues and Multiple Emotions (On Affected Writing and Ethics)

Petra Bakos, Redi Koobak, and Kharnita Mohamed

In line with the volume's overall commitment to pluriversal conversations, Part I voices *myriad tongues and multiple emotions*. The geo- and corpopolitically differently located authors of the chapters, gathered in this section, produce affected writing (cf. Helman, this volume) and reflect on the generative power of affect as a route to epistemic and ethical tussling. The exploration of affect and embodiment as critical faucets of knowledge production can make ethical demands on all involved parties; yet, these chapters turn the lens towards a less examined side of the equation: that of the researcher, the author, and the teacher. The texts testify to the power of becoming attuned to affective appeals by research interlocutors, which may bring along onto-epistemic changes in research and/or teaching and/or writing, engendering emergent methodologies. Through affect – whether affective language, the vulnerability of affected writing, and/or allowing affective modes of relationality in research and teaching – the authors come into new relationships with knowledge production itself. Furthermore, while affect as a mode of knowing offers possibilities for experimental co-creation of approaches, the chapters also show that mobilization of affect as embodied and geo-corporeal opens up avenues for feeling/sensing/thinking transnationalism, intersectionality, and decoloniality otherwise. The authors move beyond situated knowledge into a terrain that allows them to ask questions about reflexivity that is not recursive, but rather multiply angled, and dynamic.

Turning to fiction as a writing methodology, Wanelisa A. Xaba, Chapter 2, *A Black Woman Died at the Intersection(ality) Today*, powerfully laments the death of Black women. In the story, a Black woman dies at an intersection, and her body is left in the street. Using affected and affecting writing, the grasp in words of the devastating effects, which this death puts on display, Xaba rebukes the multiple and intersecting power structures that are implicated in Black women's death. She also admonishes the voyeuristic study of Black women and points to an unseemly structure of enjoyment of Black women's death that does nothing to stem the continuity of Black women's deaths as a consequence of intersections of racist, sexist, heteropatriarchal, and social relations. Through the affective force of Xaba's admonishments, we are able to enter into the vulgarity of epistemes and their accompanying

DOI: 10.4324/9781003378761-2

28 *Petra Bakos, Redi Koobak, and Kharnita Mohamed*

suggestions for methodologies that record violence but do not act to ward it off. As a methodological injunction, this chapter poses important questions about the value of academic research and the necessity for epistemologies that not only record worlds but also intervene to shore off destruction. This chapter opens up not just the potent use of affect but also what it is possible to show using creative methods. In showing the structure of research and colonial epistemologies that focus on the victim through storying, Xaba makes us aware of how inadequate and even perverse some of our methods are. The creative approach enables multiple forms of relationality to emerge and importantly, Xaba is able to humanize Black women, even in death.

In Chapter 3, *Pedagogies of Precarity*, Kharnita Mohamed uses creative nonfiction as a device to allude to how knowledge learned through precarity shapes methods. She shares encounters that traverse transnational and local intersectional relations across and in universities where her experiences of power as a precarious Black woman scholar shape her understanding of the disjunctures and contradictions within knowledge production. This chapter engages with praxis as learned through intimate encounters within the academy's power structures. Because of the unequal and hierarchical power relations within the academy, various forms of microaggression, appropriation, and other painful incidences are parts and parcels of a pedagogy that countermands stated and written ideas of freedom and liberation. Critically, the ways in which precarity shapes interactions and relationships within the academy foreclose the possibility of naming interlocutors who influence these contradictory intellectual praxes. Like Xaba's storytelling, Mohamed's affective language points to epistemic structures, to focus on those in power so as to intervene in the multiple kinds of silencing that knowledge production entails. The use of creative writing foregoes argument as the foundation, which drives academic essays. Rather, it is through the juxtaposition of examples written in affective language that makes an ethical and methodological claim, even as Mohamed retains the right to be silent as a counterstrategy to being silenced.

Like Mohamed, Redi Koobak uses creative non-fiction in her chapter, Chapter 4, *Scenes of Precarity: Where Is the Exit?* to arrive at a more nuanced understanding of how precarity shapes our understanding of the world and thereby the methods through which we produce knowledge. Koobak explores her desire and will to confront and come to terms with her experiences of precarity in relation to her privileges through affective and vulnerable writing. Weaving together various scenes of precarity, she reflects on the borders of race, gender, and class magnified by shifts in identifications, echoing June Jordan's essay "Report from the Bahamas 1982" (2003) on intersecting privileges. In particular, Koobak parallels her own experiences of precarity as a white Estonian woman who spent more than a decade working in Scandinavian academia with coming to consciousness of the difference between her personal experiences and those of her Black Jamaican partner as well as the imagined wife of a Black South African stranger she met on a research trip, each battling their own respective struggles with precarity. Affective writing, then, allows to underscore the jarring in-between moments, often bracketed or left out, when the author is produced both as precarious and implicated in structures of

Myriad Tongues and Multiple Emotions (On Affected Writing and Ethics) 29

privilege, making a clear case for mobilizing affect as embodied and geo-corporeal, as a tool through which to unpack the ethical demands of knowledge production.

The use of affect to recognize methodological limitations when researching sexual violence is poignantly explored in Chapter 5, *Affected Writing: A Decolonial, Intersectional Feminist Engagement With Narratives of Sexual Violence*, by Rebecca Helman. Helman mobilizes and conceptually frames "affected writing" to mediate her personal discomfort and understand the normalization of sexual violence and desensitization to the narratives of survivors. She advocates for a relational ethics of care that requires engaging with survivors of sexual violence affectively and in so doing engenders ethically complex modes of responsiveness. Given the pervasiveness of sexual violence in South Africa and its intricate and long-standing relationship with race that has produced differential sensibilities and responsiveness around sexual violence, interrupting normative responses is critical. In this chapter, Helman uses her own experience of being out of place as a white rape survivor, her responses to participants' narrations of their rapes and their affects in the telling, and considers how these complex affective relations are shaped by the long history of racism and sexism in South Africa. She very sensitively traverses this affective terrain and its limitations to argue for the necessity of recognizing our affectability and how it shapes our research as well as allows us to undo historical and epistemic inequalities.

Remaining on South African grounds, Chapter 6, *Notes From My Field Diary: Revisiting Emotions in the Field*, Susheela Mcwatts argues that affects generated in the field, if carefully and reflexively integrated into research methodology, have much to offer to both the researcher and the interlocutors. Close reading of her field diary used during her doctoral studies on domestic workers' political activism and international union building, based on interviews with domestic workers' union leaders worldwide (Mcwatts 2018), Mcwatts reflects on her past positionality by considering what inter-relationships could have been forged with the interlocutors had emotions been consciously related to in the field, and also what it could have meant for the process of knowledge production if she had practiced *Ubuntu*, African humanism (Clear 2022), while doing research. Next, she contemplates the impact such an integration of affects could have had on her research and arrives to envisioning an emergent methodology which veers from the postcolonial towards the decolonial. Her chapter well illustrates the value of reflection and the passage of time in discerning new methodological opportunities.

Affectivity and reflections on its interventions in research processes are also key issues in Chapter 7, *Whiteness as Friction: Vulnerability as a Method in Transnational Research* by Heather Tucker. This chapter is based on a multi-sited queer feminist ethnography that the author carried out in Accra, Ghana, for eight months in 2015. She was working with what she refers to as a group of working-class queer women and their uneasy relationship with transnationally funded non-governmental organizations (NGOs). Tucker pays specific attention to the binary of the outsider/insider in transnational research addressing key ethical elements of the power dynamics between a white queer Western researcher and local queer communities in postcolonial Ghana. In focus is a highly affective moment where Tucker

30   Petra Bakos, Redi Koobak, and Kharnita Mohamed

unexpectedly became emotionally vulnerable in front of her research participants. She asks: What are the ethical considerations to take into account in a transnational queer feminist research project that was chosen and led by a white Western queer woman in a postcolonial context? Contemplating these questions of ethics, the author reflects on the role and meanings of affect, vulnerability, and power and their relation to ethics and the outsider/insider binary in research. She considers how both affective relationships and forms of vulnerability that can deconstruct the power divide and the outsider/insider binary in research can also simultaneously confirm these divides.

Chapter 8, *From Affective Pedagogies to Affected Pedagogues: A Conversation*, also engages with the potential of feminist classrooms. As the title suggests, it discusses affective pedagogies centring on the experience of the affected pedagogues in classrooms delicately placed along the Global North–Global South and Global East–Global West axes. In their conversation, Redi Koobak, Petra Bakos, and Kharnita Mohamed revisit Redi and Petra's academic and creative writing workshops held for residency participants in the international collaboration (STINT project) that led to this volume. In these workshops, Redi and Petra approached writing as an embodied form of thinking that taps into abstract cognition as well as the visceral layers of emotions and memories. Despite being well equipped with theoretical knowledge and practical tools to encourage and inspire self-reflexivity and self-positioning in writing, Redi and Petra had to take on some of their own most pressing challenges of reflecting on their own positionality as workshop facilitators. The conversation, facilitated by scholar and novelist Kharnita Mohamed, swirls around these events and in particular those "hot" teaching moments Redi and Petra encountered therein, which in retrospect turned out to represent also "hot" learning moments for them as pedagogues.

Chapter 9, *"I will Meet You at Twilight." On Subjectivity, Identity, and Transnational Intersectional Feminist Research*, by Edyta Just, offers a further theoretical backdrop to the previous chapters' reflections on affect and embodied pedagogy. Focusing on connections between embodied and embedded subjectivity, identity, and research, Just approaches the figure of the researcher via the prism of matter understood as material locatedness. She reflects on different ways in which matter and social context may matter for subjectivity and knowledge production, emphasizing that there are connections between mental activity, meaning-making, logic behind meaning-making, embodiment, embeddedness, matter, and social context. Combining neuroscientific theorizing (Lindquist et al. 2012; Barrett et al. 2014) and the philosophical framework of Gilles Deleuze and Felix Guattari (1987), Just conceptualizes subjectivity through the prism of axes of differentiation and their corresponding identity markers. Offering a piece of creative and affective writing as part of this chapter, Just not only theorizes but also shows us how she herself lives and subjectively experiences the connections. Her closing reflections on the correspondence between lived subjectivities and research bring on board overarching themes of the volume suggesting how the theoretical framework and her personal story about her way of living it may facilitate thinking about transnational intersectional feminist research.

Myriad Tongues and Multiple Emotions (On Affected Writing and Ethics) 31

Chapter 10, *Living an African Feminist Life – Decolonial Perspectives: A Conversation*, is an interview where affectivity and autophenomenographic storytelling figure prominently. Redi Koobak and Nina Lykke interview Victoria Kawesa, focusing on African and decolonial feminisms against the backdrop of Victoria's life story as an anti-racist, feminist activist, writer, and scholar. Victoria has been based in Sweden since she arrived there as a nine-year-old in 1984, with her mother and siblings as political refugees from Uganda, a country steeped in civil war at the time. The interview aligns itself with the affective and personal–political–theoretical approach of Victoria's research, and its use of the method of autophenomenography (autoethnography with a phenomenological focus on embodiment, emotions, and affect; Allen-Collinson 2010), combined with creative storytelling. Working its way from Victoria's childhood in Black-normative Uganda to her experiences of racism in white-normative Sweden, the conversation links glimpses of her life history as told and analysed in her thesis (Kawesa In Press), with the theoretical and political frameworks also developed there. Victoria unfurls her views on African decolonial feminisms and the practice of Obuntu Bulamu, which she defines as a corpo-affective intensity of our deeply entangled beingness, related to Ubuntu, but with an Indigenous focus also on more-than-human worlds which Victoria learned to value through her grandmother. She also emphasizes the need for differentiation within Black Feminism to make space for African and decolonial feminisms with other genealogies than the middle-passage epistemologies dominating US contexts.

What does it mean to write with affect? Why is affective writing important for transnational, decolonial, and intersectional feminist analyses? The contributors to Part I give different answers and use different writing styles, when addressing these questions, yet they share a commitment to experimental approaches. Writing with affect and using writing as an affective method of inquiry (Richardson 2000) is not a once and for all given and fixed recipe, but an emergent, postqualitative method (St. Pierre 2018; Lykke 2022), which is entangled with processes of knowledge production in research, teaching, and activism. Affect's experimental potentialities as the multiple emotions connected to researching, teaching, and/or activist practicing of transnational, intersectional, and decolonial feminisms, which the authors of Part I share with the readers are therefore consciously articulated not only through a choir of myriad tongues but also through differing styles of writing and modes of establishing transgressive conversations.

References

Allen-Collinson, Jacquelyn. 2010. "Running Embodiment, Power and Vulnerability: Notes Towards a Feminist Phenomenology of Female Running." In *Women and Exercise: The Body, Health and Consumerism*, edited by Eileen Kennedy and Pirkko Markula, 280–98. London: Routledge.

Barrett, Lisa Feldman, Christine D. Wilson-Mendenhall, and Lawrence W. Barsalou. 2014. "A Psychological Construction Account of Emotion Regulation and Dysregulation: The Role of Situated Conceptualizations." In *The Handbook of Emotion Regulation* (2nd ed.), edited by James J. Gross, 447–65. New York, NY: Guilford.

Clear, James. 2022. "How to Be Happy? A Surprising Lesson on Happiness From an African Tribe. Life Lessons." Accessed May 8, 2022. https://jamesclear.com/how-can-i-be-happy-if-you-are-sad.

Deleuze, Gilles, and Felix Guattari. 1987. *A Thousand Plateaus: Capitalism and Schizophrenia*. London and New York, NY: Continuum.

Jordan, June. 2003. "'Report From the Bahamas, 1982.' The Legacies of Colonialism and White Supremacy." *Meridians* 3 (2): 6–16.

Kawesa, Victoria (in prep.). *Black Masks/White Sins: Becoming a Black Obuntu Feminist*. Linköping: Linköping University Press.

Lindquist, Kristen A., Tor D. Wager, Hedy Kober, Eliza Bliss-Moreau, and Lisa Feldman Barrett. 2012. "The Brain Basis of Emotion: A Meta-Analytic Review." *Behavioral and Brain Sciences* 35: 121–202. https://doi.org/10.1017/S0140525X11000446

Lykke, Nina. 2022. *Vibrant Death. A Posthuman Phenomenology of Mourning*. London: Bloomsbury.

Mcwatts, Susheela. 2018. "Yes Madam, I Can Speak!" A Study of the Recovered Voice of the Domestic Worker." Doctoral Thesis. Cape Town: University of the Western Cape. http://etd.uwc.ac.za/xmlui/handle/11394/6164

Richardson, Laurel. 2000. "Writing as a Method of Inquiry." In *Handbook of Qualitative Research* (2nd ed.), edited by Norman K. Denzin and Yvonna S. Lincoln, 923–48. London: SAGE.

St. Pierre, Elizabeth Adams. 2018. "Writing Post Qualitative Inquiry." *Qualitative Inquiry* 24 (9): 603–8.

2 A Black Woman Died at the Intersection(ality) Today

Wanelisa A. Xaba

"Has anyone thought of getting my daughter some fucking medical attention?" *The Grandmother* screams. "Look at all of you! All these damn books that you've read and not enough sense to call an ambulance when a Black woman is dying?"

There is blood everywhere on Liberty Square. The blood forms intricate deep red velvet rivers and thin scarlet silk streams into the four main streets that join at Liberty Square. The lunchtime traffic swooshes this way, that way, and that other-other way as if someone is not dying under a monument engraved "No justice? No peace" at the intersection. Honestly, there is no busier or more preoccupied place on earth than a busy intersection where lies the bleeding body of a Black woman whose life needs saving.

"Phila, please pass me *intsimbi zam*[1] and the Philodendron leaves", *The Grandmother* asks Phila, the Chief Oracle.

"Five hundred years later and we are still dealing with the same fuck-shit", Phila, the Chief Oracle mutters heavily under her breath. She hands *The Grandmother* her blue beads and five Philodendron leaves.

The Grandmother pulls the bleeding body of the Black woman to the centre of the intersection. She places her head underneath the bold yellow "liberty" of the Liberty Square sign. *The Grandmother* kneels by the Black woman's right arm and then crushes the five heart-shaped leaves on her left palm with her thumb. She opens her mouth wide and lets out a howl. A blood-curdling scream that prickles and vibrates underneath the skin. As she wails, silver bullet tears fall from her eyes. She lifts her left palm to her eyes so the tears can fall into the crushed leaves.

Can you imagine *elonyala*[2]? The shame of a wailing old grandmother crying silver bullet tears into her palms over a dying Black woman at the intersection? Especially with the Booksmarts who let the Black woman die, standing at the edge of Liberty Square, blood on their hands?

"When? When did this happen?" The Grandmother asks her voice raw with silver bullet tears.

"Three white men did it, Makhulu",[3] the Black man responds, his hands dripping with blood. "Yes, it was three white men named History, Legacy and Perpetuation who came running".

"I am asking when did this happen and not who did it", *The Grandmother* interrupts the Black man.

DOI: 10.4324/9781003378761-3

34 *Wanelisa A. Xaba*

"At nine in the morning, Makhulu".

"So she has been here for four hours?!" The Grandmother exclaims. "Phila spread her arms apart. Please be gentle".

After the Chief Oracle spread the Black woman's arms, *The Grandmother* gently rubs the tear-stained leaves inside her armpits.

After all, the Black woman was not born bleeding and dying at a busy intersection. Oh no, she was born laughing and swinging her arms. It surprised the doctors at the Somerset Hospital maternity ward too. "Hayini[4]! What kind of baby leaves the womb laughing and jiggling her arms?" the nurses exclaimed and passed her around the ward. It was decided that she would probably grow up to be a dancer and would jiggle her arms into audiences' hearts around the world.

The world is unkind to Black girls born laughing and jiggling their arms. How dare she laugh? Who gave her permission to jiggle her ugly Black arms like that? And at birth too? Fuck it. She must bleed to death, then.

Between just you and me, the Black woman did not need to die at the intersection today. Between the three white murderers, History, Legacy and Perpetuation and *The Grandmother's* screams, she could have survived the wounds had the Booksmarts helped. But instead, they chose to set up leather Gomma Gomma futons in a semi-circle and pulled out their laptops. After every 15 minutes the Black woman would gurgle, spit blood, and whisper, "I just might die today".

After every whisper, someone from the leather Gomma Gomma cabal would get up and explain her situation back to her. Four hours, 16 dying whispers at 15-minute intervals and no one called an ambulance. Each Booksmart was falling deeper and deeper in love with their own theories about the Black woman. "What a sight of beauty", they sighed breathlessly at the rich contrast of her red velvety blood against the bright yellow "Liberty" sign at the intersection. Her rich melanin glistening under the sun. They all agreed: no one looked as beautiful as a Black woman bleeding to death.

"I just might die today", she whispered.

"Yes, you might die. But is it not noble to die? After all the living you have been doing?" whispered the Black man carrying a Frantz Fanon book. All the while, he was breathing, living and not dying.

"I just might die today", she whispered.

"You are not dying. You are going to your heavenly Father. You will never experience the pain of this ungodly world again. Smile and worship, beloved", shouted the Black man stomping on a holy text. All the while, not in pain and not dying.

"I just might die today", she whispered.

"Yes, we are dying too. You people like to pretend you are the only people who experience pain", said the white woman from the leather Gomma Gomma futon. She did not even bother to look up.

"I just might die today", she whispered.

"That is what you get for shucking and jiving for the white man. I remember you! You used to protest with that white woman sitting over there who is now enjoying a Pinotage while you bleed to death", said the Black man wearing an Ankh necklace, enjoying his Shiraz and not calling an ambulance.

A Black Woman Died at the Intersection(ality) Today   35

"I just might die today", she whispered.

"Oh great! You are dying? This would be an amazing opportunity for you to attend our *A Million Ways To Die* three-day symposium and educate us about your unique experience! We will pay you five hundred Euros", said the white woman from the NGO holding a cheque book and a pen.

"I just might die today", she whispered.

"Funny that you mention that", the researcher laughed nervously. "I am currently conducting research on the causes of high death rates among Black women. Unlike the others, I do believe that you are dying. I was hoping you could answer a few questions for my study. I hope that when you have (obviously!) died, my research can help many more Black women in your current situation." She was solemn, determined, and sincere. Yet she also did not call an ambulance.

"I just might die today", she whispered.

"Do. Not. Die. Before. We. Fuck!" the Black man who had snitched on the three white murderers whispered while ogling her plump breasts. Not minding that they were covered in blood. Not remembering to call an ambulance.

"I just might die today", she whispered.

"Don't move! I need you to lie very still!" shouted the Black visual artist. He was biting on his paint brushes and salivating at the spectacle of it all.

Well. She died today. In the uneventful and final way people . . . just die. Fifteen minutes before *The Grandmother* and Phila, the Chief Oracle arrived at Liberty Square. While she took her last loud laborious breaths, everyone typed fast and furiously on their laptops to capture her transition. "Very uneventful" they murmured, a little annoyed, realizing they had packed way too much red wine for a couple of gurgles, loud laborious breaths, and unblinking eyes. How could a person born laughing and jiggling their arms die with so much dignity? Annoying. So. Fucking. Annoying.

Phila, the Chief Oracle turns to *The Grandmother* and asks, "Makhulu why did you use the heart-shaped leaf for this goodbye ceremony? I thought it was poisonous. Is it not?" "These sacred leaves are only poisonous when ingested. When gently rubbed in circular motions into the sweat glands, they have cleansing qualities. These Booksmart people do not understand that every time they stand at the edge of the intersection with bloody hands while a Black woman dies, we have to cleanse her before she transitions into an ancestor. Every Black girl is born with an army of five thousand spirit guides and when she dies, she joins a legion of angels." The Grandmother pauses and blows blue dust into the Black woman's unblinking eyes.

"Five thousand angels who intercede on our behalf. Tirelessly taking our prayers from our mouths directly to God's ears". The Grandmother continues with blue dust residue on her lips. "People don't care that most Black women transition to the other side under traumatic and violent circumstances. Which nation can ever progress with bleeding ancestors? So, we have to cleanse all these girls. I'll tell you this, it's an annoying and thankless job too. Every day and around the clock all we do is wail and cleanse. Wail and cleanse our girls all over these townships' fields and under the hands of these white people. Our lives as Black women are life-long street brawls for self-determination that end in us unblinking at busy intersections." The Grandmother lifts the Black woman's arms that were born jiggling and dancing, folds both her lifeless hands to her unbeating heart, and prays, "Yhuuu *Makukhanye*[5]! Qamata Makude kukhanye".[6]

A Black woman died at a busy intersection today. It could have been avoided. A Black woman was more irresistible dying than alive. If she is lucky, the leather gomma gomma cabal will write books to celebrate her. Or write books celebrating themselves disguised as celebrating her.

Notes

1 My beads
2 The shame
3 Grandmother
4 Wow!
5 Let there be light
6 God, let there be light already.

3 Pedagogies of Precarity

Kharnita Mohamed

Precarity teaches you to not name names. To be silent about those who wound you, have wounded you. Feminists teach this lesson best of all. You will learn through their silence, through the alliances they forge and continue to commit to despite what they know, that what they proclaim is not for you. You will smile anyway. Precarity demands no less.

You will not forget the betrayal. You only truly understand power afterwards. You never forget the high pitch of your voice as you are being erased, the flatness of your smile when you contain the bruises your eyes insist on sharing. No amount of Foucault would ever have soaked that knowing into your bones that the aftermath of being crushed by power, living with all the humiliation that precarity has to teach, has taught you.

It is all a game anyway. Once you would never have believed the truth of this fundamental thing to know that someone who you no longer want to name had told you. You laughed then. In the before, before the betrayals had stacked up and precarity was preferable to one more smile. You didn't know you would have to cobble your own shoes then. Today, you would make the same choices. How else would you have learned?

You cannot reference what you will come to know. You cannot cite it. You cannot even tell the story. No one writes about it. We pretend and pretend and pretend. Those who break our idealism, show us how little some of those celebrated as the thinkers of our freedom actually matter to the freedoms we must ensure. That all their big words, all the abstract shit they sell us as alternate epistemes for freedom are only good when you read their words. Watching what they do breaks your heart. Mostly you learn who not to be, which tools are utterly meaningless. It hurts your very bones to know that someday, someone will read your words and not know that you didn't learn this from a book, that the lessons are people with faces and names.

That the lesson was in a sneer when the famed scholar accused you of ignorance even though you read all the same books and thus learned how deep epistemic violence goes. The lessons were in smiling conversations where all due respect was observed with people in rooms where promises were made and broken and denied.

That the lesson was in the maniacal laughter in the world-famous scholar when they were talking about the lives of people they spent a career on othering and acting as if they were on the side of freedom. Or in that same American university,

DOI: 10.4324/9781003378761-4

38   Kharnita Mohamed

the looks, raised eyebrows touching their foreheads, that your two white feminist classmates would give each other every time you had to remind people that a text was fundamentally racist. That you would learn here how otherness gets made and reproduced and those same people would claim to be the foremost thinkers on the many peoples whose unfreedom gave them the room to bounce their ideas on.

Or the small, contemptuous smile the skinny white feminist at a European restaurant had when she looked at your plate and your fat black body. And you learn that you might sit at the same table but that your corporeality is always in the room. The life of the mind is for those whose bodies don't draw attention.

Or that small, tiny giggle on a different continent after being told to shut up by another white feminist, flush with confidence in your precarity. Another lesson in power by someone who likes to write about decoloniality as if writing and doing are the same thing.

And what about the men you ask? Black men who you labour with towards a new world? Black anti-racist patriarchs are oh so good at thinking about their liberation and subsuming you under it, burying you with their mouths that have ready answers when sometimes a slow awakening might be better. Your utterances will be named a politics of survival and so erased and ignored. The desire for survival is not intellect, is not a place from which thought comes. Bloodless in their abstraction, lessons in rationality learnt from their white male enemies and passed on to you as if it were wisdom. You will nod and note that no-one is immune, no matter how radical their chants are, from reproducing oppression. Reimagined as a new politics because it passes through a different kind of body, it is shat out nonetheless to foul up new solidarities. You will smile through your brokenness. You will say thank you very nicely for shitty wisdom. You have learned your lessons too well.

Or in the work academic liberators with power leave you to do, so they may free their precious time. And you do it. Fill your time with more than one human life can contain and sacrifice love and family and health so they may be great people with time to think great thoughts and have all the things you forego. And they do not have to be burdened with doing things they get to fail at which you do not because security and radical thinking allows you to do less and yet be more.

And you watch them do it to others and you no longer say anything. Some of those people are in the early stages of learning their lessons. And your lessons are not welcome. Your lessons will take away their shine of feeling useful and seen.

Once you were them, when being asked to do anything, was to be affirmed. Even if nothing you made belonged to you. Even though there were all those long long hours of busy busy busy with little that truly in the end mattered, little that truly changed even one life other than yours. You were reshaped. You learned to be in the world, asking for little, doing much, having less time for love and family and all the things making healthy communities, healthy societies need. Doing work, too much work, was the reward. You didn't know that it was a game. One of those shell games, perhaps, where you move the princess' pea around and around between empty cups, except the pea was never there and everyone's sleep is disturbed.

Another lesson in the smile you didn't give the benevolent black patriarch that you were punished and berated for is where you learned what praxis actually

Pedagogies of Precarity 39

entails. There are many many lessons about praxis. Many teachers of praxis. I worry that some day I will teach my students about the necessity for praxis. I so long for my words and actions to have integrity with each other, to have harmony.

Or when the person you think is a friend only cares about how she can use your thinking to write those papers no one cares about. Because that is what the academy demands. To earn your place, you must put your time and energy in proving your worth over and over and over. Like Sisyphus pushing your rock up that hill only to have to start all over when it tumbles down. Producing work for people too worn out by pushing their own rocks and all they can do is shape words that pretends they are keeping up with the storm of paper we are sending into a void. The only worth all your energy has is to show your commitment to this place, this way of being so that it might offer you belonging. This is the world academic precarity has built, where the brightest minds of a generation are having to write more than any-one can read. Where they have to find shortcuts to thinking by mining their friends and lovers and idle pleasures as ruthlessly as any mine-owner who is extracting the labour from exploited miners.

And so it is that your relationships have an edge, across nations and differences, in a world where you are mostly thingified already. The brutality you have lived, the losses that have scarred you, the hard-won knowledge through your erasure, the history you had to have felt to fully understand, the joys that bid you rise in the morning, the people who you had hard hard conversations with to forge new under-standings where you all pulled painfully on the threads of your lives and which finally brought you home to your body, to learning, to knowing anew, to hope of a different world, are not what you ever talk to with her. And so she steals always only the turning and turning of the crucible of your life, that years later emerges in this fluid beautiful one line insight.

But, of course, you know and those who are like you know that there is more, there needs to be more than this one tiny kernel of insight. Because knowing is not living. They are related but not the same. But she who smiles as if she were your friend is weightless and empty of her own insight, afraid of plumbing what it means to live as her, accustomed in an academy that was once foremost about the administration of those without power and so used to adjudicating and feeding off the lives of others, will take your hard-won insight and write about it first. And you, because you had to fight through those broken nights and hopeless mornings and nurse those tender longings you are terrified will be crushed if you allow it to be gazed upon, coming to the page is harder for you. Not as fluid. As graceful. Because you still carry the what-ifs, the aches you cannot visit yet. White feminists teach this lesson best of all.

You will be asked for citations, sometimes you go and find it retrospectively and squeeze and squeeze the words so that this ill-fitting thing can shield you from reviewer number two who has become complicit with betrayer one and two and all their ill-fitting friends and clapping audiences.

We call them: The Academy. When we are bolder, we say: sexists, racists, elit-ists, ableists, Europeans, Americans, whites, Black men, whatever label works so that our critique does not upset an actual person with power. We are so good at

40 *Kharnita Mohamed*

abstracting away the names of the people who break worlds. Who make worlds where the right to life, to earn a living, to learn is tenuous. And at some level many of those people are broken too just like they have tried to break you into an academy in a broken broken world where violence and inequality and the stupidity of the elite flourishes.

But you, you cannot relay the contours of betrayal, the layers and layers of it. The places you don't get invited to, the conversations that are begging for what you know that you are no longer allowed to be a part of. The opportunities that will never come your way because you dared to interrupt the pleasure of not knowing.

The academy will continue without you. It cannot continue without the people whose names you were not supposed to mention. You will run into them at parties and at conferences. You are not to make a scene. You are not to refuse to attend. You are not to scream when someone uses their work as an example of how to think your way out of coloniality. You have stopped telling the stories. Those stories demand too much complexity and you lost people. You lost a whole life, you lost the right to earn a living, you lost yourself.

And you are so threadbare, you don't know how many times you can reinvent yourself. You don't know how many times you can pick your way through a room as if the floor was a minefield. You don't know how many times you can stand to find a room you long to touch with your words and thinking and not break when the door is closed.

You do not scream when the reviewer asks you why you have not cited them. You are to continue to give them life, life in the worlds thinking against them make you imagine. Life in the conversations where you cannot scream when they are invited and you are not. You have to pretend to not see the discomfort from people who know. Feminists teach this lesson best of all.

You teach your students this. The way in which power fucks us all, makes us precarious. You dare them to dream a world where naming names is possible, where slivers of violence do not build and build only to break them. You teach them that there is more than one academy. And that they have to coexist with the one everyone sees but their task, their real task is to find the people who want the same freedoms as they do and find a way to break the academy they have inherited. And until they do and we do, our tools are not yours. If you do not know what they are, then you are not part of the conversation forging them and if you want to be, you have to do the work of building relationships with people whose thinking and way of being allow you to live and for whom you provide a refuge from precarity. You will not read that in a book.

4 Scenes of Precarity

Where Is the Exit?

Redi Koobak

"My wife could do that for you".

Sweating in the afternoon sun while pushing my son's stroller up the steep hill beneath Table Mountain, I had not expected the man passing me on the street to speak to me. For a split second I was confused about what he was referring to. His explanation – "Please, miss, she needs a job" – felt like a relief but the situation was unsettling, nevertheless. Assumptions about skin colour betrayed us both. I was not one of the affluent mostly white residents of the Gardens, the inner-city suburb of the "City Bowl" of Cape Town, where our paths had crossed for a moment. He was not about to harm me.

With shame, I acknowledged to myself that this man's unexpected address had prompted a kneejerk reaction in me. Come to think of it, I had not met a single white mother on the playground where I had just been playing with my son. Unlike him, all the other children there were white, accompanied by their nannies, all of whom were Black. I shouldn't have been surprised that I was, in fact, out of place in this context. A white woman pushing a stroller up the hill in scorching heat in the middle of the day. Back in Norway where we lived at the time and where my son and I used to hike up the mountains with the stroller all the time, this would not have seemed strange at all. My whiteness would be invisible. It would be his non-whiteness that would likely cause heads to turn or prompt the occasional casual comments about his hair.

This is my consciousness of race and class and gender,[1] as I continue my walk towards the Airbnb where we were staying. As a visiting scholar affiliated with a Norwegian university, I was able to bring my family with me to accompany me on my research stay in South Africa and to stay in a neighbourhood up the hill. I tried to imagine what the man's wife was like, how long she had been unemployed for, what kind of work she would like to do, whether she had worked as a nanny before, whether she had any children. What would she make of her husband's comment? Did he really think he could get a job for her approaching a stranger on the street? Or was it more of a remark on my supposed out of placeness in this situation? Walking with my son, without a nanny, performing the physically strenuous task of pushing a stroller up the hill, in a country where my skin colour was bound to register privilege differently than I was accustomed to.

DOI: 10.4324/9781003378761-5

42   *Redi Koobak*

What would this man and his wife say if they heard of the long months of torment both my partner and I spent being unemployed during my pregnancy? Would they have believed me? I didn't look like I could be unemployed. Just as I didn't when I unwittingly hid this fact from my new mom friends at the pregnancy fitness group I attended in central Stockholm. Most of them were white and as I imagined, comfortably placed and timed in life, just as the group's name Mom in Balance suggested. *This is my consciousness of race and class and gender* as I recall trying to shake off the feeling that I might be an unfit mother even before the birth of my child because of failing to secure a permanent position at a university where I had been given one short-term contract after another until one day there were no more. That whole situation had been mortifying. Despite knowing otherwise, I couldn't help feeling it was my own fault. My students got organized and wrote a letter of support. A touching gesture, but all in vain. The decade of commitment made no difference. "You will receive the documents for the unemployment office in due time", the administrator said dryly on my last day. I swallowed tears. And then wept out loud behind the closed doors of my office.

The layers of misrecognitions in my encounter with the South African man whose wife was looking for a job added a visceral quality to my awareness of my structural position and precarity. The historical oppression of poor Black people in South Africa made it very likely that his wife did not have the kind of security blanket that I was able to fall back on when I became unemployed. I had the moral support from the Swedish Association for University Teachers and Researchers who arranged a job coach for me to help me figure out my next steps and I could count on the regular arrival of unemployment checks that were actually enough to live on. I was able to recover relatively fast from the shock of unemployment after finally landing a job just days after the baby was born. While precarity still continued to hover over me like a constant looming reality for a number of years, I did enjoy the freedom to start the new position when I felt ready because the state covered for my parental leave and the university that hired me had an open starting date. *This is my consciousness of race and class and gender* as I contemplate how what I initially perceived as the man's misrecognition of me individually was not, in fact, a misrecognition of where I am placed structurally.

While I could still provide for my family during my unemployment, I struggled with the paralysing anxiety, deep self-doubt, and perpetual questioning of the choices I had made in life. How did I get into this situation? Was I not good enough as an academic? Was I not committed enough? As we are repeatedly told, to secure a permanent position, you need to produce a book. I had not finished my book. I had spent too much time on collaborative projects which don't count as much as the individual ones. What is more, to produce a book, you cannot be producing anything else at the same time – particularly not birthing and caring for a child, as I had been warned on numerous occasions by more established colleagues. Becoming a mother doesn't align well with becoming a tenured academic.

My thoughts shift to my partner and the many years he was unwillingly unemployed in Sweden and Norway. Just as my precarity as a scholar juggling endless short-term contracts in the age of the neoliberal university, his is a story of not

Scenes of Precarity 43

his individual failings but a reflection of broader issues of our broken world. As precarious subjects, we shared the frustration over being made to feel dispensable, superfluous, useless, like failures on our own account. I keep going back and forth between the moments of despair I experienced during these years of uncertainty about my employment and how these clashed with the fact that I will always hold several privileges in a way that my partner never will. There is always another layer to dispensability that as a white person I will never experience. But I have come to know this in my gut, in all its stomach-churning constant ache that I have witnessed him go through when facing the systemic and underacknowledged racism of the Scandinavian labour market, not willing to make accommodations for well-educated Black male émigrés to the point of quite literally telling them to delete their higher education from their CVs, as it happened to him. What's more, his is not a unique story. He tells me many stories of Black and "foreign-born" men who find themselves in situations just like him. At best, they are channelled to low-paid precarious service jobs. In most cases though, they spend years waiting and struggling. He also tells me that in the Swedish society, shaped by a kind of white feminist saviour complex, Black women, though undoubtedly experiencing precarity, are more likely to get employed than Black men. *This is my consciousness of race and class and gender* as I observe the way the society attempts to fix us in hierarchies.

I'm thinking back to a particularly hot August day when I had to go to the *Arbetsförmedlingen* office in the neighbourhood where we lived back then to get registered as unemployed. On my way there, I kept checking Google maps on my phone to make sure I was in the right place. Coincidentally, it turned out to be in the building right next door to the already familiar place where I had been going for my monthly pregnancy check-ups. I had never been to an unemployment office before but had heard my partner lament over how completely useless these meetings with the caseworkers were in terms of actually finding employment. I was frustrated with having to go through this ordeal but made sure I was on time and looked professional. I kept fixing my hair, smoothing my dress, and checking my bag for the hundredth time to convince myself that I had all the required paperwork with me. Entering the building, I became highly aware of how I was somehow out of place. The academic job market doesn't work this way. Jobs are few and far between, and they wouldn't be advertised in the channels that this office uses. My whole body resented being there. I noticed that I was the only white woman in the waiting area. I felt highly visible with my six-month pregnant belly and my Swedish passing appearance. I imagined eyebrows raised at my presence in this office, as if asking what a pregnant Swedish woman might be doing here. But that was probably all in my head. While waiting patiently by the door to be called in, I tried hard not to think of my last day at the university. But my mind was circling back to the deep sense of loss and disappointment and helplessness I had experienced. After all this time, just a cold "good luck!" and bye. Clutching on to my papers as I was called in to the office, I put on a smile and a chill relaxed persona. No big deal, I'm going to be on parental leave soon anyway. I can survive this.

The caseworker was a man in his late forties or early fifties, and he tried to look attentive. He congratulated me in a jolly mode on my soon-to-be born baby,

44   *Redi Koobak*

in Swedish. I smiled apologetically and said firmly that I would like to stick to English in this meeting to feel more professional. He didn't mind and proceeded to ask me where I was from. Upon hearing Estonia, he shared that he was actually from Finland and tried to create a sense of camaraderie between us around the fact that we were both natives of the same language group. Then he continued with the business of the day: assessing my needs on the job market and setting me up in the system as a job seeker. When inquiring me about my language skills, he tried again to speak to me in Swedish, as if testing me. I refused politely for the second time, but this time he responded by crossing out *all* my knowledge of Swedish from my CV, advising me strongly to work on my Swedish. It was clear he had no idea about the academic job market, and he didn't even realize how his peculiar "language test" undermined his own strategy – to convince me I should actively re-evaluate my futile desire for an academic job and look for alternatives. Not recognizing my refusal to speak Swedish as an act of active resistance to the ridiculousness of the situation, he wiped out my actual language skills that might have given me access to other jobs. I couldn't help but feel what I imagined so many of the people I had seen as I was entering this office go through: this frustration that irrespective of your qualifications and skills, dreams and desires, this office channels all the non-Swedes to the same path: the unskilled labour market.

As I write these scenes that prompt me to think about the entanglement of various forms of precarity, academia, motherhood, and intimate relationships, I immediately want to retract my words. To stop myself from making a huge blunder. I doubt the point and use of articulating these private experiences and struggles, particularly through producing an imaginary figure of a nameless precarious Black woman looking to secure employment as a nanny for a white woman and evoking my partner's personal agonies about precarity in contrast to my own, which suddenly, then, don't seem so agonizing in comparison. Do we ever really know precarity through contrasts?

I am often bracketing, leaving things out, beginning to spell out all what is troubling me, and again stopping myself in the tracks. For fear of doing the wrong thing. Of saying the wrong thing. Of being too direct. Or reverse, not direct enough. Of being afraid to be too confrontational, causing trouble. My being more critical in private than in public speaks volumes of white privilege. My survival and dignity are never seriously threatened by not being critical, not taking a stance. I sometimes even wonder if I didn't challenge the way precarity happened to me precisely because I had come to believe my situation was not that bad. It wasn't and it isn't. Yet not challenging the system that produces my precarity contributes to maintaining everyone's precarity. This process of bracketing, the urge to bracket whether it gets suppressed or sometimes not, is tied to being implicated in the structures of privilege.

My precarity only seems to become jarring in those in between moments, and it is indeed connected to my ambition to secure a job in the field that I was trained in. At the same time, with my education and professional experience I would – no doubt – have no problem finding a job outside academia. I have the resources to sustain myself and my family even if I don't get my dream job. Where does one

Scenes of Precarity   45

find moments of resistance in these situations? How do we survive these moments of despair that undo our very beings? How do we repair the broken world?

Two years after beginning this chapter and not having known for the longest how to conclude it, I find myself contemplating: precarity does not end with finally succeeding in getting a permanent position. It has indeed become so normalized, that it is no longer the exception but the very condition of our times. I am still searching for exit routes from the effects of austerity politics in academia that affected me for so many years and that continue to affect so many of my colleagues. This search for ways out must be a collective endeavour and a joint effort. I know in my gut with that same visceral feeling that used to keep me up at night, worrying about yet another job application, that solidarity got a whole new meaning for me when to my great disappointment, my very first lecture at the new job got cancelled due to the University and College Union's strike action which has been extended further. My stability and privilege need to be disrupted until among other issues gender and race pay gap and casualization of contracts are addressed fairly.

This is my consciousness of race and class and gender as I look around those who have joined the picket line and consider those who are not even in this picture – and why. And I am reminded of Tina Campt's reflections on implication and adjacency, "the reparative work of transforming proximity into accountability; the labour of positioning oneself in relation to another in ways that revalue and redress complex histories of dispossession" (Campt 2019). While I could now for the first time acknowledge with a sigh of relief that I don't have to worry about my next gig for a while and neither does my partner for that matter, I need to continue showing up consistently against precarity to say, even if it feels futile: enough is enough.

Note

1 I'm evoking this recurring phrase from June Jordan's essay "Report from the Bahamas" (1982/2003) as a way of affectively connecting the various scenes I am working through.

References

Campt, Tina. 2019. "Political Concepts: Adjacency." Lecture, Brown University, Providence. Accessed February 12, 2023. www.youtube.com/watch?v=3uFtRdVsEJI
Jordan, June. 1982/2003. "Report from the Bahamas." *Meridians* 3 (2): 6–16.

5 Affected Writing

A Decolonial, Intersectional Feminist Engagement With Narratives of Sexual Violence

Rebecca Helman

We are sitting in the kitchen of my house. Tanya[1] sits in the armchair next to the kitchen door. I sit on one of the wooden chairs at the kitchen table, facing towards her. She begins talking, without any prompt from my interview questions. She speaks frankly and composedly about how the rape has affected her life. After a few minutes she begins to recount what happened to her, nearly 30 years ago. Her voice begins to shake and she speaks more and more quietly, as if she is having difficulty getting the words out. She does not look at me but I can see that her eyes have filled with tears. I sit rigidly in my chair, not knowing where to look, consumed by a deep sense of shame.

(Excerpt from my research diary, RH)

Tanya is one of the 16 womxn[2] I interviewed for my PhD research project, focusing on experiences of sexual violence in South Africa. As I have attempted to highlight in this recollection, doing research on sexual violence is deeply uncomfortable. This discomfort is entangled with shame, silencing, and the dismissal of harm which are produced by intersecting raced, classed, and gender (among other) inequalities which characterize "postcolonial" contexts such as South Africa. In this chapter, I attempt to use my discomfort about researching and writing about rape to propose a decolonial, intersectional, feminist approach to sexual violence, which I am calling "affected writing". I present examples of an affective engagement with the narratives of the womxn I interviewed. By focusing on how I am affected by doing research on rape, I attempt to write against colonial, patriarchal "scientific" and "objective" accounts which have contributed to the construction of sexual violence in South Africa as normalized and therefore unaffecting. Therefore, I propose affected writing as a more socially just way of knowing (Law 2016), as it enables possibilities for reflecting on how our research is constituted by the intersecting inequalities which we often seek to critique. This chapter is woven together from various threads, including extracts from mainstream media, critical scholarship, interview transcripts, and excerpts from my research diary. The combination of threads is intended to highlight, at least partially, the complex and multiple layers of doing research on sexual violence, as well as the ways in which I affect and am affected by this work. I have attempted to differentiate these multiple layers via different textual forms for ease of reading: all media and academic extracts are clearly

DOI: 10.4324/9781003378761-6

referenced, extracts from interviews are explicitly indicated, and excerpts from my research diary are italicized.

The Discomfort of Writing About Rape in South Africa

South Africa is globally recognized as "the rape capital of the world"[3] (Moffett 2006; van Schalkwyk 2018). Frequently, in both local and international media, the country is represented as the home of various grotesque and extreme acts of sexual and gender-based violence. For example, an article published by BBC News noted:

> South Africans have been outraged by a spate of gruesome rapes and murders of women in recent weeks – including that of a schoolgirl who reportedly had her head staved in, and a university student who was bludgeoned to death.
>
> (BBC News 2019)

It is undeniable that rates of gender-based violence, including sexual violence, are unacceptably high in South Africa. However, decontextualized representations of South Africa as inherently sexually violent contribute to racist, colonial depictions of Africa and Africans as "naturally" more barbaric and less human (Boonzaier 2017). Current rates of sexual violence, as well as depictions of South Africa as an "inherently" sexually violent context are intimately intertwined with violent legacies of colonialism and apartheid. Within this context, I am mindful of writing about rape in ways that, rather than highlighting these structural conditions per se gives priority to ways of disrupting the normalizing powers of statistical figures through a focus on affect and affectivity.

Western colonial science has contributed in significant ways to the construction of African people in dehumanizing and problematic ways. One particularly painful example of this is the case of Sara Baartman, a young Khoikhoi[4] womxn who was taken from South Africa to Europe in the late 1800s to be exhibited (Crais and Scully 2009). In Europe, Sara was labelled the "Hottentot Venus", and much attention was focused on her sexual parts (Abrahams 1996; Qureshi 2004). These representations of Sara's genitals were employed as "scientific proof" that Black[5] womxn were naturally inferior, lewd, and primordial (McKittrick 2010). Following her death, Sara's body was dissected by Georges Cuvier, the French anatomist, and her remains were displayed in Paris at the Musée de L'Homme (Abrahams 1996). Cuvier had tried to examine Sara while she was alive. However, she had refused to allow him to examine her genitals (Crais and Scully 2009). Postcolonial scholar Sadiah Qureshi has written about how the exhibit in the Musée de L'Homme was constructed as "objectively scientific":

> [H]er skeleton and body cast stood side by side and faced away from the viewer. Above her head rested images of black people. The display exemplified her perceived values as a scientific specimen. The painted tones of the body cast simulated skin whilst the knowledge it was moulded directly from

48　*Rebecca Helman*

her corpse and the presence of her skeleton contributed to the illusion of objectivity.

(2004: 245)

The exhibition is one example of how colonial science constructed African people as *objects* of curiosity (Young 2015). Through focusing primarily on the "bizarre" and the "barbaric", colonial science sought to demonstrate that colonial intervention was required in order to interrupt the savagery of Indigenous peoples (Tamale 2011). Scientific representations of African sexualities were a key mechanism of establishing notions of difference between Europeans and Africans (Gilman 1985). The construction of African people as "primitive", "lustful", "bestial", "lascivious", and "immoral" established them as closer to nature, uncivilized, and less human than Europeans (Epprecht 2009; Tamale 2011). Abrahams (1997) has argued that the "genital encounter" between Sara and European scientists has fundamentally shaped how Black womxn, not only in Africa but across the diaspora, have been constructed.

Feminist and decolonial scholars have highlighted how colonial (mis)representations of African womxn persist in contemporary South Africa. With respect to Anene Booysen, a young Black womxn who was raped and murdered in a small South African town in 2013, Boonzaier (2017) writes: "while the lived and imagined life of Anene Booysen is absent, we are confronted – pornographically and repeatedly – with the gruesome details about how she died and the horror of her injuries" (2017: 477). In the same way as Sara Baartman, Anene Booysen enters public discourse through her dead body (Boonzaier 2017). While Sara Baartman is constituted through her displayed body and the notes of her autopsy, Anene Booysen is constituted through the description of her injuries and the state of her broken body (Abrahams 1997; Boonzaier 2017). Both Sara and Anene's subjectivities are erased by the colonial gaze on their bodies and through this gaze the violence that is perpetrated against them becomes less affecting.

At the office I read endless academic articles about rape in South Africa: "41,583 rapes reported to police in 2018/2019 . . . an average of 114 rapes . . . each day"; "SA has one of the highest incidences of rape in the world". I try to imagine the womxn these statistics are referring to all lined up in neat rows, like they are in the diagrams shared on Facebook depicting what percentage of womxn experience rape in their lifetime. I drive home from work I am confronted again and again by newspaper posters proclaiming: "Half-nude teen found dead in toilet" and "Raped by five men in one day". Some days I feel it a sharp force in my stomach, as if I've been punched. Some days I feel faintly nauseous as I read these horrifying statements. Other days I just feel tired. Sometimes I feel nothing.

(Excerpt from my research diary, RH)

However, as Abrahams (1997) has articulated, the scientific depictions of Sara only tell part of the story. What is left out of these seemingly "objective" accounts

Affected Writing 49

is how Sara must have felt during her examination by a group of white colonial male scientists: "the tears and sheer intimidation of being a woman alone with seven men, all of whom had most dishonourable of intentions" (Abrahams 1997: 45). By focusing on the affective, Sara emerges not as "scientific proof" that Black womxn were "naturally" lewd, inferior, and primordial (McKittrick 2010), but as a young womxn who was violated by a racist and patriarchal practice of colonial science. Similarly, the ways in which rape affects womxn, in multiple and intense ways, are obscured by media representations which focus only on their battered and broken bodies.

Disrupting a Colonial Gaze

In the library of the University of Cape Town, the university where I studied for six years, there was, until 2018, a sculpture of Sara Baartman. The sculpture was made by Willie Bester, a Black South African artist[6], based on the plaster cast of her body that was displayed until 1976 at the Musée de L'Homme in Paris (Abrahams 1996; Black Academic Caucus 2018). In this way, the sculpture was an attempt to problematize the violence and dehumanization produced by scientific representations of Sara (Buikema 2009). However, there has been considerable debate about whether the sculpture instrumentalizes Sara's body in problematic ways (Black Academic Caucus 2018).

> As I proceed up the first flight of stairs in the library I see the sculpture come slowly into view. It is dense and mechanical. I see the breasts protruding sharply. The face is looking away from me. I see the bits and pieces of broken, bent metal welded together. I do not see her. I carry on past the sculpture without stopping and climb the next flight of stairs.
> (Excerpt from my research diary, RH)

In early 2018, the sculpture was de-robed by William Daniels, a white man working as a university librarian. The sculpture had previously been robed on two occasions by a group of Black and queer students and staff in order to restore Sara's dignity (Kessi 2019). In response to Daniels' de-robing of the sculpture, the Black Academic Caucus, a collective of Black academics committed to transforming higher education, based at the University of Cape Town, stated: "taking the robes off so unceremoniously is to shame all of us, reminding us once again, how black women's bodies easily become the repository for violent histories" (2018: n/p). I read the de-robing of Sara as deeply enmeshed in colonial representations of Black womxn, which have rendered them as "less than human". Simultaneously, the robing of the sculpture is an act of resistance to these representations; an act of collective rage that seeks to destabilize the shame that has been inscribed on the bodies of Black womxn for hundreds of years. For me, the robing and de-robing of the sculpture produces a wave of discomfort, this time in relation to my failure to be affected by the sculpture of Sara. As I have highlighted earlier, this lack of affect is constituted by "neutral", "objective" colonial modes of scientific enquiry,

50 *Rebecca Helman*

as well as my positioning as a white, middle-class womxn. As I walk up the stairs I can look away from Sara, as she, through discourses of sexualized racism, has been constructed as "different" and separate from me.

From Discomfort to Affected Writing

In the remains of the chapter, I attempt to use my discomfort to propose an alternative engagement with rape. I ask how engaging *affectively* with the experiences of womxn who have been raped can both highlight and disrupt an unaffected response to rape. This approach is firmly rooted in a relational ethics of care, which I articulate below.

My approach to affected writing draws on affect as Sara Ahmed has articulated it: "[e]motions . . . involve bodily processes of affecting and being affected" (Ahmed 2015: 208). I understand affect and affectivity as related to what bodies can, and do, do in relation to other bodies (Lykke 2018). I am interested in how my affective responses to the narratives of my participants produce relationality, stickiness and movement, as well as specific relations of "away-ness" and "toward-ness" (Ahmed 2015; Seigworth and Gregg 2010). This included focusing on how specific bodies carry burdens of meaning, ability, and expectation, as I have highlighted in relation to Sara Baartman earlier (Sharp 2009).

It is significant that acts of resistance, such as those embodied by the re-robing of Sara Baartman, are occurring within universities which have historically served as (colonial) institutions of knowledge and "truth". Social movements across the globe (for example, #RhodesMustFall in South African and at Oxford University; #RoyallMustFall at Harvard University, and #AsiGanaChile at universities across Chile) are demanding the decolonization of such spaces (Boonzaier and van Niekerk 2019). As the Rhodes Must Fall student movements have so powerfully articulated, it is the affective experience of inhabiting spaces steeped in images and practices of anti-blackness that has promoted demands for higher education institutions to transform (Kessi 2019). The robing of Sara is thus a disruption of the affective infrastructure of the university (Kessi 2019). These kinds of disruptions provoke critical reflection on the ways in which practices of knowledge-making are implicated in the (re)production of intersecting structures of exclusion and inequality. Working within these contexts thus requires a critical, intersectional approach.

Articulating a Decolonial, Intersectional Feminist Approach

Intersectionality has been developed as a framework for understanding oppressions and inequalities as constituted by multiple axes of power. Lykke (2010) has described intersectionality as both a theory and a method which can be used:

> to analyse how historically specific kinds of power differentials and/or constraining normativities, based on discursively, institutionally, and/or structurally constructed socio-cultural categorisations such as gender, ethnicity, race, class, sexuality, age/generation, dis/ability, nationality, mother tongue and so

Affected Writing   51

on, interact, and in so doing produce different kinds of societal inequalities and unjust social relations.

(Lykke 2010: 50)

In articulating a decolonial, intersectional feminist approach to engaging with narratives of rape, I wish to highlight the complex ways in which colonialist legacies continue to constitute gendered and sexualized power relations and subjectivities (Lugones 2010; Oyěwùmí 1997). That is, how racism and sexism, among other systems of oppression, intersect in powerful and violent ways to produce particular kinds of dehumanization. Simultaneously, a decolonial intersectional feminist approach is intended to interrogate the ways in which "an imperial racial economy, with its gendered, sexualized and classed intersections, continues to underwrite dominant ways of knowing, interpreting, and feeling" (Wekker 2016: 2–3). As I have demonstrated earlier, I am interested in how dominant constructions of sexual violence in the South African context produce a particular affective response – one characterized by a kind of unaffectedness, particularly in response to the violation of poor, Black womxn. The "de" in decolonial gestures towards an undoing which opens up possibilities for a different doing (Bacchetta and Maese-Cohen 2010). Thinking through a decolonial intersectional feminist lens creates the possibility for seeing the commonalities in womxn's experiences of rape, while simultaneously not glossing over the ways in which these experiences of rape are constituted differently by virtue of womxn's intersecting social positionings.

Writing Carefully

In opposition to decontextualized, patriarchal and Western-centric conceptions of research ethics as abstract notions of "harm", "consent", and "beneficence", feminist and decolonial scholarship has called for a broadening of ethics to include examinations of the ethics of knowledge *itself* (Gillies and Alldred 2002). The disruption of violent and colonial research practices requires a broader focus on ethics, including more messy and complex engagement with the hierarchies of power, politics of difference, and conflicting concerns in which research is embedded (Posel and Ross 2014). Gilligan's (1982) "ethics of care" has been important for centring the relational nature of the research encounter and for proposing more reciprocal relationships between researchers and participants (Dutt and Kohfeldt 2018). I understand care as María Puig de la Bellacasa has articulated it: "[c]aring in this context is both a doing and ethico-political commitment that affects the way we produce knowledge about things" (Puig de la Bellacasa 2017: 66).

I am concerned with the ethical complexity of doing research on rape in South Africa. I have asked my participants to share intimate and painful stories, in a context in which rape is still deeply steeped in shame. Simultaneously, in South Africa, sexual violence has become almost "ordinary" (van Schalkwyk 2018); there is the potential for voyeuristic and uncompassionate engagement with the experiences of womxn who have been raped (Cvetkovich 2003). This is perhaps particularly pertinent with regard to the experiences of Black womxn who are repeatedly represented

52 *Rebecca Helman*

as the "inevitable" victims of sexual violence. Here, it is necessary to acknowledge the politics of writing about their violations. Within this context moments of discomfort represent important opportunities to interrogate that which is constructed as normative and comfortable (Ahmed 2015). I have written elsewhere about the deep discomfort that I felt as a result of an encounter at a healthcare centre after I was raped:

> A month after I was raped I am sitting in the waiting room of the Heideveld Thutuleza Care Centre[7] waiting to have an HIV test. On the couch opposite me, there is another womxn. She looks about eighteen. She is Black. In her hand she is holding the care package and the information book that I received when I came in a month ago, a few hours after I was raped. The nurse approaches the two of us in the waiting room. She turns to me, "Who are you bringing for an appointment?" I look at her confused. "Who is the patient?" she asks. "I am the patient". "Oh", she says. She looks surprised. In a context in which the bodies of poor Black womxn are repeatedly constructed as the sites of sexual violence the nurse is unable to recognise my white, middle-class body as the site of such violence.
>
> (Helman 2018: 403)

My discomfort of being "out of place" at the Thuthuzela Care Centre sharply surfaces assumptions about who is and isn't rapable. In the same way, by engaging with moments of discomfort produced in my engagements with other womxn who have experienced rape, I seek to disrupt the ways in which sexual violence has become normalized and therefore unaffecting in South Africa, "the rape capital of the world". This approach to affected writing recognizes the ways in which research, for example, in the form of colonial "science" which constructs itself as "objective truth", has contributed to rending rape (and the rape of certain womxn in particular) unaffecting. Using my own discomfort as a starting point, I ask the possibilities are for knowing and feeling differently about rape (Campbell 2002; Law 2016).

Affected by Rape

My discomfort in my interview with Tanya, which I introduced at the beginning of this chapter, was produced by a deep sense of shame. I "catch" Tanya's shame as she re-tells her experience of violation (Probyn 2005). Just as she is unable to look at me as she struggles to articulate what happened to her, I am compelled by a deep desire to look away from her. Therefore, hearing her shame becomes a shaming experience for me (Tantam 1998). To avoid this sense of shame, I turn away from her (Ahmed 2015). My desire to separate myself from this shame, and from Tanya who has become the object of shame, reflects a broader social desire to separate and disengage from rape. Processes of shaming womxn who experience rape serve to attribute the cause of rape to victims' individual behaviour, thereby

Affected Writing 53

creating a separation between "us" and "them". The notion that rape only happens to certain womxn creates a (false) sense of comfort for others that they can prevent themselves from being raped by adhering to certain behaviours, for example, not wearing "provocative" clothes, not drinking too much, not walking in public late at night (Campbell 2002; Moffett 2006).

Simultaneously, the construction of some communities as more dangerous and violent serves to demarcate areas of "risk". For example, in South Africa as a result of the spatial legacy of apartheid, middle- and upper-class suburbs (which continue to be predominantly inhabited by white South Africans) remain safer spaces than working-class townships (Mlamla 2019). Sympathetic media representations and public horror in response to the rapes of white and middle-class womxn reinforces the notion that these womxn should be "safe" from rape. In contrast, the violence that happens in poor, predominantly Black, townships tends to be constructed as "normal" and therefore to some extent "acceptable". The construction of these communities as hopeless spaces, in which rape is a frequent "normal" occurrence, is rooted in colonial notions of Africa and African people as inherently "evil", "anti-human", and "barbaric" (Boonzaier 2017). I am ashamed of the shame I feel in response to Tanya. My response reifies the idea that being raped (and daring to talk about it) is shameful. This served to intensify the attachment of shame to womxn who are raped rather than to those who rape them (Moffett 2006). This realization creates an intense sense of fury in me. The shame should not be ours to carry! I am reminded of the increasingly palpable rage of womxn in South Africa in recent years, expressed through protests across the country – collective refusals to be shamed, similar to that enacted in the re-robing of Sara Baartman. Young womxn display their breasts and march in their underwear as part of the RU (referring to Rhodes University) Reference List[8] protest at the University Currently Known as Rhodes (UCKAR) demanding "enough is enough – we are tired of this violence" (Gouws 2018). Womxn coming together to march in both Johannesburg and Cape Town after the murder of Uyinene Mrwetyana, the 19-year-old student from the University of Cape Town, who was raped and killed at a post office, by one of the post office workers, when she went to collect a parcel (Khumalo 2019). I remember one of the posters from the march in Cape Town, which proclaimed "your penis should be in your jockey [underwear], not in my vagina". I remember Sam[9] telling me in our interview about one day when she screamed at a man in the street who was following her and her friend:

> This guy followed us then touched our thighs and carried on walking. [Inhales] And then he followed us again and was getting closer to us. . . . This was like post-rape. It was this year. And then when he got close to me I started *screaming* like . . . b- like bloody murder [Rebecca: Mhmm] like at him. And it's a new response.

I imagine her standing there in the busy street, compelled by both terror and rage that this man *dare* touch her. That he has no shame in assaulting her on the street in

54   *Rebecca Helman*

the view of others. Once again proof that the shame of sexual violence attaches to victims and not perpetrators. As Holloway has written:

> In the beginning is the scream. We scream. . . . The starting point of theoretical reflection is opposition, negativity, struggle. It is from rage that thought is born, not from the pose of reason, not from the reasoned-sitting-back-and-reflecting-on the-mysteries-of-existence that is the conventional image of "the thinker".
>
> (2002: 2)

Alongside shame, rage has been a central affect of the discussions between my participants and I. In my interview with Nomvula,[10] we spoke about the man who had raped her and then offered to help her get a morning after pill the next day:

Nomvula: I woke up in the middle of the night and there was someone on top of me . . . nak- and I was naked [Rebecca: Mhmm] . . . and I was confused . . . so he tried to convince me that we were having sex . . . and he told me that he used a condom to begin with and then he removed it . . . so I knew that I needed to . . . you know um . . . at least get a morning after pill [Rebecca: Mhmm]. . . . So . . . he offered to help me get one.
Rebecca: Oh how generous of him!
Nomvula: Coz he's such a kind person. Because . . . he's done this horrible thing to me [R: Yeah] but he's so compassionate.

We laugh at the absurdity of the situation – a man calmly and composedly accompanying the womxn he has raped to the pharmacy the next day so that she does not get pregnant. Our laughter is full of rage and contempt – not only for him but also for a society that so easily dismissed the harm that rape does to womxn, a society that has confused and distorted our own understandings of our violations, where we so much more easily feel shame than rage at what has been done to us. We laugh ourselves free of this absurdity, we laugh our rage into being. But of course, embodying this rage is complex and steeped in discomfort. We are not all equally titled to express our rage. Some of us are "already stereotyped as rageful, violent, or shrill" (Srinivasan 2018: 136). As feminist and decolonial scholars have demonstrated, "legitimate rage" is raced, classed and gendered in significant ways (Cooper 2018; Palmer 2017). While white masculine rage is increasingly institutionalized and weaponized, the rage of poor Black people, and womxn in particular, is positioned as "disruptive", "inconvenient", and "excessive" (Boyce Kay and Banet-Weiser 2019). This work highlights the way in which an uneven distribution of affect (Bargetz 2015) creates different possibilities for responding to sexual violence. The positioning of certain instances of rape as "deserving" of collective attention and rage remains deeply political, intertwined with intersecting racialized, classed, gendered (among others) social structures.

Limitations of My Approach

While I attempted to create affective connections between my experiences and those of my participants within the interviews, it is also important to acknowledge the limitations of this affective approach. As Hemmings has argued, "[a]ffects do not only bring us together, whatever our intentions; they also force us apart or signal the lack of any real intersubjective connection" (2012: 153). As I have shown with regard to shame, being affected by the experiences of others does not necessarily create solidarity. To elaborate this point further, I shall reflect on a moment of being unaffected or failing to be appropriately affected in my interview with Nomvula. This example highlights the complexity of working affectively in a context constituted by both material and discursive inequalities. The particular exchange emerged as Nomvula was telling me about her most recent experience of rape, during her explanation I jokingly interjected a remark about how men try to convince womxn to have sex with them:

Nomvula: And then this year um . . . I was . . . I'd just come out from a night of drinking with my friends [Rebecca: Mhmm] . . . I don't remember how I got into the car . . . um . . . he [the taxi driver] was saying stuff to me [inhales] "you're so beautiful. You're so pretty can I just have one night with you?" Then I was like . . . "no. I just wanna go home" [Rebecca: ja]. Then he was like um "I'll pay you if you want? I'll give you x amount – "

Rebecca: Oh because [Nomvula laughs] that'll make it ok.

Nomvula: [laughing] and I was like "ja. O – x amount whatever". Then I was like . . . "ok I can do that. If you're gonna pay me I don't mind because I'm very broke right now" . . . So . . . we go . . . we do what we do and then he refuses to pay me [Rebecca: Mhmm]. So for me . . . I don't know . . . you know the logistics of rape or whatever but . . . for me I felt like I was raped.

I realized immediately after I had made the joking remark that I had made a deeply insensitive and damaging assumption. Another moment of squirming discomfort produced by deep shame. This time produced by my own economic position of privilege, which renders a situation in which I would need to provide sex for money almost unimaginable. This is an example of how structural inequalities constrain the ability to witness the experiences of others (Wise 1987). Simultaneously, this comment is also constituted by dominant narrative of what "real rape" (Estrich 1987) looks like. I had anticipated that Nomvula was going to say that when she refused the taxi driver's advances he became angry and resorted to violence. In a context in which extreme forms of physical violence are ever-present, "where babies and old women are raped on a daily basis, where young girls' maimed bodies are found dumped on empty fields" (van Schalkwyk 2018: 1), it becomes easy to anticipate these kinds of stories, at the cost of not hearing others. The exchange between Nomvula and me is therefore also about the power of hegemonic rape narratives to silence alternative experiences by rendering them "less affecting". The

56 *Rebecca Helman*

deep sense of discomfort and shame that I felt in relation to my comment to Nomvula has been instructive for thinking about the limitations of an affective approach which focuses only on symmetry and what is shared between myself and my participants. As feminist scholars have argued that focusing on congruence, while paying insufficient attention to difference, risks constructing a falsely homogenized understanding of social phenomena (Gillies and Alldred 2002). A focus only on what is shared or similar in womxn's experiences of rape risks glossing over the uneven social context in which rape occurs. As I have attempted to show, a decolonial intersectional feminist engagement allows me to connect with and get closer to the experiences of my participants, while simultaneously highlighting the gaps that exist between our experiences of rape. An engagement with the discomfort that is produced by these gaps or moments of becoming both affected and unaffected is therefore a central part of affected writing.

Concluding Feelings

In this chapter, I have attempted to show how an affected approach to research and writing creates possibilities for knowing differently. If we want to know differently, we have to feel differently and use these feelings to write differently (Hemmings 2012). I have shown how doing research on rape is deeply uncomfortable, as it should be in light of the significant effects that rape has on the lives of those who experience it. By engaging with the ways in which we, as researchers, are affected by our research we may be able to engage with and disrupt the (re)production of social inequalities, including those that are (re)produced by our research practices. Affected writing, as a decolonial, intersectional feminist approach, may be particularly useful within the context of transnational research. As I have demonstrated earlier, colonial knowledge practices continue to perpetuate global inequalities between "North" and "South", with the Global South frequently represented as the home of particularly extreme and grotesque forms of sexual violence. Within this context, an engagement with discomfort (both individual and collective) may serve as an important starting point for destabilizing the normalized, intersecting hierarchies of power within which we and our research are embedded.

Notes

1 Pseudonyms have been used to protect the identities of participants. Tanya is a white, middle-class, Afrikaans-speaking womxn in her fifties.
2 I am using the term "womxn" to refer people who identify as women, female, femme, or trans to highlight the fluid and diverse way in which gender is constructed and experienced.
3 This term has been widely used to refer to South Africa as a whole and not a specific city within the country.
4 The Khoikhoi, who are also referred to as the Khoisan, are the Indigenous inhabitants of South Africa (Abrahams 2003).
5 The uses of the terms "Black" and "white" are deeply problematic in South Africa, given their utilization in the system of apartheid. I therefore use these terms here tentatively and with much discomfort. I recognize that while race is a social construction rooted in colonial relations of power, racialization operates as a social reality with significant

Affected Writing 57

discursive and material effects. I use the term "Black" to refer to all people who were classified as "non-white" by the racist legislation of apartheid.

6 Bester's status as a Black artist is significant given that historically the works of Black artists have been excluded from institutional spaces such as universities, in light of colonialism and apartheid. The display of this particular sculpture in 2000 (made by a Black artist and reflecting on such a powerful example of racism) can be seen as an attempt to disrupt or at least call into question the coloniality of the University of Cape Town.

7 Thuthuzela Care Centres (TCCs) are multi-service or "one-stop" facilities for those who have experiences rape. The centres are intended to reduce secondary victimization and to support successful prosecution.

8 The RU (referring to Rhodes University) Reference List was an online list of the names of 11 male students at UCKAR who were well known for sexually violating womxn students. The release of the list was in response to the University's failure to take action against these students (Gouws 2018).

9 Sam is a white, middle-class womxn in her late twenties.

10 Nomvula is a Black womxn in her mid-twenties. She described herself as being between working and middle class in light of the instability of her financial situation.

References

Abrahams, Yvette. 1996. "Was Eva Raped? An Exercise in Speculative History." *Kronos* 23 (1): 3–21.

Abrahams, Yvette. 1997. "The Great Long National Insult: 'Science', Sexuality and the Khoisan in the 18th and Early 19th Century." *Agenda* 13 (32): 34–48. https://doi.org/10.1080/10130950.1997.9675585.

Abrahams, Yvette. 2003. "Colonialism, Dysfunction and Disjuncture: Sarah Bartmann's Resistance (remix)." *Agenda* 58 (3): 12–26. https://doi.org/ 10.1080/10130950.2003.9674488

Ahmed, Sara. 2015. *The Cultural Politics of Emotion* (2nd ed.). London: Routledge.

Bacchetta, Paola, and Marcelle Maese-Cohen. 2010. "Decolonial Praxis: Enabling Intranational and Queer Coalition Building." *Qui Parle: Critical Humanities and Social Sciences* 18 (2): 147–92.

Bargetz, Brigitte. 2015. "The Distribution of Emotions: Affective Politics of Emancipation." *Hypatia* 30 (3): 580–96. https://doi.org/10.1111/hypa.12159

BBC News. 2019. "Sexual Violence in South Africa: 'I Was Raped, Now I Fear for My Daughters'." *BBC News*, September 12. www.bbc.co.uk/news/world-africa-49606146

Black Academic Caucus. 2018. "The Place of Sara Baartman at UCT." *Thought Leader*, March 26. https://thoughtleader.co.za/blackacademiccaucus/2018/03/26/the-place-of-sara-baartman-at-uct/

Boonzaier, Floretta. 2017. "The Life and Death of Anene Booysen: Colonial Discourse, Gender-Based Violence and Media Representations." *South African Journal of Psychology* 47 (4): 470–81.

Boonzaier, Floretta, and Taryn van Niekerk. 2019. "Introducing Decolonial Feminist Community Psychology." In *Decolonial Feminist Community Psychology*, edited by Floretta Boonzaier and Taryn van Niekerk, 1–10. Cham: Springer.

Boyce Kay, Jilly, and Sarah Banet-Weiser. 2019. "Feminist Anger and Feminist Respair." *Feminist Media Studies* 19 (4): 603–9. https://doi.org/10.1080/14680777.2019.1609231

Buikema, Rosemarie. 2009. "The Arena of Imaginings: Sarah Baartman and the Ethics of Representation." In *Doing Gender in Media, Art and Culture*, edited by Rosemarie Buikema and Iris van der Tuin, 78–93. New York: Routledge.

Campbell, Rebecca. 2002. *Emotionally Involved: The Impact of Researching Rape*. New York, NY: Routledge.

58   Rebecca Helman

Cooper, Brittney. 2018. *Eloquent Rage: A Black Feminist Discovers Her Superpower.* New York, NY: St Martin's Press.

Crais, Clifton, and Pamela Scully. 2009. *Sara Baartman and the Hottentot Venus: A Ghost Story and a Biography.* Princeton, NJ: Princeton University Press.

Cvetkovich, Ann. 2003. *An Archive of Feelings: Trauma, Sexuality, and Lesbian Public Cultures.* Durham, NC: Duke University Press.

Dutt, Anjali, and Danielle Kohfeldt. 2018. "Towards a Liberatory Ethics of Care Framework for Organising Social Change." *Journal of Social and Political Psychology* 6 (2): 575–90.

Epprecht, Marc. 2009. "Sexuality, Africa, History." *The American Historical Review* 114 (5): 1258–72.

Estrich, Susan. 1987. *Real Rape.* Cambridge, MA: Harvard University Press.

Gillies, Val, and Pam Alldred. 2002. "The Ethics of Intention: Research as a Political Tool." In *Ethics in Qualitative Research*, edited by Melanie Mauthner, Maxine Birch, Julie Jessop, and Tina Miller, 33–52. London: SAGE.

Gilligan, Carol. 1982. *In a Different Voice: Psychological Theory and Women's Development.* Cambridge, MA: Harvard University Press.

Gilman, Sander. 1985. *Difference and Pathology: Stereotypes of Sexuality, Race and Madness.* Ithaca, NY: Cornell University Press.

Gouws, Amanda. 2018. "#EndRapeCulture Campaign in South Africa: Resisting Sexual Violence through Protest and the Politics of Experience." *Politikon* 45 (1): 315–29. https://doi.org/10.1080/02589346.2018.1418201

Helman, Rebecca. 2018. "Mapping the Unrapeability of White and Black Womxn." *Agenda* 32 (4): 10–21. https://doi.org/10.1080/10130950.2018.1533302.

Hemmings, Clare. 2012. "Affective Solidarity: Feminist Reflexivity and Political Transformation." *Feminist Theory* 13 (2): 147–61. https://doi.org/10.1177/1464700112442643.

Holloway, John. 2002. *Change the World Without Taking Power: The Meaning of Revolution.* London: Pluto Press.

Kessi, Shose. 2019. "Towards a Decolonial Psychology: Defining and Confining Symbols of the Past." *Museum International* 71 (1–2): 80–87. https://doi.org/10.1080/13500775.2019.1638032

Khumalo, Thuso. 2019. "South African Declares 'Femicide' a National Crisis." *VOA News*, September 20. www.voanews.com/africa/south-africa-declares-femicide-national-crisis.

Law, Siew Fang. 2016. "Unknowing Researcher's Vulnerability: Re-searching Inequality on an Uneven Playing Field." *Journal of Social and Political Psychology* 4 (2): 521–36.

Lugones, Maria. 2010. "Towards a Decolonial Feminism". *Hypatia* 25 (4): 742–59.

Lykke, Nina. 2010. *Feminist Studies: A Guide to Intersectional Theory, Methodology and Writing.* New York, NY: Routledge.

Lykke, Nina. 2018. "When Death Cuts Apart: On Affective Difference, Compassionate Companionship and Lesbian Widowhood." In *Affective Inequalities in Intimate Relationships*, edited by T. Juvonen and M. Kolehmainen, 109–24. London: Routledge.

McKittrick, Katherine. 2010. "Science Quarrels Sculpture: The Politics of Reading Sarah Baartman." *Mosaic: An Interdisciplinary Critical Journal* 43 (2): 113–30.

Mlamla, Sisonke. 2019. "Crime Stats: Despite 6% Decrease in Cases, Nyanga Still Remains the Murder Capital of SA." *IOL*, September 12. Accessed June 6, 2019. www.iol.co.za/capeargus/news/crime-stats-despite-6-decrease-in-cases-nyanga-still-remains-the-murder-capital-of-sa-32852205.

Moffett, Helen. 2006. "'These Women, They Force Us to Rape Them': Rape as Narrative of Social Control in Post-Apartheid South Africa." *Journal of Southern African Studies* 32 (1): 129–44. https://doi.org/10.1080/03057070500493845

Oyěwùmí, Oyèrónkẹ́. 1997. *The Invention of Women: Making an African Sense of Western Gender Discourses*. Minneapolis, MN: University of Minnesota Press.

Palmer, Tyrone. 2017. "'What Feels More Than Feeling?': Theorizing the Unthinkability of Black Affect." *Critical Ethnic Studies* 3 (2): 31–56.

Posel, Deborah, and Fiona Ross. 2014. "Opening Up the Quandaries of Research Ethics: Beyond the Formalities of Institutional Ethical Review." In *Ethical Quandaries in Social Research*, edited by Deborah Posel and Fiona C. Ross, 1–26. Cape Town: HSRC Press.

Probyn, Elspeth. 2005. *Blush: Faces of Shame*. Minneapolis, MN: University of Minnesota Press.

Puig de la Bellacasa, María. 2017. *Matters of Care: Speculative Ethics in More Than Human Worlds*. Minneapolis, MN: University of Minnesota Press.

Qureshi, Sadiah. 2004. "Displaying Sara Baartman, the 'Hottentot Venus.'" *History of Science* 42 (2): 233–57. https://doi.org/10.1177/007327530404200204.

Seigworth, Gregory, and Melissa Gregg. 2010. "An Inventory of Shimmers." In *The Affect Theory Reader*, edited by Melissa Gregg and Gregory J. Seigworth, 1–28. Durham, NC: Duke University Press.

Sharp, Joanne. 2009. "Geography and Gender: What Belongs to Feminist Geography? Emotion, Power and Change." *Progress in Human Geography* 33 (1): 74–80. https://doi.org/10.1177/0309132508090440.

Srinivasan, Amia. 2018. "The Aptness of Anger." *The Journal of Political Philosophy* 26 (2): 123–44. https://doi.org/10.1111/jopp.12130

Tamale, Sylvia. 2011. "Researching and Theorising Sexualities in Africa." In *African Sexualities: A Reader*, edited by Sylvia Tamale, 11–35. Cape Town: Pambazuka Press.

Tantam, Digby. 1998. "The Emotional Disorders of Shame". In *Shame: Interpersonal Behaviour, Psychopathology and Culture*, edited by P. Gilbert and B. Andrews, 161–75. New York, NY: Oxford University Press.

van Schalkwyk, Samantha. 2018. *Narrative Landscapes of Female Sexuality in Africa: Collective Stories of Trauma and Transition*. Cham: Palgrave Macmillan.

Wekker, Gloria. 2016. *White Innocence: Paradoxes of Colonialism and Race*. Durham, NC: Duke University Press.

Wise, Sue. 1987. "A Framework for Discussing Ethical Issues in Feminist Research: A Review of the Literature." In *Writing Feminist Biography 2: Using Life Histories*, edited by V. Griffiths, 47–88. Manchester: University of Manchester Press.

Young, Sandra. 2015. *The Early Modern Global South in Print: Textual Form and the Production of Human Difference as Knowledge*. New York, NY: Routledge.

6 Notes From My Field Diary

Revisiting Emotions in the Field

Susheela Mcwatts

At a seminar for postgraduate students in Cape Town, one of the persistent questions asked was how one incorporates emotions into research and how one writes one's own voice into research. I reflected on the fact that voice and emotions had significance for me too when writing my thesis, and this was probably due to Black South Africans having their voices and emotions shut down and policed for hundreds of years through the legally enforced system of apartheid. I remembered when writing my own story in the preface of my thesis, that it felt surreal that I could so freely write about a period of my life where my voice was silenced through an oppressive regime, because I was black and because I was a woman. Thus, when writing on the activism of domestic workers in my doctoral thesis, I felt a sense of liberation in being able to listen to their voices without claiming neutrality or objectivity, as demanded by a positivist framework. Rather, the strength of feminist methodology and reflexive research in Steve Biko's (1970) words allowed me to write what I liked.[1]

I devoted an entire chapter, titled *Stories of the Heart* in my doctoral thesis (Mcwatts 2018), to the stories of the domestic worker leaders. Stories straight from the heart have the potential to create a greater "empathic understanding" (Farrelly and Nabobo-Baba 2012: 1). However, while reading through my field diary five years later and reflecting on my thesis, I realized that the participants' emotions and feelings in their narrative accounts, although empathetically understood by me, were nevertheless mostly erased by me, mainly due to my not having the conceptual and methodological tools to incorporate these in my research.

When reading through my study and field diary, I took heed of anthropologists Anderson and Smith's (2001: 7) exhortation that "there are moments where lives are so explicitly lived through pain . . . that the power of emotional relations cannot be ignored", and that is when I decided that I had to revisit the emotions prevalent in the field. I was reminded of renowned anthropologist Ruth Behar's (1996) ethnographic memoir, *The Vulnerable Observer: Anthropology That Breaks Your Heart*, in which she speaks of the anxiety and how ethically charged it is to get close to the lives of your participants, just to leave when the funding dries up or when the summer vacation comes to an end. She says, then you are required to "please stand up, dust yourself off, go to your desk, and write down what you saw and heard" (Behar 1996: 5). Indeed, in the conclusion of my thesis, I wrote "there were many moments in this project that I could not capture, that I wished I could" (Mcwatts 2018: 152).

DOI: 10.4324/9781003378761-7

The aim of this chapter is thus to revisit my field diary and analyse the emotions that were prevalent in the field through the lens of reflexivity. I captured my thoughts in my field diary while conducting interviews in August 2015, so five years have since elapsed. Revisiting my field diary makes me reflect on my own growth – as a feminist and a scholar and as an empathic human being that believes that emotions play a fundamental role in all social phenomena. It comes to me that to practice reflexivity only during the course of a study but not during writing is to miss the point. In my present understanding, reflexivity is on a recursive loop, free from the constraints of time, therefore each time I return to my research I am rewarded with richer insights, especially gained which may have eluded me in the previous rounds.

Post-Study Reflexivity: Emotions as Discourse

The aim of my doctoral thesis was to shift the debate away from the victim status assigned to domestic workers through an exploration of contemporary domestic worker leaders' activism and to understand how domestic worker leaders' experiences shape their agency and activism (Mcwatts 2018). All of the domestic worker leaders in my study were marginalized women of colour mostly from the Global South and Asian countries. At the same time, these women's activism often crossed regional, national, and international boundaries.

As a Black South African, who once was an activist and marginalized herself, I realized that I was privileged that these women trusted me with their stories and journeys of their activism to change their own lives and those of future domestic workers. As marginalized subjects usually suffer multifaceted oppressions, novel ways of doing research are usually required, even more so if the researcher wants to empower the subjects by eliciting their voice and agency, because of the political commitment of feminist research. During my research, I struggled to be a producer of knowledge without being trapped into the reproduction of patriarchal ways of knowing. By patriarchal ways of knowing I mean "positivist social scientific research methods, [which] often either ignore the emotions of the researcher, or argue that emotional expressions are to be avoided in research, even when the topic is thought to inspire intense feelings" (Cain 2012: 396). Having being schooled in the positivist tradition and only learning about and using feminist methodologies in my doctoral research, I did not have the epistemological tools to communicate the emotions inherent in the research process nor to critically examine my emotions and those of the participants. This was unfortunate, given that "research is an emotional process" (Evans 2012: 503) and emotions are important in the performative undertaking that fieldwork is. Furthermore, since my study was on the activism of domestic worker leaders, being able to communicate the emotions in the field as they arose may have provided richer data since emotions, which result from social situations and facilitate social action influence thoughts, actions (Lutz and White 1986) and future behaviour and may have also revealed the concealed, intersectional exercizes of power. This contention is supported by human geographers Laliberte and Schurr, who argue that when examining the politics of knowledge

62 *Susheela Mcwatts*

production and power relations, as I did in my research, it would be possible "to make visible how the power relations of sexism, racism, capitalism, nationalism and imperialism permeate and constitute emotional spaces in the field" (2016: 1).

It was also important to take into account the geopolitical situatedness of both myself as a researcher and the domestic worker leaders as participants, which provided more accurate and situated narratives, while I conducted my research. Of significance too, was the culture that produces emotions as a discourse and in my writing, the culture of activism and, in particular, the culture of women of colour fighting against their oppression. As anthropologist Nancy Scheper-Hughes (1992: 430) argues:

> emotions do not precede or stand outside of culture; they are part of culture and of strategic importance to our understanding of the ways in which people shape and are shaped by their world. Emotions are not reified things in and of themselves, subject to an internal, hydraulic mechanism regulating their buildup, control and release. . . . In other words emotions are discourse; they are constructed and produced in language and in human interaction. They cannot be understood outside the cultures that produce them.

I now turn my attention to my field diary.

Revisiting the Field Diary

Reading through my field diary, I remembered three encounters most vividly and the feelings and emotions they evoked and still do. I present here three extracts of narratives of these encounters as well as my thoughts and feelings about these narratives as captured in the field diary after I conducted the interviews. First, I engage in an intersubjective reflection to capture these encounters and their emotional dimensions, and then I will assess the implications these reflexive accounts have for a revised methodology.

A vivid recollection of my encounter with Myrtle[2], a domestic worker leader and activist from South Africa who was very involved with the anti-apartheid struggle, was the question I posed to her – I asked her whether she was ever scared. It must be noted that this question was not included in my interview schedule, but I felt impelled to ask her given the line her story during the interview was taking in terms of the anti-apartheid struggle. I also asked her that question because of my own memories. I remembered the fear I felt of the anti-apartheid police, and I was curious to find out whether a global, larger than life activist sitting in front of me also experienced the vulnerability and fear as I did.

This is how Myrtle answered:

> The only time I got scared was one night when my daughter phoned me and my daughter said that the police were there and Peter, my baby son, said to the cops "my mommy is tired of you". He was still a child. My daughter said she thought the cops were going to hit Peter and that was the only time I felt

scared. The second time was when they locked me up with Allan Boesak[3], Desmond Tutu[4] and them. We were locked up for talking about our rights. I remember it was my birthday and the cops started singing and I got so angry, how dare they? They still said to us "you will not have Kentucky[5], you will have pap[6]" because they liked to terrorize us.

After listening to Myrtle's story, I wrote in my field diary the following:

That was hard listening to. I can still remember the fear I felt when picked up by the special branch of the police services for my political activities and the threats they made against the family. I remember that grinning imbecile, Loots, who tried to instil the fear of the devil in me and how I tried to act brave. I can still feel the fear viscerally – especially for Thata[7], who they threatened and who tried to bribe them with whisky just so that they do not harm me. Myrtle must have felt so scared, not only for herself, but also her family. But then again, she said she felt anger and so did I. A curious mix of emotions. I remember that this did not stop me. In fact, if anything, their dirty tactics made me angrier, their threats against my family made me resolute, I was going to show them that apartheid has made us strong and that we will overcome. That's probably what Myrtle felt too.

Indeed, it is those aggressions and assaults against my personhood that impelled me to take on leadership positions in the struggle against apartheid, to make my voice heard and become an executive member of the Cape Town branch of the African National Congress. Myrtle and I shared a history, albeit a painful one, that deepened our bond and contributed to the richness of our connection and the subsequent data elicited from such connection. I could identify with her struggles and she with mine. Comparing our lived experiences was done, as so eloquently put by anthropologist Crapanzano (2010: 65), "neither out of egoism or as a confession, but because the consideration of field encounters requires intimate understanding".

Indeed, renowned psychoanalyst–psychiatrist Laub (1992) maintains that it is through this experience of "witnessing" the participants in one's research that enables the researcher to partially feel the pain, fears, and other emotions, which allows an emotional bond to be forged and the production of new, but complementary knowledge. It is important that Laub maintains that the researcher and the participant stop to think about these memories as they come up, "so as to reassert the veracity of the past, and to build anew its linkage to, and assimilation, into present-day life" (1992: 76). However, geographer Woon cautions though that cognizance must be taken of the fact that the researcher who becomes a "participant and co-owner of the event, he/she is also a separate human being and will experience personal hazards and struggles" (2013: 33).

Indeed, Myrtle's narrative opened up old wounds in me, which haunted me for days. Sharing a bond with Myrtle and having a shared past strengthened the trust relationship we already had and certainly contributed to the new knowledge that Laub speaks about. However, the emotional bonds between me as the researcher

64 *Susheela Mcwatts*

and Myrtle as the research participant which contributed to richer data were not acknowledged in my thesis although no doubt influenced my positionality. In my thesis, I only referred to how Myrtle and I met and that we did indeed share a trust relationship. In retrospect, since the main theme of my thesis was the analysis of domestic worker leaders' journeys to activism, it might have strengthened my study to delve further into the past and analyse whether the pain and hurt contributed to both of us later assuming leadership positions in activists organizations, thereby paying attention to the link from past to present, as recommended by Laub (1992).

The second extract is from the narrative of Sonu, a domestic worker leader from Nepal, who started working as a child labourer at the age of seven:

> When I was first hired, I was told that I would be playing with the other kids and taking care of the kids, but from the very first day, I was never allowed to play or look after the kids. I had to do all the household chores, like cleaning the dishes, washing clothes, cleaning the house. When I was seven years old, I didn't know how to wash properly, and I had washed the dishes near the well, they had a family water well, then the dishes was still dirty, so when the grandmother of the house saw the dirty dishes, she slapped me.

They were a big family, and she had seven other siblings. She says:

> When I was first taken, actually, the employer spoke to my father, and my father was ill at the time, so he let me go easily. Later on, when I complained to my father that my employer does this, my father did not show any reaction. I think it may be that my father was ill. My mother did not care at all.
>
> They never paid me, it was like, my mother used to come every week, and they used to give her some uncooked rice, about two or three kgs. They used to give that as payment, and sometimes, they would give my mother old clothing.
>
> Then my father got sick and passed away. In our religion, you had to have funeral rights for 13 days, and for that my family needed money. Maybe at that time, my family took money from the employer, and I then had to work there to pay off everything that my family owed. I used to ask my employer often, if the debt was repaid, and they always said no, I haven't repaid the debt yet. I ran away from that house. I don't know whether the money was repaid or not.

In my field diary, I wrote the following:

> *"When I was taken", there right there, is the crux of all their stories. It is reminiscent of being a slave, in fact she was a slave being sold against her will under the threat of violence. Her youth, her freedom, her life, her very being sold, stolen. She still looks so vulnerable. Here she is, a woman of 29 years old, with a hard-fought for degree, still working as a domestic worker – why? Strangely, I don't feel angry, just incredibly sad. She looked sad too. Maybe*

that's because we both realize that it is the reality of so many marginalized people, and there is not much we can do. No, actually, this is what the thesis is about, what they are doing to change lives – brave, strong women.

I remember how I shut down my emotions during apartheid as well, how they lay dormant for many, many years, because I was too young to deal with it. What was the use of being emotional? Her story is so much sadder than mine could ever be. But that was our reality, we had to be strong and brave. Is that what unconsciously led to my being an activist? All these deep seated and hidden emotions? Her story has resonated with me.

As with Myrtle, Sonu and I had a shared empathetic understanding. Pacific researchers Farrelly and Nabobo-Baba maintain that "empathy is an intersubjective and embodied experience which is vital to [ethnographic] research" and argue that such research constitutes "an intentional, embodied, emotional, and intersubjective process between the researcher and the participant", which has "the potential to enhance shared understandings between all human beings and that it provides a meaningful contribution to decolonising research methodologies" (2012: 1). Sonu and I spontaneously engaged in an empathetic dialogue about our experiences, as she was interested in my being a third-generation Indian living in South Africa. The interview thus veered from the questions I had prepared. I did not steer the interview in a particular direction, and questions relevant to my thesis were asked after our discussion. I did not want to subject Sonu to a line of questioning which could be intrusive given her very painful past. Rather, I let our encounter spontaneously develop into a dialogue, where we both shared experiences and I probably received more data than I would have had in a standard interview. However, in my thesis I did not analyse the merits of an empathetic dialogue, only the data obtained.

The final extract is from Antonio, a migrant domestic worker leader. Migration is a simple word, but yet encompasses so many life-changing and life-determining events, all multi-layered and multifaceted and all filled with emotion. Yet, reading back the transcripts of my interviews with migrant workers, the emotions felt at the time are obscured by the simple words expressed. For instance, Antonio said the following to me:

The lady treated me very badly. They didn't like that I ate the bread that they ate. She preferred that it was spoilt, rather than have the women eat it. Two other ladies also worked there. She would buy a different type of bread for us. It was a cheaper type of bread that she bought for the maids.

In my field diary, I wrote:

I could sense that Antonio felt embarrassed and hurt by this, she averted her gaze and did not make eye-contact. This makes me so angry, if she felt humiliated, the embarrassment is not hers to feel! This reminds me of Motala's (2010) study that was done in South Africa, where domestic workers lamented the fact that dogs ate and slept better than them. One even said

66   Susheela Mcwatts

that she cooked chicken (it had to be roasted), but she ate it before she gave it to them. This perception of domestic workers as being less than human is so pervasive amongst friends and family, so wide-spread in society. How can we change the attitudes among employers and make them introspect? Make them see that these are human and vulnerable souls working for them?

I sensed and understood Antonio's emotions and empathized with her at the humiliation she had to endure. In retrospect, if I had shared my feelings on the subject with her, it may have strengthened our empathetic bond. Sharing the South African Community Agency for Social Enquiry's (CASE's) researcher, Mohamed Motala's (2010) study with her too might have been useful in emphasizing that hers was not a unique situation, but that such instances occurred in my country and many other geopolitical locations as well. It was an opportunity for both of us to learn about the conditions domestic workers had to live with globally, while still acquiring agency, becoming activists, and preparing for taking up leadership positions. In addition, it was an opportunity to make the transnational linkages that obviously existed more tangible.

Furthermore, in retrospect, if I had taken the emotions in the field into account, I could have explored more widely the emotional bonds that the participants may have developed towards their employers and charges. These emotional bonds are recognizable in the excerpts below.

Antonio:

I wanted to study or something like that, and I went back to another job taking care of an elderly lady, she suffered from Alzheimer's, but I liked taking care of her. If she didn't treat me well, I would think that she is just sick.

For example, she would confuse me with someone at the factory that belonged to her husband. She thought that the husband had an affair, and she confused me with that lady, so she would try to kick me out of the house, or hit me with a broom or stab me with a knife. After a while, I wanted to earn a little bit more money, but I didn't move, because the husband could not find someone else who was as patient with the lady as I was, so I had to stay for another year.

Myrtle:

I was working with this family and their one child was badly burnt, and I loved her very much so I stayed with them for 12 ½ years . . ., I had a girl. I had her in town, in District Six, and I took her to my employer and my employer let me stay in the house with her because my employer had this little child that was burnt and the child cried very badly, but after a month I couldn't cope with two children. My employer had this child that was burnt and she wanted my attention, I had a baby, I was not married at that time and my employer was going to birth again soon, and when she gave birth,

Notes From My Field Diary 67

my child had to be away. So my child went to stay with my mother and she stayed with my mother until she was 11 years old.

In my field diary, I wrote:

Antonia and Myrtle are the embodiment of Ubuntu[8]. How heart-breaking it must have been for Myrtle to give up taking care of her own child to look after another, how selfless. Yet, she did not show any resentment. That's probably because her own daughter turned out so well and she was able to embrace her own and her employers' humanity and live her compassion, despite being a subjugated domestic worker. Antonio too showed so much Ubuntu – so much compassion, that despite the hardships she endured under the old woman with Alzheimer's, she put her own wellbeing at risk to ensure that this woman had the care she needed.

In this extract, I refer to Antonio and Myrtle's selfless behaviour as *Ubuntu*, as they put the need of their charges first and above their own – their humanity is bound, and inextricably linked to others. Extracts from Myrtle and Antonio's narratives are just two of the many examples where domestic worker leaders displayed compassion in the face of adversity. As a South African, Myrtle certainly understands the concept of *Ubuntu*. Had I delved deeper into understanding whether this cultural phenomenon impacted on the decisions she made, the analysis and findings of my study would have been richer.

Reflecting on these new insights, next I will retrospectively assess the changes I could have made to the methodology I employed.

Methodological Imperatives: From Postcolonial to Decolonial

In my PhD research, in examining the events that occurred in the lives of the participants, I was concerned with positionality and power relations, and limited myself to focusing on the voice and agency of domestic workers. Revisiting my field diary, I realized that by neglecting the role of emotions the methodology I employed produced a limited version of what actually occurred in the field. It obfuscated the immediacy and emotional effects of these events (Punch 2012), which then impacted on knowledge production.

As a woman of colour living in South Africa, I shared a geopolitical situatedness with most of the participants and culture with some of the participants. I realized that my own personal life events drew me to the study that I was involved in and this I wrote about in the preface to my thesis. I made clear my positionality and understood that these life events impacted on the research process. What I did not make clear though was that the "emotional knowledge" (Ng 2017: 409) that I gathered through my experiences contributed to my having a good understanding of the emotions evoked by the participants' narratives and thus "enriched the research process". It also assisted me in understanding the participants in context (Ng 2017).

68　*Susheela Mcwatts*

However, having an understanding is still not enough, more is demanded of the researcher. In retrospect, I consider that I could have:

- Acknowledged the emotional reactions verbally, my own, and those of the participants.
- Incorporated the participants' emotions and feelings in my interview questions, by asking them how they feel and/or felt when these events occurred, to give them space to talk about their emotions.
- Acknowledged their emotional journeys in my research, a by-product of which would also have been richer data.
- Shared my own life experiences, when appropriate.
- Shared my positionality and acknowledged my privilege.

Had I used the tools earlier, I would have been practising *Ubuntu* in my research, a quality that is embodied in the Nguni[9] slogan *Ubuntu ngumtu ngabanye abantu*, which is translated as "a person is a person through other people" and "calls us to mirror our humanity for each other" (Flippin 2012: n/p). Using these tools would outwardly have demonstrated that my research is conducted in the "spirit of willing participation, unquestioning cooperation, warmth, openness, and [respect for] personal dignity".[10]

Practising *Ubuntu* in one's research is empathetic research, and the latter, according to Farrelly and Nabobo-Baba (2012: 4), allows for "epistemological and ontological underpinnings of the lived realities of our individual participants within their specific cultural contexts". Showing empathy would elicit more responses from the participants who would feel more understood and deepen the connection between the researcher and the research participants. Indeed, as sociologist Cain (2012: 403) maintains, "researchers are embodied, and acknowledging our embodied experience throughout the process of research enriches the quality of data and our theoretical conclusions". However, I am cognizant of the belief that one has to remain vigilant as there is the possibility of empathy becoming "imperialistic", if we are lulled into projecting our own beliefs onto the participants' experiences (Hoggett 2006: 149–50). In order to prevent this from happening, it is important to understand that the interview is much more than a data gathering exercise. Opening up a space in which to discuss emotions provides an avenue to explore further lines of questioning and open up certain topics (Wilkins 1993, cited by Ng 2017), and this also provides an opportunity to question and understand the participants' beliefs about their own experiences.

Furthermore, sharing personal stories, as McKay (2002) argues, "created a sense of affirmation and social support" (cited in Ng 2017: 412). Indeed, I concur, as sharing my own life experiences as I did with Sonu and Myrtle strengthened the bond between us, increased trust, and facilitated a more open relationship. I do recall Myrtle telling other participants at a meeting that she knew me well and that they could trust me.

Prior to my interviews, Myrtle did share with me her annoyance of being interviewed several times, in particular, she complained about an academic from a more privileged institution of higher learning, whose research on domestic workers would benefit him greatly, but there was nothing in it for them. She had a different reaction to me though. She knew that I wanted to interview the leadership of the domestic workers and told me about a conference that was being held in Jakarta in Indonesia, which was going to be attended by most of the leadership. She personally got me an invitation from the organizers and ensured that I had access to interview the domestic worker leaders. After the completion of my thesis, she attended my graduation party with other domestic workers from the union, because by that time we had developed strong emotional bonds. I was a woman of colour who also was an activist who shared an apartheid past. Thus, the other aspects of my identity did not matter as much as she understood my motivations for my research, unlike the other researcher whom she criticized. This I did not write about in my thesis.

Conclusion

Although the type of research that takes emotions into account is widely acknowledged as being enriching to knowledge production, it was once labelled as "epistemologically irrelevant" (Barter and Reynold 2003, cited in Evans 2012: 503). In the positivist framework, emotion was also linked with irrationality (Davies and Spencer 2010). With the Cartesian rationalist emphasis on dualism and the separation of mind and body, emotion was seen to be counterintuitive to thought and reason.

Proponents of using emotions in research though believe that knowledge and emotion are mutually constitutive (Jagger 1989, cited in Holland 2007). Furthermore, anthropologist Monchamp argues that "fieldwork is based on information gathered through relationships, and therefore the emotional elements of those associations are relevant to the ethnographic writing that is produced" (2007: 1). Emotion in the field, if treated with the same intellectual rigour as other sources of information, can act as an available source of information that can provide rich data to accompany more conventional methods of research (Davies and Spencer 2010). Indeed, social researcher Holland (2007) argues that emotion is necessary for knowledge and according to behavioural scientists Hubbard, Backett-Millburn, and Kemmer that "whilst an emotional way of knowing may be contrasted with an objective, scientific approach, it is more appropriate to perceive our emotional and cognitive functioning as inseparable" (2001: 126).

Although sociological researchers such as Schutt (1999) warned researchers against allowing emotions to enter the field of data collection as it might derail the interview process, if effective strategies to deal with these emotions in sincere and appropriate ways are developed, it will in effect add to the authenticity of the research. Furthermore, ethical considerations require one to acknowledge these emotions and hold the participants in a safe space. It does not mean that researchers should be emotionally entangled in the lives of the participants, but rather a consideration that participants come to the research process not only able to answer interview questions but also as human beings with emotional responses to life situations. To police these emotions or try to avoid them being expressed verbally or non-verbally could be considered unethical. Indeed, Hutchinson et al. (1994), for

70   *Susheela Mcwatts*

example, maintain that there are many advantages for the participants in research, which include catharsis, self-acknowledgement, sense of purpose, self-awareness, empowerment, healing, and providing a voice for the disenfranchised (cited in Hubbard et al. 2001: 124).

In sum, in this chapter I have argued that drawing on the emotions generated in the field has much to offer both to researchers and to participants if carefully included in the research methodology. By employing self-reflexivity and examining the field diary I used for my doctoral studies, I re-considered my positionality by reflecting on what I hold as lost opportunities in the field and during writing, then speculated on the impact it would have had on my research and thus on knowledge production. Thus, this chapter illustrates the value of reflection and the passage of time to discern new methodological opportunities. I conclude and agree with Hubbard et al. (2001: 119) that "emotionally-sensed knowledge" is an essential part of research and "that unless emotion in research is acknowledged, not only will researchers be left vulnerable but also our understandings of the social world will remain impoverished".

Notes

1 Steve Biko was an apartheid activist that was brutally murdered by the apartheid police. In his book, *I Write What I Like* (1970), he discusses the need for black solidarity to liberate the Black people of South Africa from servitude and the apartheid regime.
2 All participants in my study wanted me to use their real names.
3 A cleric and anti-apartheid activist at the time.
4 An archbishop and anti-apartheid activist.
5 Kentucky Fried Chicken, a popular brand of fast food.
6 An Afrikaans word for maize porridge.
7 An Indian term for grandfather, also a Xhosa term for old man.
8 A quality that includes the essential human virtues: compassion and humanity. South Africans understand Ubuntu in the context of Desmond Tutu's explanation: "Africans have a thing called ubuntu. We believe that a person is a person through other persons. That my humanity is caught up, bound up, inextricably, with yours. When I dehumanize you, I dehumanize myself. The solitary human being is a contradiction in terms. Therefore you seek to work for the common good because your humanity comes into its own in community, in belonging" (https://jamesclear.com/how-can-i-be-happy-if-you-are-sad).
9 The Nguni are Zulu, Xhosa, Ndebele, and Swazi people who predominantly live in South Africa.
10 Explanation is derived from online Oxford Dictionary.

References

Anderson, Kay, and Susan Smith. 2001. "Editorial: Emotional Geographies." *Transactions of the Institute of British Geographers* 26 (1): 7–10.
Behar, Ruth. 1996. *The Vulnerable Observer: Anthropology That Breaks Your Heart*. Boston, MA: Beacon Press.
Biko, Steve. 1970. "I Write What I Like: We Blacks." Frank Talk, SASO Newsletter. Digital Innovation: South Africa. Accessed June 18, 2023. https://disa.ukzn.ac.za/.
Cain, Cindy L. 2012. "Emotions and the Research Interview: What Hospice Workers Can Teach Us." *Health Sociology Review* 21 (4): 396–405.

Notes From My Field Diary   71

Crapanzano, Vincent. 2010. "At the Heart of the Discipline: Critical Reflections on Fieldwork." In *Emotions in the Field: The Psychology and Anthropology of Fieldwork Experience*, edited by James Davies and Dimitrana Spencer, 60–1. Stanford, CA: Stanford University Press.

Davies, James, and Dimitrana Spencer (eds.). 2010. *Emotions in the Field: The Psychology and Anthropology of Fieldwork Experience*. Stanford, CA: Stanford University Press.

Evans, Monica. 2012. "Feeling My Way: Emotions and Empathy in Geographic Research With Fathers in Valparaiso, Chile." *Area* 44 (4): 503–9.

Farrelly, Trisia, and Unaisi Nabobo-Baba. 2012. "Talanoa as Empathic Research." Paper for presentation at the International Development Conference, Auckland, December 3–5.

Flippin, William E. 2012. "Ubuntu: Applying African Philosophy in Building Community." *Huffpost*, April. www.huffpost.com/entry/ubuntu-applying-african-p_b_1243904.

Hoggett, Paul. 2006. "Pity, Compassion, Solidarity." In *Emotion, Politics and Society*, edited by Simon Clarke, Paul Hoggett, and Simon Thompson, 145–61. London: Palgrave Macmillan.

Holland, Janet. 2007. "Emotions and Research." *International Journal of Social Research Methodology* 8 (20): 151–60.

Hubbard, Gill, Kathryn Backett-Milburn, and Debbie Kemmer. 2001. "Working With Emotion: Issues for the Researcher in Fieldwork and Teamwork." *International Journal of Social Research Methodology* 4 (2): 119–37.

Hutchinson, Sally, Wilson Margaret, and Wilson Holly. 1994. "Benefits of Participating in Research Interviews." *IMAGE: Journal of Nursing Scholarship* 26 (2): 161–4.

Laliberté, Nicole, and Carolin Schurr. 2016. "The Stickiness of Emotions in the Field: Introduction." *Gender, Place and Culture: A Journal of Feminist Geography* 23 (1): 72–8.

Laub, Dori. 1992. "An Event without a Witness: Truth, Testimony and Survival." In *Testimony: Crises of Witnessing in Literature, Psychoanalysis and History*, edited by Shoshana Felman and Dori Laub, 75–92. London: Routledge.

Lutz, Catherine, and Geoffrey M. White. 1986. "The Anthropology of Emotions." *Annual Review of Anthropology* 15: 405–36.

McKay, Deirdre. 2002. "Negotiating Positionings: Exchange Life Stories in Research." In *Interviews in Feminist Geography in Practice: Research and Methods*, edited by Pamela Moss, 187–99. Oxford: Blackwell.

Mcwatts, Susheela. 2018. " 'Yes Madam, I Can Speak!' A Study of the Recovered Voice of the Domestic Worker." Unpublished Doctoral Thesis, University of the Western Cape.

Monchamp, Anne. 2007. "Encountering Emotions in the Field: An X Marks the Spot." *Anthropology Matters Journal* 9 (1): 1–7.

Motala, Mohammed. 2010. "Domestic Workers in South Africa: It's Modern Day Slavery." www.sacsis.org.za/site/article/473.1.

Ng, Isabella. 2017. "When [Inter]Personal Becomes Transformational: [Re-]Examining Life Course-Related Emotions in PhD Research." *Area* 49 (4): 409–14.

Punch, Samantha. 2012. "Hidden Struggles of Fieldwork: Exploring the Role and Use of Field Diaries." *Emotion, Space and Society* 5 (2): 86–93.

Scheper-Hughes, Nancy. 1992. *Death Without Weeping: The Violence of Everyday Life in Brazil*. Berkeley, CA: California University Press.

Schutt, Russell K. 1999. *Investigating the Social World: The Process and Practise of Research*. Thousand Oaks, CA: Pine Forge Press.

Woon, Chih Yuan. 2013. "For 'Emotional Fieldwork' in Critical Geopolitical Research on Violence and Terrorism." *Political Geography* 33: 31–41.

7 Whiteness as Friction

Vulnerability as a Method in Transnational Research

Heather Tucker

In 2015, I carried out a multi-sited queer feminist ethnographic research project in Accra, Ghana, for eight months. The project's aim was to understand the ways queer women were positioned in terms of manoeuvring neoliberal transnational frictions, including the increasing involvement of donors interested in funding gender and sexuality projects, most especially LGBT projects. In my use of friction, I am referring to Anna Tsing's concept, as the "heterogeneous and unequal encounters", of processes of globalization which "can lead to new arrangements of culture and power" and "zones of awkward engagement" (2005: 5). In my analysis of the neoliberal transnational frictions which occurred as "zones of awkward engagement", I include my own research process and those who participated as a part of this transnational phenomenon.

As a white American "obruni" (the Twi term for outsider) in the postcolonial, NGOized context of Accra, both I myself and my research project, and the relations it required were inherently embedded in transnational and neo-colonial forms of power. While reflexivity and participation are ways of dealing with power inequalities, I acknowledge that they do not absolve them, and that I am also a part of the "friction" that I seek to interrogate (Hodžič 2017). In fact, anthropologist and African studies scholar Jemima Pierre contextualizes the term, *obruni* in Ghana, as "associated with class and cultural standing of whites (and whiteness) in Ghana", but also points towards a particular racialized identity which assumes not only a higher class but also a higher "cultural standing, education level, and outlook" (2012: 77). This meant that my racialized whiteness and education were relationally constituted in the context as having a higher cultural standing which required consistent reflection. In fact, whiteness in research requires a consistent intersectional analysis of power in any context (Faria and Mollett 2016).

In this chapter, I focus more specifically on one particular moment in which, as an *obruni* outsider, I became emotionally vulnerable during an unplanned visit with my research participants. It was at a time in which I myself was experiencing the end of a queer relationship, and because of its abrupt ending, I was visibly emotionally upset in front of my research participants. This led to an unplanned and sudden sharing of my heartbreak and the situation with the small group. This vulnerable moment opened up stories of loss, betrayal, cheating, and what this felt like as a queer woman in Ghana. Through this vulnerability, queer women shared stories of

DOI: 10.4324/9781003378761-8

Whiteness as Friction 73

heartbreak and the emotions of relationships and everyday struggles, which was met with a sensitivity, vulnerability and attention to well-being of those who shared their time and thoughts with me (Behar 1996). My own emotional vulnerability was a means to complicate my outsider status as well as the relationality of power between the researcher and researched through sharing stories of queer heartbreak. However, I want to acknowledge that the ability to create this vulnerability, in this particular research project, was mine to have, and therefore was mine to will. I was in control of when and if I became vulnerable, which is also a critical point to reflect on here. The price of vulnerability for myself was little, while my research participants' vulnerability with me could have both emotional and material consequences. My argument and/or exploration suggests that queer vulnerability offers a route to exploring and breaking down "frictions" within transnational research, while not eliminating them.

"We Are Scared"

During the month that I was in Accra, my position as a white or *obruni* outsider who was interested in speaking with queer women and those who participated in NGOs working on sexual rights in Accra had brought about sceptical responses from those who would speak frankly with me about it, and this was most definitely justified. I heard stories about well-meaning white outsiders who had visited those within the NGO circles, and had made devastating decisions that often meant life or death to queer Ghanaians. One particular story stood out. A documentary filmmaker from an NGO intended to be a watchdog of the Global Fund had produced a documentary film about the effects of HIV/AIDS on individuals, and their ability to access medicines and counselling. The verbal agreement of participants in the film was based on the understanding that the film would not be shown in Ghana. However, the film was posted on Vimeo and made its way back to the community, outing a well-known activist who was HIV positive and identified as gay. The activist was outed to his employer, and eventually his family against his wishes. When queer Ghanaians sought to hold the documentary filmmaker accountable for this, she replied that they had all given their verbal consent to participate. No apologies or redresses were made, and devastatingly, the activist died a month later.

This story highlights the inherent vulnerability of queer Ghanaians who participated in projects conducted by well-meaning researchers, filmmakers, and NGO workers who travel to the country. Feminist transnational scholar Sherene Razack asks that individuals reflect upon the ways in which we are relationally constructing ourselves as "saviours" or "progressive" in opposition to those who are less fortunate or in need of saving (2001: 170). In the case of this particular filmmaker, the need to save and the desires to "advocate" and/or produce a product, led in the end, to violence on the ground. In the case of my own research, this called for critical reflection upon the ways in which my own queer feminist inclinations to read the lives of my research participants and my desire to produce knowledge about their lives were not necessarily the solution, nor were they always appropriate, considering the

74 *Heather Tucker*

inherent material vulnerability to various forms of violence my research could have unearthed. Meanwhile, despite these inevitable frictions and the significant material inequalities between myself, the researcher, and those whom I am researching, what can be gleaned from this research encounter that might make a contribution to feminist transnational methodologies on sexuality, gender, and race?

Queer Vulnerability and Queer Heartbreak

It was no surprise that the response from some of those who were able to be frank with me when I asked how they felt about an *obruni* outsider coming in to do research was: "many are scared". This starkly highlighted the power inequalities and susceptibility to violence and control that an outsider's influence could have on an already vulnerable group. Despite these legitimate concerns from various "community members", after a few months in Accra, I was welcomed as a queer woman into the lives of a core group of research participants, with whom I developed relationships within the process: primarily Rebel, Lady, Patricia, and Obaara (all names are pseudonyms for the research participants in order to keep their identities anonymous). It was through this core group that most of this multi-sited ethnography took place, via participant observation in bars, homes, NGO offices and training venues, funerals, parties, and WhatsApp. It was just after these first few months that I came to a moment through which my own vulnerability enabled a deconstruction and re-orientation of the ways in which I formed relationships with my research participants. Throughout these first few months of fieldwork, I had sought to maintain a professionalized and objective perspective as a researcher and, in many ways, had been responded to accordingly, as an outsider who was often met with respect, but also silence and/or ambivalence from many queer women.

Lady, whom I had known for about a month at the time, had taken me under her wing as a part of her friendship group, approaching me enthusiastically as a potential friend and embracing my interests as a researcher. Socially, she was a leader in her social circle of queer women, assertively ushering everyone together for various events, myself included. Upon our first meeting at a local bar in Osu, and her knowing that I was there to research "women" and their relationships, she had flipped the script between the researcher and researched, and unabatingly asked me questions about my sexual desires. "Are you a top or a bottom?" she asked, wondering where in the puzzle I would fit within her social circle, despite my being a white *obruni* outsider, and my being a researcher on the topic. She was interested in my desires, my identity, and also my inclusion.

After I slowly got to know Lady and, eventually, her social circle, she took the initiative to invite me to a street party in central Accra. On that same Friday, I received a skype call from my then girlfriend who lived in Budapest. She shared with me that she had slept with someone else and that she was breaking up with me. I immediately became overwhelmed with grief after the call and realized that I was due to attend a "white" party that evening at the invitation of Lady. I decided that my research was certainly more important than sitting at home and feeling sorry for myself, and so I walked a few blocks to a local container store where Lady,

Patricia, Obaara, and a few other queer women with whom I wasn't as familiar were having pre-party drinks. While we were all sitting in plastic chairs under the awning on the small concrete porch, Patricia – who was typically very outspoken and frank with me – asked me how I was doing. I had spent a lot of time with her in the past, hoping to get to know more about her relationships, what her experiences were like in Accra, and how she felt being in various spaces throughout the city. At this point in our relationship, I felt that she was not someone who shared a whole lot. I felt that it would be important to be honest with her, to challenge my researcher positionality and my expectation that those whom I wanted to research would share with me. When I shared with her that I had just received the news that I had been cheated on, tears began to run down my face uncontrollably. To my surprise, Patricia responded like any good friend – with justified anger. "Oh she's useless! Don't worry about her, she's no good". It felt like I was being protected and cared for. Patricia then sought to console me though sharing stories of her own heartbreak, elaborating on a story about a person she was with for five years who suddenly decided to cheat on her. "Five years of my life, five years! You have to just move on, it's not worth it".

In this moment, what felt at the time like a breakdown of professionalism as a researcher led to the small group gathering around and sharing their stories of heartbreak in response to my own. It was a moment through which my own vulnerability and my willingness to move through and past the notion of a "professionalized" approach to research opened up routes through which queer women and myself connected through shared experiences, despite my outsiderness. Also, the core research participants opened up to me due to my identifying as a queer lesbian, and this vulnerability on my part was an essential queer and feminist ethnographic choice. By this, I mean that my identifying as queer and lesbian with my informants challenges my outsiderness as a queer ethnographer (Roscoe 1996: 204) and creates a vulnerability as a feminist ethnographer (Behar 1996).

This breakdown of the duality of the researcher and the researched challenges and opens up "frictions" in the research encounter, but importantly, it is also critical to interrogate the material inequalities between my own vulnerability and the emotional labour that came from this particular encounter. While this vulnerability offered a moment in which emotional memories and stories of heartbreak were shared, I can by no means equate my own vulnerability to that of the queer women I spoke with. While I was experiencing an emotional vulnerability, I was able to express this loss with my social network outside of Accra as well, and I was able to receive emotional support. Access to counselling services and material support were slim if present at all for many of those I spoke with. Many of the material vulnerabilities due to the ending of a relationship experienced by queer women in Ghana include the depletion of an entire social safety net, including housing, access to income, and/or food. Because of the interwoven nature of many same-sex relationships in Ghana, the repercussions of loving and losing are frequently interwoven with the loss of material well-being. Feminist transnational scholar Sherene Razack's calls for feminist critical reflection on the ways in which our positionalities are embedded in global relations of inequality in transnational research projects

76 *Heather Tucker*

(2001: 170). These material inequities, as well as my ability to travel in and out of Accra and to ask questions about Ghanaians sexual identity, desires, and ways of being inevitably highlights the continuing colonial racialized divide between my research participants and myself.

> Emotional labour that racialized minorities provide for whites.
> What was the cost of my presence?
> What was the labour?
> But also the vulnerability?

References

Behar, Ruth. 1996. *The Vulnerable Observer: Anthropology That Breaks Your Heart.* Boston, MA: Beacon Press.

Faria, Caroline, and Sharlene Mollett. 2016. "Critical Feminist Reflexivity and the Politics of Whiteness in the 'Field'." *Gender, Place and Culture* 23 (1): 79–93.

Hodžič, Saida. 2017. *The Twilight of Cutting: African Activism and Life After NGOs.* Oakland, CA: University of California Press.

Pierre, Jemima. 2012. *The Predicament of Blackness: Postcolonial Ghana and the Politics of Race.* Chicago, IL: University of Chicago Press.

Razack, Sherene. 2001. *Looking White People in the Eye: Gender, Race, and Culture in Courtrooms and Classrooms.* Toronto, ON: University of Toronto Press.

Roscoe, William. 1996. "Writing Queer Cultures: An Impossible Possibility?" In *Out in the Field: Reflections of Lesbian and Gay Anthropologists*, edited by Ellen Lewin and William L. Leap, 200–11. Urbana, IL: University of Illinois Press.

Tsing, Anna. 2005. *Friction: An Ethnography of Global Connection.* Princeton, NJ: Princeton University Press.

8 From Affective Pedagogies to Affected Pedagogues

A Conversation

Petra Bakos, Redi Koobak, and Kharnita Mohamed

At the end of the collaborative, transnational project (STINT), on which this book is based, Kharnita Mohamed spoke to Petra Bakos and Redi Koobak about the writing workshops that were an integral part of the project from its inception. Each of the workshops was embedded in a residence period, thus there were writing workshops in Linköping (2016, facilitated by Nina Lykke), in Bergen (2017, facilitated by Redi and Nina), Budapest (2018, Redi and Petra – separately), and Cape Town (2019, Redi and Petra – together). The workshops were planned to support PhD students in their research and writing process from the initial conception of their contributions to this volume to the finalization of the chapters. At the same time, these workshops also offered spaces for the contestation of the "publish or perish" attitude in academia because of the project's commitment to pluriversality and post-disciplinarity as well as the facilitators' long history with creative writing modalities. They did so through a variety of approaches: by engaging with the emotional aspects of writing; acknowledging the challenges inherent in straddling feminist convictions and academic expectations; by reflecting on the impact of various social and geopolitical locations on one's research and by addressing modes of giving good and generous feedback. For these reasons and because of openness to both visiting participants and local PhD students, the workshops truly provided opportunities for worlds to collide through words – sometimes painfully so.

Kharnita: So it's taken us three years to get here. Maybe we want to take a breath and reflect on this long journey. Before we go into the pedagogies for the project, and how your pedagogies were framed towards the project, I'm going to ask you to start us off with thoughts about your own pedagogy in general and where it is now? We can also talk about how it's changed over the last three years and then go back to thinking about how you were approaching the pedagogical framework of the project.

Redi: You're catching me in a moment where my academic self is thrown into a completely new situation and I'm barely catching up with things. As I have just started a new job in an academic system new to me and still learning how everything works here, it's a very challenging question to think about. I feel like I'm floating in many ways because I have uprooted myself from contexts I am used to and haven't taken root in

DOI: 10.4324/9781003378761-9

78 *Petra Bakos, Redi Koobak, and Kharnita Mohamed*

this new place yet. So, maybe Petra wants to start while I gather my thoughts.

Petra: Alright. It just dawned on me that the Cape Town workshop in 2019 was the last time I taught in person. From the spring of 2020 everything was closed down and for the next two academic years I was exclusively teaching online. I taught classes and courses and various workshops but I never met my students in person, and I, like many others, found teaching under these circumstances really challenging. Teaching, as well as the facilitation of writing workshops has always been a rewarding experience for me, yet via online work I learned that much of the rewarding bit of teaching was closely tied to classroom presence.

Redi: I have been teaching since that workshop both in person and online. The last time I taught was actually my first class here at my new university a few weeks ago. It was focused on the role of experience in feminist research. I felt a little bit rusty or out of habit, but once I got there, met the students and established a connection with them, it flowed, flowed from there. I totally take your point about the preference for embodied teaching or embodied pedagogies because you can't reach the students the same way online as when you're teaching in person. I've been trying to write a little bit about that in relation to a course that I taught in 2020, a course I designed to be in-person but which was disrupted by the pandemic and had to move online, unplanned. This experience taught me that there's a huge gap between the embodied and the virtual. We understand the virtual as having all these opportunities of connectivity or at least we have that illusion. But without people gathering in the same space, a lot of it falls apart.

Kharnita: A big emphasis of the writing workshops was on embodiment. For instance, I remember you had us doing some yoga moves. But it wasn't embodiment in the way in which you mean now, right? The sense of being in a space.

Petra: It's both.

Kharnita: Do you want to reflect on some of that? About the loss of community and the necessity for being in the same space?

Petra: During the past years, I devoted much research and classroom time to exploring embodied pedagogies and embodied writing practices with a focus on acknowledging how the individual learners' or writers' bodies participate in creative processes. My recent experience with online teaching urged me to dig deeper into the way the collectivity of bodies influences a creative process even when the process itself is not necessarily collaborative. When I'm present in the classroom, even when the students or the workshop participants are staring at the paper in front of them or at the screen, there is a way to sense when someone feels frustrated or when someone experiences difficulty, but also when someone gets the sparks. It is possible to feel all these various dynamics, because

From Affective Pedagogies to Affected Pedagogues   79

being present in the classroom you are tuned in empathetically with the process. None of that was accessible online. Giving writing exercises in an online classroom meant that I watched the participants with their heads buried in their notes, but I could not sense whether they just hovered over the paper, whether they doodled, whether they wrote, or whether they cried. It was terrible. I felt so detached. And I was so sorry for this loss of opportunity.

Redi: As Petra was talking, I was reminded of when we met in Cape Town before the writing workshop to talk about how to frame it and what kind of exercises to include. And our main concern was a little bit different back then and, Petra, you were saying that it would be nice to include some of these very bodily elements, even though we were meeting in-person and it was not an issue to become attuned to the participants. So, we started out with this creative imagination exercise and we called the workshop "Alive in writing: From stuckness to structure". So the stuckness part was somehow the starting point and becoming alive was the goal, and you were arguing and I agreed that we need to do something with our bodies and to get our minds unstuck. Like more physical exercises. Since you facilitated this part, maybe you can say more about that process.

Petra: Two decades ago as a student I discovered that I cannot stay seated for a long time without getting irritated, and it really, really hinders my creative process if I must stay put. I started to explore possibilities, mainly by trial and error, of acknowledging the body's needs while writing and teaching. There was not much research done in this regard back then yet, or perhaps I wasn't aware of it. I was relying on my own resources, like deep experiences of dance because I used to dance for two decades, and yoga, which I started practicing as a teenager to eventually become an instructor. Through my dance background, I knew that bodies moving together may bring along a sense of gentleness and comfort and confidence, which can open up the creative venues of the individual and also of the collectivity. So, I was interested if any of this can be transferred to the academic setting and started to include various exercises involving the body and space into classes and workshops. What I found was that in an academic setting a little could go a very long way. A few minutes of conscious breathing or some simple stretching or self-administered massage, exercises that are accessible to most bodies at almost any location with simple means may evoke a sense of aliveness which can do wonders. Other exercises were meant to offer a chance for participants to relate to their usual working space with curiosity and deliberation, instead of accepting their place behind a desk as their sole possible vantage point. I found that these explorations, at least temporarily, freshly reconnect people to their senses, which is an absolute necessity for writing but for any sort of creative engagement. So, the embodied exercises that I suggested

80   *Petra Bakos, Redi Koobak, and Kharnita Mohamed*

for the Cape Town workshop were meant to enhance awareness of our placement in space, which we lack in particular since we are so digital, then our placement in collectivity, and then our placement in our own bodies.

Kharnita: It's fantastic. Redi, do you want to add anything?

Redi: I'm trying to transport myself mentally back into that space when we had that workshop and how I experienced it myself both as a co-teacher and as someone who was taking part in the workshop. We were drawing something, right? What else did we do?

Kharnita: We were drawing.

Redi: And we covered our eyes.

Petra: Indeed. I usually propose a gentle lead meditation with the eyes covered. It is meant to offer a little break from the dominance of vision, which can lead to sensory deprivation on other levels. For instance, we are less and less aware of smells, but actually smells are very much influencing how comfortable we feel in a space or next to a person. On the other hand, these short inward travels allow us to scan our current physical and emotional status and to arrive at the shared space of the workshop with a sharper sense of where we are at now.

Redi: Right, I remember that moment very vividly. When we closed our eyes, I came to this strong realization that, as a new mother – my son was just about to turn one at that time – I had been experiencing a complete sensory overload, particularly of touch. So, I remember when we did this exercise, I realized I had not been alone for such a long time, experiencing just myself in my body. I was overloaded by constant physical closeness and touch. It was like closing my eyes in that guided meditative space, I felt myself becoming alive in my body again, feeling that my body was my own again. I think this came up also in the drawing exercise. So, the reflexive, body-focused part of the workshop was very effective.

Kharnita: What was your writing journey? That was the question leading into the drawing exercise, to draw your writing journey. But then some of the questions were framed as, what do you want to say in this paper? Those were almost like layman's questions into academic reasoning.

Petra: Yeah, some questions were coming from Redi's workshops because her workshops were more oriented towards academic writing.

Redi: Exactly. Since the aim was also to encourage everyone to think about working towards a book chapter for the edited volume, hence we included "structure" in the title and content of the workshop.

Petra: All the writing workshops were hybrid in some sense as they tried to balance between various goals of the project, some rather productivity oriented, while others rather liberatory. In my praxis as a workshop facilitator, I approach writing primarily as a thinking tool. As such it can be really useful in academia, but it can be useful for other things too, for instance, for gathering yourself at the end of the day or before a challenge. The drawing exercise that you mentioned was inspired by

From Affective Pedagogies to Affected Pedagogues   81

a course in pedagogical psychology, where we learned about the evolution of writing in our lives: we start from doodles that is the nonfigurative, then we go through a phase of being figurative, that is we draw, and then from there we go to the abstract expression of things through symbols, letters, and words. I often try to simulate this process in workshops, because after a sensory experience gained through movement or meditation I do not wish to jump immediately into the abstract which is using words which are using categories, instead I wish to keep the space of exploration open in between for a little while. So that's why I introduced drawing because it's a beautiful and for most people easily accessible intermediary on this bridge.

Kharnita: Right. And then, Redi, can you run us through your questions? What were those aimed at?

Redi: Yes, the first step was: What do you most hope to write? and the second step: What do you most hope to read? So, shifting perspectives: from what I desire to put on page to what I hope somebody would take from it when they're reading it, imagining myself in a reader's role. I think that was it: these were the writing prompts.

Petra: And this was great. I thought it was so amazing. Those shifting perspectives were really inspiring for me, especially the one about reading. Writing my PhD, I was solely focused on output, which is ironic given that as a fiction writer one of my mottos for years now has been by Toni Morrison (1981): "If there's a book that you want to read, but it hasn't been written yet, then you must write it". Yet I never considered my dissertation from the reader's side, from the receiver's side – it exemplifies how deep those disciplinary and generic chasms run in us. . . . So when you proposed that exercise it was as if a plug had been removed and words started flowing.

Redi: It's interesting that you perceived my workshops as being more oriented towards academic writing because I always thought that I tried to stay away from conventional academic abstract writing, focus on bringing the I and the body into the writing and that my exercises supported that. But I take your point. That's why our approaches complemented each other so well, because you really brought the body and the sensory into the workshop.

Petra: Yeah, but I think your approach also changed. I participated in your workshop in Bergen in 2017 and that was more like a "proper" academic writing class though it certainly had a creative edge to it, it had playfulness to it. But in my view in Cape Town your questions were much more subtle and evocative. They allowed space for emotions that are oftentimes totally excluded from academic writing and these enabled a very nice connection to the sensorial and feeling based approach that I use. Although the previous workshops, like the one in Bergen and those in Budapest were also bringing quite some fragility and tension to the surface.

82 *Petra Bakos, Redi Koobak, and Kharnita Mohamed*

Redi: The Bergen workshop – there was a really difficult moment there, wasn't there? In terms of emotions, there were a lot of unexpected affects and breakdowns even, which I did not anticipate at all when I designed that workshop or not in that way.

Kharnita: Do you want to tell us? Because my next question was going to be, to run us through the progression of the workshops. What were the shifts across the different workshops? I'm also interested because for me STINT was supposed to be about peer-to-peer learning but I didn't take any of the classes that other student participants did, so I'm curious what forms they took. I'm also interested in the dynamic of shifting from a student into somebody who's also now an instructor. What do you think about that?

Redi: As I was based in Linköping when the project started, my position in the project was conceived of as that of an ambassador of sorts as the project's "home" was in Linköping. My task became to connect the different universities and create links between the PhD students and postdocs involved in the project, those who were doing the residencies. And because I was interested in creative writing methodologies, it seemed like a good contribution to the project to offer the opportunity for the PhD students to participate in writing workshops. In each of the participating universities' locations that was my main job during our meetings. So the Bergen writing workshop was the first one, on the politics of location. I think that was the title.

Petra: That was the heated one.

Redi: Yes, I remember I was using some exercises from the book *Writing Academic Texts Differently: Intersectional Feminist Methodologies and the Playful Art of Writing* (Lykke 2014), edited by a wonderful group of feminist scholars, writers and writing teachers led by Nina Lykke, that I had been part of as a PhD student. So, it was like a modification of one of those exercises I had proposed in that book. The way I usually organize these writing workshops is that I first share something of my own experiences in order to encourage students to share theirs. The task this time was to think about geopolitical positioning and relate that to one's choice of a research topic. I encouraged the students to zoom in on how their politics of location was affecting the kind of knowledge they were able to produce. I asked them to write for about five minutes, and then each of them was invited to share. It was during sharing these writings that we reached an unexpected moment of a breakdown. But it's so hard to talk about it without implicating specific participants.

Kharnita: Perhaps you can talk through some of it so that we can get to some of the abstract ideas involved.

Redi: Without wanting to go into details, let's just say that the difficult moment involved tears and sharing feelings of guilt and shame after reflecting on whiteness and racism that came up in the writing exercise. Honestly, I have been haunted by my memory of that moment,

From Affective Pedagogies to Affected Pedagogues   83

even to the extent that when I participated in a pedagogical course "Hot Moments in Teaching and Learning" several years later, I ended up using this example of a "hot moment" in my teaching in the forum theatre assignment that formed a major part of that course. I scripted that difficult scene again, shared it with others in the group and we then acted it out in order to take it apart and see how it could be turned into a learning moment in teaching. That experience really made me think about what happens to bodies in the classroom in an academic setting when strong feelings suddenly come to surface, particularly around whiteness and race, and how I as a teacher or facilitator navigate these affective responses, including my own. Knowing all too well the stories from intersectional, decolonial, and anti-racist feminist groups where white people often take up too much time to focus on their own feelings and use the space to overcome their white guilt. I did not want to obfuscate the painful experiences of students of colour living in racist societies. It made me take pedagogies of discomfort seriously as there was a lot of discomfort for me in that moment, wanting to do the "right thing" but not knowing what that was. I don't think I dealt well with it in that moment or I am not sure what "dealing well" in that situation actually entails but staying with discomfort, lingering over it a little bit longer and not immediately trying to smooth things over seems important. I thus have spent a lot of time considering how I might have acted differently as the facilitator, and it has certainly had a deep impact on how I navigate classrooms since then.

What is also interesting is how this "hot moment" impacted Nina's workshop on autophenomenography and scene writing that took place right after my workshop. As she reminded us in a personal email communication, "when thinking back on the whole thing, I think that the disruption in the morning actually somehow became very concretely productive in the sense that it 'co-generated' the intense cathartic moments in the afternoon". So there was continuity and movement between the different workshops.

Kharnita: So, in terms of feminist community, what is left? What I'm curious about is how do you think the writing workshops produced feminist community or produced the space because a lot of the project was about building transnational relations. And we've actually seen that a lot of them failed, a lot of the relationships actually didn't quite pan out. So, do you think the space of the writing workshops created a particular form of feminist community or a method for thinking about making feminist knowledge? Was it a pedagogical goal to create feminist community?

Redi: I'm not sure. The idea initially was to offer tools for PhD students to connect to the main topics of the project, that is, transnational feminisms, through writing and then thinking about their own work. And not all workshops worked out, at least in Budapest, the writing workshop failed because only two people showed up.

84   *Petra Bakos, Redi Koobak, and Kharnita Mohamed*

Petra: But in Budapest there were two writing workshops because you had one, and I had one later.

Redi: Right, I wasn't there for the whole duration of the PhD students' residency, I was there for 3–4 days I think and only two people showed up for the writing workshop I had planned. They said they were exhausted by the programme that CEU had already provided them in the first week. But one of the two students who came had a breakdown and cried. So, it was another crying moment, but [this time] because they were so stuck in their PhD process and they were thinking about quitting. So that workshop ended up being a support session, a space to listen and share. Thus, some sort of feminist community building did take place almost by itself, unplanned.

Petra: My workshop in Budapest was for CEU's PhD students and for the STINT students together, so there were like ten participants. It took place in two parts, the first part was in the garden that is on top of the Budapest CEU campus, where we engaged in walking and drawing exercises. The second part was in a classroom setting, and there we worked with poetry reading and writing prompts. The focus of that workshop was the joy of reading, because I discovered among peer PhD students that they were reading nothing else than the scholarly literature of their specific fields. It seemed that as they increasingly turned into professional readers they were less and less capable of reading fiction or poetry, they lost reading as a source of joy, fulfilment, and inspiration. Since the workshop examined how we can bring reading back into our lives as professional readers, and I thought that poetry might pave the surest way in, I experimented with a poetry-based writing exercise that actually worked out well for many. I proposed one line from a poem by Anne Sexton as a writing prompt, and when I felt that the momentum was waning, then I gave the second line to push them further, and then the third, and so on. These dense and oftentimes cryptic quasi one-liners really acted like little wings carrying their writing forward. So, there was a lot of spark in that workshop but there was crying too. For instance, when a student remembered that the last time she read happily was before she started her PhD . . .

Redi: Yeah. So three out of four workshops had intense crying in it.

Petra: God yeah.

Kharnita: How would you reflect on that? These were writing workshops with other feminists. What is it about the writing workshop, the space of the writing workshop, that produces this intensity? It seems that all the workshops were centred around stuckness. There was one around conflict, one around who I am as a writer, and the other one was about confronting oneself as a scholar. So, the starting position each time said "this is a difficult thing", and an assumption about stuckness was at the centre of the workshop. I wonder what it is actualizing or where that comes from.

Redi: But the first one wasn't really about stuckness. It was about the politics of location.

From Affective Pedagogies to Affected Pedagogues 85

Kharnita: Yes, but nonetheless the assumption was that the PhD students came to the workshop because they have problems, tensions, or frictions. But what makes the writing workshop into a space that catalyses these kinds of emotions? Even though the incidents are different, it seems the writing workshop catalyses the potential in some ways for difficult and complex emotions to erupt as a public event.

Petra: You asked earlier how these workshops contributed to a feminist collectivity, or the creation of a feminist collectivity. While editing this book I found that it was much easier for me to work with texts by people whom I had encountered in the workshops. During the workshops we were writing together, we shared pieces of our writing, and reflected on the process of writing. I felt that with all that we had established some foundation for thinking about texts together, for relating to texts in a way that is unconventional in the academic setting, for instance by acknowledging that our emotions also affect the editorial work. As if an ongoing workshop was created, which extended into the editorial process, and we could go quicker deeper. On the other hand, these workshop spaces engendered a sense of safety, while writing intimately brings forward a deep connection to oneself. So, I think it was the exploration of one's connection to oneself embedded into the sense of safety offered by the workshops that contributed to those moments when someone allowed themselves to break down, allowed themselves to be emotional, allowed themselves to be fragile. But say in Cape Town there was no crying, there we laughed a lot. That was the most cheerful workshop of all.

Kharnita: That's because I was there. (laughing)

Petra: Because you were there, of course. But it's an interesting question, isn't it? Why were we so honed in on stuckness? Because it's important what Kharnita says that we frame the whole space if we start from stuckness. Instead of arriving at it as a potential problem, we predisposed that.

Redi: I think partly the focus on stuckness as a starting point happened because of my book chapter on writing in stuck places (Koobak 2014) in the volume *Writing Academic Texts Differently* which I have used a lot in teaching and a lot of my students have found very useful. So that is why Nina had suggested I do a workshop on stuckness. And yes, Cape Town was different, but there we also had another aim. One of my tasks for the workshop was to talk through questions like how to convert some part of a PhD thesis into a book chapter? So that was the "from stuckness to structure" part of the workshop. As editors of the volume, we wanted people to experiment more with creative things rather than produce something that is taken from a PhD, which usually doesn't allow so much space for experimentation.

Kharnita: How does the framing relate to your own writing practices or challenges? Because I know when I do writing workshops, I usually work from my own challenges. And I also teach from my own struggles, so it removes shame in many ways. I think about writing related to the times

86   *Petra Bakos, Redi Koobak, and Kharnita Mohamed*

when I felt ashamed of not being able to write in the way the academy imagines and I don't want my students to feel that shame, so I teach from that place. And so, I am curious how your own writing challenges or joys come into the teaching of writing, because I think it's important. Being a writing instructor doesn't mean that you don't struggle to write, right?

Petra: I never thought of it this way, but there seems to be a correlation between how a workshop is framed and what kind of emotions emerge. So those that were structured around stuckness or the one in Budapest which was titled *The Joy of Reading*, but actually it asked why PhD students don't enjoy reading any more, those turned into tearful workshops. And then there was the one in South Africa which was framed around creativity, and turned out to be much more playful, even amusing, yet inspiring. That's something to reflect on pedagogically, I think. Not to say that we must frame workshops with positive concepts at all times, rather that we should be aware of this correlation and prepare accordingly. But to come back to your last question: in the Budapest workshop I was placing one of my greatest pleasures at the centre, something that gave me so much fulfilment and so much joy in life, that is reading. And because of that, despite the fact that the process raised loads of various emotions that I had to navigate through, I remember leaving the premises super charged. It was really nice to work from a place where I felt confident. But I think that was the one time. Usually, I also go to the places where I struggle. Another thing to ponder.

Kharnita: What I'm also finding very interesting is a hierarchical framing of your relationship to the workshop. Given that a number of the participants were accomplished writers and are novelists, poets, and creative non-fiction writers. Most of the Black South African participants, for example, are creative writers. I am a novelist, Pralini and Tigist are exceptional poets and Wanelisa merges fiction, creative non-fiction and theory in the most incredible ways. I am sure across the workshops and other PhD candidates, there were a range of experienced writers. In some ways, there was also an instrumentalist engagement with what we were to produce at the end, which is a very neoliberal academic notion. So, there was a particular framing and I'm curious whether that shifted over time. Whether the forms of relationality that you were speaking about in the beginning changed, i.e. the kinds of relationality and embodiment that are necessities for creating community, particularly given that this was a transnational project and over time we've all scattered to different parts of the world. We're in contact now because we have the book project but part of STINT was about creating a network of feminist scholars, right? So, I'd like you to reflect on some of that, the power dynamics, the hierarchies within the workshops, because when I think about the creation or crafting of a feminist community, it is about the abolishment of those hierarchies themselves and it's also about the

From Affective Pedagogies to Affected Pedagogues 87

move away from instrumentalist forms of engagement. At the same time, you've got to produce the chapter which is a fairly instrumentalist engagement but again, we wouldn't have the book without that as a materialization of our relationality. So, would you reflect on your pedagogy in relation to that, in relation to the classroom or the space of a writing workshop where a lot of the people were your peers in many senses right, Petra?

Petra: Yeah. My placement was particular in the sense that I was not designated as an instructor from the beginning of the project. I was invited to hold a workshop in Budapest by Professor Jasmina Lukić from the Department of Gender Studies at the CEU because she knew that I've been working with creative writing methods in CEU's Roma Graduate Preparation Program. And yes, within the STINT workshops I always worked with my peers, I worked with PhD students like me. At the same time, although they were my peers, most of them were much younger than me and basically all of them shifted from university setting to university setting. So, what differentiated me mainly was that before joining the PhD programme I've worked professionally as a teacher of literature and as an editor of books and as a translator and a yoga instructor. The Cape Town workshop was a very pleasant surprise in that regard too, because there I met people who also arrived at the doctoral school with considerable professional experience behind them. Plus, most Cape Town team members, as you said, were poets or writers, people for whom writing is central, as for myself. Unfortunately, I only learned about that after our last workshop. In hindsight, it could have been fruitful to have some kind of preliminary communication with future workshop participants and involve them in the workshop design. What I'm sure about is that I would still wish us to experience writing as a form of embodied thinking. Whenever we could tap into that, even if only temporarily, I felt that it was a wholly successful endeavour. I never felt the pressure to push myself or the participants towards academic production. If our work had that side effect, oh that's much better.

Redi: I think we need to pose the question about hierarchies to the whole project and the meetings we held together with all the project participants, which were separate from the writing workshops Petra and I facilitated where only some of the PhD students and postdocs participated. Particularly in our meeting in South Africa we had workshops with the whole group where we discussed our initial drafts for the book collectively and these were open discussions, not facilitator-led writing workshops. But indeed, those meetings were framed by this very neoliberal end goal: to produce a book as a result or proof of our collaboration to justify the good use of funds given to us for feminist network building. That's the challenge of walking the fine line between what the funders require and what kind of work we as feminists want to do together, right?

Kharnita: My final question is going to be why does writing matter? And why does providing tools to write matter? Does it matter and why does it matter to teach writing tools?

Redi:	Oh, I feel like this question requires an eloquent quote which I am not really able to give off the top of my head now. My mind is blank. But the first thing I would say though is, of course, it matters. I mean, I have invested a lot of myself in perfecting the art of affective, critical, creative academic writing and also trying to guide my students towards writing more affectively, starting from themselves, grounding themselves in their situatedness. Often, I find that the best tool I can offer is to create space for an open discussion about writing that doesn't come off like giving instructions: do this, don't do that. Though in academic settings, like in master's or PhD thesis writing process, there is a lot of that too. But sharing our vulnerabilities, being transparent about our own struggles in writing, being explorative and curious is what matters in pedagogical settings. Writing matters because it can be both a method of inquiry, to understand something about the world and ourselves in it, and a tool for communication and empowerment, a means of connection. People need these tools.
Petra:	I would like to answer with a quote by Fatema Mernissi (2023): "Writing is one of the most ancient forms of prayer. To write is to believe communication is possible, that other people are good and that you can awaken their generosity and their desire to do better". With all their necessary limitations and unnecessary fallacies, these writing workshops and the making of this book strengthened my conviction that "communication is possible". And I'm grateful for that.

References

Koobak, Redi. 2014. "Writing in Stuck Places." In *Writing Academic Texts Differently: Intersectional Feminist Methodologies and the Playful Art of Writing*, edited by Nina Lykke, 194–207. New York: Routledge.

Lykke, Nina, ed. 2014. *Writing Academic Texts Differently: Intersectional Feminist Methodologies and the Playful Art of Writing*. New York: Routledge.

Mernissi, Fatema. 2023. "Fatema Mernissi." Accessed February 21, 2023. https://fatema-mernissi.com/.

Morrison, Toni. 1981. "Speech at the Ohio Arts Council." In *Toni Morrison: The Power of Fiction in the Arc of Progress*, edited by Cecilia M. Ford. Accessed February 21, 2023. https://womensvoicesforchange.org/toni-morrison-the-power-of-fiction-in-the-arc-of-progress.htm.

9 "I Will Meet You at Twilight"

On Subjectivity, Identity, and Transnational Intersectional Feminist Research

Edyta Just

Podczas zmierzchu rozmywają sie kontury.
Niby są a jednak zacierają się linie demarkacyjne.
Mnogość.

In the twilight, the contours blur.
It seems that the contours are there and yet the demarcation lines are blurring.
Multitude.

Edyta Just 2020

Is it too much to say that we are embodied and embedded, yet always and already about connections, difference, and change ourselves? Can I accept that, even though my subjectivity is embodied and embedded, the matter/social context/logic behind meaning-making can deprive my subjectivity of identity? Or engender a new and temporary identity that is always prone to change? Or fix my identity for some time, although never forever, and by extension influence the way I do my research? Do I need the twilight to sense this better?

In this chapter, I would like to focus on embodied and embedded subjectivity and identity and reflect upon the connections between embodied and embedded subjectivity, identity, and research. I seek to discuss how those reflections can help me to think about transnational intersectional feminist research. It is important to stress that I am not implying that intersectional feminist theories and research are focused solely on subjectivity and identity. However, for me, intersectional feminist research entails, among other things, reflections and discussions concerning the researchers' and research subjects' axes of differentiation and corresponding identity markers, as well as reflections on their geopolitical location (understood here as particular spatio-temporally located societal and power relations, beliefs, discourses, and practices regarding various forms of embodiment, gender, sex, sexuality, ethnicity, racialization, age, and class). Yet I am curious about the possible content of those reflections and discussions when problematized through the lens of subjectivity and identity. Moreover, I am curious as to how such research can be conceptualized when subjectivity and identity are taken into consideration.

Whenever I consider my research topic and my research goals, objectives, and questions, I always have in mind feminist theorist Donna Haraway's (1988)

DOI: 10.4324/9781003378761-10

90 *Edyta Just*

concepts of situated knowledges, partial perspectives, and embodied epistemologies. Haraway's concepts necessarily bring to the fore the subjectivity of a
researcher and its role in knowledge production. In this text, similarly to Haraway,
I take subjectivity as embodied and embedded. To approach subjectivity in such a
manner is to acknowledge that embodiment and embeddedness matter for subjectivities and knowledge production. In this chapter, I approach the embodiment and
embeddedness of a researcher via the prism of matter, understood here as material
locatedness, yet with matter defined *only* as physical or corporeal substance in
general (the substance or substances of which any physical object consists or is
composed), and situate them within a social context. Social context is discussed
here mainly in terms of geopolitical location with all its spatio-temporally located
societal and power relations, beliefs, discourses, and practices regarding various
forms of embodiment, gender, sex, sexuality, ethnicity, racialization, age, and
class.[1] Thus, I reflect upon the different ways in which matter and social context,
thus defined, may matter for subjectivity and knowledge production.

Alongside matter and social context, I recognize the logic behind meaning-
making as crucial for subjectivities and knowledge production. Hence, in this text
I refer to a neuroscientific theory known as a psychological constructionist account
of the brain as the basis of emotions – the conceptual act model (Lindquist et al.
2012; Barrett et al. 2014), which discusses meaning-making in a very transpar-
ent manner. The idea of also referring to the field of neuroscience stems from my
strong belief in combining knowledge from different fields. Such undertakings, in
my opinion, support the attempt to produce daring epistemologies that can challenge my own conceptual framework and push my thinking further. In the text, I
emphasize that there are connections between mental activity, meaning-making,
the logic behind meaning-making, embodiment, embeddedness, matter, and social
context. My desire to discuss such connections is influenced by the work of feminist philosopher Rosi Braidotti, who defines subjectivity "as both materialist and
relational, 'nature-cultural' and self-organizing" (Braidotti 2013: 52).

To illustrate these connections, in the first part of this chapter, I begin with
a reflection upon embodiment, embeddedness, matter, social context, and mental
activity. Second, I present the process of meaning-making using the aforementioned neuroscientific theory.

In the second part of this chapter, I take my reflections on subjectivity from the
first part to yet another level by using the philosophical framework of French phi-
losophers Gilles Deleuze and Felix Guattari (1987). Here, I focus on subjectivity
through the prism of axes of differentiation such as gender, sex, sexuality, ethnicity, racialization, age, and class, approached through their corresponding identity
markers. I ask the question: What if a researcher lives hir subjectivity as "imperceptible", "assemblage-like", and/or "stratified" (Deleuze and Guattari 1987) with
regard to these various axes of differentiation and their corresponding identity markers? The concepts of imperceptibility, assemblage, and stratum will be explained
in the second part of this chapter. For now, I want to indicate that, if I think about
embodied and embedded subjectivity with regard to various axes of differentiation
and corresponding identity markers in terms of imperceptibility, I think about it as
deprived of identity or non-identity (identity markers "disappear"). If I think about

subjectivity in terms of an assemblage, I think about it as a new and temporary identity that is always prone to change. And, finally, if I think about subjectivity as stratum, I think about identity as more fixed yet never fully static or unvarying.

I have decided to refer to the philosophy of Deleuze and Guattari because, in a very challenging manner, it problematizes the concept of identity and adds significantly to our understanding of the concept of subjectivity. Importantly, their concepts deepen my comprehension of embodied and embedded subjectivity as prone to connections, change, and difference. Furthermore, it seems that, even if subjectivity is embodied and embedded with regard to various axes of differentiation, it can become "imperceptible", that is, deprived of identity. Thus, I argue that sometimes material locatedness and social context may lead to a complete freeing from identities of any kind, and against this background I ask: How can this kind of lived subjectivity correspond with one's research topic, questions, discussions led, and comments made?

Certainly, I do not propose that this is *the way* of conceptualizing subjectivity. On the contrary, it is an experiment influenced by Deleuzian and Guattarian scholarship. Furthermore, it is crucial to point out here that I am not claiming that there is any obvious, direct, essentialist, or deterministic link between embodied and embedded subjectivity, identity, and research. Rather, I am interested in examining and reflecting upon the possible connections and their consequences. In this chapter, I want to suggest that different experiences of subjectivity with regard to the axes of differentiation and corresponding identity markers may result in various kinds of research (research topic, questions, discussions, comments) that seem to be: (1) unspecified (as a result of subjectivity lived as imperceptibility), (2) trembling (as a result of subjectivity lived as assemblage), and (3) fixed (as a result of subjectivity lived as stratum) with regard to the axes of differentiation of the researcher/research subjects and their potential reflections on geopolitical location (i.e. spatio-temporally located societal and power relations, beliefs, discourses, and practices regarding various forms of embodiment, gender, sex, sexuality, ethnicity, racialization, age, and class). Furthermore, I think that a researcher can produce different forms of research on different occasions, or even concurrently. In order to avoid giving prescriptions that could be applicable for everybody, in the second part of this chapter I focus on the ways in which I experience my own lived subjectivity with regard to my axes of differentiation, and on how I do research. I do this in a poetic way to make the concepts and my argument tangible and comprehensible.

In the third part of this chapter, I discuss how the reflections upon embodied and embedded subjectivity and identity, and upon the connections between embodied and embedded subjectivity, identity, and research can help me to think about transnational intersectional feminist research.

On Mental Activity, Meaning-Making Processes, Embodiment, Embeddedness, Matter, and Social Context[2]

Let me start by reflecting upon embodiment, embeddedness, matter, and mental activity. I sympathize with the identity position, or monism, which claims that "mind is *brain activity*" and that one "cannot have mental activity without brain

92   *Edyta Just*

activity" (Kalat 2009: 6). Furthermore, I take the body and the brain (understood as a part of the body) to be the foundation of cognition, perception, action, thinking, emotion, and memory, that is, both conscious and unconscious, volitional and automatic mental processes. Let us think about eyes and ears, optic and auditory nerves, visual and auditory cortex – which are important for processing visual and auditory information, respectively – or the skin's receptors, which respond to touch and temperature. Concomitantly, it is important to remember that the body is in constant internal motion and that, within the brain, within the body, and between the body and the brain, there are innumerable matter-based connections that matter for mental activity. It is enough to think about a thyroid condition that can influence one's mood, or a full bladder, toothache, or back pain. Moreover, the brain and the body are always embedded in a physical environment and as such undergo ceaseless encounters with external matter (the substance or substances that compose any physical object and that stem from the outside of the body). Dark rooms, bright lamps, noisy air conditioners, dysfunctional heaters (either over-heated or too cold), medicines taken, sweet chocolates eaten, cups of coffee or glasses of wine drunk, viruses, and bacteria invading – all of these matter for mental activity. To sum up, the body and the brain, the interactions between internal matter and the encounters with external matter, all *matter* in relation to mental activity.

When it comes to embodiment, embeddedness, social context, and mental activity, it is also important to stress one's geopolitical location, with all its societal and power relations, beliefs, discourses, and practices regarding various forms of embodiment, gender, sex, sexuality, ethnicity, racialization, age, and class, which all affect one's body and therefore one's mental activity. In different geopolitical locations, certain forms of embodiment, genders, sexes, sexualities, racializations and ethnicities are still marked negatively, excluded, and discriminated against due to patriarchy and its visible and invisible power mechanisms, and other insecting historical, political, economic, and cultural conditions. Encounters with harmful and discriminatory beliefs, discourses, and practices can never leave one's body, brain, or mental activity indifferent.

Now, let me say a few words about the meaning-making process (certainly a mental activity) and its logic. The theory I am working with is a psychological constructionist account of the brain's basis of emotions – the conceptual act model (Lindquist et al. 2012; Barrett et al. 2014). This neuroscientific theory focuses on the processes involved in the meaning-making of both external and internal sensations, including the experience of emotions. It discusses how the brain processes information from the world (external sensations) and information from the body (internal sensations/core affect) to make meaning. To do so, the brain creates situated conceptualizations, which is a process of making meaning out of sensory input from the world and from the body "using representations of prior experience" (Lindquist et al. 2012: 125; Barrett et al. 2014). These "representations of prior experience" are also referred to as "stored" or "conceptual" knowledge (Barrett et al. 2014). This conceptual knowledge can fuse with "impinging sensory input" because "knowledge is stored and represented in the same format . . . as the sensations" (Barrett et al. 2014: 451). This shows that conceptual knowledge, or – to put it differently – past experience, plays a significant role in the process of meaning-making. Importantly, conceptual knowledge can add novel features and modify sensorial input (Barrett et al. 2014: 448), but it can also be altered by the incoming sensorial information. Furthermore, conceptual knowledge about a given category develops for properties, relations, rules, other objects, setting, actions, words, events, or internal states related to that category (Barrett et al. 2014: 452). Therefore, in order to process both external and internal inputs, the brain uses the conceptual knowledge "associated with relevant concepts" and "produces a conceptual state using multimodal information about entire situations" (Barrett et al. 2014: 452). This indicates that to produce meaning is to think, to feel, and to act.

The process of meaning-making is accompanied by another process called executive attention. This is "the process by which some representations are selectively enhanced and others are suppressed" and the process that "foregrounds certain core affective feelings [information from the body] and exteroceptive sensory sensation in a moment, and guides which situated conceptualizations are brought to bear to make meaning of those sensations in the given context" (Lindquist et al. 2012: 125). Importantly, executive attention "can be exerted both volitionally and without the conscious experience of volition" (Lindquist et al. 2012: 125). This indicates that meaning can be produced in both an automatic and a volitional way. Furthermore, the process of conceptualization is "represented as a distributed brain state (with both cortical and subcortical contributions), or even a series of brain state transitions across time" (Barrett et al. 2014: 455). This leads to the conclusion that "mental causation is not mechanistic per se, but probabilistic" (Barrett et al. 2014: 455). This indicates a realization that it cannot be easily foreseen or predicted how meaning-making from external and internal sensations will advance or proceed.

The past, and the present here and now, matter in the process of meaning-making – that is, the ways in which one thinks, feels, and acts matter. Present experiences can alter and/or add to previously accumulated conceptual knowledge. Importantly, even though meaning-making (i.e. ways of thinking/feeling/doing) can occur automatically, it can also occur as the result of a volitional action. Finally, even though one can, to a certain extent, predict (or try to predict) the kind of meaning that may be produced, still one can never be certain about the ways in which one may think, feel, or act.

Matter and social context *matter*. Without the body (and here I also mean the brain), conceptual knowledge could not be stored or internal and external sensations experienced. Furthermore, bodily matter conditions whether and how sensations are experienced and made meaning of. Moreover, as the internal matter remains in constant motion, afflictions such as Parkinson's disease or any chemical imbalance in the brain can affect mental activity and the meaning-making process. In addition, an inflow of internal sensations, for example, back pain or stomach ache, could become the only thing one can focus on.

Then there are constant interactions with external matter. When one is making meaning – let us say when attending a play at the theatre – the antihistamines taken that morning or a viral infection may matter, as may an un/comfortable chair or dysfunctional loudspeakers in the venue. The connections and interactions between the body, the brain, and external matter condition how the sensations are

94   *Edyta Just*

represented and stored and how both internal and external sensations are made meaning of. They matter for the ways in which one thinks, feels, and acts.

When it comes to social context, then, practices, discourses, beliefs, and power relations all result in personal experiences that create one's conceptual knowledge. Personal experiences, one's accumulated conceptual knowledge, matter in the process of making meaning. Therefore, it can be stated that the discourses and power relations that formed one's experience influence meaning-making practices and thus one's ways of thinking, feeling, and acting. Meaning-making is probabilistic and one's conceptual knowledge can alter the arriving input. It can happen that incoming sensations (e.g. a large room with an audience) may not be directly linked to encounters with harmful discourses/practices, and yet they will be interpreted as such. If you were told that speaking in public must not/cannot be your thing, then when you find yourself needing to speak in front of a large audience, you may feel frightened and want to leave the room, and you may even do so. Furthermore, in cases where the incoming sensations are directly linked to discriminatory and abusive practices, then previous experiences can not only completely influence the meaning-making process but also solidify it further.

Yet, meaning-making is probabilistic and can be either automatic or volitional. Therefore, the ways in which one thinks, feels, and acts cannot be entirely predicted, but they can be volitionally monitored and executed. One may decide not to "listen" to former oppressors and not to give in to the fear but to stand up, face the audience, and deliver the speech. Then perhaps, next time, the fear will no longer be experienced, or will at least lessen. The manners of thinking, feeling, and acting, as well as the accumulated conceptual knowledge, can change, transform, and become anew.

Mental activity, meaning-making, the logic behind meaning-making, embodiment, embeddedness, matter (the body, the brain, internal matter interactions, external matter), and social context (existing discrimination, exclusionary and harmful beliefs, discourses, and practices regarding various forms of embodiment, gender, sex, sexuality, racialization, ethnicity, age, and class) are intertwined, constituting subjectivities that, to refer to Braidotti (2013) again, are materialist, relational, "nature-cultural", and self-organizing. Now, what if subjectivities are lived as imperceptible, assemblage-like, and/or stratified with regard to their various axes of differentiation? How do such lived subjectivities of researchers correspond with their research?

On Subjectivity and Research

Ways of thinking, feeling, and acting are influenced as much by the past as they are by the present. They are a result of both automatic and volitional processes, and as much as they can be predicted – indeed, sometimes we can predict how certain situations will make us think/feel/act – still, they cannot be easily foreseen. Furthermore, the body, the brain, internal matter interactions, encounters with external matter, and social context – with all its discriminatory, exclusionary and harmful beliefs, stereotypes, discourses, and practices – matter for mental activity, and for manners of thinking, feeling, and acting.

"I Will Meet You at Twilight" 95

Following my general approach, I shall now enter into an experiment, contemplating subjectivity as following the logics of imperceptibility, assemblage, and stratum with regard to axes of differentiation. I will first outline the concepts of becoming, imperceptibility, assemblage, and stratum. Second, based on my own experience and in a poetic way, I will make an effort to bring to the fore the ways in which I become a lived imperceptibility, assemblage, or stratum in relation to my own axes of differentiation and corresponding identity markers. Finally, I will try to reflect upon how my becoming imperceptible, assemblage-like, or stratified may correspond with the research that I produce.

Imperceptibility, Assemblage, and Stratum

Every becoming is linked to difference, change, and connections. As Stagoll in *The Deleuze Dictionary* puts it, becoming is "the continual production of difference", not "a product, final or interim . . . [but rather] the very dynamism of change, situated between heterogeneous terms and tending towards no particular goal or end-state" (2005: 21). Importantly, "each change or becoming has its own duration, a measure of the relative stability of the construct, and the relationship between forces at work in defining it" (Stagoll 2005: 22).

For Deleuze and Guattari (1987), one can become imperceptible, an assemblage or a stratum. To become is to change, and every becoming (e.g. becoming imperceptible, assemblage or stratum) is about connections, difference, and change. Braidotti describes *becoming-imperceptible* as:

> the point of fusion between the self and his or her habitat, the cosmos as a whole . . . the point of evanescence of the self and its replacement by a living nexus of multiple interconnections that empower not the self, but the collective, not identity, but affirmative subjectivity.
>
> (2006: 261)

Importantly, during this becoming-imperceptible one is exposed to "the unexpected and unprogrammed"; the social identity dies and selfhood is delegated "to something that you may call transcendence, except that it takes you into embodied and embedded perspectives, into radical immanence, not into further abstractions" (Braidotti 2006: 261–2). Becoming-imperceptible "is the absolute form of deterritorialization" and "it marks the death of the self to any notion of identity" (Braidotti 2006: 262). One becomes an ultimate expression of difference and change. Long before Deleuze and Guattari, Virginia Woolf pointedly described imperceptibility when she wrote in *Mrs Dalloway*:

> She would not say of any one in the world now that they were this or were that. She felt very young; at the same time unspeakably aged. She sliced like a knife through everything; at the same time was outside, looking on. She had a perpetual sense, as she watched the taxi cabs, of being out, out, far out to sea and alone; . . . and yet to her it was absolutely absorbing; all this; the

96 *Edyta Just*

cabs passing; and she would not say of Peter, she would not say of herself, I am this, I am that.

(2005 [1925]: 6)

Concerning an *assemblage*, one of the most popular concepts in Deleuzian and Guattarian writing, Elizabeth Grosz writes: "[a]ssemblages . . . are heterogeneous, disparate, discontinuous alignments or linkages brought together in conjunctions (x plus y plus z) [they] are the provisional linkages of elements, fragments, flows of disparate status and substance: ideas, things – human, animate, and inanimate" (1994: 167). Assemblages, similarly to imperceptibility, are about connections, difference, and change. However, in contrast to imperceptibility, an assemblage is not linked to full deterritorialization. Nevertheless, there is a peculiar likeness between these two because every assemblage involves processes of deterritoriali-zation. Reflecting upon the correspondence between an assemblage and identity, I approach becoming-assemblage as an actualization of a new identity. It is not a death of the self to identity, but rather an engendering of something new that nonetheless can always disappear (a moment of imperceptibility or full deterritori-alization) to again form a new shape that is never finished but always in a process "towards no particular goal or end-state" (Stagoll 2005: 21).

Deleuze and Guattari link a *stratum* – or, in the plural, strata – to *something* that is "ordered by rigid schemata and point-to-point connections ensuring a linear and fixed structure" (Semetsky 2009: 451). Strata:

consist of giving form to matters, of imprisoning intensities or locking sin-gularities into systems of resonance and redundancy, of producing upon the body of the earth molecules large and small and organizing them into molar aggregates. Strata are acts of capture . . . They operate by coding and ter-ritorialization upon the earth; they proceed simultaneously by code and by territoriality.

(Deleuze and Guattari 1987: 40)

Furthermore, strata "make [one] a kind of organism, or signifying totality, or deter-mination attributable to a subject" (Deleuze and Guattari 1987: 4). Similarly, as in imperceptibility and assemblage, I can also detect connections and difference within a stratum. Moreover, I can also sense a promise of change, yet it seems valid to say that strata are very stubborn about resisting deterritorializations and change. In this sense, when I think about becoming-stratum, I think about identity as rela-tively fixed, yet never fully static or unchanging.

My Lived Imperceptibility, Assemblage, and Stratum

Imperceptibility. It is of a different duration. It can last just a moment or somewhat longer. It can happen once a day or twice a month. It has been occurring for as long as I can remember. Most of the time, it seems to be beyond my conscious control. It is a moment of merging, of disappearing, and of losing all my borders, contours, and shapes. Concomitantly, I am nothing and I am everything. Scary moment. Precious moment. Empowering moment. My meaning-making, my thinking, feeling, and doing appear to make no sense as they seem not to be related to any territory. Yet I think and I feel. I think and feel the unnamed. It could be due to my body/brain matter and its internal and ceaseless connections that facilitate those moments. It could be due to the always-incoming external matter that the body/ brain takes in and to which it responds acutely and intensely. It could be due to my past, my present, and the ways in which my past meets the present. Too many or too few cups of coffee drunk? Too little oxygen? Too intense a green in the trees or blue in the ocean? Too much noise? Too many or too few memories attached to this particular building or that certain street? Too harsh the words of a lover? Too tired of names, frames, labels, and boxes? Too much of this? Too little of that? Or perhaps, just right? I do not know. In those moments, there is no identity of any kind, no gender, sex, sexuality, racialization, ethnicity, age, or class. They lose their grip. They do not matter. They do not count. They are not there. A moment similar to the one experienced by Septimus, one of the main characters in Woolf's *Mrs Dalloway*, "the flesh was melted off the world. . . . [the] body was macerated until only the nerve fibres were left" (Woolf 2005 [1925]: 49). Shapes and contours are gone. I become a pure expression of connections, difference, and change. What is thought, felt, and done remains unnamed and exists beyond known words or images.

My body/brain and the world form a huge assemblage consisting of a thousand of *pieces*. These pieces vary. They are the body/brain matter, external matter, discourses and practices, experiences, memories, internal and external sensations. They are in me. I am in them. We form a territory, a temporary and trembling territory; yet, we have a shape, we have a contour, we exist. The pieces matter differently on different occasions. They are like ebbs and flows. They change position, sometimes without a volitional act from me. Sometimes, I explicitly ask them to come closer or move a little further away. My desire for coffee overshadows any pondering about gender or sexuality. Because I have experienced acts of discrimination, the victory of a right-wing party makes me scream in anger for women's rights and criticize any signs of homophobia or xenophobia. In my assemblage, I can easily become a breakfast, a shower, a Polish woman, a 40-something-year-old body, a crime book or a chocolate. This is not relativism; it is the beauty of connections, difference, and change. Every time a piece gets closer or more distant, I am a little bit different. My thinking, feeling, and acting are a little bit different. The medicines in my body/brain, back pain, a flight, a walk taken, a small discussion in an office corridor, the gaze of a neighbour, a question from a border control officer, a comment from a doctor, feedback from a language teacher, each makes the pieces matter differently and shapes me into a pain, a fear, a tree, a cloud, a woman, a Polish-speaking person, or a chocolate (when a friend happens to have a chocolate while chatting with me in a corridor). I am not either this or that, I am and . . . and . . . and . . . – sometimes interchangeably, sometimes concurrently, yet never for too long. Frequently, imperceptibility (of a different duration) enters the scene and my trembling and temporary territory disappears in an act of full deterritorialization. I think and feel the unnamed. Once that moment is over, I reterritorialize

98   *Edyta Just*

again. I and the world have a shape, a contour, once again – but some pieces may never meet again, some are gone forever, some have departed but may return, though never the same, and some new aspects have entered the territory. Maybe, when seeing a tree, I will not become a tree any longer but a leaf. Most probably, I will never become that Edyta I was in 2006. Perhaps I will walk again that *same-different* street in Utrecht. Possibly now, in the mornings, for a while, I will keep on becoming titanium or maybe an hour-long sleep.

"The assemblage is between two layers" (Deleuze and Guattari 1987: 40). On one side, it "faces . . . the body without organs" (Ibid.), that is, the moments of imperceptibility, of deterritorialization. On the other side, "it faces the strata" (Ibid.). I am on the move. I am an assemblage (I am a Polish woman, or darkness for a day). I am an imperceptibility (I am of unspecified gender, ethnicity, and age). I can also be a stratum (I am a woman or a chocolate for a month). Sometimes, my body/brain matter, internal matter connections, external matter, discourses and practices, experiences, memories, and internal and external sensations form fixed connections. Even though, in my volitional or automatic becoming a stratum, I am still an outcome of connections and difference, I can nonetheless be very resistant to change. For some reason, the pieces connect in a certain manner and remain connected in this way for long periods. They last persistently. This does not mean that change, deterritorialization, or dismantling of the me-stratum is not possible or is not occurring. Yet, as already explained, such undoing does not occur easily. I can be a woman or a chocolate for long periods of time.

My Research and My Lived Imperceptibility, Assemblage, and Stratum

In my becomings, everything matters, although it may matter differently during different periods of time: the body/brain matter, external matter, discourses and practices, experiences, memories, and internal and external sensations. Therefore, as a *result* I can be as much *nothing* as I can be gendered or with a particular ethnicity or as I can be a tree, titanium, or a chocolate. I am an assemblage between two layers. I have no identity. I have various and temporary identities. I can become attached to some kinds of identity for long periods of time. This is again not a relativism. It is certainly not madness. It is an assemblage between two layers. It is connections, difference, and change. It is subjectivity in relation to axes of differentiation that is lived in an imperceptible, assemblage-like, and stratified manner.

Certainly, as Berrett, Wilson-Mendenhall, and Barsalou suggest, I cannot "gain introspective access to the processes in [my] brain" (2014: 449). I cannot control or know *in what I will result* (although sometimes one can try to find the patterns and try to predict or exercise volitional acts). Whenever I consider my research topic and questions, whenever I lead discussions or make comments, I operate within volitional acts (or at least, so it seems). However, as discussed earlier, my body/brain, external matter, discourses, experiences, and sensations have their say, and quite often their *say* is executed automatically without, or rather beyond, my rational and conscious control. Since I am living my life as an assemblage between two layers, since I happen to have no identity, multiple and temporary

"I Will Meet You at Twilight" 99

identities, or occasionally I am attached to some kinds of identity for longer – I sometimes employ my volition to allow all, or parts, of this to govern and influence my research topic, questions, discussions, and comments. Furthermore, it can also happen that the way in which I am living my life (as imperceptible, assemblage-like, and stratified) becomes, automatically and beyond my conscious control, reflected, and embodied in my research. Hence, it happens that sometimes my research does not reflect upon geopolitical location or researcher/research subjects' axes of differentiation. This does not mean that they do not matter. Rather, it means that the freedom and *potentia* I find in imperceptibility, in full deterritorialization, in having no identity of any kind, in a pure expression of connections, difference and change somehow finds its way into a text. I am aware that, in those instances, my research may seem unspecified, but this is not how I experience it. To me, it is rather a plenitude, a possibility, a release, and an escape from the frames, boxes, and labels into a powerful nothingness that nonetheless promises everything: "Give me the possible, or else I'll suffocate" (Deleuze 2007: 234).

Sometimes my research (topic, questions, discussions, and comments) brings to the fore geopolitical locations and researcher/research subjects' axes of differentiation. The subjects' location and their shapes and contours become visible. Yet these shapes and contours are never fixed; rather, they are multiple, of different durations and prone to deterritorialization. I am an assemblage, and my research becomes an assemblage with regard to locations and identities. The territories are there, yet they are trembling, and they deterritorialize and reterritorialize to take on yet another shape, yet another contour. Volitionally or automatically, these seem to be strategic gestures because, to me, both territories and deterritorializations are necessary in order to make a statement and encourage change. In those instances, my research becomes a trembling territory with moments of deterritorialization, and it welcomes identities (including those that go beyond intersectional axes of differentiation), which are nonetheless never fixed but always temporary and prone to transformation. It embodies connections, difference, and change on its way to infinity.

It may also happen that my research will fix and freeze a location or researcher/research subjects' axes of differentiation. It may fix an identity of some kind. Me-stratum, my research-stratum. Volitionally or not, sometimes it is not easy or possible to detach myself from a fixed territory, either because I love it so much or because I dislike it too much. Like me, my research topic, questions, and discussion about locations and identities can become a fixed territory that still embodies connections and difference, yet is somewhat resistant to transformation. Importantly, it is crucial to mention that, as in life, so in research: imperceptibility, assemblage, and stratum can occur separately (the duration and order of their existence may differ) or even concurrently.

Transnational Intersectional Feminist Research

In this chapter, influenced by Haraway, Braidotti, and neuroscientific theory, I have shown that mental activity, meaning-making, the logic behind meaning-making, embodiment, embeddedness, matter, and social context are intertwined to

100   *Edyta Just*

constitute materialist, relational, and "nature-cultural" subjectivities. Thus, I have focused on subjectivity through the prism of the axes of differentiation and corresponding identity markers such as gender, sex, sexuality, racialization, ethnicity, age, and class, and reflected upon how matter (understood here as material locatedness, yet with matter defined only as physical or corporeal substance in general; the substance or substances of which any physical object consists or is composed), social context (discussed here mainly in terms of geopolitical location with all its spatiotemporal societal and power relations, beliefs, discourses, and practices regarding various forms of embodiment, gender, sex, sexuality, racialization, ethnicity, age, and class), and the logic behind meaning-making matter for subjectivity and knowledge production. Referring to Deleuze and Guattari and my own experience, and in a poetic way, I have discussed subjectivity lived as imperceptibility, assemblage, and stratum with regard to various axes of differentiation. I have emphasized how matter, social context, and the logic behind meaning-making result in subjectivities that are about connections, difference, and change and, furthermore, in embodied and embedded subjectivities that can nonetheless be deprived of identity, or imbued with a new and temporary identity that is always prone to change, or with a fixed identity for some time, although never forever. I have also tried to reflect upon how becoming imperceptible, assemblage-like, and stratified may correspond with research.

I have concluded that the way in which I live my subjectivity with regard to axes of differentiation can result in research that is unspecified, trembling, and fixed in terms of identity markers, related to the axes of differentiation of the researcher/ research subjects and reflections on their geopolitical location (understood here as particularly located societal and power relations, beliefs, discourses, and practices regarding various forms of embodiment, gender, sex, sexuality, racialization, ethnicity, age, and class). As stated at the beginning, I am claiming neither that this is *the* way to conceptualize subjectivity nor that there is a straightforward link between subjectivity, identity, and research; I am simply experimenting. Nor am I saying that this is *the* manner in which subjectivity (with regard to axes of differentiation) can be lived and research conducted – quite the opposite, I present my own experiences in order to avoid giving prescriptions applicable to everybody. Although certainly I wonder whether any of my readers can sense some similarities, and whether what I am writing about resonates in some way with my readers' experiences.

Now, I want to discuss how those reflections can help me to think about transnational intersectional feminist research. I think that embodiment and embeddedness will always have a say in how one experiences one's own subjectivity and does research. Yet the very fact that one is embodied and embedded somehow shows that one is always already about connections, difference, and change. The logic behind meaning-making, body/brain matter, external matter, discourses and practices, experiences, memories, and internal and external sensations all bring about and stand for connections, difference, and change. They bring about and stand for non-identities, identities of different kinds, and temporarily fixed identities of different types. All of these embody connections, difference and change, resulting from the logic behind meaning-making, from the dance of the body/brain matter, external matter, discourses and practices, experiences, memories, and internal and external sensations. Like life, research embodies difference, connections and change, non-identities, identities of different kinds, while temporarily fixed identities of different types, and unspecified/trembling/fixed reflections upon geopolitical locations occur separately or concurrently. One may sense shapes and forms, but it is enough to play with light to start sensing differently. *In the twilight, the contours blur*. Would it not then be an ethical gesture to think about transnational intersectional feminist research as embodying and welcoming difference, connections and change, non-identities, identities of different kinds, temporarily fixed identities of different types, and differing (unspecified/trembling/fixed) reflections/discussions on geopolitical location? Research accounting for the role that the logic of meaning-making, the body/brain matter, external matter, discourses and practices, experiences, memories and internal and external sensations play in engendering epistemologies? Transnational intersectional feminist research that is aware of the fact that a researcher can produce diverse forms of research on different occasions, or even concurrently?

I Will Meet You at Twilight: when we listen to our fellow researchers and when we read each other's research – in a dim light – the contours may blur and we may sense the beauty and the power of the connections, difference, and change, and perhaps in those moments we can understand each other a little better. Perhaps.

This text is not a prescription. It does not suggest that this is *the* way of thinking about subjectivity, identity, research in general, or transnational intersectional feminist research in particular. I hope that this chapter situates itself on the plateau of forever, daring others to generate feminist scholarship that is committed to the engendering of innovative epistemologies able to inspire practices that result in positive transformations and change.

Notes

1 In this chapter, I take social context seriously into consideration. However, in the empirical section, I do not analyse it or discuss it specifically with all its differentiating powers.
2 This paragraph is based on the text: Just, Edyta. 2020. "The Body and the Brain in Classrooms: On Matter and Social Context." *Creative Education* 11: 693–709.

References

Barrett, Lisa Feldman, Christine D. Wilson-Mendenhall, and Lawrence W. Barsalou. 2014. "A Psychological Construction Account of Emotion Regulation and Dysregulation: The Role of Situated Conceptualizations." In *The Handbook of Emotion Regulation* (2nd ed.), edited by James J. Gross, 447–65. New York, NY: Guilford.
Braidotti, Rosi. 2006. *Transpositions: On Nomadic Ethics*. Cambridge and Malden, MA: Polity Press.
Braidotti, Rosi. 2013. *The Posthuman*. Cambridge and Malden, MA: Polity Press.
Deleuze, Gilles. 2007. "May'68 Did Not Take Place." In *Two Regimes of Madness: Texts and Interviews 1975–1995*, 233–36. New York, NY and Los Angeles, CA: Semiotext(e).
Deleuze, Gilles, and Félix Guattari. 1987. *A Thousand Plateaus: Capitalism and Schizophrenia*. London and New York, NY: Continuum.

102   *Edyta Just*

Grosz, Elizabeth. 1994. *Volatile Bodies: Toward a Corporeal Feminism*. Bloomington, IN and Indianapolis, IN: Indiana University Press.

Haraway, Donna. 1988. "Situated Knowledges: The Science Question in Feminism and the Privilege of Partial Perspective." *Feminist Studies* 14 (3): 575–99.

Just, Edyta. 2020. "The Body and the Brain in Classrooms: On Matter and Social Context." *Creative Education* 11: 693–709. https://doi.org/10.4236/ce.2020.115051

Kalat, James W. 2009. *Biological Psychology* (10th ed.). Boston, MA: Wadsworth Cengage Learning.

Lindquist, Kristen A., Tor D. Wager, Hedy Kober, Eliza Bliss-Moreau, and Lisa Feldman Barrett. 2012. "The Brain Basis of Emotion: A Meta-Analytic Review." *Behavioral and Brain Sciences* 35: 121–202. https://doi.org/10.1017/S0140525X11000446

Semetsky, Inna. 2009. "Deleuze as a Philosopher of Education: Affective Knowledge/Effective Learning." *The European Legacy* 14 (4): 443–56.

Stagoll, Clifford Scott. 2005. "Becoming." In *The Deleuze Dictionary*, edited by Adrian Parr, 21–2. Edinburgh: Edinburgh University Press.

Woolf, Virginia. 2005 [1925]. *Mrs Dalloway*. London: Hogarth Press.

10 Living an African Feminist Life – Decolonial Perspectives

A Conversation

Victoria Kawesa, Redi Koobak, and Nina Lykke

Victoria Kawesa is an anti-racist feminist activist, writer and scholar. She has been based in Sweden since she arrived there, as a nine-year old, in 1984. She came together with her mother and siblings as political refugees from Uganda, a country embroiled in a civil war at the time. As a practising Catholic, Victoria's father was brutally murdered by the secret police of the then Ugandan leader, Idi Amin. Victoria's current doctoral research and writings on African feminism from decolonial perspectives takes an autobiographical point of departure, using the method of autophenomenography (autoethnography with a phenomenological approach). Our interview conversation aligns itself with this personal-political-theoretical starting point of Victoria's research. It links glimpses from her life history that she tells in her forthcoming thesis Black Masks/White Sins: Becoming a Black Obuntu Feminist, with the theoretical and political perspectives that she also develops there. In particular, we asked Victoria to address key issues of And Words Collide from a Place, and the ways in which different forms of corpo-political and geopolitical situatedness matter for transnational feminist cartographies, onto-epistemologies and opportunities for alliance building.

Becoming a Feminist Through My Grandmother

Redi: A good point to start from could be: How did you become a feminist? Perhaps you could spell it out, starting with a biographical note?

Victoria: I became a feminist due to being a part of the women in my life, but specifically my grandmother. She's the one who inspired me and made me understand the link between power and gender oppression. From when I was five years old, she made me aware of domestic violence. She told all her grandchildren that she had been subjected to domestic violence by her husband, and that she had thrown him out of her home. She also told us that she would never marry again. She was wearing a cross and pointed to Jesus: "He is my husband now". That memory stuck with me. I understood that there was gender oppression, and that my grandmother had to act against it. I became more observant and started analysing and recognizing gender oppression in my life.

Nina: Did you witness the violence and abuse that your grandmother was subjected to?

DOI: 10.4324/9781003378761-11

104 *Victoria Kawesa, Redi Koobak, and Nina Lykke*

Victoria: I witnessed violence and abuse through the women around me. We often heard women talking about abuse from their husbands. I witnessed that through my mother. That's when I saw it with my own eyes, when she was abused several times by different men in her life. For example, the first abuse I witnessed was when I was six years old, and I woke up in the middle of the night to hear my mother crying. It was dark, so I went to see where the crying was coming from. I saw my mother lying on the floor in her bedroom. She was completely covered in dark patches all over her body. My grandmother and auntie were pressing ice on her body because she was so swollen. She was crying and crying. When I saw her lying there, naked, swollen, and bruised, I picked up from their conversation that it was her boyfriend who had beaten her. I really understood then that there's something going on whereby women are subjected to this kind of abuse. That made me very aware, and it became a part of my analytical framework, the way I looked upon the world, the way I understood gendered power relations and that men held a certain power which they misused.

Nina: But I guess that resistance was also part of the feminism you got from your grandmother?

Victoria: Yes, exactly. It was the resistance and acknowledgement that violence against women is wrong. Otherwise, I wouldn't really have understood what it was, but Granny made it very clear when she gathered all her grandchildren during the war,[1] and we were many grandchildren at her home. She told us that she had a big announcement to make, and even the smaller ones, like me, were part of the meeting. Normally, I was never called for anything important, but this time, we were all gathered. She then told us: "This is wrong". It was that acknowledgement that it's not right, and I'm doing something about it, that made me aware of how important resistance is.

Redi: This sounds brave, taking a stance, like: I won't tolerate this.

Victoria: I think that's what made this such a strong memory in my life, encouraging me to resist oppression.

Redi: I don't think a lot of women have that in them, to take that stance.

Victoria: Exactly, and many can't financially afford to kick out abusive men. My grandmother owned her home and her land, which she had inherited from my great-grandmother. She was able to kick him out, and wasn't ashamed about it, and she could verbalize and talk about it. Like you said, resistance is another move, which means not only accepting but also doing something or speaking back. That's what I see as the feminist movement. The speaking out and speaking back and resisting. My grandmother taught me that through her actions.

Nina: Was this feminist resistance related to Obuntu Bulamu[2] and to what you would perhaps consider to be African feminism?

Victoria: My experience of domestic violence in the Ugandan communities is that people around don't want to get involved. They see it as a private

Living an African Feminist Life – Decolonial Perspectives   105

matter, between the spouses. Obuntu Bulamu, the way I look at it, involves acknowledging the abuse that women are subjected to, and taking a stance against it. My grandmother acknowledged it in front of us all, and said: "This is wrong, it shouldn't happen". She broke this taboo barrier that we don't take a stance; we don't care; we don't have this concern for each other. Obuntu Bulamu is very much about being concerned about others and really doing something to override or overcome all these barriers, all these oppressive barriers through care. It was a caring act when Granny told us: "You should never accept this". She saved us because I wouldn't have understood so early in my life how important it is to care through taking a stance against oppression.

African Feminism, Spiritual Activism, and Obuntu Bulamu

Nina: In your dissertation, you also write about another episode from your childhood in Uganda, related to your grandmother and the ways in which she practised Obuntu Bulamu – and African feminism. Perhaps you could spell this story out here as well?

Victoria: If we talk about Obuntu Bulamu as African feminism, and conceptualize it as comprising both resistance and care, then it's also about survival through overcoming barriers. This event illustrates what I mean when I talk about Obuntu Bulamu, as a lived experience of resistance not only in the sense of an oppositional mode of consciousness but also as a feminist tactic, based in a differential mode of consciousness that acts as an ethical care principle.[3]

During the war, we left the city, and we were staying with my grandmother. We were around 30 grandchildren living with Granny, so the house was full. Food was very scarce, and I was hungry all the time. One evening we were sitting down in the kitchen, waiting for dinner, when I heard somebody knocking on the door. I saw my grandmother walk towards the door and open it. I could see a woman standing there with a little child holding her hand, and another child on her back. Granny was talking to them, and the woman was saying: "Just for one night, please. Just for one night". I got furious, I walked over to them, annoyed that the woman with these children wanted to stay overnight when we hardly had any food. I pulled my grandmother's skirt, and told her: "Granny, we can't take in more". Then she stopped and kneeled in front of me and looked straight into my eyes. She held my face between her palms and said: "Nankinga [my Ugandan name], we should never deny anybody food, ever. We share the little we have". I was shocked; I couldn't even grasp her thinking because for me what should be done was very clear, and she was telling me something completely different. It shifted my consciousness in that very moment. It changed my perspective on the way I understood the meaning of sharing and giving.

106 *Victoria Kawesa, Redi Koobak, and Nina Lykke*

That you can be humble even in the most difficult times. She shifted my worldview in that instant. This moment became the point of departure from which my social ethos stems. It became my guiding principle when she concluded: "We must have Obuntu Bulamu".

Nina: And she mentioned this concept of Obuntu Bulamu?

Victoria: Yes, she said: "We must have Obuntu Bulamu". The meaning of this concept in Luganda is the same as the South African term "Ubuntu". As Ugandan Afro-feminist and decolonial scholar Sylvia Tamale explains it, it is a term that refers to the maxim "I am because you are", and "sums up the reciprocity and interconnectedness that is alive in the world view of most Africans" (Tamale 2020, 221). This is in contrast to the Cartesian Western philosophical worldview, which is based on the maxim: "I think, therefore I am". What is common to both of these expressions is that they're grounded in a humanistic philosophical worldview which is different from my grandmother's practice and understanding of Obuntu Bulamu. Her rural roots formed her belief system about the interconnectedness and reciprocity of all life, which includes human life, as not separated from nature, spirituality, or our dead ancestors as part of the world of the living. My concept of Obuntu Bulamu is derived from my grandmother's practice, which transcends modernistic, humanistic African understandings of Ubuntu/Obuntu Bulamu.

Nina: Could you tell us more about how Obuntu Bulamu, in this broadened sense that you use it, has become a keyword for your research?

Redi: . . . and activism?

Victoria: It's like when we talk about pluriversality.[4] It's part of Indigenous knowledges that can also be activated to intersect with notions of resistance and oppression within anti-racist work. Anti-racist feminist work is also about resisting and overcoming oppression, about survival. But for me, I can't survive oppression and continue resisting if it's only living a life in opposition. I need something that can vitalize me, and that's where my notion of Obuntu Bulamu comes in. It's a vital source of spiritual presence. The power that I get from my beloved dead father, for example, is a kind of spiritual activism, which is a practice of Obuntu Bulamu, as a corpo-affective intensity of our deeply entangled beingness. This way of living with the dead is pulled from the Indigenous practices of becoming with the dead. Thus, Obuntu Bulamu should not merely be understood as a concept that explains knowledge at the periphery of the Western hegemonic discourse of modernity. Rather, as a pluriversal concept, it's a decolonial shift from universal concepts to what Madina Tlostanova and Walter Mignolo define as the "geo- and body politics of knowledge", rather than the Western "geopolitics of reason" (Tlostanova and Mignolo 2012). Spiritual activism is a term that I borrow from Gloria Anzaldua,[5] but I link it to Obuntu Bulamu as well – as something that is connected to pluriversality and Indigenous knowledge as a way of surviving through resisting and

Living an African Feminist Life – Decolonial Perspectives   107

overcoming. The way I do it is through corpo-affectivity work, which helps me to release some of the trauma and find the necessary healing from colonial wounds[6] such as war, death, poverty, racism. Spiritual activism occurs, for example, when I call on my father and talk to him, his presence then revitalizes my spirit and soul.

Nina: Does he speak to you, and what does he say?

Victoria: I'm trying to develop that in my work. I've noticed that the co-existence with my father helps to vitalize and regenerate my sense of being in the world. For example, I talk to him when I feel sad or stuck. I can say: "Dad, I feel bad, I don't know what to do", and by starting a conversation with him, I start hearing him. I get into this corpo-affective space whereby I sense myself opening up. I can sense all this warmth, his voice telling me: "I'm here with you, I'm holding your hand. I'm going to be with you while you're writing". Then I create a safe space with him, and writing starts to flow. So that's an example which helps me move forward from stuck places.

Nina: So, can you also establish that safe space with your grandmother?

Victoria: Yes. But now, I'm very anxious about my grandmother, especially with COVID-19, she might not be here for much longer.

Nina: Because she's old now?

Victoria: Yes, she's 86 and has dementia, she doesn't recognize us any longer. But when I talk to her about what she means to me, she always reminds me that I've already inherited her spirit, we are one, which really gives me joy and comfort.

Nina: And she will not die.

Victoria: She will not die.

Nina: She will not disappear, vanish for good. She will be there in another way for you . . .

Victoria: Yes. Writing my thesis has been a journey of embodying her spirit. It's like she's giving me her spirit so that I can spell it out, share it with others, through the notion of Obuntu Bulamu. That's the whole purpose of writing my thesis.

Nina: I know, because you must do it, otherwise she will vanish.

Victoria: Exactly!

A Political Murder

Redi: Could you say more about your father and his role in terms of shaping your activism and research? You talked about your grandmother, but you didn't really tell the story of your father.

Victoria: The reason I'm in Sweden is really because my father was murdered. We came as refugees after his death. He was murdered in Uganda during the Idi Amin war, in 1978. I was three years old then. The soldiers came to our home and took him. They threw him in the trunk of his

108 *Victoria Kawesa, Redi Koobak, and Nina Lykke*

	car and drove him away. We never saw him again. His body was never found or buried. We just know that he was killed. Brutally murdered.
Nina:	By Idi Amin's secret police?
Victoria:	Yes. My mother was pregnant with my little sister when they took him. They told her that he was in prison. She went there almost all the time and tried to get him out. They wanted more money and for a whole year she was going back and forth trying to get him out and paying the money, but we later found out that he had already been killed a month after they arrested him.
Nina:	So, they just squeezed money out of your mother, pretending that your father was still alive?
Victoria:	Yes, for a long time. When she found out that they had killed him, our lives were in danger, and we had to leave the country.
Nina:	But that was also why your mother took you to your grandmother – to hide the family outside of town?
Victoria:	Exactly. Because we were living in another town, in a smaller town called Masaka, where I was born. After my dad was killed, the soldiers took everything, our house, everything. So, my mother had to move back to Granny in the countryside close to Kampala. So we were hiding out there, and that's when I was with my grandmother a lot, and she taught me about Obuntu Bulamu. I was my father's last child. I resemble him very much – I wear his face and carry his bones. People who knew him always reminded me of how much he loved me. I made it a mission to live my life so that his life wouldn't be forgotten.

Encountering Whiteness and Swedish White Normativity

Nina:	Perhaps we should now turn to your life in Sweden, and your encounters with whiteness and white normativity. What were your first encounters with whiteness like?
Victoria:	We moved to Sweden when I was nine years old in 1984. Growing up in Uganda, in a Black-normative society, we didn't talk about being Black or white. You were either European or African or from a specific ethnicity. For example, I am a Muganda, from the Baganda people, who belong to the Buganda kingdom. I grew up having no interactions with white people because even though Uganda was part of the British Empire, it wasn't a settler colony where British people lived. Uganda was a protectorate, meaning that Ugandans were the ones administrating the colony for the British. When I started kindergarten, I noticed that all the books were from Britain. The school system was organized according to the British system. We had books like *Jack and Jill went up the hill*, *Cinderella*, and *Snow White*, which all had images of white children. All the images of the angels and Jesus were also white. It was a huge contrast to my reality, and I used to wonder: why were only

Living an African Feminist Life – Decolonial Perspectives 109

Europeans in heaven? I wanted to see an angel that looked like me, but they were always babies with blue eyes. Seriously, I used to wonder if there was a European heaven and an African heaven . . . you know? I didn't understand it. Nobody really explained that. At school, I was shocked that we were forced to speak only in English. We couldn't speak Luganda; we would get punished for speaking our mother tongue at school.

When we came to Sweden, I had all of that in mind, and suddenly, I was in a space where my skin colour was not only different but also devalued, and I became really confused. The first white people I saw were in our village in Uganda. They were in a jeep, driving by very fast, and I remember how all the children ran to the road. Everybody was excited, waving, and shouting: "White people, white people are here!" I thought it was a strange thing to do, clapping and waving when they saw visitors in our village.

The first day of school in Sweden was horrific. I later found out that I was the first Black person in that school. During a break, when we were playing, the children surrounded me in the schoolyard. They made a circle around me, and I was standing in the middle of this circle. They were all looking at me, as if I was this weird, different, scary person. I didn't understand their fear. I was trying to understand it and that's when I became aware that it was my skin colour that made me different. Before then, I didn't attach any meaning or value to my skin colour. I didn't understand that white perspective of blackness as something devalued and I began to understand the experience of becoming black in a white-normative society.

Becoming an Anti-racist Feminist Activist

Nina: You've been talking about becoming a feminist, so when did you become an anti-racist?

Victoria: When I was kicked out of a posh school in Stockholm in the eighth grade. I was living in the Stockholm suburb of Tensta, which is a poor migrant neighbourhood. But I was going to school in the city centre with all these white middle-class children. I was abused and bullied a lot. They really tortured me there. They called me the n-word, threw my books in the dustbin, always harassing me. I skipped school for almost a whole year. Then finally the school principal called my mother for an appointment and told her they didn't want me to attend their school anymore. They told her that it would be better for me to attend a school where we lived, "over there", as they said. I had reached out several times, told my teachers. I was going to a school counsellor, but nobody was doing anything to stop all this abuse and bullying. When they kicked me out of their school, my mother was sad and disappointed

110   *Victoria Kawesa, Redi Koobak, and Nina Lykke*

	with me, and that's when I realized: I am going to be treated like this, I'm going to be subjected to racism, and nobody is going to help protect me or take any responsibility for it. I need to help myself and find ways to navigate a way through racism.
Nina:	How old were you at that time?
Victoria:	I was 14. I realized that I needed to navigate this racist space myself, since no one else was acknowledging the problem of everyday racism. If I didn't take charge, if I couldn't navigate through racism, they were going to destroy my education. We were sitting on a bus, on our way back home. My mother was crying, telling me that I'd destroyed my education by being thrown out of the nice posh school. Then I told her: "Don't worry, in Sweden, we all go to the same universities at the end of the day. The most important thing is that I get good grades from high school and then I'll meet those posh white bullies at the university".
Nina:	And at that time, you wanted to become a lawyer to work with social justice?
Victoria:	Yes. To change the racist system. I became like a social justice warrior.
Nina:	Did you have any friends who also wanted to resist the system?
Victoria:	I became involved politically in a local Marxist group called *Offensiv*.
Redi:	Where? In Stockholm?
Victoria:	In Stockholm.
Nina:	When you were 14?
Victoria:	I was 14 or 15 years old. I remember it was the first time that I'd met people who talked about the systemic Imperialist Capitalist Colonial relations between Europe and the African countries, and the way in which the African countries pay more money in debt than they receive in funds.
Nina:	So it was at that time that you started to become politically aware of the structural dimensions of oppression? Because it's one thing to resist individually, but another to understand the structures?
Victoria:	That's when I started to be more aware of oppression from a Global North/South perspective.
Nina:	Through this Marxist group?
Victoria:	Yes. During this time there was a lot of resistance against skinheads, especially when they marched in Stockholm on 30 November 1991.[7] The Marxist group organized protest marches on that day in Gamla Stan (the historic part of Stockholm's inner city). The police surrounded us, blocked us off completely, and squeezed us into a corner so that we couldn't move. The skinheads could march freely while we were squeezed into a corner. That was an eye-opening experience.
Nina:	Was the group, the Marxist group, mainly white?
Victoria:	Yes, only white middle-class people.
Nina:	Could you tell more about your relation to this group and how it evolved?

Living an African Feminist Life – Decolonial Perspectives   111

Victoria: The Marxist group wanted me to speak about their work at my school to mobilize more students into their political movement. One of their political demands was that grades should be abolished from schools. I remember thinking that it was not good policy to encourage children in poor neighbourhoods to oppose grades. How would we get into higher education? I refused and explained to them that good grades were the only way for us to get into university because we couldn't score high on the high-school test, since it was culturally designed for white Swedish people. I had only lived in Sweden for nine years at that time. I knew that my Swedish wasn't good enough to score well on the high-school test. I noticed that they never talked about their white middle-class Swedish privilege, and I eventually left the Marxist group.

Redi: Was feminism a part of the discussion?

Victoria: No. They didn't talk about feminism either, or structural racism, but rather about white extremism.

Nina: So when did you meet people who talked about structural and institutionalized racism? When did you expand your analysis of the world to include race as a structuring principle?

Victoria: The TV series *Roots*[8] was the first eye-opener when I was nine years old. *Roots* made me conscious of the white gaze and what it saw when looking at me. I gained a historical background to racism, which became an important framework that helped me early on to know that the problem was not me, but rather how white people were conditioned to see me. That understanding helped me navigate racism and develop my anti-racist perspective.

Nina: When did you meet people who also had an anti-racist perspective?

Victoria: The first time was when I was 25 years old, and got involved in *Mana*, an anti-racist feminist magazine in Malmö.[9] By then, I was working as an activist in the African community with HIV/AIDS prevention work in Malmö. I was interviewed by Lawen Mothadi[10] about my work with the African diaspora and HIV prevention. After the interview, she asked me if I wanted to join the editorial board of *Mana*.

Nina: Where are we timewise?

Victoria: Around 2000.

Redi: And the group was mostly white Swedes again?

Victoria: No, they were migrants and racialized people. I started writing articles for the magazine about Black Feminism. I wrote an article entitled "Anti-racist grand-slam!" (Kawesa 2004) about Serena and Venus Williams and the black female body.

Nina: "Anti-racist grand-slam!" That's a very good title (laughs).

Victoria: Then I wrote an article entitled "Ain't I my hair?" (Kawesa 2006) and that's when I started giving seminars about whiteness.

112 *Victoria Kawesa, Redi Koobak, and Nina Lykke*

Politically Focusing Whiteness

Redi: Can you say more about your shift to whiteness as a political issue? Did it come from the frustration with the Marxist group: that they weren't really addressing this?

Victoria: My shift to focusing on whiteness started when I was 19 years old. I had just started studying law at Stockholm University. The first day, I entered this big auditorium and saw only white middle-class students staring at me. I was the only black person. When I realized that, my whole body froze. I couldn't move. I started panicking and couldn't enter the room. I had to mobilize all my strength to enter. That's when I realized the power of whiteness as a spatial thing. I sensed how whiteness was a brick wall, which I was running up against, as Sara Ahmed[11] explains this experience of whiteness being a barrier that stops black bodies in their movements. I hit the famous white wall, becoming rejected by the room, and I never returned to that Law School. This incident made me realize that racism had caused me to internalize a fear of white people and to experience extreme discomfort in white rooms. I spent a whole year trying to figure out what to do. I applied to Black universities in the USA, planning to study African and Black history. But then I realized that running away was not the answer if I really wanted to understand whiteness. I had to find a way of being comfortable with white people and white spaces, so I applied to Lund University,[12] with the intention of overcoming my fear of whiteness and navigating white spaces. I stayed. And I'm still fighting!

Nina: That's what I was going to say! You've done that ever since.

Redi: To say the least.

Doing Black Theorizing From Different Geopolitical Locations

Redi: Shifting this conversation to academic debates and theory, you've often said that the theory you can find in Sweden about racism and anti-racism is very US-centred or US-based. Like, a lot of the role-models for Black people in Sweden somehow come from the States, and you've been very critical of that. Could you say more about this issue?

Victoria: The Black Feminist movement is very much focused on being a counter-hegemonic discourse to White Feminism, and in this way it's very much focused on a Western cultural understanding of blackness and whiteness; that is, it's caught in a binary opposition. Blackness here becomes very much defined by whiteness, and Black women are always put in opposition to white women. But I don't see us as defined by white people at all, and I find this perspective very limiting and Americanized.

Redi: That reminds me of an anecdote a colleague of mine told me. She's based in South Africa, at the University of Cape Town, where they get exchange students from the States, often Black Feminists. They

Living an African Feminist Life – Decolonial Perspectives   113

come to Africa because they want to find authentic African feminism. But then they become so disappointed when they're assigned readings by African American feminists such as bell hooks (laughs).[13] They're like, "Why are we reading bell hooks? We came here to find authentic African feminist voices".

Victoria: I think South Africa is very different from the rest of Africa since whiteness plays a huge role in the daily lives of South Africans, compared to someone like me, who comes from a Black-normative society. I can see why South Africans easily relate to US Black Feminist ideas, since they are caught in this oppositional space to whiteness. In Uganda, bell hooks might not make sense in the same way since we don't experience the Black/white binary on a structural or everyday basis.

Nina: We've been talking about the problems with anti-racism in Sweden, and the Americanization of Black Feminism. So where do you see your allies in terms of political struggle and theorizing? Do you, for example, feel connected to the work of African feminists like Sylvia Tamale?[14]

Victoria: What I like about African feminists, such as Sylvia Tamale, is that their focus is on patriarchal oppression, which is also where my feminist journey started, through the experiences of domestic violence in my family. One of the misconceptions is that feminism is a white woman's theory, in contrast to African feminism, which is considered to derive from the lived experiences of women on the African continent. But does that imply that feminism is a white woman's struggle? We need to create our own decolonial identities, connecting to our Indigenous knowledges, and different ways of creating knowledge production through feminist frameworks, so that we can survive and overcome multiple oppressions, different from, but not in opposition to white European and US feminism. When we talk about decolonial work, we always talk about the Western world and whether the Western world is doing this or doing that, but we also need to really talk about toxic masculinity in our own countries. Feminism is understood as something that comes from white women, and patriarchal oppression is seen as coming from the colonizers: "Before the colonizers came, we didn't have a patriarchal society. We had only beautiful matriarchal societies, where all the women and the men shared everything. Then, the white people came and destroyed it all and taught us how to hate each other". This is an illusion! Still, that's the story that Black Feminism is always selling. bell hooks sells that idea in her books. In the States that's something they always say [speaking in ironic imitation of a sermon]: "Before we came on the boat, black men and black women loved each other, and then we got on the boat and got off the boat, and then they crushed the love and racism destroyed the love between the black woman and the black man and now we hate each other". I'm just like, "No! We've always hated each other" (laughs). There is no love lost between us.

114 *Victoria Kawesa, Redi Koobak, and Nina Lykke*

That's a fantasy, and it's really irritating, the way the Black struggle in the US is always building this fantasy about pre-slavery, and then we also have some African feminists trying to promote this pre-colonial unity, and it's very frustrating, and I feel like that makes things very difficult. Then we always talk about the white person as bringing us all these problems, and if we get rid of the white people, then everything would be fine, but that's not true.

Nina: This story also constructs white people as having far too many super-powers. Of course, white people have been powerful, in colonialism, but this story boosts the image of white people, reproducing an image of white people being the agents of everything.

Victoria: Exactly! It becomes, like, idolizing white people to the extent that they're made to believe that everyone wants to be like them.

Nina: I think the Ugandan term "muzungu", confused, for white people that you told me about, is much more to the point.

Victoria: The phrase "muzungu zungu" means to be confused and disoriented. When white people came to Uganda, they always seemed to be asking for directions and seemed confused, so they were called "muzungu zungu". This phrase is so much to the point, and when using it to specify my take on whiteness, I recall Gloria Anzaldúa (1987), who uses her mother tongue, Spanish, to conceptualize her feminist ideas, which are rooted in her Indigenous knowledges.

Nina: You have a broad set of theoretical inspirations. Could you say a bit more about the way you go beyond theorizing from a mere oppositional space?

Victoria: Next to Anzaldua, I also like another Chicana feminist Chela Sandoval's (2000) notion of differential consciousness. This concept articulates an important mode of resistance that's different from a mere oppositional mode. Sexual difference theory is also important to me, especially Rosi Braidotti's (1994) ideas of subjectivity, and how to revitalize our sense of selves while being in the struggle, by not only engaging in being deprived, the negative part of resistance, but also trying to find spaces whereby we can be corpo-affectively attuned to the world.

Nina: Could you also say more about your way of thinking Black Theory and Black Feminist theory that's different from US-based versions?

Victoria: When your history begins with the trans-Atlantic slave trade, which it does for African Americans, for the Caribbeans, for the West Africans, and for the South Africans, it's different from being a Muganda, from the Buganda Kingdom, that welcomed the first white people to arrive in Buganda in 1877. It's different, for example, from West Africans, who can connect with African-Americans, since they have that continuation of the trans-Atlantic slave trade. When we talk about Africa, people think that white colonization and the slave history have been the same all over. This is, however, absolutely not the case. The Kingdom

Living an African Feminist Life – Decolonial Perspectives   115

of Buganda, for example, became a British protectorate in 1890 and had existed for hundreds of years before white people became involved in our political, cultural, and social system.

Nina: Your way of framing this is historically different but also different in an epistemological sense; you situate the gaze and the body in a different location – instead of just opposing the white gaze through a universalizing black counter-gaze.

Victoria: Exactly. I want to avoid this universalizing move, which has also excluded Africa as being something in the past, that you go back to and revisit. As Baganda people, we have always stayed in Africa, we haven't moved. Against this background, it becomes very strange to think that, for example, I should wear African clothes as a means of opposing whiteness. I don't wear my clothes to oppose whiteness. That's not why I wear my clothes! I wear my African clothes for special occasions like birthdays, as tradition. It's not politicized in the context of the struggle against whiteness. Using African heritage as a form of authenticity is, as I see it, just a way of being stuck in a binary oppositional consciousness to whiteness.

African Feminism and Decolonial Perspectives

Nina: What do you think about decolonial strategies? How does decolonial feminism resonate with your view of African feminism? Both in terms of what you said about the importance of Indigenous knowledges, and perhaps also in relation to transnational collaboration, alliances across differences, different histories, different trajectories, and pluriversality rather than universality?

Victoria: Talking about decoloniality in a pluriversal context makes me think of the role that Christianity still plays in colonizing our imaginations in African societies. This has made it very difficult to talk about Indigenous knowledges, and it has disconnected us from our vital spiritual energies and our sense of belonging and being in the world. One of the greatest struggles that we have on the African continent is to decolonize our imaginations, since Christianity colours it white and male. It's very difficult if you can't even allow yourself to talk about how we used to talk about spirits. I can see, for example, when I talk to my mother, how scared she becomes.

Nina: Why? How?

Victoria: If I talk about astrology, energies or about speaking to my dead father, or if I talk about inheriting my grandmother's spirit; these things really scare her because they go against her Christian worldview.

Nina: Even though, she as a Christian probably believes in angels?

Victoria: Exactly! (laughs) My mother's generation internalized the westernized colonial concept of capitalism and religion as liberation. My mother

116 *Victoria Kawesa, Redi Koobak, and Nina Lykke*

always tells me: "Oh, now we go deep into the villages, and we minister to the people in the villages, and now I found a widow and built her a house, and the whole village became Christians! Because they said, 'Wow! Look at her, she got a house, and this woman just helped her build the house. It's the power of God! We need to become Christians!'" And I'm like: "No! Please, stop with capitalism and your Bible, please!"

Redi: Is that why you cite your grandmother as your source of feminist influence, rather than your mother?

Victoria: Yes, because my mother is completely westernized. She was born in 1951 and belongs to a generation that was educated under the British colonial system from the beginning, being indoctrinated to love modernity, Christianity and capitalism. After Uganda got its independence from the British in 1964, they wanted to be modern, which meant preferring everything European above Indigenous cultural practices.

Redi: What's your mother's relation to feminism?

Victoria: It's taken time but she's more of an individualist, capitalist liberal feminist. At the end of the day, she believes that we're all individuals who, through God, money, and health, can survive and overcome, and this outlook is very different from my African Decolonial Feminism.

Redi: Perhaps, as a closing remark, you could sum up your views on African Decolonial Feminism, and its difference from Black Feminism?

Victoria: The difference, as we talked about, is that African feminism doesn't necessarily start by focusing on the white gaze, as Black Feminism does. Another difference is that African feminism doesn't centralize the trans-Atlantic slave trade but rather seeks its historical roots in Indigenous knowledges. A third difference is that African feminism does not inevitably focus on racism, but rather on patriarchy, colonialism, and decoloniality, whereas Black Feminism doesn't often deal with decoloniality, but rather with anti-racism.

Notes

1 The Uganda–Tanzania war lasted October 1978 until June 1979 and led to the overthrow of the Ugandan dictator Idi Amin Dada (Nayenga 1979).

2 Obuntu Bulamu is an indigenous concept practised by the Baganda people of Uganda as a means of belonging and humanity. Obuntu Bulamu implies a shared set of values that promote well-being, togetherness, and unity. The concept of Obuntu Bulamu is closely linked to the South African Ubuntu philosophy ("humanity to others"), often referred to as African humanism. The Zulu phrase, "Umuntu ngumuntu ngabantu", which means "A person is a person through other persons", captures this intersubjective meaning. The concept can also be found in other Bantu-speaking cultures, such as the Baluba of Central Africa as *Bumuntu*, the Yoruba of Nigeria as *Iwapele*, and the Shona of Zimbabwe as *Hunhu*. For further discussions of Ubuntu and African Feminism, see Tamale 2020 (on Ubuntu and African Feminism); Mbazzi et al. 2020 (on Obuntu Bulamu and disability); Hailey 2008, and Matolino and Kwindingwi 2013 (on Ubuntu and African Humanism).

Living an African Feminist Life – Decolonial Perspectives 117

3 Sandoval (2000) outlines survival skills, conceptualized as oppositional and differential consciousness, as methodologies of the oppressed in the contemporary postmodern world, where subjects, ideas, and concepts cannot be contained within fixed boundaries. The methodologies of the oppressed in the oppositional mode of consciousness are tactics identified by Sandoval as related to equal rights, as well as to revolutionary, supremacist, separatist, or differential forms of resistance. Sandoval's understanding of subject formation is active; subjects have agency to move in-between oppositional and differential consciousness and can activate the various tactics by assessing the necessary move as situational and contextual. In this sense, Sandoval's subject is empowered on a psychological level to enact a transformative resistance fuelled by love, care, and hope. Obuntu Bulamu, as a survival skill of the oppressed, is thus not merely a fixed resistance tactic, enacted as an oppositional consciousness to power and domination. Under the conditions of the postmodern world, it is necessary for subjects to develop survival skills of boundary crossing, thus enabling a differential consciousness to emerge. Obuntu Bulamu, as an indigenous differential consciousness, entails mobility, flexibility, and movement in-between different ideological systems and categorizations that permit feminist alliances.

4 Tlostanova (2017: 18) describes the concept of pluriversality as relational in terms of the coexistence and correlation of multiple interacting and intersecting non-abstract universals that are "grounded in the geopolitics and corpo-politics of knowledge, being and perception, reinstating the experiential nature of knowledge and the origin of any theory in the human life-world. Pluriversal critique targets not the concrete constellations of race, gender, and class but rather the aberration" (Tlostanova 2017: 18). According to Tlostanova and Mignolo (2012), pluriversality demonstrates how multiple cosmologies connected and entangled in power differentials, while linked to the logic of coloniality, become disguised by the rhetoric of modernity. The term is used as a critique of the concept of universality, through which the West conceptualizes itself as universal through the rhetoric of modernity. Hidden behind modernity is the agenda of coloniality; thus, coloniality is constitutive of modernity. Pluriversality is enabled by border thinking and by a shifting from "the geography of reason to geo- and body politics of knowledge" (2012: 65–6).

5 According to Keating (2009: 323), Anzaldua did not coin the term "spiritual activism", but "used it to describe her visionary, experimentally based epistemology and ethics", which Anzaldua understands as grounded in "listening to an inner order, the voice of real intuition [that] allows it to come through the artist's body and into the body of the work" (Keating 2009: 292). Anzaldua describes the relation between these bodily energies and spiritual activism like this: "the artist transmits and transforms inner energies and forces, energies and forces that may come from another realm, another order of intelligence. These forces use la artista to transmit their intelligence, transmit ideas, values that awaken higher states of consciousness. Once conocimiento (awareness, conciousness) is reached, you have to act in the light of your knowledge. I call this spiritual activism" (Keating 2009: 292). According to Anzaldua, spiritual activism activates spirituality for social change and acknowledges our differences and commonalities as a catalyst for transformation.

6 Mignolo (2011) borrowed the concept of the "colonial wound" from Gloria Anzaldúa, who constructed "the U.S.-Mexican border as 'una herida abierta', an open wound where the 'Third World grates against the first and bleeds'" (2011: xxi). This is an experience of the colonial wound, but, as Mignolo explains, there are different "modes of experiencing the colonial wound" (2011: 109).

7 30 November is the commemoration of the Swedish King Karl XII's Day of Death. This commemoration is one of the most long-lived traditions among the extreme nationalist and National Socialist groups in Sweden. In her analysis of Nazism in Sweden 1980–1999, Swedish author Heléne Lööw (2000: 388) describes the clashes between

118   *Victoria Kawesa, Redi Koobak, and Nina Lykke*

Nazi groups and anti-racist demonstrators on 30 November 1991, and states that the commemoration has long traditions dating back to the 1930s among Swedish right-wing nationalist groups.

8 *Roots* is an American TV miniseries (Jones 1977), based on Alex Haley's novel *Roots* (1976). The series first aired in January 1977. It tells the story of captured Africans, how they survived the slave ships to America, and about their lives in slavery in the United States. The main character is Kunta Kinte, who was captured in Gambia, and arrived in Maryland in 1767.

9 *Mana* is an anti-racist cultural magazine, which examines oppression in all its forms and offers an anti-racist intersectional perspective with a focus on structural racism, in Sweden and internationally. http://tidskriftenmana.se/om-mana/

10 Lawen Mohtadi is a Swedish journalist, writer, director, and publisher.

11 Sara Ahmed analyses how whiteness has become a barrier: "It's history that has been cemented and become a barrier that is now massive and palpable" (2011: 10). This "barrier" stops the movement for some people, while others do not sense its presence, and it becomes invisible to those bodies that can "flow through". She argues that we can best understand the hegemony of whiteness if we think of whiteness as that which we collide against (Ibid.).

12 Lund University is a public research university in Sweden and is one of Northern Europe's oldest universities.

13 Gloria Jean Watkins, better known as bell hooks, was an African-American author, professor, Black feminist, poet, and social activist. The name "bell hooks" is borrowed from her maternal great-grandmother, Bell Blair Hooks. Her books, such as *Ain't I a Woman? Black Women and Feminism* (1981), have inspired generations of Black women to become feminists. hooks coined the notion "Imperialist White Supremacist Capitalist Patriarchy" in order to "define interlocking political systems of oppression that work together to maintain domination" (e.g. 2013: 4).

14 Sylvia Tamale is a Ugandan professor, human rights activist and the first female dean of the Law Faculty at Makerere University, Uganda. In her book, *Decolonization and Afro-Feminism* (2020), Tamale links the philosophies of Ubuntu and Feminism in order to open up a space for the possibilities of a decolonialized Afro-Feminism.

References

Ahmed, Sara. 2011. *Vithetens hegemoni*. Hägersten: TankeKraft förlag.

Anzaldúa, Gloria. 1987. *Borderland/La Frontera: The New Mestiza*. San Francisco, CA: Aunt Lute.

Braidotti, Rosi. 1994. *Nomadic Subjects: Embodiment and Sexual Difference in Contemporary Feminist Theory*. New York, NY: Columbia University Press.

Hailey, John. 2008. *Ubuntu: A Literature Review* (Document). London: Tutu Foundation.

Haley, Alex. 1976. *Roots: The Saga of an American Family*. New York, NY: Doubleday.

hooks, bell. 1981. *Ain't I a Woman? Black Women and Feminism*. Boston, MA: South End Press.

hooks, bell. 2013. *Writing beyond Race: Living Theory and Practice*. New York, NY: Taylor & Francis.

Jones, Quincy. 1977. *Roots: The Saga of an American Family*. New York, NY: A&M Records.

Kawesa, Victoria. 2004. "Om svart femininitet och identitet; Antirasismens Grand Slam." *Mana* 3&4, n.p.

Kawesa, Victoria. 2006. "Ain't I My Hair? Black Femininity and Identity." *Slut*, 1.

Keating, AnaLouise (ed.). 2009. *The Gloria Anzaldua Reader (Latin America Otherwise)*. London and Durham, NC: Duke University Press.

Lööw, Heléne. 2000. *Nazismen I Sverige: den rasistiska undergroundrörelsen: musiken, myterna, riterna 1980–1999*. Stockholm: Ordfront Förlag.

Matolino, Bernard, and Wenceslaus Kwindingwi. 2013. "The End of Ubuntu." *South African Journal of Philosophy* 32 (2): 197–205.

Mbazzi, Femke Bannink, Ruth Nalugya, Elizabeth Kawesa, Harriet Nambejja, Pamela Nizeyimana, Patrick Ojok, Geert Van Hove, and Janet Seeley. 2020. "'Obuntu Bulamu': Development and Testing of an Indigenous Intervention for Disability Inclusion in Uganda." *Scandinavian Journal of Disability Research* 22 (1): 403–16.

Mignolo, Walter. 2011. *The Darker Side of Modernity: Global Futures, Decolonial Options*. Durham, NC and London: Duke University Press.

Nayenga, Peter F. B. 1979. "Myths and Realities of Idi Amin Dada's Uganda." *African Studies Review* 22 (2): 127–38.

Sandoval, Chela. 2000. *Methodology of the Oppressed*. Minneapolis, MN: University of Minnesota Press.

Tamale, Sylvia. 2020. *Decolonization and Afro-Feminism*. Ottawa: Daraja Press.

Tlostanova, Madina. 2017. *Postcolonialism and Postsocialism in Fiction and Art: Resistance and Re-Existence*. New York, NY: Palgrave Macmillan.

Tlostanova, Madina, and Walter Mignolo. 2012. *Learning to Unlearn: Decolonial Reflection from Eurasia and the Americas*. Columbus, OH: Ohio State University Press.

Part II

Portals of Possibility (On Methodologies)

Swati Arora, Petra Bakos, and Nina Lykke

Methodological considerations are embedded in all the chapters of this volume. They cut across its ongoing conversations on transnational, intersectional, and decolonial feminist efforts to counteract methodological nationalisms and research designs that are uncritically governed by Western vantage points. Nevertheless, we have chosen to devote this short middle part specifically to methodological issues – in order to explicitly foreground the book's open-ended approach to methodologies as "portals of possibility" (Naidoo, this volume), that is, as malleable guides to knowledge-shaping processes that are grounded in transformative practices and pave the way for social and environmental justice-to-come. In very different ways, the three chapters, we have gathered here, argue for approaches that do away with understandings of methodologies as fixed straitjackets, implemented from the perspective of distant, and disconnected viewing positions. Across differences, they share an approach to methodologies that considers them to be mouldable and changeable phenomena. They underscore that methodologies need to be carefully and (self-)critically situated, and handled as completely open to change in resonance with transformative, ethico-political tasks to be accomplished. Taken together, these chapters also make it clear that it is difference, rather than a new uniformity or disciplinary purity, that emerges from transnational, intersectional, and decolonial feminist conversations on methodologies as "portals of possibility".

In Chapter 11, *Can Methodologies Be Decolonial? Towards a Relational Experiential Epistemic Togetherness*, Madina Tlostanova problematizes Euromodern/colonial epistemic frameworks. She reflects upon alternative decolonial instruments of analysis and broader practices of knowing and making sense of the world, which escape conventional methodological definitions. Moreover, she criticizes methodology as a specific classifying operation that is rationally limited by default and experienced as distorting by those who are not part of Euromodern sameness. Revisiting decolonial and Indigenous texts that claim to do away with modern/colonial methodologies, or enter into an intense debate with them, this chapter engages with a corpus of core decolonial feminist texts (e.g. Anzaldúa 1987; Smith 1999; Sandoval 2000; Lugones 2003; Simpson 2013) that have engaged in dialogue with each other and framed major methodological issues. Tlostanova argues the case for emerging transversal decolonial agendas that help to imagine a redirected future, a

DOI: 10.4324/9781003378761-12

122 *Swati Arora, Petra Bakos, and Nina Lykke*

world-making that becomes possible through communities and coalitions striving for re-existence.

In Chapter 12, *Reading Transnationally: Literary Transduction as a Feminist Tool*, Jasmina Lukić enters the discussion on methodologies from another angle. Engaging with the decolonial notion of thinking from the borderlands (Anzaldúa 1987) and feminist border thinking (Tlostanova et al. 2016), Lukić suggests the concept of transduction, borrowed from literary theory (Doležel 1998), as a methodology that can be productively recycled in the context of feminist transnational thought, while also taking into account locational feminism (Friedman 2001) and utopian perspectives. Through a literary analysis of the novel *A Concise Chinese-English Dictionary for Lovers* by Chinese novelist Xiaolu Guo (2007), Lukić argues that the concept of transduction, when applied to feminist theory, can reveal its potential for foregrounding processes rather than fixed states of affairs, and allow for a complex approach to the dynamics of transnational encounters and interactive events that produce transculturation through chains of open-ended interpretations – both converging and diverging.

The interview conversation – Chapter 13 – *Writing Love Letters Across Borders: A Conversation on Indigenous-Centred Methodologies*, by Hema'ny Molina Vargas, Fernanda Olivares Molina, Camila Marambio, Nina Lykke, and Kharnita Mohamed, reflects upon Indigenous-centred, feminist, and decolonial methodologies. The interview tells the story of a set of loving transnational feminist relations that unfurled across borders, marked by apparently incommensurable difference, starting at a writing workshop in Chile and eventually resulting in a co-authored article, "Decolonising Mourning", for the journal *Australian Feminist Studies* (Vargas et al. 2020). The storytelling presented in this chapter is a contemplation on methodologies by the co-authors of that journal article: Hema'ny Molina Vargas, a poet-philosopher of the Selk'nam people of Tierra del Fuego, Chile; Camila Marambio, a Chilean curator, scholar, eco-activist, and Selk'nam ally; and Nina Lykke, a white queerfeminist professor from the Global North, and also a supporter of the Selk'nam cause. The interview conversation explores how commitments to transversal relations, loving friendships, trust, ancestrality, bodily materialities, embodied storytelling and poetry writing, ongoing relations with the dead, passionate commitments to decolonization, and a planetary ethics of sustainability became key methodologies for a shared writing practice.

The chapters making up Part II encompass different approaches, yet they share a vision of methodologies as portals of possibility for research that is committed to justice-to-come. These chapters also revolve around the theme of borders. Albeit in different ways, both Tlostanova and Lukić take inspiration from the border thinking of queerfeminist and decolonial scholar Gloria Anzaldúa (1987), and her exploration of how living in the borderlands makes people see things from more than one perspective. For Tlostanova, border thinking is linked to her plea for pluriversal approaches, while it leads Lukić towards an argument for literary transduction as a transnational feminist tool. In the interview conversation about Indigenous-centred feminist methodologies by Vargas, Olivares, Marambio, Lykke, and Mohamed, a multiplicity of material and epistemological borders and boundaries

Portals of Possibility (On Methodologies) 123

are also addressed in the stories of transversal relations and transnational feminist and decolonial coalitions that were established during poetic co-writing and co-publishing across intersecting differences. The interview conversation highlights commitments to love and trust as pathways towards undoing the barriers created by borders.

Alongside borders and border thinking, two related themes are also addressed in Part II. One of these is translation as a means of cross-cutting borders. All the chapters deal with the ways in which languages – ranging from native tongues and vernaculars through disciplinary formats, epistemic habits (including epistemological ignorance), and the organization of cultural institutions – change across borders. However, the authors also show that, although border crossings engender change, change may also cross borders – facilitated among other things by the trickster-like and playful work of translators and translations. In addition to translations, Part II also prompts us to engage with another feminist trickster methodology related to borders; namely, smuggling – bypassing disciplinary, epistemic, and other kinds of border-policing, while carrying concepts, epistemologies, languages, and cultural goods across. From a more utopian perspective, Part II suggests that such trickster methodologies can work as portals of possibility that may eventually undo borders.

References

Anzaldúa, Gloria. 1987. *Borderlands/La Frontera: The New Mestiza*. San Francisco, CA: Aunt Lute Books.

Doležel, Lubomír. 1988. *Heterocosmica*. Baltimore, MD and London: Johns Hopkins University Press.

Friedman, Susan Stanford. 2001. "Locational Feminism: Gender, Cultural Geographies, and Geopolitical Literacy." In *Feminist Locations: Global and Local, Theory and Practice*, edited by Uredila Marianne DeKoven, 13–36. New Brunswick, NJ: Rutgers University Press.

Guo, Xiaolu. 2007. *A Concise Chinese-English Dictionary for Lovers*. London: Vintage Books.

Lugones, Maria. 2003. *Pilgrimages/Peregrinajes: Theorizing Coalition against Multiple Oppression*. New York, NY and Oxford: Rowman and Littlefield.

Sandoval, Chela. 2000. *Methodology of the Oppressed*. Minneapolis, MN: University of Minnesota Press.

Simpson, Leanne Betasamosake. 2013. *Islands of Decolonial Love*. Winnipeg: ARP.

Smith, Linda Tuhiway. 1999. *Decolonizing Methodologies: Research and Indigenous Peoples*. London and New York, NY: Zed Books.

Tlostanova, Madina, Suruchi Thapar-Björkert, and Redi Koobak. 2016. "Border Thinking and Disidentification: Postcolonial and Postsocialist Feminist Dialogues." *Feminist Theory* 17 (2): 211–28.

Vargas, Hema'ny Molina, Camila Marambio, and Nina Lykke. 2020. "Decolonising Mourning: World-Making With the Selk'nam People of Karokynka/Tierra del Fuego." *Australian Feminist Studies* 35 (104): 186–201.

11 Can Methodologies Be Decolonial?

Towards a Relational Experiential Epistemic Togetherness

Madina Tlostanova

In loving memory of María Lugones, who always finished her sentences with a question mark and never thought in linear ways.

Since Audre Lorde wrote her famous words on the impossibility of dismantling the master's house with the master's tools (Lorde 1984), African American, Chicana, Indigenous, and other women of colour feminists have insisted on the necessity of coming up with alternative instruments of analysis that could allow us to accomplish this task. However, in decolonial feminism, the idea was further reformulated to focus not so much on the dismantling of a particular master's house as on questioning the "hegemony" as such, "the mastery itself which will then cease to maintain its imperial status" (Walsh and Mignolo 2018: 7). Decolonial feminists seldom use the term "methodologies" because they see methodology as a product of the coloniality of knowledge and of thinking. Methodology as a specific classifying operation that is rationally limited by default is seen as distorting for those who do not belong, who are not part of the Euromodern sameness.

Therefore, the urge to do away with methodology is justified. Yet we still need some set of practices to make sense of the world and the question persists: can we decolonize methodologies, as Chela Sandoval (2000) and Linda Tuhiwai Smith (1999) attempted to do in their ground-breaking works, or should we make a more radical shift in the "geography of reasoning" (Gordon 2010) and reject methodology altogether? What would we be left with then? To be honest, most texts that claim to be decolonial are less radical than they promise, as they are still using Euromodern tools to convey their ideas. The sporadic use of Amerindian concepts does not change the overall Euromodern structure or logic of decolonial reasoning (Mignolo 2002; Vázquez 2017). This can be partly explained by the fact that these texts still need to be competitive in academic journals that are informed by the coloniality of knowledge. This makes any academic decolonial intervention partial and opportunistic, promising delinking but in fact performing a kind of mimicry (Bhabha 2004).

There are also a few decolonial feminist texts that attempt to go deeper and truly delink from every contaminated Western concept, term, and method (Lugones 2003; Simpson 2011). This is a challenging choice because it leaves one either

DOI: 10.4324/9781003378761-13

126   *Madina Tlostanova*

working exclusively with Indigenous or non-modern/colonial concepts and erased epistemic models, or starting from scratch and inventing completely new words, narrative modes, and kinds of discourse, to convey the required meanings and cognitive operations. Such a radical conceptual decolonization may lead to hermeticism, preventing any dialogue with those unfamiliar with decolonial parlance (including both the Western and the postcolonial and other critical non-Western researchers). I argue for a less purist but more honest position that is aware of the fact that, right now, building alliances and looking for understanding is more important than focusing on incommensurabilities or trying to prove to each other whose suffering is more important.

By a more honest position, I mean that we need to stop promising radical delinking from Euromodern theorizing when in fact we are still very much embedded in it, both methodologically and theoretically, particularly in academic interventions. Dismantling the mastery remains a crucial task, and no one can claim to be able to undo modernity/coloniality on their own. What we can realistically do is to continue destabilizing the system from within through mastering and then remaking its discourse, not to assimilate and merge and not to curse and condemn, but rather to try to overcome the suffocating system existentially, intellectually, and affectively.

The feminist element in decolonial thinking further complicates its relations with other critical discourses on and in modernity/coloniality, while also performing an internal critique of the heteronormative male versions of decoloniality, as evidenced in Lugones' exemplary works (Lugones 2007). This brings us back, once again, to the question of strategic alliances and "deep coalitions" (Lugones 2003: 98) in our decolonial struggles that merge political, ontoepistemic, ethical, and affective tools.

Methodology as a Defamiliarizing Move?

When it comes to decoloniality, the question of methodologies really becomes a larger issue of decolonial ways of relating to the world, of making sense of other people, other species, and the planet. These ways of relating and making sense could be regarded as micro- and macro-level tools, with some of them reaching a meta-level of reprogramming the overall knowledge structures and disciplinary taxonomies. Functioning together in a complex, dynamic, transversal way, these tools ultimately work to achieve a decolonization of thinking and of knowledge, and attempt to reunite knowledge production and distribution with the actual life world, human and other, and with acting upon it.

If we look closely at decolonial methods of inquiry, we will see that the most frequent operation is far from being exclusively decolonial. I mean defamiliarization, which later became German playwright and prominent experimental theatre theorist Bertolt Brecht's Verfremdungseffekt ("estrangement or distancing effect") (Brecht and Bentley 1961). It is a technique that does not allow the audience to identify with the characters and become fully engrossed in the performance. The effect is achieved through using special tools (such as the famous songs that interrupted Brecht's plays and other ways of destroying the so-called fourth wall that divides the actors from the spectators). These special effects encourage the public to always keep the position of a critical observer whose active presence is constantly acknowledged. In some ways, defamiliarization intersects with French poststructuralist philosopher Jacques Derrida's notion of "différance" (Derrida 1982), that is, a mixture of differentiation and deferral allowing to question the actual presence and self-evidence of the embodied logos (or in other words, the absolute truth) that is accessible to the contemporary subjects only through traces. In decolonial discourse, this sort of disassembling and estrangement are never disembodied rational operations. Rather they are formulated from a clearly contextualized perspective of the colonial difference. Defamiliarization disturbs one's habitual perception of reality; it renders the familiar in unfamiliar terms to slow down automatic perceptions. Coined by Russian formalist Viktor Shklovsky in 1917 in his essay "Art as technique" (Shklovsky 1929), defamiliarization subsequently came to signify a technique of presenting common things in an unfamiliar way in order to enhance and de-automatize their perception, thus acting as a form of political or artistic contestation.

In a way, decoloniality at large is grounded in a defamiliarization of the assumptions of modernity as well as its epistemic and methodological tools. One of the possible ways to do this is to try to practise pluritopical (Mignolo 1995) or multispatial (Tlostanova 2017) hermeneutics, in which the Euromodern hermeneutical horizon is destabilized by the active presence of other epistemic genealogies.

Decolonial Hermeneutics?

Hermeneutics in its simplest terms is the art of interpretation and is a habitual tool of the humanities. This is in contrast to epistemology, which is often defined as the art of explanation and hence marks the sciences. Hermeneutics, as argued by the philosopher Hans-George Gadamer in his *Truth and Method* (Gadamer 1975), assumes that people have a historically and culturally affected consciousness that is firmly grounded in the (Western by default) "tradition", which acts as a necessary condition for the fusion of horizons. This universalist and monotopical understanding of hermeneutics neglects the presence and the rights to existence of other cognitive *topoi* (spaces/sites) and other traditions, which are then controlled and subsumed into the normalized Euromodern model that defines itself by inventing its exteriority – the other.

Pluritopical or multispatial hermeneutics is based on the previously proposed diatopical hermeneutics coined by the philosopher and theologian Raimundo Panikkar. He defines diatopical hermeneutics as the art of coming to an understanding "across places" (*dia-topoi*) or traditions that do not share common patterns of understanding or intelligibility (Panikkar 1975). Panikkar is referring to an understanding of the radically different other – an understanding that does not assume that the other has the same basic self-understanding as the self/subject. It is the ultimate human horizon that is at stake here, not merely differing specific contexts. Therefore, Panikkar rethinks the logic of the monotopical Western hermeneutics (monotopical both in morphological sense, i.e. in relation to form, and diachronically, i.e. in

128   Madina Tlostanova

relation to the passage of time) based as it is on Gadamer's assumption that there needs to be a certain degree of pre-understanding (horizon) to be able to fully make sense of any phenomenon.

In intercultural or, better yet, inter-cosmological contexts, such an anticipation or a pre-understanding, as the basis for a hermeneutical circle (a key phenomenological concept describing and claiming the circular nature of the human understanding preconditioned by specific existential and historical contexts which have shaped particular presuppositions of the understanding subject) is not possible and a diatopical hermeneutics comes into play. Such a hermeneutics is intended to help us understand something that does not belong within our hermeneutical horizon and therefore cannot be grasped with the preconceived tools of understanding, standards of truth, and value criteria stemming from only one tradition or culture. The open and unfinished process of bringing these radically different human horizons or *topoi* together is described by Panikkar as "dialogical dialogue". This implies a bearing in mind of cognitive differences and a penetrating of *logos* to reach a dialogical, translogical realm of the heart (in most traditions), via which we can communicate and which ultimately allows understanding as standing within the same horizon of comprehensibility (Panikkar 1979: 9). Diatopical hermeneutics operates by way of an onto-mythic symbolism that stands in between (narrow rational) *logos* and (prerational) *mythos*, and connects subjectivity and objectivity, understanding and interpretation, the heart and the mind, rational thought, and the spirit that flies free, breaking through all rigid mental schemes (Panikkar 1979: 6f).

Diatopical hermeneutics begins with the realization of pain stemming from alienation and radical difference. It discards the idea of radical otherness, which too often acts as an excuse for not trying to understand the other while enjoying one's epistemic privilege of belonging to the monotopical, Euromodern, hermeneutical tradition. Panikkar prefers to talk about radical relativity in the sense of relationality, of the initial links between all human cognitive traditions that we must decipher and make work in the building of an intersubjective, inter-traditional form of communication that is not grounded in epistemic taxonomies or measuring rods emerging from delocalized vantage point (Panikkar 1995: 174).

Panikkar was painfully aware of the asymmetry between the monotopical, Euromodern, hermeneutical tradition, and all other traditions. He was very critical of the colonialist traces in comparative studies that always start from the notion of the normative Euromodern universal tradition, against which everything else is compared. He suggested replacing them with non-hierarchical im-parative (not com-parative) approaches (from Latin imparare – to learn in an atmosphere of plurality). This is a form of dialogical and experiential (not interpretative as in Euromodern hermeneutics) learning from and with the other, thus enriching our thinking through the intuitions and revelations of the other (Panikkar 1988). It is grounded in homeomorphic equivalence – a functional equivalence that we trace through a topological transformation. In other words, he is describing an ability to perceive several different symbols at once. Panikkar refers to this principle as homological as opposed to analogical and based on diatopics rather than dialectics (Panikkar 1978: 33). The dialectical method as a reasoned argumentation or debate

Can Methodologies Be Decolonial? 129

in quest for the one correct answer (the truth) is radically replaced in Panikkar's work by the actual praxis of dialogue – (diatopics) in existential encounters.

Walter Mignolo's early reflection on the colonial semiosis (meaning-making) attempts to apply Panikkar's general idea to a concrete colonial situation of meaning production in South America (Mignolo 1995: 11). He claims that this positionality in fact gives the colonial other a hermeneutical privilege that a monotopical imperial self is lacking. This privilege is connected to the potential of thinking from one's body and experience and subsuming the imperial reason that dehumanized this person in the first place. Within colonial space, the strangeness of the other constantly erodes the realm of the same, does not leave it impenetrable, and eventually finds its way into the metropolis to destabilize its own idea of the self and of the same. Hence comes the colonial semiosis that is based on the interactive production of culture and knowledge by means of different traditions. From this complex positionality emerges a decolonial pluritopic hermeneutics as an act of understanding someone else's philosophy, cosmology, ethics, culture, or language. It presupposes a self-conscious parallelism that not only involves the two or more terms that are being considered together but also questions the very act of comparison itself, its mechanisms, its ideologies, and the relativity of its points of view. Thus, it reflects the very process of constructing the space that is being cognized. The understanding subject is placed at the colonial periphery, which disturbs the easy and clear rendering of hermeneutical tradition or the naturalized point of reference (Tlostanova and Mignolo 2009).

However, this complication of hermeneutical procedures does not have to always be rendered via the literally embodied colonial difference. The questioning of the position and homogeneity of the understanding subject can be linked with other forms of modern/colonial otherness that do not necessarily have to be placed outside the zones of sameness or regarded as unquestionable others. What matters are the social, political, and ontological dimensions of any theorizing and any understanding, the questioning of the naturalized Euromodern locus of enunciation that, being provincial and arbitrary, has still successfully masked itself as universal and delocalized, and the striving to retrace and reconstruct via Panikkar's homeomorphic equivalence, the different yet equal loci of enunciation and the multiple ways of making sense of the world. The latter also opens up an ethical dimension of pluritopical hermeneutics that reinstates the epistemic rights of other truths and draws attention to their persistent inequality due to the coloniality of knowledge, power, being, sensing, and gender.

Love as a Decolonial Analytical Tool?

Reflecting on the trajectory from diatopical to pluritopical hermeneutics, I could not help noticing that another strand of decolonial hermeneutical reflections was left aside. This is a neglected strand that in fact has more in common with Panikkar's initial ethical, existential, and epistemic stance than with Mignolo's radically delinking position. This forgotten strand is a decolonial queer feminist one and its most interesting examples are to be found in the works of the queer Chicana thinker

130 *Madina Tlostanova*

and poet Gloria Anzaldúa, Queer Chicana theorist and activist Chela Sandoval, and decolonial diasporic Argentinian queer feminist philosopher María Lugones. These works are crucial for today's situation and for a refuturing in which a decolonial radical delinking should be balanced against a more pronounced re-existential, in Adolfo Alban's (2009) understanding, and dialogical stance. Both Sandoval and Lugones begin their hermeneutical reflections in Anzaldúa's metaphorical notion of the *Coatlicue state* (La herencia de Coatlicue). This is a specific condition of complex and contradictory anger of a divided self on its way to becoming, which is a queer Chicana twist on a core pre-Columbian myth laden with numerous historical layers of specific mestisaje and borderland affects and experiences (Anzaldúa 1987: 53–4).

In Lugones' famous essay, "Playfulness, 'World'-Travelling, and Loving Perception" (2003), she regards love as a basis for interpersonal communication, which she sees as a specific kind of non-agonistic playing that is akin to Panikkar's diatopic hermeneutics. Lugones links her concept of love with the idea of travelling to other people's worlds and knowing them. Lugones sees love as a special method of inquiry that is rooted in a genuine interest in the other and an urge to know them, when she says that "by this traveling we can understand what it is to be them and what it is to be ourselves in their eyes. Only when we have travelled to each other's 'worlds' are we fully subjects to each other" (Lugones 2003: 97).

In her later essay on Anzaldúa, Lugones returns to hermeneutical issues in her characteristic circular way, attempting to define the complex method of resistant knowing and making sense of the world and of one's own split self in relation to other border selves. This is a never-ending and never quite successful recurring process. In this process, the borderland as a space for dialogical meaning production acquires a crucial role as a "resistant terrain" and a "vague and undetermined" space where borderland hermeneutics is actually in the making – both individually and collectively. This space "is also a coalitional journey" for, as she reinstates, "it is this knowing each other that makes life livable" (Lugones 2005: 85). In Lugones' view, the Coatlicue method of remaking oneself cannot be a solitary process and does not stop at stasis, anger, or delinking as these are too simple, straightforward, and rationalized options. Instead, it vacillates between fear and germination, directed at the creation of an *other* self and "a counter-universe of sense" (Lugones 2005: 95). It then goes further and attempts an overcoming, an emancipation, a metamorphosis of the forever changing, and unstable border self that is regarding the multiple versions of itself and must never forget its complex relationality with others.

Chela Sandoval, in her seminal *Methodology of the Oppressed*, states that the apparatus needed for the launching of the global decolonization of consciousness will be an apparatus of "love, understood as a technology for social transformations" and as a form of hermeneutics (Sandoval 2000: 2). Her book remains one of the few examples of decolonial thinking that attempts an actual dialogue with Euromodern critical theories through looking for major connectors in the development of human thought and agency, understood in many ways as Panikkar's homeomorphic equivalence. The main functional equivalence (homology) for Sandoval

Can Methodologies Be Decolonial? 131

is the methodology of the oppressed and the corresponding oppositional consciousness, grounded in the idea of the differential, which she finds and deciphers in various places – from the women of colour feminism to French deconstruction.

Sandoval presents love as a political technology, as a corpus of knowledge, arts, and practices, and as a social movement for remaking the self and the world. She echoes Anzaldúa's visionary overtones in her understanding of the hermeneutics of love, which always has an additional meaning of rupture and temporary but profound unsettlement, a state of neither/nor or both/and. Sandoval opts for a refusal to make a final choice. Instead, she is attracted by the open hermeneutical *topoi* of oppositional consciousness, where an explosion of meaning and its subsequent temporary convergences and solidifications take place, where meaning escapes from any finalized definition or fixation, which allows it to penetrate the shifting contours of power (Sandoval 2000: 180). The way in which she describes the process of revelation, preparing for the hermeneutics of decolonial love, brings us back to the aforementioned estrangement effect. It starts by disturbing the complacency and normalcy of the dominant system of power and its status quo society with the help of the oppositional consciousness that reveals alternative, erased, forgotten, never-realized, round-about paths, and options that suddenly enable us to grasp a more complete picture of the world we are striving to make sense of. Sandoval also devotes some time to criticizing the academic apartheid of narrow specializations, prescribed disciplines, methods and approaches, that prevent us from forming genuine political and intellectual coalitions, and, we might add, reinstate the modern/colonial agonistics which, in the case of colonial difference, often takes the shape of a toxic victimhood rivalry that prevents hermeneutical revelations, instead locking the smaller and smaller groups of others inside their respective hermeneutical ghettoes.

Questioning Method-Centrism and Remaking the Disciplines

This latter potentially dangerous limitation has also stood at the centre of Afro-Caribbean philosopher and prominent Fanon scholar Lewis Gordon's attention, both in his critique of disciplinary decadence, which I address later, and in his reinstatement of the politics of love as an open potentiation instead of the endless moral indignation that is used as a fuel for competition. Gordon claims that, along with political responsibility, the world badly needs this peculiarly political form of love for the lives of those who remain anonymous to us, or perhaps beyond our understanding (Gordon and Tlostanova 2021: 135).

Gordon's critique of disciplines is a good example of decolonial phenomenological analysis of the Euromodern superstition of method-centrism and an attempt to remake and rethink disciplines in order for them to start making sense again. Since Gordon believes that reason is broader than rationality, he is sceptical of any method-centrism. Regarding method as a deontological categorical imperative (following Immanuel Kant's idea of an absolute moral law that everyone must follow at any times and under any circumstances; Kant 1785) is a form of disciplinary decadence, marking the death of the discipline's teleological impetus and its failure

132   *Madina Tlostanova*

to engage the world any longer. Gordon demonstrates the negative consequences of such deontologization of method and its ossification in narrow methodologies cut off from reality, which is typical of philosophy and other classical Euromodern disciplines. Suggesting a shift in the geography of reasoning (Gordon 2010), he imagines it as a way back into the world, including the human life world. Methodology then should be reconsidered in less institutionalized forms of transient events and contextual applications, rather than as stable, solidified scholarly approaches that only generate more and more solipsistic disciplines that are narrowed down and down and rationalize themselves as a myth. Solipsistic disciplines turn their practices into rituals in which methods collapse into a closed methodology or a secularized theodicea (or ratiodicea as Gordon refers to it, meaning that instead of god as a focus of theodicea – a framework which strives to prove the existence of all-powerful, omniscient, and omnibenevolent deity as possible and plausible, ratiodicea has rationality as its core). Gordon suggests that, in order to dispose of this "disciplinary decadence", we need to practise a teleological suspension of disciplinarity, with its specific methodological claims, through revamping and revisiting the open goals and ideas that existed at the origins of disciplines (Gordon 2006). Questioning disciplinary decadence as a manifestation of ratiodicea means suspending our own methodological claims and problematizing the ontological status of our own methods, while simultaneously cultivating respect for evidence, conclusiveness, and responsibility in the social world and in the world of inter-subjective relations. Echoing many Indigenous pedagogical and cognitive tools, the call to end disciplinary decadence is grounded in the principle of relational–experiential rationality, reuniting the thinkers with the world and making them aware and critical of their own vantage point.

The Geopolitics and Corpopolitics of Knowledge and of Being and/or Intersectionality and Situated Knowledges?

The relational–experiential principle also forms the foundations of the decolonial parallel to intersectionality as a long-established feminist methodological tool and to "situated knowledges" (Haraway 1988) as a related concept in feminist theory. By this, I mean the geopolitics and corpopolitics of being, of knowledge, of sensing and of gender – a specifically decolonial way to express the idea of situated knowledges and dynamically entangled discriminations and resistances. The geopolitics here refers to the local spatial and temporal foundations of knowledge. Corpopolitics can be defined as the individual and group biographical grounds of understanding and thinking, rooted in our local histories and trajectories of origination and dispersion. Decolonial corpopolitics necessarily includes the re-inscription of history inscribed in non-European bodies in a world dominated by the White male heterosexual body. "The interconnections between geohistorical locations (in the modern/colonial order of things) and epistemology, on the one hand, and body-racial and gender epistemic configurations, on the other, sustain" (Tlostanova and Mignolo 2012: 71) the geopolitics and corpopolitics of knowledge that are put forward in any decolonial attempt at pluriversality (Escobar 2017).

Decolonial pluriversality has strong links with various Indigenous concepts of relationality, which stress the centrality of maintaining a coexistence and correlation of many different interacting and intersecting positions with equal rights to existence. Pluriversality is also a conscious effort to reconnect theory and theorists with experience, to reinstate the experiential nature of knowledge and the origin of any theory in the human life world. Pluriversal critique does not target concrete constellations of race, gender, or class and other power asymmetries, but rather the aberration of the universal as such, thus bringing us back to defamiliarization as the main decolonial trope.

Decoloniality attempts to turn the usual subject-object hierarchy upside-down, and question the Western imperial epistemic duress which is complicit in maintaining the established knowledge-producing institutions and measuring rods. It does so from the positions of those who have been denied subjectivity and rationality and regarded as mere tokens of our culture, religion, sexuality, race, or gender. Decolonial critique is pluriversal rather than universal, and constantly aware of its own positionality while addressing the "hubris of the zero point" which, according to S. Castro-Gómez, is a specific Eurocentric positionality of the sensing and thinking subject. It occupies a delocalized and disembodied vantage point which eliminates any other possible ways of producing, transmitting, or representing knowledge, enabling a worldview to be built on a rigid essentialist progressivist model (Castro-Gómez 2007: 433).

This agenda obviously intersects with intersectionality and situated knowledges. But in decolonial rendering it is important to always remember to ask: Who speaks in and of intersectionality and from what position is this enunciation made? Who is the enunciator of intersectionality? Is the enunciation in intersectionality a new discipline? And in what intersection of intersectionality does the enunciation take place? Thus, it becomes more important to focus on different tangential genealogies of knowledge, being, gender, and perception, and to shift the emphasis from the enunciated to the enunciation. This is the actual shifting in the geography of reasoning from the enunciated (an object to be described or explained) to the enunciator (the subject doing the describing and explaining), who can counter the "hubris of the zero point" (Castro-Gómez 2007: 433). Decolonial feminism is interrelated with intersectionality at the level of the enunciated because they are both dealing with multiple histories of discrimination, othering, and marginalization. But they may diverge at the level of the enunciation or concrete configurations of knowledges' situatedness – the geopolitics and corpopolitics of knowledge, being and perception which are linked with agents, experiences, and memories that were denied the right to act as epistemic subjects (Tlostanova 2015).

"*La Facultad*" as a Decolonial Mode of Inquiry and a Route to Re-Existence

The shifting of the geography of reasoning enacted through the geopolitics and corpopolitics of knowledge is made possible through border thinking and border existence, which allows us to make another uneven circle and come back to Anzaldúa.

134   *Madina Tlostanova*

Border positioning in the entanglement of the Western invention of modernity and its dark other is a difficult stance of the outside created from the inside, or a duboisean "double consciousness" (Du Bois 1903) as a gap between one's divided sensibility, the prescribed societal norms and standards, and the constant rejection of the people marked by difference. This includes those who make a perfect, if self-destructive, job of internalizing mainstream values, and the assertion of the geopolitical and corpopolitical epistemic rights of those who have been dehumanized by and in modernity based on its racial and gender hierarchies and ontologized differences. Border onto-epistemology, as an essentially defamilarizing tool, leads to an itinerant, forever open, and multiple positionality, marked by transformationism, shifting identifications and, once again, a rejection of either/or binaries. It turns instead to a non-exclusive duality, which is to be found in contemporary models of conjunctive logic in many Indigenous cosmologies of the Global South, and in diasporic trickster identifications overcoming the previous Ariel-Caliban dichotomy (following Shakespeare's iconic *The Tempest* (1610–1611) with its tamed/ assimilated Ariel who is willingly serving the master Prospero and the unsubdued Caliban hatching plans for revolt and revenge and stereotypically represented by Shakespeare as a dehumanized savage) in various indirect and ironic forms of activism. Anzaldúa famously refers to this specific subjectivity in a set of powerful images of the borderlands people that opens her seminal book:

> A borderland is a vague and undetermined place created by the emotional residue of an unnatural boundary. It is in a constant state of transition. The prohibited and forbidden are its inhabitants. Los atravesados live here: the squint-eyed, the perverse, the queer, the troublesome, the mongrel, the mulato, the half-breed, the halfdead; in short, those who cross over, pass over, or go through the confines of the "normal".
>
> (Anzaldúa 1987: 3)

These border dwellers are the ones who, after an angry moment of Coatlicue, ultimately come to a more creative and insightful visionary moment of *la facultad*. Anzaldúa's *la facultad* is a mode of thinking, understanding, and (re)making that can be seen as a decolonial replacement of traditional methodology. She defines it as the "capacity to see in surface phenomena the meaning of deeper realities, to see the deep structure below the surface" (Anzaldúa 1987: 60). This hypersensitivity of the oppressed and those experiencing prejudice, like the Coatlicue state, is also rooted in fear, yet it has clear potential to grow into a positive, re-existent condition of remaking the self and the world, a special kind of understanding: "Confronting anything that tears the fabric of our everyday mode of consciousness and that thrusts us into a less literal and more psychic sense of reality increases awareness [*la facultad*]" (Anzaldúa 1987: 61). *La facultad*, as a form of double vision, enabling us to see the forest for the trees and reconnecting with the collective ancestral memory, is the opposite of the conventional archive as a modern/colonial instrument of the meaningless accumulation and biased selection of data. La facultad is a knowledge-generation mechanism that germinates in systematically dehumanized

Can Methodologies Be Decolonial? 135

but resistant, and ultimately re-existent, bodies and not in pure hermetic rationality. Thus, it overcomes the artificially imposed Euromodern boundaries between thinking and acting, thinking and being, feeling, and thinking.

Indigenous Decolonial "Methods" of Knowing and Being in the World

There are also more specific decolonial tools to be found in different, mostly Indigenous, cognitive practices that deserve to be mentioned here and later analysed using Panikkar's homeomorphic equivalence approach. One such tool is Linda Tuhiwai Smith's appeal to *Kaupapa* research. According to Graham Smith, this can be viewed as a locally rooted version of critical anti-positivist theory and ethics grounded in Maori cosmology, focused on the critique of societal inequalities and power asymmetries, and aimed at the struggle for autonomy over Maori cultural well-being (G. H. Smith 1990). The underlying principle of Kaupapa Maori research is the *whanau* principle of correlational communal knowledge production and agency. Linda Tuhiwai Smith stresses that *whanau* can be a way of organizing a research group, of incorporating ethical procedures that report back to the community, a way of giving voice to the different sections of such communities and a way of debating ideas that impact upon the research project (L. T. Smith 1999). The roots of this "specific modality" of research go back to precolonial cosmological and ethical principles, epistemic frames, existential models, and forms of social organization characteristic of Maori people, and cannot be reduced to simply anticolonial political struggles. We can, perhaps, interpret *Kaupapa* as an equivalent of epistemology since it functions at a meta-level of reflecting upon the framing and structure of Maori knowledge, whereas *whanau* is a more concrete methodological tool used to implement this general epistemic principle. However, working together, they can be viewed as a non-traditional methodological tactic with the clear goal of social benefit, and of positive change for Maori societies, which are necessarily active participants in decolonial research.

Another relevant example of more local decolonial methods of inquiry can be found in the works of Canadian Indigenous (Nishnaabeg) feminist scholar, musician, poet, and activist Leanne Betasamosake Simpson, who not only reinstates a relational–experiential cognitive model grounded in complementarity and reciprocity, by referring to a dynamic Indigenous relationship with the land, cosmos, and communal agency but also brings us back to the hermeneutics of love through a metaphor of the "islands of decolonial love" (Simpson 2013). In her critically acclaimed *Dancing on Our Turtle's Back*, Simpson (2011) refers to *Biskaabiiyang* as a specific Nishnaabeg onto-epistemic methodology. The word *Biskaabiiyang* literally means to look back, but the method is not a simple return to the past as most Euromodern interpreters would automatically assume. For Simpson and her fellow Indigenous researchers, it is an essentially decolonial and convoluted method which means "returning to themselves" in order to evaluate how they have been affected by colonialism in all their realms of being (Simpson 2011: 49–50). It involves a complex and often painful process of resurgence, psychological reunification and

136 *Madina Tlostanova*

re-identification with delegitimized and forgotten ancestral bodies, genderings, wisdoms, memories, oral histories, stories, testimonies, and ways of being, not as an object of research but as a way of ensuring survival and revival. Importantly, Simpson stresses that *Biskaabiiyang* is not just a research methodology that one can forget after the project is over, but a method that one needs to keep present in one's mind and that helps Nishnaabeg people to carry out their daily lives, to walk their ways through the world, in their current, still-occupied state. Biskaabiiyang is both a deeply individual and a collective process. It is not about returning to the past, but rather about "re-creating the cultural and political flourishment of the past to support the well-being of our contemporary citizens", "reclaiming the fluidity around our traditions", "encouraging the self-determination of individuals within our national and community-based contexts", and "re-creating an artistic and intellectual renaissance within a larger political and cultural resurgence" (Simpson 2011: 51).

Refuturing?

This contextually specific Nishnaabeg method resonates with the emerging broader decolonial agendas of shifting towards imagining a redirected decolonial future (Tlostanova 2020) that would come to life through the agency (and not just discursive intersections) of the change communities and coalitions incorporating different actors – from the Global North and the Global South as well as the semi-periphery, scientists, scholars and activists, local communities, and artists. Decolonial communities of change would have to shift away from the past and turn more towards a transnational and transmodern present that we hope to refuture. They would have to overcome the immobilizing locality of continental and national ontologies and the modern/colonial predicament, to counter the bleakness of the post-pandemic world of normalized states of exception and new forms of biomedical coloniality, and to face the inevitability of humbling our thoughtless consumption and growth. This collective re-existent endeavour would begin, of necessity, in a state of unsettlement, a new negatively global version of the Coatlicue state that we should strive to make into a positive move of resurgence – not only for a specific Indigenous community and memory but also for the entirety of our fragile and unstable, injured and distorted, complex, and unfathomable world that we need to learn to make a communal home again.

References

Albán, Adolfo. 2009. "Artistas Indígenas y Afrocolombianos: Entre las Memorias y las Cosmovisiones. Estéticas de la Re-Existencia." In *Arte y Estética en la Encrucijada Descolonial*, edited by Zulma Palermo, 83–112. Buenos Aires: Del Siglo.

Anzaldúa, Gloria. 1987. *Borderlands/La Frontera: The New Mestiza*. San Francisco, CA: Aunt Lute Books.

Bhabha, Homi. 2004. *The Location of Culture*. London and New York, NY: Routledge Classics.

Brecht, Bertolt, and Bentley Eric. 1961. "On Chinese Acting." *The Tulane Drama Review* 6 (1): 130–6.

Castro-Gómez, Santiago. 2007. "The Missing Chapter of Empire: Postmodern Reorganization of Coloniality and Post-Fordist Capitalism." *Cultural Studies* 21 (2–3): 428–48.

Derrida, Jacques. 1982. "Différance". In *Margins of Philosophy*. Trans. A. Bass, edited by Jacques Derrida, 3–27. Chicago, IL: University of Chicago Press.

Du Bois, William E. B. 1903. *The Souls of Black Folk*. Chicago, IL: A.C. McClurg & Co.

Escobar, Arturo. 2017. *Designs for the Pluriverse*. Durham, NC: Duke University Press.

Gadamer, Hans-George. 1975. *Wahrheit und Methode. Grundzüge einer philosophischen Hermeneutik*. 4. Auflage. Tübingen: J.C.B. Mohr.

Gordon, Lewis. 2006. *Disciplinary Decadence: Living Thought in Trying Times*. Boulder, CO: Paradigm.

Gordon, Lewis. 2010. "Philosophy, Science, and the Geography of Africana Reason." *Lichnost. Kultura. Obschestvo* [Personality, Culture, Society] 12 (3): 46–56.

Gordon, Lewis, and Madina Tlostanova. 2021. "Epilogue: Conversation With Decolonial Philosopher Madina Tlostanova on Shifting the Geography of Reason" In *Freedom, Justice and Decolonization*, edited by Lewis Gordon, 127–35. London: Routledge.

Haraway, Donna. 1988. "Situated Knowledges: The Science Question in Feminism and the Privilege of Partial Perspective." *Feminist Studies* 14 (3): 575–99.

Kant, Immanuel. 1785. *Grundlegung zur Metaphysik der Sitten*. Riga: Verlag J. F. Hartknoch.

Lorde, Audre. 1984. "The Master's Tools Will Never Dismantle the Master's House." In *Sister Outsider: Essays and Speeches*, edited by Audre Lorde, 110–3. Berkeley, CA: Crossing Press.

Lugones, María. 2003. *Pilgrimages/Peregrinajes: Theorizing Coalition Against Multiple Oppression*. New York, NY and Oxford: Rowman and Littlefield.

Lugones, María. 2005. "From Within Germinative Stasis: Creating Active Subjectivity, Resistant Agency." In *Entremundos/Among Worlds: New Perspectives on Gloria E. Anzaldúa*, edited by A. Keating, 85–100. London: Palgrave Macmillan.

Lugones, María. 2007. "Heterosexualism and the Colonial/Modern Gender System." *Hypatia* 22 (1): 186–209.

Mignolo, Walter. 1995. *The Darker Side of the Renaissance*. Ann Arbor, MI: The University of Michigan Press.

Mignolo, Walter. 2002. "The Enduring Enchantment: (Or the Epistemic Privilege of Modernity and Where to Go From Here)." *South Atlantic Quarterly* 101 (4): 927–54.

Panikkar, Raimundo. 1975. "Cross-Cultural Studies: The Need for a New Science of Interpretation." *Monchanin* 8 (3–5): 12–5.

Panikkar, Raimundo. 1978. *The Intra-Religious Dialogue* (1st ed.). New York, NY: Paulist Press.

Panikkar, Raimundo. 1979. *Myth, Faith and Hermeneutics*. New York, NY: Paulist Press.

Panikkar, Raimundo. 1988. "What Is Comparative Philosophy Comparing?" In *Interpreting Across Boundaries: New Essays in Comparative Philosophy*, edited by Gerald James Larson and Eliot Deutsch, 116–36. Princeton, NJ: Princeton University Press.

Panikkar, Raimundo. 1995. *Invisible Harmony*. Minneapolis, MN: Fortress Press.

Sandoval, Chela. 2000. *Methodology of the Oppressed*. Minneapolis, MN: University of Minnesota Press.

Shklovsky, Viktor. 1929. "Isskustvo kak priyom" (Art as Technique). In *O Teorri Prozi* (On the Theory of Prose), edited by V. Shklovsky, 7–23. Moscow: Federatsia.

Simpson, Leanne Betasamosake. 2011. *Dancing on Our Turtle's Back: Stories of Nishnaabeg Re-Creation, Resurgence, and a New Emergence*. Winnipeg: ARP.

Simpson, Leanne Betasamosake. 2013. *Islands of Decolonial Love*. Winnipeg: ARP.

138 *Madina Tlostanova*

Smith, Graham H. 1990. "Research Issues Related to Maori Education." Paper presented to NZARE Special Interest Conference, Massey University, reprinted in 1992, The Issue of Research and Maori, Research Unit for Maori Education, University of Auckland.

Smith, Linda Tuhiwai. 1999. *Decolonizing Methodologies: Research and Indigenous Peoples*. London and New York, NY: Zed Books.

Tlostanova, Madina. 2015. "Toutes les femmes sont russes, tous les Caucasiens sont des hommes? Intersectionalite, pluriversalite et les autres genre-e-s des frontiers eurasiennes." In *Les Cahiers du CEDREF. Intersectionalite et colonialite. Debats contemporains*, edited by J. Falquet and A. Kian, 97–124. Paris: Universite Paris Diderot – Paris 7.

Tlostanova, Madina. 2017. *Postcolonialism and Postsocialism in Fiction and Art: Resistance and Re-existence*. Cham: Palgrave Macmillan.

Tlostanova, Madina. 2020. "Of Birds and Trees: Rethinking Decoloniality Through Unsettlement as a Pluriversal Human Condition." *ECHO. Rivista Interdisciplinare di communicazione. Universita degli studi di Bari aldo modo* (Special Issue: Semiosis of Coloniality and Cultural Dynamics at the Time of Global Mobility) 2: 16–27.

Tlostanova, Madina, and Walter Mignolo. 2009. "On Pluritopic Hermeneutics, Trans-Modern Thinking, and Decolonial Philosophy." *Encounters: An International Journal for the Study of Culture and Society* 1 (1): 11–27.

Tlostanova, Madina, and Walter Mignolo. 2012. *Learning to Unlearn: Decolonial Reflections From Eurasia and the Americas*. Columbus, OH: Ohio State University Press.

Vázquez, Rolando. 2017. "Precedence, Earth and the Anthropocene: Decolonizing Design." *Design Philosophy Papers* 15 (1): 77–91.

Walsh, Catherine E., and Walter Mignolo. 2018. *On Decoloniality*. Durham, NC: Duke University Press.

12 Reading Transnationally

Literary Transduction as a Feminist Tool

Jasmina Lukić

Borders and Security in Times of Crisis

While I make final revisions to this text, the world around me moves slowly, as if in a haze; it's the age of the coronavirus pandemic, and in Budapest, like in so many other cities across the globe, the streets are empty, as we are all locked up in our houses and apartments hoping for the virus to just go away and for a return to what was once considered "normal" life. Yet, at the same time, we are inundated with messages as to the "new normal" that is here to stay; we wear beak-like masks which make us look like strange birds; and following requirements for keeping "social distance", we refrain from contacts with other people in actual spaces. And while virtual life takes over, very real, physical borders are suddenly being erected all around us. State borders are closing down, planes are grounded, and physical distances are again looming large.

The old/new state borders, firmly (re)established, also divide most of my small transnational family scattered across Europe. While we connect daily, grateful for miracles of modern technology that make it possible for us to see each other and be sure all is fine, I am painfully aware of how difficult it might be to travel if the need arises (travel for other reasons, like the simple wish to be together or to offer emotional support, being put on hold now). Thus, I personally experience the relevance of Arjun Appadurai's claims on new forms of interconnectedness between technology and migration (1996). At the same time, the title of my recent edited volume on transnational literature, *Times of Mobility* (Lukić et al. 2019), sounds all of a sudden like a cruel joke, when so many cannot venture beyond their own street or even their own doorstep due to restrictions imposed by the pandemic – and when too many others, due to wars, forced migration, or extreme poverty do not even have that doorstep and a home to get sheltered in in the face of the then-unknown illness.

The COVID-19 pandemic adds a strange new twist to the recent history of border crossing in Central and Eastern Europe. Coming from Yugoslavia, a "soft socialist" country, I remember how strictness at Yugoslav borders gradually diminished throughout the 1970s and the 1980s; and the feeling of freedom my Yugoslav passport afforded me in passing borders both "East" and "West", a liberty that many of my colleagues from socialist countries behind "the iron curtain" did not share. But later on the situation radically changed both for my colleagues and for

DOI: 10.4324/9781003378761-14

140   *Jasmina Lukić*

myself. While borders opened up for the former socialist bloc after the fall of the Berlin Wall, the wars for Yugoslav secession in the 1990s led to the creation of several nation-states with hard borders between them and between them and other neighbours. Living between Belgrade, Zagreb, and Budapest, I had to learn the hard way about the hardships of getting visas every time I wanted to travel. So when Hungary joined the Schengen Treaty, it was a new phase of fully open borders for me. Until now – when I once again witness the return of hard borders due to pandemic and I am startled at the ease with which it is being done.

The new reality of reemergent borders has been taken by nationalists in many countries as a strong sign that the nation-state has proven to be the best, if not only, way to organize communal social life. In this new reality, feminist theory can offer critical tools to address the new perils of forcibly closing borders in the name of people's protection and security. In response to that situation, which in its own way creates dystopian possible worlds we never thought would be a part of our life experiences, I propose using the concept of literary transduction[1] (Doležel 1998) within the larger framework of feminist transnational studies. The new significance given to national borders amid the global COVID-19 pandemic imparts new meaning to transnational perspectives, which is interpreted here as a dynamic open series of interactions challenging or probing previously established borders, political, or otherwise. These interactions are interpreted here as a form of transduction in Doležel's sense of the term, emphasizing the transformative power of border thinking and transculturation.

On Border Thinking, Feminism, and Transnational Studies

In this new situation created by the COVID-19 crisis, discourses on security soon became a cover for local power struggles, an excuse for serious attempts at introducing mechanisms of control, including those limiting women's reproductive rights or the human rights of LGBT populations. A few examples from the beginning of the pandemic clearly demonstrate this, showing as well how the crisis itself and related security measures are deeply gendered. In Hungary, a new law was passed early in the pandemic as if it were a matter of urgency; it mandates "sex at birth" for life and thus annuls the rights of transgender persons to decide their gender.[2] The Polish government also used the new situation to tighten already extremely restrictive legislation on abortion, doing this at a time when the coronavirus crisis made massive public demonstrations practically impossible.[3] The Serbian government demonstrated extreme ageism in its first measures against pandemic, locking people over 65 years old in their homes for prolonged periods of time and justifying excessively strict isolation of this particular social group with a need to "save the lives of our elderly citizens".[4] The state authorities behind all of these decisions called upon "the national good" to justify such moves.

Current reinforcement of borders in the name of protecting the nation from the pandemic means that borders are being reestablished in their traditional role as state instruments of separation and exclusion. But it is not a simple process, and the current coronavirus pandemic seems to renew and reactualize the tension between

Reading Transnationally 141

the border as a traditionally "protective" or exclusionary zone and the border as a zone of interconnectedness and communication, as border studies point out.

The significance of Gloria Anzaldúa's seminal work *Borderlands* (1999 [1987]) for rethinking the very concept of the border cannot be overemphasized here; for Anzaldúa the border is a space characterized by its openness towards difference in which a new kind of mestiza identity is created. Margaret R. Higonet describes the border as

> a complex construct that defines and localizes what it strives to contain or release. It is rarely a smooth seam; an edge may revel, gape open at interstices, or leak in both directions. Borders mark sites of rupture, connection, transmission, and transformation.
>
> (Higonet 1994: 2)

Drawing upon Martin Heidegger and Homi Bhabha, as well as Gloria Anzaldúa, Noha Hamdy sees the border as a "location-in-movement" and "third space" (Hamdy 2010: 216–7), emphasizing that "most contemporary borderland configurations are grounded in epistemologies which reinforce concepts of transnationalism, hybridization, heterogeneity and mestizaje rather than teleological and homogeneous cultural formations" (2010: 218).

Prominent border theorists Walter Mignolo and Madina Tlostanova underline the artificiality of all kinds of borders and the concomitant need to deconstruct their legitimacy (2006: 208). From that understanding comes also a request for a new epistemology:

> Border thinking is the epistemology of the exteriority; that is, of the outside created from the inside; and as such, it is always a decolonial project. . . . Border thinking brings to the foreground different kinds of theoretical actors and principles of knowledge that displace European modernity (which articulated the very concept of theory in the social sciences and the humanities) and empower those who have been epistemically disempowered by the theo- and ego-politics of knowledge.
>
> (Mignolo and Tlostanova 2006: 206–7)

Mignolo and Tlostanova call for pluriversality, which "is only possible from border thinking, that is, from shifting the geography of reason to geo- and body-politics of knowledge" (2006: 210). And in order to perform the required epistemological shift, we are required "to think from the borders themselves" (2006: 214).

How such a shift works in practice can be seen in a project of Madina Tlostanova, Suruchi Thapar-Björkert, and Redi Koobak (2016), which turns to feminist border thinking as an important tool in feminist knowledge production:

> Feminist border thinking is a horizontal transversal networking of different local histories and sensibilities mobilised through a number of common, yet pluriversal and open categories. The positive impulse behind border thinking replaces the negative stance that entraps women in multiple oppressions with

142   *Jasmina Lukić*

the re-existent position of building an alternative world in which no one will be an other.

(2016: 217)

Although they speak from different contexts – with Hamdy focusing on border subjectivity through a critical reading of Anzaldúa's *Borderlands*, while Mignolo and Tlostanova (2006), and later Tlostanova et al. (2016), investigate strategies of decolonial thinking – these theorists all acknowledge the dialogic potential produced by occupying the border position. In Hamdy's case, the recognition of such a position calls for a transnational perspective, while in the case of Tlostanova et al. (2016), it is the multiplicity of spaces evoked through "different local histories" that leads to a similar conclusion (the three authors came to Sweden, where they work together, from diverse geographic locations and with different personal histories). But in both cases it is the "local" perspective that opens their understanding of "border thinking" towards transnational perspectives.[5]

The connection between border thinking and transnational perspective brings into focus the significance of the local and the particular. By saying this, I do not intend to negate differences between the various approaches to transnationalism, nor the different disciplinary and topical directions that the "transnational turn" has taken. Moreover, as Laura Briggs (2016) points out, transnationalism is not an uncontested term within the larger field of women's and gender studies. Yet leaving these debates aside, I would like to argue here that the transnational approach offers an interpretative framework in which specific and general perspectives interact in dialogic fashion.

The relation between specific and general perspectives is also examined by Susan Friedman in an essay in which she argues for the concept of "locational feminism" (2001). In this text, Friedman calls for a "reinstitution of *feminism in the singular*", which does not aim to erase differences between women, the social conditions in which they live in, or the feminist traditions that they create, but emphasizes that various forms of feminism share political practice based upon theories of gender and social justice (2001: 15).

To distinguish her idea from older forms of essentialism in feminist theory, Friedman introduces the term "locational feminism", which is both local and global. Always located in particular spaces, with local specificities and trans/local connections, feminism, she argues, is also a global phenomenon in the way in which its Indigenous formations are created and in the way they travel, and influence one another (2001: 15). Thus, the concept of locational feminism "acknowledges the historically and geographically specific forms in which feminism emerges, takes root, changes, travels, translates, and transplants in different spatial/temporal contexts" (2001: 15).

Friedman underlines that feminism can be understood only through the interaction of its multiple origins and locations:

The notion that a given social order privileges the masculine does not, I believe, have a single origin. Nor does the advocacy of gender equity. Rather, these constitutive components of locational feminism have emerged differently in particular times and places and have traveled from one culture to another, producing hybridic cultural formations of indigenous feminism influenced by other traveling forms of feminism. Such syncretic practices result from ongoing processes of what anthropologists often call "transculturation", whereby one culture absorbs and redefines within its own terms what it takes from others as an effect of multiple contact zones.

(2001: 16)

These multiple contact zones, furthermore, are not nation-bound; they belong to different cartographies that need not be based on given or assumed borders built upon traditional ethnic or other group identities. Likewise, the transnational perspective I am arguing for here is not based on recognizing and reinforcing a static, given "national" identity to be counterpoised to another equally static and essentialized identity. In other words, a transnational perspective is not based upon a given set of relations but, rather, a dynamic open series of interactions through which a referential framework for both personal and group identifications is created, one that continually challenges or probes previously established borders of some kind.

In order to move away from an understanding of transnationalism as an interaction between nation-states, Bill Ashcroft proposes the concept of "transnation", defined "not [as] an ontological object but [as] a way of understanding the possibility of ordinary people avoiding, dodging, circumventing the inevitable claims of the state upon them" (2010: 13). Transnation, he further argues, is "the fluid, migrating *outside* of the state that begins *within* the nation". It is an "in-between" space, which "contains no one definitive people, nation, or even community, but is everywhere, a space without boundaries" (2010: 16). Ashcroft recognizes that the nation is an "apparatus of enormous symbolic power" but emphasizes its limitations and the loss of its relevance in times characterized by "fluidity and movement", the "transnational character of culture", and "the transformation of the global at the level of the local" (2010: 16). The last point brings Ashcroft's understandings of the global imaginary and transnation close to Susan Friedman's understanding of the locational as both local and global, and feminism as transnational by definition. At the same time, Ashcroft's emphasis on the transnation's potential for subverting binary relations between centre and periphery (2010: 26) evokes Shu-mei Shih and Françoise Lionnet's arguments on "minor transnationalism" as a tool for overcoming the centre/margin dyad in postcolonial theory (2005).

Yet what particularly interests me is the utopian aspect of the concept of transnation. A utopian moment is also present in Mignolo and Tlostanova and, importantly for this analysis, it is connected to the idea of multiple possible worlds: "De-colonizing being and knowledge is a way towards the idea that 'another world is possible' (and not alternative modernities). That world, as the Zapatistas had it, will be 'a world in which many worlds will co-exist'" (2006: 219). We can also recognize the utopian promise in Tlostanova et al. (2016) when they speak of border thinking as a tool for building alternative worlds in which no one will be seen or treated as Other. And yet, there is an important difference here, which I would like to use not only as a point of

144 *Jasmina Lukić*

comparison but also as a starting point for extending the discussion on the transnational perspective and its significance for feminist theory.

Feminist Utopia, Possible Worlds, and the Power of Literature

For Tlostanova et al. (2016), the utopian potentiality of border thinking comes from agency and from praxis. In this chapter, they examine border thinking alongside disidentification, viewed as:

> transformative tools coming from different genealogies and disciplinary cultures. While they are based on the same ground and outlook, border thinking works on a more general epistemological level, whereas disidentification acts more as an immediate praxis. Both deliberately blur boundaries between agency and knowledge, although structurally they pertain to differentiable planes. Border thinking often requires and leads to disidentification as a mode of political agency in order to be fully embodied and realised.
>
> (2016: 223)

For Ashcroft, the realm of utopia is the realm of literature. Following Ernst Bloch, Ashcroft sees literature as "inherently utopian because its *rasion d'etre* is the imagining of a different world" (2010: 26). That different world is produced by narrative; if produced by utopian thinking and utopian narrative, it brings about the conception of a radically changeable world (2010: 25). In this type of writing, the question is not "what the text *may mean* but what it *can do*", which is especially a characteristic of postcolonial and diasporic literature (2010: 26).

Recent work by Debjani Ganguly deals with contemporary literature from a perspective close to that of Ashcroft when it comes to understanding the way literature operates in society. Looking to the end of the 20th century and beginning of the 21st century, Ganguly sees a new novelistic genre that responds to some of the most urgent problems of our time:

> My primary thesis is that around historically significant threshold of 1989,[6] a new kind of novel as a global literary form emerged at the conjuncture of three critical phenomena: the geopolitics of war and violence since the end of the Cold War; hyperconnectivity through advances in information technology; and the emergence of a new humanitarian sensibility in a context where suffering has a presence in everyday life through the intermediacy of digital images.
>
> (2016: 1)

Ganguly names this new genre the "world novel"; in the context of globalization, the emphasis is upon the "world" as the new chronotope, and on worlding processes and world building. The main questions for Ganguly are: How is the world conceptualized through "the genre of novel"? And what can the novel tell us about our being in the world (2016: 24)? In answering these questions, she underlines how her approach differs from that taken by Edward Said, for whom, as she puts it, the world was "primarily the material domain of economic and political interest" (2016: 21). For Ganguly, rather, there is an emphasis on the difference between the worlds of fiction and the actual world we live in, where the world is "related to, but not synonymous with its material and chronotopical coordinates" (2016: 21). In this respect, Ganguly accepts the main postulates of possible world theories, from Leibnitz to Thomas Pavel and Ruth Ronen. Thus, "world" is seen here "as a linguistically finite set of entities and relations marked off by worlds made up of other finite set of entities and relations" (2016: 21); the novel is understood as "a world-enclosing total system" (2016: 21); and the actual world is "but one of the conditions of possibility for creation of the fictional world and not the sole determinant of its *realism*" (2016: 22).

The position Ganguly takes here enables her to investigate the ways in which the contemporary novel engages with the actual world but without reducing the novel to mere "reflection" of experiential reality. In other words, fictional worlds are seen here as nonmimetic in relation to our experiential reality. At the same time, they are profoundly involved with this reality, and the world novel as a genre is defined here through this involvement. In that sense, Ganguly's idea of world novel displays an agency that Ashcroft calls for and recognizes primarily in postcolonial and diasporic literature. Taking the timeline indicated by Ganguly and the choice of novels that she associates with the genre of world novel, one can see that she has similar understanding of the potentiality for engagement of postcolonial literature.

The complex interaction between "actual world" and the worlds of literature as worlds which have ontologies of their own has been extensively discussed by Lubomir Doležel. For him, that interaction is a "bidirectional exchange", since "the poetic imagination works with 'material' drawn from actuality", while "fictional constructs deeply influence our imaging and understanding of reality" (Doležel 1998: x). According to Doležel, the material which comes from reality into the worlds of fiction has to undergo substantial change: "Because of the ontological sovereignty of fictional worlds, actual-worlds entities have to be converted into nonactual possibilities, with all the ontological, logical, and semantic consequences that this transformation entails" (1998: 21).

The ontological sovereignty of fictional worlds makes it not only possible but also necessary to preserve the consciousness of the specific nature of literary texts while reading. Doležel distinguishes between two types of texts, those he terms worldimaging texts and those he terms worldconstructing. The difference between them is based on their relationship to the actual world, which exists "prior to, and independently of, textual activity". Thus, world-imagining texts are those which offer a representation of the actual world, or provide information about it, while "constructing texts are prior to worlds; it is textual activity that calls worlds into existence and determines their structures" (1998: 24).

For Doležel, fictional texts are world-constructing texts; hence, even when they tend to remain very close to the actual world as we know it, they can never be fully translated back into it. At the same time, even when they tend to be as distant from our actual world as possible, fictional worlds have to keep a connection with it in

146   *Jasmina Lukić*

order to remain accessible to the reader. In reading, fictional worlds are accessed through a "semiotic channel", which assumes "crossing somehow the world boundary between the realms of the actual and the possible" (1998: 20). The actual world is always present in fictional worlds in a number of ways, but that material has to "undergo substantial transformation at the world boundary" (1998: 21).

This transformation is not the only one that occurs in the process of interaction between possible worlds. Understanding literature as a "specific form of communication" (1998: 202), Doležel extends the simple triadic scheme Author–Text–Reader to include fictional worlds as an outcome of this process. The author "is responsible for text production and world construction; his [sic] text functions as a kind of score in which the fictional world is inscribed. The reader's text processing and world reconstruction follow the instructions of the score" (205). This model is further extended with the help of the concept of literary transduction. Transduction is a process that "takes the literary work beyond the communicative act into an open, unlimited chain of transmission" (1998: 205). In the scheme proposed by Doležel (1998: 204), the emphasis is on conversions that occur between fictional worlds in the process of literary communication. It is a process in which the experiences of the previous world building become a part of the next act of world creation. The prototype of transduction is literary translation, which necessarily involves a certain transformation of the original text in the process of making it accessible to readers in another language (1998: 205).

Reading Transnationally: Transduction as a Feminist Tool

Transduction as a literary concept brings together several important points relevant both for transnational perspective and for feminism. As a transfer of information that implies translation/transformation/conversion from one world to another, transduction speaks both to border thinking and to locational feminism in Friedman's sense of the term. Addressing processes and not given states of affairs, transduction offers a useful model for understanding transnationalism as a series or chain of transmissions leading to complex processes of transculturation. All of these make the concept of transduction particularly useful for feminist interpretations of transnational literary texts.

My example here will be *A Concise Chinese-English Dictionary for Lovers* by Xiaolu Guo (2007). As its title suggests, this novel is organized as a kind of dictionary, a collection of short narrative fragments, each associated with a particular word quoted from an English dictionary and followed by a prose fragment describing the personal experiences of a young Chinese woman named Zuangh Xiao Qiao, who came to London to learn English. Zuangh Xiao Qiao is the narrator and the main protagonist of the novel. At the beginning, the novel mimics the genre of trivial romance, with the promise of the familiar girl-meets-boy storyline with a happy ending. But their relationship is full of misunderstanding, at first, due to Zuangh Xiao Qiao's precarious grasp of English, but later on, due to divergent cultural norms that make her and her partner understand very differently what various words are supposed to mean. The "misunderstanding" section is telling:

"That's how all starts. From a misunderstanding. When you say 'guest' I think you meaning I can stay in your house. A week later I move out from Chinese landlord" (Guo 2007: 54). This key moment signals a departure from conventional or stereotypical romance; the distancing from the plot of a trivial romance gets more and more obvious as various other genres are evoked, from diary to travelogue, bildungsroman, and consciousness-raising feminist autofiction. The narrator, at first completely focused on her lover, gradually widens her perspective and becomes an observer of the "Western"[7] way of life and the values it is based on. At the same time, the newly acquired perspective and facility for language she obtains, thanks to her London life, enable her to look back on her previous life in a different, more critical manner. Thus, she finds herself in a "third" zone, in between two cultures that seem so different, at moments even incompatible. In the end, it is obvious that this experience has profoundly changed her, as well as her lover, whose silent presence at the edges of the narrative indicates a number of possible alternative positions to be taken in this strange (mis)communication between them, from sexual obsession to indifference and final separation. The narrator continually feels that she lacks real closeness, a real intimacy with her lover, which leads her to experiment with her body and to challenge him with her acknowledgement of this experimentation. But this bodily experiment is at the same an act of rebellion against her own culture and tradition, a fast-track to sexual liberation that she needs to go through.

What makes this novel a piece of transnational literature is not simply the fact that a Chinese woman and a British man meet in London but, rather, the way in which two different cultural traditions meet, clash, and interact with one another. The English language serves here as a kind of a borderline that divides the two protagonists and the symbolic spaces they occupy; yet at the same time it also serves as a powerful tool to establish the third space of communication. But it is not about a simple opposition between China and Britain. The novel brings together two very different characters. The narrator is an educated woman from a small town who even before coming to London has to negotiate her communist education and her small-town family traditions, while her partner is a young man from the "alternative" arts scene of 1990s London. The depth of their misunderstanding arises not solely from the differences in their national traditions but also from their own complex social identities that make them see the world differently. It is obvious that the two protagonists are positioned differently when it comes to the ways their identities have been constructed, and this is the difference, being constitutive for the world of the novel, that calls for intersectional reading.

The narrator, Zuangh Xiao Qiao, stands for a possible world of communist China as it is seen from her geographical and class location, and in accordance with views of an individual who lives a life of an ordinary, socially integrated person. Before coming to London, she was employed and lived close to her family. Apart from these defining points in her personal life, there is a whole set of interlocked customs and traditions which can be generally and very vaguely named here the "Chinese way of life", indicating a form of collective identity that the narrator at the beginning uncritically accepts as her own.

148   *Jasmina Lukić*

She starts her travels to England confident in the values she grew up with. But with time spent in another country – which is like another possible world for her – she is forced to reconsider many of her previous assumptions. A year later, when she finally goes back to China, she finds a world very different from the one she left behind and feels, predictably enough, very much out of place. This new China she returns to is a country in transition, with replicas of so-called "Western" life everywhere around her. The country has changed, but so has she (2007: 352). Her partner does not have much of a voice in the novel. We always hear him through her, but the novel's closing letter, the last she receives from him, clearly indicates that he has changed as well, and in a direction that she would be happy to see and be a part of.

The deep changes that both characters go through can be seen as an outcome of shared living in third space, an individual transformation for both of them. And already on that level, it is possible to speak about a form of transduction. With Doležel's communicational model in mind, we can say that each of the protagonists offers their own possible world to the other as a "reader" of that world, reconstructing it. Here, the symbolic role of the "dictionary" as a tool of translation/communication gains added relevance. But this reading/translating/reconstructing of one partner's possible world by the other partner can only happen in a form of transduction, a transformative process in which the border between the inside and the outside is turned into an osmotic-like communication channel.

Both characters represent more than themselves in the novel. Or, as Jonathan Culler puts it, the power of literary representation lies in its ability to combine specific singular cases with exemplarity (2007: 35). For the reader, Zuangh Xiao Qiao and her partner raise more questions than those surrounding their own personal destiny, ranging from issues related to national, ethnic, and gender identity, as well as questions of selfhood, intimacy, love, and sexuality. Another set of questions opens up if the reader decides to look at the two main characters as metonymic representatives of much larger interactive (ex)changes between China and the so-called West. For the reader who takes the title literally, this novel is a love story (a "dictionary for Lovers"); for a reader attuned to larger contexts, it is about the interaction between two world-changing cultures and traditions. Such a reader would engage in her reading a more general picture of global processes, especially of the ways in which Chinese industry and export of goods profoundly changed global trade. In my view, this geopolitical subtext is "silently" present in the same way as the voice of the narrator's partner is toned down. Reading further along these lines, it is possible to say that Guo's novel grows from love story into a much more complex narrative, a version of the world novel, as Ganguly understands the genre.

Such a change of perspective is possible because the novel counts on the reader's knowledge and her contribution in widening the scope of the narrative. Speaking of possible worlds' properties, Umberto Eco underlines that:

a fictional text abundantly overlaps the world of the reader's encyclopedia. But also, from the theoretical point of view, this overlapping is indispensable,

Reading Transnationally   149

and not only for fictional world. It is quite impossible to build a complete
alternative of world or even to describe our "real" one as completely built up.

(1983 [1979]: 221)

The semiotic channel, through which fictional worlds can be accessed, enables
bidirectional mediation of information (Doležel 1998: 20). The reader obtains
from the fictional text, as it were, a set of instructions on how to build a possible world; but she also furnishes that world with the knowledge from her own
"encyclopedia".

A Concise Chinese-English Dictionary for Lovers has numerous connections
with well-established genres of women's literature. As a form of fictional auto-
biography, it can be read as an autofiction of a literary character; and the careful concealing of the name of the narrator for the majority of the novel supports
such an interpretation. The novel also reads as a feminist consciousness-raising
text through pointed references to gender, the body, and sexuality, as well as to the
legacies of feminism. The narrator explores her body and her sexuality in a number
of ways, in a challenging opposition to her family tradition and the education she
has received, both of which came together to control her body and her sexuality
throughout her upbringing.

Leaning about her sexual organs is an act of agency, a border-crossing action
she undertakes in the manner of second-wave feminists from the early 1970s.
The difference is that Zuangh Xiao Qiao is alone: she does not have a consciousness-raising group to support her. Instead, in a boundary-breaking move, she
goes to a peep show and compares her body with what she sees in the exposed
body of a sex worker. Contrary to her upbringing, she engages freely in sexual
relations beyond monogamy and finally discovers masturbation as a form of
repossessing her own body, the ultimate confirmation that she has acquired her
independence:

And I scream.
On my own. With myself. I did it. It is like dream.
For the first time in my entire life, I came by myself.
I can be on my own. I can. I can rely on myself, without depending on a man.

(245)

The realization that she can "rely on herself" is obviously not only about her sexuality but also about learning through the body and learning to see herself outside
group identities. The scene clearly evokes a range of feminist ideas concerning
women's bodies and sexuality, confirming the power of the body to produce gendered knowledge. Within such a reading, the play with the genre of trivial romance
comes back, but in a different light. Seen by critics and publishers as a genre for
female readers, trivial romance is evoked in order to be disputed on various levels,
from the level of the plot (the ending is not what is expected in romance) and a
questioning of the very concept of romance, to turning towards feminist strategies

150   *Jasmina Lukić*

of narration and subject formation. In this way, the text creates a whole network of references to feminism, women's literature, and popular culture. As a feminist text, it also lends itself to interpretations in which feminist border thinking and the concept of disidentification can be useful tools.

Instead of a Conclusion: On Transduction and Singularity

The position from which Zuangh Xiao Qiao narrates her novel can be very helpful to address one more useful category introduced by possible worlds theory, that of accessibility. It is used to deal with the problems of communication between possible worlds, where the so-called actual or real world of reference is also understood as a possible world (Eco 1983 [1979]: 222). Eco defines the "actual world" as "every world in which its inhabitants refer to it as the world where they live in" (1983 [1979]: 223). Within the actual world of Zuangh Xiao Qiao, the English language is a semiotic channel, which allows for accessibility between the world of small-town communist China that she came from and the world of London in which her partner lives. This channel of accessibility is not simply given; it changes with time and with her increasing fluency in English. Nevertheless, there are always certain meanings which escape her due to differences between the two worlds that come together in her experience. So the process of translation proves to be a process of transduction in Doležel's sense of the term. Within the actual world of the novel, Zuangh is the author of a narrative in which a young Chinese woman with certain ideas and values that constitute her world comes to London as to another reality. She offers her understanding of the world to her partner as a "text" he has to translate/reconstruct, which he can only partially do. And the other way around, Zuangh has to translate/reconstruct the messages/instructions for reading/reconstructing her partner's world of London, which is only partially accessible to her. Both of them perceive and construct for themselves their actual worlds differently, and their worlds are related, but not synonymous. In both cases, a form of transformation occurs in the process of translation; the concept of transduction helps us understand this process as a chain of events, each of them requiring some form of conversion.

"Possibleworlds semantics uses the concept of accessibility for formally representing contacts between possible worlds", Doležel argues, adding that it tells us nothing about contacts between *actual* persons and *fictional* worlds (1998: 20–21). In the proposed reading of Guo's novel, its protagonists are treated both as fictional characters and as "real" readers in their actual world of reference. In the same way as we read the novel as a possible world of its own, they experience the other culture they confront as a possible world they can only partially access.

This turning of protagonists into "readers" enables us to look into the logic of their actions without violating the ontological sovereignty of the fictional text. At the same time, it brings into the focus the problems of theorizing the individualized reading process that escapes the logic of theoretical generalizations. Derek Attridge addresses this problem through the concept of singularity understood as the inherent quality of a "potential work of art", that is, a text which could be read as such.

Singularity, he argues, produces "otherness" that challenges habitual processes of thoughts and emotion (Attridge 2004: 27).

> The otherness that is brought into being by an act of inventive writing – an argument, a particular sequence of words, any imagined series of events embodied in a work – is not just a matter of perceptible difference. It implies a wholly new extent that cannot be apprehended by the old modes of understanding, and could not have been predicated by means of them; its singularity, even if it is produced by nothing more than a slight recasting of the familiar, and thus of the general, is irreducible.
>
> (Attridge 2004: 29)

The "event of singularizing" takes place in the process of the reader's reception of a given text (2004: 64). For Attridge, the reception that leads to such an event is highly individualized and dependent upon the context, time, and space in which one lives and experiences singularity. In order to explain the more closely particularized perspectives associated with singularity, Attridge introduces the concept of "idioculture"; such refers to the "embodiment in a single individual of widespread cultural norms and modes of behavior", which shapes and mediates one's grasp of the world (2004: 21). Singularity is not a constant; it is highly contextual and always gets reproduced "differently" with different readings. More precisely, as Attridge puts it:

> singularity exists, or rather *occurs*, in the experience of the reader (including writer-as-reader), understood not as a psychological subject (though singularity has its psychological effects) but as a repository of what I have termed an idioculture, an individual version of the cultural ensemble by which he or she has been fashioned as a subject with assumptions, predispositions and expectations.
>
> (2004: 67)

In this way, an act of individual reading is connected to a more general set of experiences that establish the ground for experiencing singularity, while singularity itself as a *potentiality* remains a specific quality of the given work of art.

It is obvious that idioculture as Attridge understands it can be related to politics of location in so far as it assumes a need to understand the individual subject's positioning, which impacts the reading. In this case, it is my own life experience as a migrant feminist scholar interested in transnational literature and women's writing which influences my choice of *A Concise Chinese-English Dictionary for Lovers* as a relevant example here. My experience as a migrant person living and working in another language makes me sensitive to the position of the novel's narrator, and my experience as a feminist literary scholar helps me to establish a chain of references indicating the generic conversions that are constitutive of the possible world of the novel. This chain of references operates as a form of transduction, since in the case of each genre referred to in the novel the reader is invited to reconstruct

152   *Jasmina Lukić*

the basic plot and characteristics of the given generic model and to follow the ways in which it is used/translated/converted within the narrative.

Similarly, Zuangh's idioculture guides her reading of the world of London that is presented to her. Her reading translates/transforms the city named London into a fictional world of her translation. And later on in the novel, when she moves back to China, it is her idioculture, changed by her London experiences, which affects her feeling of displacement. Her reading of the new China turns out to be a form of conversion of the two worlds she knew before as distinct ones. In my reading of the novel, I recognize the source of singularity in the ability of the text to mark clearly these points of conversion, indicating the spaces of in betweenness that characterize the transnation.

The concept of transduction, with its emphasis on the processes by which chains of interpretative events produce a series of conversions, can reveal multiple complexities: namely, those of transnational encounters, of transculturation as an inherent part of these encounters, and of transnation in Ashcroft's sense of the term. Or, to put it differently, the concept of transduction proves useful as a tool to address complexities involved in border living and border thinking.

Going back to the utopian moment involved in feminist projects, and understanding feminism[8] as an open set of possible worlds with the one shared aim that no one ought to be treated as Other, as Tlostanova et al. (2016) put it, we can look at transduction as a process which is constitutive of feminist utopian thinking. If feminism designates a political project with utopian potentiality, we can see feminism's different locational manifestations as its various possible worlds. The way in which such worlds communicate and translate each other's political practices, projects, and visions is always much more than a simple act of communication. Travelling from literary to feminist theory, the concept of transduction can help unpack the far-reaching transformative effects of these processes.

Notes

1 During the COVID-19 pandemic, "transduction" has gained in potency, as it especially refers to "the transfer of genetic material from one microorganism to another by a viral agent (such as a bacteriophage)" (*Merriam-Webster's Dictionary*).
2 As Shaun Walker (2020a: n/p) explains, "the new law defines gender as based on chromosomes at birth, meaning previous provisions whereby trans people could alter their gender and name on official documents will no longer be available".
3 For more details, see Shaun Walker (2020b).
4 From 17 March to 7 July 2020, there were several public speeches where Serbian President Aleksandar Vučić emphasizes that "we are doing it all to protect our elderly", as if the entire society is sacrificing for them; see, for example, the statement from 17 March as presented on N1 tv station at http://rs.n1info.com/Vesti/a579045/Vucic-Zabrana-kretanja-od-20h-do-5h-ujutro-pocinje-od-sutra.html. During the first lockdown (17 March–6 May 2020), people older than 65 years were forbidden to go out for days, being allowed to go shopping only occasionally at odd hours (4–7 a.m.). On these measures, see, for example, www.penzin.rs/vreme-izlaska-i-kupovine-za-starije/.
5 I am saying this although Tlostanova et al. (2016: 213) are critical of transnational feminism ("global and transnational forms of feminism have declared their faithfulness to

Reading Transnationally 153

dialogue, but have offered limited tools to bridge theorising and oppositional praxis").
Such criticism lies outside my line of argument here.

6 Interestingly, Ganguly emphasizes that 1989 as a temporal landmark is not primarily related to the fall of the Berlin Wall or communism, but with a more complex and far-reaching set of event that started to develop as early as the 1960, growing exponentially until 1989 (6).

7 Despite its problematic connotations, I use the term "West" since it is used in the novel.

8 After Friedman, I employ "feminism" in the singular: "What I mean by feminism in the singular is a locational feminism that is simultaneously situated in a specific locale, global in scope, and constantly in motion through space and time. A locational feminism is one that acknowledges the historically and in geographically specific forms in which feminism emerges, takes root, changes, travels, translates, and transplants in different spatio/temporal contexts" (2001: 15).

References

Anzaldúa, Gloria. 1999 [1987]. *Borderlands/La Frontera, the New Mestiza*. San Francisco, CA: Aunt Lute Books.

Appadurai, Arjun. 1996. *Modernity at Large: Cultural Dimensions of Globalization*. Minneapolis, MN: University of Minnesota Press.

Ashcroft, Bill. 2010. "Globalization, Transnation and Utopia." In *Locating Transnational Ideals*, edited by Walter Goebel and Saskia Schabio, 13–29. New York, NY: Routledge.

Attridge, Derek. 2004. *The Singularity of Literature*. London: Routledge.

Briggs, Laura. 2016. "Transnational." In *The Oxford Handbook to Feminist Theory*, edited by Lisa Disch and Mary Hawkesworth, 990–1009. Oxford: Oxford University Press.

Culler, Jonathan. 2007. *The Literary in Theory*. Stanford, CA: Stanford University Press.

Doležel, Lubomír. 1998. *Heterocosmica: Fiction and Possible Worlds*. Baltimore, MD: Johns Hopkins University Press.

Eco, Umberto. 1983 [1979]. *The Role of the Reader: Explorations in the Semiotics of Texts*. London: Hutchinson.

Friedman, Susan Stanford. 2001. "Locational Feminism: Gender, Cultural Geographies, and Geopolitical Literacy." In *Feminist Locations: Global and Local, Theory and Practice*, edited by Marianne DeKoven, 13–36. New Brunswick, NJ: Rutgers University Press.

Ganguly, Debjani. 2016. *This Thing Called the World: The Contemporary Novel as Global Form*. Durham, NC: Duke University Press.

Guo, Xiaolu. 2007. *A Concise Chinese-English Dictionary for Lovers*. London: Vintage Books.

Hamdy, Noha. 2010. "The Border as Third Space: Between Colonial Gaze and Transnational Dislocation." In *Locating Transnational Ideals*, edited by Walter Goebel and Saskia Schabio, 217–27. New York: Routledge.

Higonet, Margaret R. (ed.). 1994. *Borderwork: Feminist Engagements With Comparative Literature*. Ithaca, NY and London: Cornell University Press.

Lukić, Jasmina, and Sibelan Forrester, with Borbála Faragó (eds.). 2019. *Times of Mobility: Literature and Gender in Translation*. Budapest: Central European University Press.

Mignolo, Walter D., and Madina V. Tlostanova. 2006. "Theorizing From the Borders: Shifting to Geo- and Body-Politics of Knowledge." *European Journal of Social Theory* 9 (2): 205–21.

Shih, Shu-Mei, and Françoise Lionnet. 2005. "Introduction." In *Minor Transnationalism*, edited by Françoise Lionnet and Shu-Mei Shih, 1–26. Durham, NC: Duke University Press.

154   *Jasmina Lukić*

Tlostanova, Madina, Suruchi Thapar-Björkert, and Redi Koobak. 2016. "Border Thinking and Disidentification: Postcolonial and Postsocialist Feminist Dialogues." *Feminist Theory* 17 (2): 211–28.

Walker, Shaun. 2020a. "Hungary Votes to End Legal Recognition of Trans People." *Guardian* (International Edition), May 19. www.theguardian.com/world/2020/may/19/hungary-votes-to-end-legal-recognition-of-trans-people.

Walker, Shaun. 2020b. "Polish Parliament Delays Decision on New Abortion Restrictions." *Guardian* (International Edition). www.theguardian.com/world/2020/apr/16/polish-parliament-delays-decision-on-new-abortion-restrictions.

13 Writing Love Letters Across Borders

A Conversation on Indigenous-Centred Methodologies

Hema'ny Molina Vargas, Fernanda Olivares Molina, Camila Marambio, Nina Lykke, and Kharnita Mohamed

The aim of this interview-conversation is to reflect upon creative and indigenous-centred, feminist and decolonial methodologies. Our point of departure is a border-crossing, poetic co-writing practice: the article "Decolonising Mourning: World-Making with the Selk'nam People of Karokynka/Tierra del Fuego", co-authored by Hema'ny Molina Vargas, Camila Marambio and Nina Lykke (Vargas et al. 2020). *This article, and the conversation about it, marks a transnational feminist collaboration that has unfurled lovingly and transversally across borders of apparently incommensurable difference. Hema'ny is a poet-philosopher, with Selk'nam ancestry, from Karokynka (named Tierra del Fuego by the colonizers), Chile. Hema'ny and her daughter, Fernanda, who acts as translator here, are activists in the Selk'nam struggle for Indigenous rights and decolonized spaces for cultural revitalization. Camila is a Chilean curator, founder of the art/research/ecoactivist platform Ensayos*[1], *queerfeminist scholar and Selk'nam ally. Nina is a white, queerfeminist professor from the Global North, who also supports the Selk'nam cause. The interviewer, Kharnita, is a black Muslim feminist, who teaches anthropology at the University of Cape Town and grapples with the contradictions of living in post-apartheid South Africa. The interview-conversation took place online, and was conducted in a mixture of English and Spanish. The two bilingual participants (Fernanda and Camila) translated back and forth between the two languages, helping Kharnita and Nina, who do not speak Spanish, and Hema'ny, who does not speak English, to overcome language barriers. Afterwards, the full interview-conversation was transcribed, and the English parts were translated into Spanish, and the Spanish parts into English, to ensure that all participants, including those of us who only understand one of the languages, have had access to the full text when decisions were to be made about editing.*

Round of Presentations

Kharnita: I'm Kharnita. I'm an anthropologist, teaching anthropology, at the University of Cape Town. I'm in the process of finishing my PhD, which looks at the making of death, disability, and debility in settler colonial contexts. Lovely to meet you.

DOI: 10.4324/9781003378761-15

156   *Hema'ny Molina Vargas et al.*

Camila:	I'm Camila. Right now I'm in Stockholm as part of a post-doc fellowship. I'm looking forward to the conversation.
Hema'ny:	I'm Hema'ny, a native Selk'nam. I'm a writer, poet, craftswoman, a follower of ancestral knowledge, I can sing, I can dance. I do many things. However, what I like most in life is writing, and I think it's what I have the least time to do. . . . But, thanks to the chance that Camila is offering me, which I greatly appreciate, a door has been opened for me to start materializing a part of me that was disrupted and abandoned. The political issues, the Indigenous cultural issues, the Selk'nam cause, have been an important part of my life experience, but I haven't written about any of this before. So, a new chapter in my life has started, and now I'm taking time away from other things to write. Our first writing experience, when the three of us – Camila, Nina, and I – met at a workshop and co-wrote the article which is the point of departure for this conversation, was really enthralling. It was the first time I had lived this experience of being able to write and meet people who truly valued a skill that I had.
Fernanda:	I'm Fernanda. I'm acting as translator here. I'm Selk'nam, too, and live in Tierra del Fuego, trying to help with all the advances we're now experiencing regarding the Selk'nam people and our recognition. I don't write. I dance, but only at night, and I don't sing unless I'm drunk, and I'm almost never drunk. . . . Nice to meet you.
Nina:	I'm Nina. I'm retired. I enjoy being retired because it gives me lots of time for writing and doing the things I want to do in terms of writing poetry, writing about death, writing about changing the world. I'm honoured to have been part of this co-writing process together with you two, Camila and Hema'ny. I truly believe in loving transnational feminist decolonial solidarity, and I think that our co-writing was a manifestation of that. So, thank you very much for letting me be part of this community.

The Materialization of a Process of Border-Crossing Feminist Co-Writing

Kharnita:	My first question concerns the relationship between the three of you, Hema'ny, Camila, and Nina. How did you come to engage in this collaborative writing methodology?

Writing Love Letters Across Borders 157

| | Could you talk about the process of starting to co-write and co-publish this article for *Australian Feminist Studies*? |

Hema'ny: Well, I'll explain it the way I experienced it. I think it was different for each of us. Similar, but different. I was at home on a regular day, just doing stuff. I received a strange WhatsApp message from an unknown number that said: "Hello, I'm Camila. Is this the number of Hema'ny Molina?" I always respond to everyone. I don't like leaving people hanging, so I replied: "Yes, I'm indeed Hema'ny". And she said: "Can we talk?" "Yes". She called me on the phone, and we talked for about an hour. And we were on a roll, blah, blah, blah, and agreed to meet the following day. Camila told me about a workshop that was to be held at the University of Chile, a workshop that would be based, among other things, on the anthropologist Anne Chapman's work on the Selk'nam people[2] . . . and, of course, Camila encountered a barrier here, because: "I don't like Anne Chapman and I have lots of things against Anne Chapman". So it was like, phew! We arranged to meet the following day, and here Camila introduced me to Nina, who could not speak Spanish. So it became a funny meeting, because I was like "what did she say? what did she say? what did she say?" The workshop was going to be in English, and Camila and Nina invited me to it, which really surprised me a lot. I am used to doing things because I feel I have to do them, and because they come forward from within me, and I love what I do. But I never see how important my work can be for other people. I don't have that perspective.

So, they invite me to the workshop, and here I see that one of the requirements for the people who attend is to speak English, and I was the only person who didn't speak English. But then, everything got turned upside down, and it was all done in Spanish. I really saw how complicated it was for some people who didn't speak Spanish well, and, wow, I valued that a lot because I was the only one who couldn't say a word, had it continued in English. I also brought critical materials, and I felt that I tore apart some people's emotions who held the anthropologist Anne Chapman in high regard. I felt it as though I had shot down some people's plane. It was like "damn, what should I do?" It was an important experience for me. I've always given high priority to the visions and perspectives that come from my people and my Selk'nam culture, and I've experienced how official historiography,

158   *Hema'ny Molina Vargas et al.*

including the writings of Anne Chapman, have distorted all this. So, passing on my people's visions and perspectives to people who wanted to listen to them, and who valued them, was very intense. I even brought a recording of Selk'nam elder Abuela Lala, in which she scolded people who exploit and misuse our culture. It really had an impact on me how people at the workshop responded with intense interest to everything I told them, but I also saw how they started to feel bad about the ways in which they had looked at Anne Chapman's work before. One person even said: "I don't think I want to continue to think about Anne Chapman". I think these responses helped me to start being more tactful in the way that I said things, because I was really combative and tough that day. That's what I remember, and then Camila and Nina invited me to participate in this article co-writing process, which, at first, I found strange because I didn't know that kind of work, but it was also easy, right? I accepted, and the truth is that it was a very nice experience. That's it.

Nina: One thing to add about the workshop event at the University of Chile is that it was also a writing workshop, and we laid the foundations for our writing together there. As part of the poetic writing at the workshop, Hema'ny wrote a very beautiful poem. I just wanted to mention this.

Camila (in Spanish to Hema'ny):   Did you understand what Nina just added, Hema'ny? She points out that the event at the University of Chile was not only a workshop on Anne Chapman but also a writing workshop, and we were all encouraged to write poetic texts, and the text you wrote there was so touching and beautiful. The initial invitation to you to participate in the workshop was because you're a Selk'nam woman and president of the Selk'nam Corporation of Chile, and it was just and necessary to have you at a workshop that attempted to criticize Anne Chapman's work, and present problems surrounding her anthropological approach to Selk'nam culture. You clearly had to be the person at the forefront of that issue. But then your writing and your writing talent stood out so clearly, when we did that poetic writing exercize together. This made us want to also explore this space together with you.

Hema'ny: Oh, how nice, really, that you say this. And you know what? I'll tell you something. I don't even remember what I wrote. Because I never keep the things I write.

Camila (in English):	Yeah. Hema'ny writes like she talks, you know, with such ease. *(Camila continues in Spanish):* What I observe in you as a writer, Hema'ny, is that you write with such ease, you write like you breathe, very naturally. For some writers, me included, sometimes it's clumsy, but I can tell that in all the exercises we do together you produce texts with such spontaneity and sincerity . . . a Selk'nam thing, no doubt.
Kharnita:	Thank you for elaborating on how your methodology of co-writing came about. But, how was your relationship established in the first place? Camila, can you perhaps tell us about the process of finding Hema'ny? How did you come to this relationship where you have Hema'ny's phone number, and you're calling her and being so nice that she's talking to you for an hour and then comes to the workshop? There's a process prior to your meeting.
Camila (in English):	From the article in *Australian Feminist Studies*, you know a little bit about my engagement, my love of Tierra del Fuego, the ancestral land of Hema'ny and Fernanda, and how, from my very first travels there over 10 years ago, I felt the absence of Selk'nam culture. I felt uncomfortable with the official myth of Selk'nam extinction, but I didn't do much with that discomfort until much later. At first, I did something that I now see as rather traditional: I decided to go to the literature about the extinction, and that's how I arrived at Anne Chapman's work, and started to read between the lines there, saying "what is Anne Chapman saying, and what is she not saying? Where can I find more traces of Selk'nam survival?"

And when I met Nina, I started to tell her about my quest, and Nina, with all of her experience of queering texts and histories of all sorts, helped me to sit with that work. It became an important part of my PhD research and, out of that, was born this workshop. The first time that Nina and I gave the workshop was in Melbourne, Australia, where I did my PhD. We invited a group of women to a workshop there, and we asked them to help us think about the problem. We said to them: "Here are these texts by Anne Chapman representing the anthropological canon on the Selk'nam history of extinction. But the message they convey doesn't feel right. What's wrong with it?" We worked on this issue during the workshop in Australia and wanted to do so again later in Chile, when Nina visited me there. That's when it became very important for us that, when questioning the Chapman texts, and taking seriously the idea that what they say about Selk'nam culture and its extinction is a fallacy, then we had to find a Selk'nam person.

I had tried to google "Selk'nams today" before, without result. But now, again, I did a Google Search, and boop! an article from *Revista Paula* (Di Girolamo 2018), a women's fashion magazine, appears. This was in January 2019, and in the latest issue of the magazine there was an article, and a picture of Hema'ny and a couple of other people from the Selk'nam community, together with a short narrative telling their story. It said that Hema'ny was the president of this community, of the corporation that was fighting for their representation and rights. I copy-pasted her name, looked it up, and found a website where she was making available some soaps, shampoos, and other products that she makes with natural materials, and there was a telephone number. I took that telephone number and . . . No, first, I went to Nina, who was at my house. We were preparing to do the workshop a couple of days later, and we were really trying to make it into not just another academic experiment, but real in the sense that it would push us to the level of again having to really question the way in which the myth of Selk'nam extinction was operating in ourselves, as well. And Nina says: "We must get in touch with her". So I text Hema'ny, she responds, we talk for an hour and, like Hema'ny said: We hit it off.

And Hema'ny is so patient; she's such an amazing listener and such a critical mind, and she immediately engaged with the critical aspect of our work. We agreed to meet over coffee the next day in Santiago, and I believe that she trusted us, Nina and me, at that first meeting. Hema'ny probably felt something with her deep intuition, and she said: "Okay, I'll take part in the workshop", knowing that she was, as she said, kind of the odd one out. She didn't speak English, she was going to be there as a Selk'nam woman, and the rest of the participants were all academics . . . And Hema'ny took part in that workshop with so much integrity, pride, and courage, and then produced this incredible text and really schooled all of us regarding Anne Chapman's work and the myth of extinction it had conveyed – she schooled us in ways that were very much needed, so much needed.

From there, our friendship was born. That's my version of the story.

Writing Love Letters Across Borders   161

Fernanda (in English):	Can I add something? I think probably Hema'ny really trusted you on the phone, Camila, because otherwise she'd never have agreed to meet you. She's my Mom, and I've known her for 30 years. So, yeah, had she not trusted you on the phone, this conversation would probably never have happened.
Fernanda (in Spanish):	I'm telling them, Mom, beautiful Mommy, since I know you so well, that if you hadn't actually trusted them from the first moment, you wouldn't have met them in person after that hour-long phone call.
Hema'ny:	That's true.
Kharnita:	Nina, for you, how did this come about? We meet lots of people, but to place an in-depth commitment in a relationship that evolves over time is a lot.
Nina:	There's also a long story to Camila and me meeting . . .
Kharnita:	Please, tell that story. I think transnational feminism is fundamentally about relationships – relationality and committing to relations are crucial methodologies.
Nina:	Camila and I met through cancer. My lesbian life partner had died from cancer some years before, and I had been mourning her very strongly. Camila has had cancer, and we came to talk about this while we were both taking part in an evaluation of an artistic PhD, which was being defended in a very strange place in Stockholm, Sweden – an under-earthly place, a former nuclear reactor hall, now transformed into a performance space.

In this strange place, Camila and I started to compare notes on our existentially different experiences of cancer, Camila having had cancer in her own body, and I having been very close to my partner when she died from cancer. Out of these conversations grew a strong friendship, a loving friendship, due to which we committed ourselves to writing a book on our experiences with the horrors of cancer (Marambio and Lykke, Forthcoming), and how they can be translated into an in-depth ecological critique and resistance to the ways in which, for decades, carcinogens have been spread all over the world due to capitalist extractivism and the unsustainable chemicalization of production.

Out of this loving friendship, there also came an interest in Camila's PhD research, her passionate engagement with Tierra del Fuego, and her commitment to the cause of the Selk'nam people and their ancestral land. I have visited Camila in both Australia and Chile, and Camila has visited me in Denmark and Sweden. Camila is very

162 *Hema'ny Molina Vargas et al.*

good at engaging people all around the world in important causes, and through her I became more and more committed to Tierra del Fuego and the Selk'nam cause. So, it became politically important for me, too, to find ways to undo the myth of Selk'nam extinction, which all the anthropological sources insisted upon, with Anne Chapman's canonized work figuring prominently among them. So, I was as excited as Camila, when she told me about her phone conversation with Hema'ny.

I believe in the world-changing capacities of transnational, loving, passionate feminist relationships and in learning about other people's causes and doing all you can from where you are located to support them. So this is my entrance.

Creative Writing Practices and Ancestral Knowledges

Kharnita:

You have a commitment to creative writing practices, all three of you. I find this interesting because I'm a novelist (Mohamed 2018), and love reading beautiful writing. So I'd like to hear how creative practices figure in your methodological approach.

I also have a very specific question for Hema'ny. It came out of our conversation. One of my friends is a historian. She's been instrumental in having the South African Khoisan people recognised. In South Africa, we have a similar situation to the one you describe in Chile. It was also believed that our Indigenous first people had been erased. A lot of my friend's work has aimed at showing that the Khoisan people have not in fact disappeared. But she ended up leaving academia to make soap. She said that the soap is the theory. As a historian, she found so many old recipes in the archives, Khoisan recipes, among them recipes for soap-making. Against this background, she has made natural, organic, carbon-free soap. I'm intrigued by that, and I became especially intrigued by the connection when you told that you met Hema'ny through her soap-making. So I wanted to know more about this, in terms of creativity and connecting to the past through a material practice.

Camila (in English):

That's a wonderful observation. I'm sure Hema'ny will have the perfect explanation (Camila continues in Spanish): Speaking about your creativity, Hema'ny, Kharnita thought of a South African historian, a friend of hers, who,

Writing Love Letters Across Borders   163

like you, raised a similar cause in terms of recognition of her people, one of the Indigenous peoples of South Africa, the Khoisan people, who were also believed to have been made to disappear through the process of colonization. She did this through academic work, going over historical documents. She also studied economics and history to see how the decisions to erase the Khoisan people had come about, and how it had to do with the economic colonization of the country. She was successful in her work. But, at a certain point, she left academia, and instead dedicated herself to soap-making, based on old Khoisan recipes that she found in the historical archives.

So, when Kharnita heard that I found you on a website where you sold soaps, her head almost exploded and she started thinking: "Oh, look, how is it that Hema'ny understands creativity? She also sees it as associated with material life, such as soap-making, and to work that's not just writing and words, but instead has to do with a more natural, material knowledge". This South African historian says that the recipes she uses when making her soaps are ancestral recipes that were found in the historical documents. This is how she started to make these soaps. Nowadays she devotes all of her time to soap-making and says that this is her iterative political practice.

Hema'ny: Wow! Well! What can I say about that? Look, I don't really know how old I was when I realized that I wanted to write. It was when I was 11 or 12 years old. I was in love, head over heels in love with a boy, and I breathed, gave off, and even exuded verses for him through my very pores. That's when I realized my desire to write, and, due to that, I also started to write short stories and silly things that my grandfather listened to and that made me soar. I always had an imagination that made me soar, and then I started to write it down.

But, since I was very little, when a character I wrote about was, for example, expressing pain, I imagined what that pain would be like, but that wasn't enough. I would go out and twist a leg, fall down, make myself feel that pain, to write about it. I realized that, if I just imagined it, I wasn't content with what I wrote. I always liked writing about real things, transcribing things, real experiences. So I also started to listen to people and devote my time to transcribing what they told me, transforming it into stories by adding elements that made it fun. And that's how I slowly started.

164   *Hema'ny Molina Vargas et al.*

There was also a time when I was more devoted to poetry. But I always wrote many short stories, too. I've made a few attempts to write novels as well. I have three novels, actually. There they are. But it's paper. The only thing I've published is a small book of poems, *Madre Tierra* (Molina 2010). In the end, I paid for it and had it made in Argentina, because it was easier there than here in Chile. And then, I stepped away from all of that due to different circumstances in life. However, I took it up again when I met you, Camila and Nina.

Here in Santiago I was a member of the poets' and writers' organization, Chile País de Poetas, for many years. But I didn't like the atmosphere of people who think they do everything well and never listen to criticism. It was an atmosphere in which the men were in charge. They said my work was very good, but I didn't get along with them, and I left. But when I found you, Camila, and we started doing these writing exercizes, I felt very comfortable with all the exercizes because I had already done such things as a child.

My writing stems from real experiences. I can't talk about love if I haven't felt it. I can't talk about my culture if I don't live it. I can't talk about an experience I haven't gone through. So, that's how writing is for me.

Camila (in English):   Hema'ny and I have been writing a lot with "Ensayos" using all kinds of creative practices, and she keeps insisting on playful creative writing.

Kharnita: And the soap?

Camila (translating into Spanish):   Sí. What about the soap? And the relationship with wider creativity, Hema'ny? Do you have any thoughts? Perhaps you could also say something about your work with plants and herbs?

Hema'ny: Let's see, it's all a combination. . . . Despite many people saying to me things like: "Oh, you had four kids! How did you do it? How terrible. Poor woman". By all means, I really enjoyed my kids. . . . I really enjoyed this life with the kids. It was taking me to a more materially grounded place. Maybe I didn't write as much as before. But I still took notes, and I grew with my children. For example, when I started to participate in literary workshops, I went there with my four children. They always went with me. They were always involved, and I saw their reactions, and they felt happy. "Oh, my mom is on stage reading a poem". They applauded me.

There was a break in my writing work, insofar as there was a time when I was mostly working on things I had already written. I'd never shown it before. I was very shy, I was really scared of showing my poetry work, my stories, anything. I was really embarrassed to show it because I felt as though everyone would know me naked. That was the feeling. So, it was very hard for me to show my work. But my children accompanied me throughout my process of growing.

However, part of my growth was, indeed, also related to my knowledge of herbs. I started to work on this from the perspective of teaching people to be self-sufficient. This part of my creative work arose from the needs of the school where I sent my children. It was a very precarious, poor school. I started to instigate social initiatives as president of the parents' association. I set up different support groups to make the school self-sufficient. And there I realized other things that I hadn't realized before – things I knew, but didn't understand before.

I started to bring out this arsenal of information that I had from my own relatives. First, I tested it out at home, with my children, with my family. I was always my own guinea pig. If I made a shampoo, a soap, a new cream, I tried it out on myself first. If nothing happened to me, if my face didn't fall off, I started to share it. But it was very hard for me to sell. I was never good at selling the things I made.

But all of this blended into an experience that has been reflected in my writing. All the social processes that I experienced strengthened my personality. Believe it or not, before my children went to school, I couldn't speak to an audience. I would go all red like a tomato and everything would hide deep inside me. I was afraid of people. So all the changes came through my maternity, and I always told my children that, if they hadn't been with me, I would never have opened up. They've been a part of my process of growing, a very important part in terms of my maturing, my coming to believe in my own words, having enough self-confidence and wanting to open up a path for them as well. All of this has been replicated and reflected in my literary work.

But it's all been a combination – also discovering my culture as a Selk'nam, and realizing that everything I had been taught as a child was part of a culture that I didn't know existed. It isn't that I didn't know I was Selk'nam,

166   *Hema'ny Molina Vargas et al.*

but rather that I didn't know that all the habits I had were part of Selk'nam culture. I didn't have any references. Discovering that was also part of what made me feel much more secure. This is all reflected in everything I continue to do today.

Kharnita: That's fascinating. I think a lot of Indigenous methodologies are methodologies that aren't verbally theorized but are carried through in memory, and people don't necessarily realize that "actually I'm a pharmacist, or I'm a". I have so much I'd like to pick up on here, but time is running quickly.

Creative Writing as an Ethico-Political Opening Towards New Ontologies and Social Relationalities

Kharnita: So, Camila and Nina, what about your creative practices? I have a section in my novel where I say that creativity isn't a good thing in and of itself, it's really the politics that underly a creative practice that may produce a different kind of opening. . . . An affective opening that has the possibility to change how people feel or see the world. So, I'd be curious to know more about how you think about creativity as an ethico-political opening towards new social relationalities, like the one you've opened up through your co-writing.

Nina: Camila, you go first.

Camila: No, Nina, you.

Nina: Okay. This is a big question. But I'll tell you what the co-writing process meant to me. Since my partner died, my creative practice has been very much related to mourning and how it was for me to work through my mourning (Lykke 2022). This has included moving from a nostalgic mourning ("oh, I miss my partner") to the creation of a different ethics and politics of mourning, where my personal need to mourn my partner, and to have something to hold onto, has moved beyond this nostalgic focus on the loss of something that was in the past.

It has been important for me, through my poetry and narrative writing, to explore ways of getting in touch with my partner in the here and now, to develop a present and ongoing relationship. But, to do so, I had to rethink the ways in which both Christianity and modern science have left us without any tools other than useless religious images about immaterial souls in Heaven, or secular ideas

Writing Love Letters Across Borders   167

of death as annihilation of the subject, and hence equivalent to a vanishing into nothingness.

During this rethinking process, the collaboration with Hema'ny and Camila, and the co-writing of the article for *Australian Feminist Studies*, was really important to me, a boost, a confirmation: "Okay, you can speak to the dead!" For me, having grown up in a culture pervaded by Christian thought, and, in particular, by the secular worldview of mechanistic science, it was a revelation to think about relationships to the dead as really materially ongoing. . . . Like what Hema'ny just said about this material concreteness, when she writes that it's not that there's fiction here and reality there. The boundaries are totally dissolved between what we call fiction and what we call reality. These boundaries are, indeed, arbitrary, but they're experienced as very real by someone like me, who grew up with a worldview crafted by positivist, mechanistic science.

The Selk'nam philosophy that Hema'ny is living, articulating, and expressing is breaking down these boundaries between what is fiction and what is reality. This means, for example, that when, in our co-written article, Hema'ny writes letters to her dead great-grandmother, then I can feel in her text how the great-grandmother is really there, alive – Hema'ny is articulating an ongoing relationship between the living and the dead in that text.

This resonated so much, really so much, with the things I was trying to tease out myself in my poems, this ongoingness, this ongoing materially real relationship to the dead – in my case, to my dead life partner. I feel this relationship in the house where I lived with my partner. I feel it when I go to the place where her ashes are scattered; when I swim in the sea there, I feel that I'm together with her.

The co-writing with Hema'ny and Camila confirmed this material concreteness for me, which I felt so strongly, but still did not really dare to believe in as really real. What these creative practices, and co-writing, have done for me is to produce this kind of reality, which some modern Western aesthetic theory would call "fictional" – in the sense of being separated from life, from actual reality. What poetry can do is to somehow break down the boundaries between "real" and "not-real", and lead you into a world where these boundaries are dissolved. Co-writing with Camila and Hema'ny helped me to enter this

168 *Hema'ny Molina Vargas et al.*

world. It really confirmed something in me, and I think it resonates very much with this material concreteness that Hema'ny described.

Kharnita: The imaginary phenomenon, that's really deeply located in everyday reality. Yeah . . . I just want to hug you, actually.

. . . And for you, Camila?

Camila: Yeah, I feel the same, I want to hug you all. I very much understand my body as a creative site, and I'm alive and words move through me, and they move me. Chemicals, hormones, listening to all of us here. Listening to Fernanda translate her mother so eloquently, and Nina speak with such clarity about the dead and their presence, and always learning more about Hema'ny and being surprised by her humour, and your ability, Kharnita, to pick up exactly on the important parts of this conversation of wild women, it does so many things inside of me. And I feel so lucky to have found communities, specific women, who want to engage with the world of what can be sensed, a world that challenges ideas, but that feels like it's providing truths about where knowledge comes from. You mentioned, Kharnita, the way in which Indigenous methodologies provide evidence that we can derive knowledge from dreamspaces and from histories that are beyond our bodies, that appear in our bodies. And, for me, creative practice is working into that, really going in, into those feelings, looking for ways to touch them, to share them, to move them around, to make them available to others. The word "play" comes up here, and I love playing as an adult. Actually, I think I like it even better than I did as a kid.

So, this is what we do, we play all the time. When I met Nina, you know, she's got this incredible head of white hair, and she's one of the people who plays the most. You'd think, "oh, as you get older you become more realistic", but it's the opposite. Or at least Nina has become more available for all sorts of joyful excursions and mysterious attempts at things that are not yet known. Nina took her first dance workshop with me a couple of months ago at her house at the age of almost 73.

And, Hema'ny and I are constantly making up writing prompts. Fernanda, Hema'ny, and I are part of a Selk'nam language group. Fernanda and Hema'ny are teaching us the Selk'nam language, and we're creating it all together. I guess that what I want to reinforce is just that creative

Writing Love Letters Across Borders   169

practice can be anything. It's about being available for it, putting yourself in that place where some people would fear doing a dance workshop with dancers if you've never done it before. But no, you just go there, you just show up. Because that's what creativity is, showing up to the unknown and allowing the future to surprise you. I've been thinking about something constantly these past few weeks, which is to never underestimate the future. Like this little cat tail that appeared behind Fernanda. What is that?

Fernanda: Yeah, he's Floki. Floki is my baby, he's two years old.

Kharnita: Something that I felt coming through very strongly in the piece that you co-wrote is that it feels like an attempt to find language across spaces of almost incommunicability, but of course you are communicating. But it feels like, in some ways, you're all trying to speak across terrain, where a particular kind of responsiveness is not possible, or rather where a secular rationality would assume that responsiveness is impossible. But of course there is a responsiveness, and most de-colonial, postcolonial, or Black feminist theorists have found ways of creating responsiveness here. I'm thinking, for example, about what Black feminist historian Saidiya Hartman (2007) did with critical fabulation. How do you speak to a history in which people have been silenced and make that history? You're all attempting to speak to the past, despite attempts to erase those worlds or states of being, through the practice of the imagination.

Final Words on the Role of Anthropology and Anthropologists

Kharnita: A last question. It struck me that the rebuke of the anthropologists, this Anne Chapman, in particular, is actually what brought you together. You might say that the moment of your coming together would not have been possible without the ethnographic archive. What do you think of this? It's a big and complex question. We could discuss it at length, but we don't have much time left, so feel free to choose any part of it.

Hema'ny: Well, firstly, I don't feel that I have to focus my work on erasing what Anne Chapman did. I'm always very respectful about that. I don't agree with many things in her work, but I prefer to say that what she said about Selk'nam history isn't wrong, it's incomplete. My work focuses on trying, through the many small cracks in Chapman's work, to demonstrate that information is missing, that there's a gap in her explanation, and you can prove that it's different. Based on that, I try to demonstrate that the history she told isn't complete, and I think this has given me results, not only with Anne Chapman's work but also with that of Martin Gusinde (1931), the other famous anthropologist who studied the Selk'nam and contributed to the myth of our extinction. However, in one way or another, you have to perform the task of reading many of their books to realize that they contradict themselves.

So, it's about taking advantage of all the cracks to demonstrate that history isn't complete and that the part that's missing is the one that, in that moment perhaps due to responsibility to a purist trend, was cherished not only by Chapman but by all the anthropologists at that time who denied miscegenation. They looked for purity. But, since then, it's been demonstrated that blood purism doesn't exist. This has led me to look for the cracks to demonstrate that we mestizas are entitled to full rights.

Secondly, though, I think we've focused a lot on anthropology's past, and that's important. But I also think it's important to highlight the changes that anthropology has undergone, and to acknowledge that many contemporary historians and anthropologists themselves take a completely different approach. For example, one of the people I trust the most nowadays in my circle of trusted people is an anthropologist, the person who has been leading the study with us, with the Selk'nam community in Chile, for six years now. So, although it's true that anthropologists and historians sealed the word "extinction" into the literature and history of Chile, nowadays they themselves are the ones who are opening the door, turning around, and supporting us in our work. I'd like to highlight this as well.

Notes

1 https://ensayostierradelfuego.net/
2 North American-French scholar Anne Chapman (1922–2010) and Austrian priest Martin Gusinde (1886–1969) contributed to the construction of the Selk'nam people, culture, and language as having become "extinct" in the 20th century, basing their scholarly writings on their discipline's (classic anthropology's) conceptualization of cultural "purity", which did not recognize mestiza existence (Gusinde 1931; Chapman and Montés de Gonzalés 1977; Chapman 2002a, 2002b).

References

Chapman, Anne. 2002a. *Hain: Initiation Ceremony of the Selknam of Tierra del Fuego*. Buenos Aires: Zagier & Urruty.

Chapman, Anne. 2002b. *End of a World: The Selknam of Tierra del Fuego*. Buenos Aires: Zagie & Urruty.

Chapman, Anne, and Ana Montés de Gonzalés. 1977. *The Ona People: Life and Death on Tierra del Fuego* (Film). San Francisco, CA: Kanopy Streaming.

Di Girolamo, Greta. 2018. "Ser selknam en el Siglo XXI." [To be Selk'nam in the 21st Century]. *Revista Paula*, November 20. Accessed February 14, 2019. www.latercera.com/paula/selknam-siglo-xxi/.

Gusinde, Martin. 2010/1931. Die Feuerlandindianer. Ergebnisse meiner vier Forschungsreisen. Band. 1. Die Selk'nam. [*The Indians of the Land of Fire: Results From My Four Research Journeys. Volume I. The Selk'nam*]. Mödling Bei Wien: Verlag der Internationalen Zeitschrift Anthropos, Unveränderter Faksimileprint.

Hartman, Saidiya. 2007. *Lose Your Mother: A Journey Along the Atlantic Slave Route*. New York, NY: Farrar, Straus and Giroux.

Lykke, Nina. 2022. *Vibrant Death: A Posthuman Phenomenology of Mourning*. London: Bloomsbury.

Lykke, Nina, and Camila Marambio. Forthcoming. *Sandcastles. A Queerfemme Proposition on Cancer Ecologies*. Manuscript in Preparation.

Mohamed, Kharnita. 2018. *Called to Song: A Novel*. Cape Town: Kwela Books.

Molina, Hema'ny. 2010. *Madre Tierra* [Mother Earth]. Buenos Aires: Mis Escritos.

Vargas, Hema'ny Molina, Camila Marambio, and Nina Lykke. 2020. "Decolonising Mourning: World-Making With the Selk'nam People of Karokynka/Tierra del Fuego." *Australian Feminist Studies* 35 (104): 186–201.

Part III

Intrepid Journeys (On the Epistemic Implications of Geopolitical Situatedness)

Swati Arora, Nina Lykke, and Kharnita Mohamed

Part III clusters together chapters which invite reflections on the implications of a pluriversality of geopolitically different epistemic points of departure in the volume's ongoing conversations between transnational, decolonial, and feminist approaches. The authors approach these conversations from "politics of location" (Rich 1986) which are shaped by the book's overall commitment to investigating meaning-making along the lines of Global North/South, and Global East/West power formations, while firmly rejecting any hegemonic, universal, definitive, and simplistic modes of operation of these axes. Insisting instead on askew dimensions and pluriversality, the contributors undertake "intrepid journeys" (Naidoo, this volume) to (self-)reflexively and critically scrutinize the geopolitics of situated knowledge production. The chapters come together in a cross-national conversation, but they do not seek a shared universal truth about the intersections of transnational, decolonial, and intersectional feminisms. What materializes in the sequence of chapters is rather a series of displacements, which, taken together, move readers through specifically embodied geopolitical locations, critiques, self-reflections, and vantage points in the Global South, North, East, and West.

In Chapter 14, *#MeToo Through a Decolonial Feminist Lens: Critical Reflections on Transnational Online Activism Against Sexual Violence*, Tigist Shewarega Hussen and Tamara Shefer bring our attention to the stakes when local digital movements against sexual violence are displaced to privilege a transnational hashtag such as #MeToo. This chapter is in conversation with debates on the politics of location and the necessity for transversal politics which centre local situations to prevent the universalization of Northern conditions (Yuval-Davis 1999). Focused on South Africa as emblematic of the Global South, the authors argue that when local activists attach their causes to global digital movements such as #MeToo to benefit from the visibility offered by a viral hashtag, they produce an "uberization of transnational activist feminism" which can entail multiple erasures of historicity. Transnational digital movements, even where intersectionality is incorporated as a feature of digital virality, undermine local digital activism, upstage local hashtags, and do not involve reciprocal movements of knowledge from the Global South to

DOI: 10.4324/9781003378761-16

174   *Swati Arora, Nina Lykke, and Kharnita Mohamed*

the Global North. Moreover, viral hashtags like #MeToo that become inscribed as epochal contain modalities of amnesia and epistemicide that are already entangled with relations of power in the Global North, such as race/class dynamics, before they are even taken up by local activists in the Global South. This chapter joins what has become an extensive literature in and for the Global South about the epistemic effects of privileging the Global North as an epistemic centre, through which we read a chronicity of digital activism on sexual violence.

Chapter 15, *Translocality: A Decolonial Take on Feminist Strategies*, by Caroline Betemps, shifts the perspective from troubled South–North interactions to the potentials and problems of South–South dialogues. In a personal essay that reflects upon experiences from a residency as visiting PhD student at the University of the Western Cape and from engagements in the networking of the project that led to this book, Betemps discusses South–South relations and translocality (Alvarez et al. 2014). Their starting point is the relations between the colonial and capitalist histories of Cape Town and the South Brazilian region in which they grew up as a descendant of poor white immigrants – "immigrants-turned-colonizers [settlers]" (Ferreira da Silva 2019: 174), that is, poor Europeans who, at the end of the 19th century, went to Brazil and other parts of Abya Yala as small farmers and cheap labourers, while also materializing a eugenic move of whitening the population after centuries of colonial oppression. Prompted by these reflections, also on their own status as migrant in contemporary Europe, and the question by a fellow PhD student from the University of the Western Cape – as to why their PhD project does not engage more with South–South relations – Betemps emphasizes the usefulness of the notion of "translocality" (Alvarez et al. 2014). They argue that this concept, rather than "transnational" which, according to Betemps, cannot throw off its neoliberal genealogies, can grasp the complex relations of belonging and (dis)identifications across class, race, gender and sexual dissidence, geopolitical locatedness, migration status, colonial and capitalist histories that need to be thought through in order to foster non-hierarchical feminist conversations and cross-border coalitions on decolonizing grounds.

Moving the vantage point to the Middle East, or West Asia, and to the powerful political signifier "Queer", Chapter 16, *Re-Routing the Sexual: A Regional and Relational Lens in Theorizing Sexuality in the Middle East (West Asia)*, by Adriana Qubaiova, offers a critique of the epistemic dilemmas that occur when privileging Queer Theory emanating from the Global North, and the United States, in particular, in attempts to understand non-normative sexualities, practices and identities in the Middle East/West Asia. Qubaiova begins with the dilemma that, on the one hand, the theorizing of sexualities, including non-normative ones, carries Global North imperial legacies of conquest, travel and the shaping of Orientalist imaginaries. On the other hand, as a queer feminist scholar from the West Asian region, passionately committed to non-normative sexual politics, Qubaiova states that she "cannot ignore the relevance of Queer Theory and sexuality studies for analysing the region's contemporary and lived realities" (Qubaiova, this volume). In West Asia, Queer Theory in conversation with local struggles has inspired activism and

Intrepid Journeys (On the Epistemic Implications of Geopolitical... 175

struggles for LGBT rights. This dilemma has created binary tensions between critical sexuality scholars in the region. However, Qubaiova offers a third way between the binaries and a more commensurable scalar dimension. Drawing on Arondekar and Patel's (2016) reflections on a queering of area studies (see Chapter 1, this volume), she demonstrates how non-normative sexual practices and lived experiences in West Asia, analysed on a regional, relational basis rather than through comparisons with the United States, offer expanded ontological dimensions. Regionalism decentres the Global North and opens up potent epistemic avenues for understanding local hegemonies and struggles against them.

Chapter 17, *Beautiful Diversity? Diversity Rhetoric, Ethnicized Visions, and Nesting Post-Soviet Hegemonies in the Multimedia Project The Ethnic Origins of Beauty* (EOB) by Dinara Yangeldina, continues the intrepid, epistemic journey of the previous chapters. Yangeldina complicates the volume's transnational feminist conversation through a focus on postsocialist difference, showing how locations in post-Soviet spaces displace agendas and frameworks. This chapter is a critical reflection on post-Soviet hegemonies and Russian imperial legacies as articulated through an ethnically essentializing and culturally racializing version of the female beauty myth. EOB, the focus of Yangeldina's analysis, is a post-Soviet multimedia project that claims to represent the ethnic diversity of the entire world through ethnically diverse representations of women's beauty, while glossing over local Russian and post-Soviet hegemonies, imperialist legacies, privileging of whiteness and Russianness, and orientalist constructions of people from the former Soviet republics of the East and South. Taking EOB as an example, Yangeldina critically examines relations of power within post-Soviet imaginary constructions of ethnicity and female beauty. She demonstrates how EOB's rhetoric of global diversity built on visuality reinforces folkloristic difference, and presents ethnicities as fixed and homogenized entities, stereotypically portrayed using female faces as icons. She identifies racialization, ethnic hierarchies, and hegemonic language politics as three sites of contention that dismantle the rhetoric of beautiful diversity advanced by EOB as rooted within a hegemonic Russian nation-building project. Last but not least, Yangeldina also pinpoints how, to some extent, EOB can be read against the grain, identifying cracks and disruptions in the project's glossy surface, when, for example, interviewees articulate painful encounters with racism.

With health and biopolitics as its pivot, Chapter 18, *Reducing Costs While Optimizing Health? Transnational Feminist Engagement With Personalized Medicine*, by Maria Temmes, critically examines a reconfiguration of the Global North/South divide, as it has been conceptualized from Western-centric, postcolonial vantage points as the divide between so-called "developed" and "developing" countries. Drawing on postcolonial feminist critic Chandra Mohanty's reconceptualizing of this divide as one between "One-Third/Two-Thirds Worlds" (Mohanty 2003: 527), which emphasizes the existence of people in precarious, marginalized, and othered situations all over the globe, Temmes focuses on personalized medicine as it is debated in two specific countries, one located in the Global North: Finland, and one in the Global South: Bangladesh. A superficial comparison seems to identify these

176 *Swati Arora, Nina Lykke, and Kharnita Mohamed*

countries as fitting the bill of an abstracted North/South divide. However, through an analysis of the establishing of biobanks and biomedical research in the two countries, the author critically assesses the statement that personalized medicine can lead to "cost-effective" and equitable healthcare planning globally. Calling for a cross-cutting approach in line with Mohanty's framework, she highlights the ways in which the development of personalized medicine is governed by capitalist market and biopolitical logics, and contributes increasingly to foregrounding individuals' responsibility for their own health in both countries, at the expense of societal and transnational actions against social inequalities in healthcare provision and exposure to environmental pollution.

In Chapter 19, *The Meanings of Chronopolitics and Temporal Awareness in Feminist Ethnographic Research*, by Christine M. Jacobsen and Marry-Anne Karlsen, the epistemic focus is again the Global North/Global South divide. Here, it is approached through a self-reflexive study of chronopolitics, the politics of time, as a marker of social inequalities between ethnographic researchers of the Global North and irregularized migrants from the Global South. With a starting point in ethnographic debates on temporal othering and coevalness, the co-authors reflect on the chronopolitics involved in their feminist ethnographic research on irregularized migrants in Norway and France. In line with the volume's overall emphasis on the need to ground transnational feminist analysis in specific and situated perspectives, this chapter argues that chronopolitics and geopolitics should be considered as entangled; the politics of location has always both temporal and spatial dimensions. Drawing on their fieldwork, the authors reflect upon their positioning as feminist anthropologists with Norwegian citizenship and its relational constituting of the spatiotemporal encounters with their interlocutors, irregularized migrants from Ethiopia and Niger, within intersecting nationalist, racialized, and gendered power structures. Recognizing the interdependency of differentially lived time, and considering how time, as space, is an always-already intersecting marker of social difference that produces othering, the authors argue for the need to develop greater awareness of how feminist knowledge production about ethnographic encounters is situated not only in uneven geopolitical terrains but also within highly powerful politics of time.

Chapter 20, *Disrupting the Colonial Gaze: Towards Alternative Sexual Justice Engagements With Young People in South Africa*, continues the reflections upon temporalities, but shifts the vantage point back to the Global South. Tamara Shefer analyses the body of research on sexual practices in the South African context during the now almost 30 years of the post-Apartheid period, particularly as directed at young people, through a post/decolonial, transnational feminist lens. Research on young people's sexualities in South Africa has been spurred on over the last few decades by the international "industry" of HIV reproductive health research and global emphases on HIV and gender-based violence (GBV). Shefer critiques this body of work to argue that it has tended to reinstate the hierarchies of power, authority and privilege endemic in colonialist, and patriarchal scholarly traditions. She writes that contemporary scholarship has been directed by what

Intrepid Journeys (On the Epistemic Implications of Geopolitical... 177

Sedgwick (2003) called "paranoid readings", which have privileged a particular academic critique, a combative, masculinist, militarized engagement with seeking power. Instead, Shefer suggests the importance of "reparative readings" (Sedgwick 2003), aiming towards efforts to achieve an ethical, just, non-extractive, and non-representational transnational intersectional feminist research praxis. A feminist ethics and politics of care and relationality, inspired by fruitful entanglements of decolonial, feminist and queer art, activism, and scholarship, is central to ethical transnational feminist scholarship, if it is engaged to disrupt the wider habits of colonial, patriarchal scholarly research practices and pedagogies.

The theme of care and relationality is also key to the unfolding of critical-affirmative, Global South feminist perspectives, as they are discussed in relation to the notion of "happiness" in Chapter 21, *Studying Happiness in Postcolonial and Post-Apartheid South Africa: Theoretical and Methodological Considerations* by Carmine Rustin. Embedding her work in conventional research methods, but with an important Black Feminist twist, Rustin suggests that a combination of qualitative and quantitative data is needed in order to effectively frame critiques of intersecting inequalities from Global South perspectives. With "happiness" as her key parameter, Rustin's research examines how intersections of gender, race, and class continue to shape inequalities between women in postcolonial and post-Apartheid South Africa. The qualitative part of the study highlights how different groups of South African women speak about happiness in their everyday lives, showing how some of the interviewees, in particular, the feminist activists among them, challenge individualistic Global-North-centred understandings. The quantitative part of the study complements the qualitative work with statistical data, which is used to map intersectional differences and inequalities. In line with the volume's overall conceptual discussions, Rustin reflects upon the values that the methodologies and methods employed in the study, hold for intersectional feminist research that is firmly situated in postcolonial, Global South epistemologies and epistemes.

In Chapter 22, *Decolonization, the University and Transnational Solidarities: A Conversation*, Redi Koobak and Nina Lykke interview Swati Arora. The conversation pivots around Arora's engagement in the ongoing Decolonize the University Movement in India, South Africa, and the UK, and addresses the ways in which she translates her situated transnational commitments into research, writing, and pedagogy in Performance Studies. Arora shares her thoughts on transnational and decolonial feminisms, which are informed by embodied experiences of inhabiting a multiplicity of different geopolitical locations in the Global South (Delhi and Cape Town) and the Global North (Amsterdam and London). She interweaves descriptions of activist practices and performances with theoretical reflections, underscoring how her transnational trajectory and overlapping situatednesses have informed her awareness of epistemic differences, silences, and erasures. She argues for a reconsideration of decolonization as a pluriversal activity that "requires a continuous commitment" (Arora 2021: 8) to social and epistemic justice and embodied challenges to the hegemonic colonial, racist, casteist, ableist knowledge-building practices, embedded in these university systems. Deploying the trickster-like

178 *Swati Arora, Nina Lykke, and Kharnita Mohamed*

feminist practice of translation as a starting point for pluriversal dialogues, Arora moves away from the monologic of universality, while sharing insights from her forthcoming book on performance cultures in Delhi, from a manifesto she wrote to decentre Theatre and Performance Studies (Arora 2021), and from her research on a feminist performance, *Walk* (Arora 2020), which engaged with translation as an act of transnational solidarity.

The epistemic journeys undertaken in the chapters of Part III bring us through a series of displacements between #MeToo in Post-Apartheid South Africa, troubled translocal, South-North and South–South relations, Queer politics in West Asia, an ethnicized beauty myth in post-Soviet Russia, capitalist biopolitics in Finland and Bangladesh, irregularized migrants from Ethiopia and Niger in Norway and France, young people's sexualities as well as differently located women's experience of "happiness" in South Africa, and, finally, arts activism in Delhi, Cape Town and London. The geopolitical and epistemic displacements and relationalites which are entailed in all of this reflect the volume's overall commitment to conversations between transnational, intersectional, and decolonial feminist approaches along the lines of Global South/North and Global East/West vectors. Each in their different ways, the contributors take into account the geopolitical configurations of power emanating from these vectors and reflect upon the ways in which they mould their specific topic and positionality to undertake research ethically. But, each from their specific situatedness, the authors also seek out possibilities for thinking critically and relationally across the borders of these crude vectors and beyond the horizon of a world split into nation-states. In this way, they implicitly explore what care might look like in a world where borders and hierarchies become undone. Deploying decolonial, intersectional and transnational feminist critiques of the extractive, reductive, individualizing, and universalizing tendencies of scholarship emerging from within privileged academic institutions, which either silence or erase minoritarian bodies, the authors offer meticulously thought-through geopolitical situatedness as an alternative mode of doing ethico-political scholarship, which can inspire a moving together in difference, on intrepid journeys towards justice-to-come.

References

Alvarez, Sonia E., Claudia de Lima Costa, Norma Klahn, and Millie Thayer (eds.). 2014. *Translocalities/Translocalidades: Feminist Politics of Translation in the Latin/a Américas*. Durham, NC: Duke University Press.

Arondekar, Anjali, and Greta Patel. 2016. "Area Impossible: Notes Toward an Introduction." *GLQ: A Journal of Lesbian and Gay Studies* 22 (2): 151–71.

Arora, Swati. 2020. "Walk in India and South Africa: Notes Towards a Decolonial and Transnational Feminist Politics." *South African Theatre Journal* 33 (1): 14–33.

Arora, Swati. 2021. "A Manifesto to Decentre Theatre and Performance Studies." *Studies in Theatre and Performance* 41 (1): 12–20.

Ferreira da Silva, Denise. 2019. *Unpayable Debt: Coloniality, Raciality, and Global Capitalism from a Black Feminist "Poethical" Perspective*. Berlin: Sternberg Press.

Mohanty, Chandra T. 2003. *Feminism Without Borders: Decolonizing Theory, Practicing Solidarity*. Durham, NC: Duke University Press.

Rich, Adrienne. 1986. "Notes Toward a Politics of Location." In *Blood, Bread and Poetry: Selected Prose 1978–1985*, edited by Adrienne Rich, 210–33. London and New York, NY: Virago and Norton.

Sedgwick, E. K. 2003. *Touching Feeling: Affect, Pedagogy, Performativity*. Durham, NC and London: Duke University Press.

Yuval-Davis, Nira. 1999. "What Is 'Transversal Politics'?" *Soundings* 12: 94–8.

14 #MeToo Through a Decolonial Feminist Lens

Critical Reflections on Transnational Online Activism Against Sexual Violence

Tigist Shewarega Hussen, and Tamara Shefer

While gender justice has been a key concern in post-1994 democratic South Africa, the country remains characterized by high rates of gender and sexual violence, homophobic violence, and sexism and racism at multiple levels of society.[1] The entanglement of sexual violence with systemic violence embedded in centuries of colonization and decades of apartheid has been increasingly noted (Gqola 2015; Boonzaier 2017; Ratele 2013).

While political and community action against sexual and gender violence in South Africa is by no means new, there has recently been a proliferation of activism, art, and performance specifically focused on sexual violence against women (Gouws 2017, 2018; Hussen 2018; Xaba 2017), which has deployed an intersectional, decolonial, and queer discourse (Disemelo 2019; Pather and Boulle 2019; Shefer 2019). Student protests beginning in early 2015 have played an important role in energizing local feminist struggles. Within the larger framework of student and public protest, a feminist and queer understanding of systems of oppression is key to the decolonial struggle. Examples include the activism against sexual violence within the Fallist movement, and ongoing intersectional and decolonial queer activism on university campuses and elsewhere (Kessi and Boonzaier 2015; Gouws 2017, 2018; Hussen 2018; Shefer 2018; Xaba 2017). The words of the trans collective in their framing narrative are a powerful example here:

> An intersectional approach to our blackness takes into account that we are not only defined by our blackness, but that some of us are also defined by our gender, our sexuality, our able-bodiedness, our mental health, and our class, among other things. We all have certain oppressions and certain privileges and this must inform our organising so that we do not silence groups among us, and so that no one should have to choose between their struggles. Our movement endeavours to make this a reality in our struggle for decolonisation.
>
> (UCT The Trans Collective 2016: n/p)

Over the last few years, student and broader community mobilization against sexual violence has grown, with events, marches, and online and media-based interventions, including #RUReferenceList, #RapeMustFall, and #NakedProtest. The more recent #TotalShutdown marches against sexual violence took place throughout the country and were mobilized by various communities outside the student movement and academic institutions.

In the highly raced South African context, where feminist discourses have been strongly associated with whiteness, middle-classness, and the Global North (Dosekun 2007; Gouws 2016), it is notable that young Black women and trans people have been particularly active in leading sexual and gender justice struggles within the decolonial movement (Gouws 2016, 2017; Omarjee 2018; Xaba 2017). It is also worthy of note that the very naming of these movements and activist events within the #hashtag format is illustrative of the central role of online strategic engagements (Hussen 2018).

While local movements benefited from and were supported by global trends and models of online mobilizations, it is not clear whether there is a relationship of causality or determination between them. Certainly, online mobilization has accompanied and strengthened material embodied activism, and some campaigns have relied on the internet not only for advocacy but also for communication and recruitment relating to planned activist events. At the same time, #MeToo has been making waves in South Africa, specifically within ruling-class white contexts. The most well-known case has been the calling out of top South African sports administrator Danny Jordaan by Jennifer Ferguson, who is celebrated as both a musician and a left-wing politician (Ferguson 2017).

During the wave of #MeToo, Ferguson wrote in great detail in her blog, notably from a Northern context where she currently lives and 24 years later, about how she was raped by her former colleague Jordaan. There are also some recent examples of young South Africans engaging in #MeToo-movement of naming and shaming, for example, at the Universities of Stellenbosch and the Western Cape in the last few years. Yet, despite not being taken up by many local South Africans as a primary vehicle for activism against sexual violence, it seems that #MeToo is currently viewed as the authoritative framework for activism against sexual violence. It has become commonplace to hear South African feminists say "in the era of #MeToo", or "in the wake of the #MeToo moment" as a clear demarcation of a historical period.

The tendency to reinstate the authority of the North/West is deeply connected to recalcitrant and inherent colonial mind-sets and power structures. This chapter argues that the power embedded in #MeToo as a "global" and transnational movement might threaten to erase the histories of local contemporary activist movements. Even though it is commonly understood that the #MeToo movement built its feminist politics on pre-existing feminist activism and scholarly work, its hypervisibility within the global arena makes it appear exceptional and novel. Thus, we critically reflect on the ways in which such emphases may serve to erase, undermine, and weaken local grassroots feminist movements in the Global South.

#MeToo Through a Decolonial Feminist Lens 183

To this end, this chapter foregrounds a "politics of location" as a structural and discursive basis for unravelling the power dynamics that can harm the transversal politics upon which contemporary transnational feminist movement-building and solidarity strategies attempt to build: heterogeneous yet opening up an equal and reciprocal knowledge transfer (Yuval-Davis 1999). We draw on decolonial feminist critique, which has identified and resisted the dominance of Northern/Western authorities on knowledge that have represented global Southern women as submissive, passive, and always already victims to be "saved" (Mohanty 1984; Spivak 1988). Within this critical framework, we explore how the neoliberal capitalist shaping of #MeToo furthers the dominant representations of the Global North as an "expert" in movement-building, advocacy, and the marketization of gender equality.

In particular, we are concerned with the way in which the dynamics of the movement have tended to reflect and reinstate global power inequalities, resulting in diminishing knowledge transfer from the South to the North so that histories of Southern-led movements become obfuscated. Consequently, African and global Southern women's struggles and knowledges are erased from the local and global public imaginary and from African feminists' collective memory. As feminist scholars located in South Africa, we are committed to a critical and decolonial feminist project that seeks to identify "new tools" towards an ethical and social justice scholarship. We suggest that, as a global movement, #MeToo offers a space to interrogate the current politics of transnational feminist scholarship across temporal and spatial inequalities. Thinking about how the movement has been deployed across multiple sites provides a valuable optic for assessing how contemporary transnational feminist meaning-making might repeat colonial logics of knowledge-making, and creates possibilities for making a difference in understanding and praxis.

Building #MeToo Moments on Stories of "The Other"

The #MeToo moment is nothing if not viral, drawing in millions and circulating around the globe. How should we understand these circulations in relation to the politics of location that frame feminisms around the world?

(Lukose 2018: 45)

The #MeToo campaign has been actively running on the internet since 24 October 2017. In recent history, this movement is by far the longest-lasting feminist form of digital activism. Most of the articles we have come across (Mendes et al. 2018; Onwuachi-Willig 2018; Gill and Orgad 2018; Nathaniel 2019) refer to the sexual assault allegations made by actress Alyssa Milano against Hollywood producer Harvey Weinstein as "the beginning" of the #MeToo Twitter trend and campaign. These scholars acknowledge the twist around "who started me too campaign first?" by stating the story of the African American women's rights activist Tarana Burke,

184 *Tigist Shewarega Hussen, and Tamara Shefer*

who created the phrase "Me Too" in 2006. But many have not dwelled on this. This brief and superficial naming of Tarana Burke deprives readers of the knowledge that her activism also primarily took place on a digital platform. In fact, she might have been one of the first feminist digital activists to use social media platforms creatively. Wolfe states that "a black woman, Tarana Burke started the Me Too movement over a decade ago in 2006 on MySpace, where she had created a page to enable 'empowerment through empathy' for survivors of sexual assault and abuse" (2018: 2). Although MySpace has been phased out, at the time it was one of the most popular social networking spaces.

Such an erasure of contextual reality should have been a signal to observe how #MeToo operates through and benefits from a politics of location. Instead, scholars simply report the #MeToo Twitter trend as "newly" founded activism by Alyssa Milano, which managed to attract 12 million tweets within 24 hours of its launch. This begs the question of why "Burke had never received anywhere near the same level of support that white feminists like Milano received from the general public" (Onwuachi-Willig 2018: 106). Perhaps the support of #MeToo by Tarana Burke herself might have distracted critical analysts from focusing their energies on the politics of the movement or narratives of its historical roots. However, as far as the politics of digital feminist activism is concerned, the missed opportunity here is situating the 2006 attempt on MySpace within the broader historical context. Perhaps comparing where it began and where #MeToo is at present could open up a more nuanced understanding of how feminist digital activism has developed to deploy multiple spaces for social change.

More recently, despite initial obsessive and impulsive support, critiques of #MeToo have surfaced regarding its political impact and multiple shortcomings. First, digital spaces, specifically hashtag activisms on social media platforms, have become a regular domain for protest, movement-building, and solidarity around the world. Many scholars (Castells 2015; Bonilla and Rosa 2015; Wolfe 2018; Gill and Orgad 2018; Mendes et al. 2018; Hearn 2018) acknowledge that "hashtag activism" is the most popular digital galvanizing strategy, especially among feminist activists. The hashtag symbol # is used to create an imaginary of community, a platform for networking and a collective response. However, as is true of other digital activisms, #MeToo was criticized for representing the lived experience of sexual violence only among those who are connected to the internet and various social media platforms. In relation to this, Raiva and Sariola's (2018: 13) critical insight on the digital subject is instructive:

> From a point where the digital formed one increasingly important part of the political landscape, of the materiality of political action, and political subjectivity, in the aftermath of the #metoo movement, we see what might be considered the mechanism of enclosure – whereby rather than being one part of the landscape, the digital becomes *the* landscape itself. Here we have a situation where politics is contained within the digital, and the only political subject that remains legible is the digital subject. The affect and intimacy of embodied collective action is not simply diminished in its significance

#MeToo Through a Decolonial Feminist Lens   185

– it is evicted from the newly sequestered realm of the political itself. With this comes the fact that the conditions of political subjectivity in the digital is overdetermined by the logics of the digital – of which there are many elements.

The #MeToo movement does not represent those who are not connected to the digital world; those who do not have access to technology; those who live under social, religious, and/or cultural laws that ban speaking out against sexual assault and rape culture on social media or in public spaces. Yet the movement took advantage of the culture of hashtagging on Twitter. Once it had gained massive popularity, it expanded to other social media platforms, like Instagram and Facebook, all of which are more accessible to a small group of relatively privileged women across intersecting levels of class, geopolitical, cultural, religious, age, and other locations, who have the necessary resources, technological and otherwise, including a personal sense of confidence, agency, and safety. Notably, Statistics South Africa (2018) report that only 10.4 percent of South Africans have an internet connection in their home. While there is a need to recognize and affirm the role of this digital feminist activism, "key ideas of the movement, and means of mobilisation . . . [s]olidarity and sense of unity were at stake" (Raiva and Sariola 2018: 11).

Second, since the movement was re/initiated by a white, upper-class woman from Hollywood, the movement un/intentionally centred on stories of sexual violence against cis-heterosexual, white, upper-class women in the Global North. Therefore, #MeToo has been widely criticized for excluding stories of women of colour, poor women, queer individuals, and trans communities in the movement, thus reproducing heteronormativity and other forms of privilege. For example, Gill and Orgad (2018: 1319) write:

> #MeToo promotes an understanding of sexual gendered violence as primarily experienced through a binary between men and women, thus undermining broader coalitions of those facing harassment in the face of masculinist dominance, including cis-women, trans* men and women and gender non-conforming subjects and queer subjects of colour.

Beyond the absence of an intersectional feminist approach, the framing of the #MeToo movement, primarily focusing on the workplace, also exacerbated the fixation on sexual violence in one place. This contributes to the effective exclusion of sexual assault cases in other, non-institutional, public spaces and violence in the domestic sphere. Perhaps the extension of these critiques is the way in which #MeToo may then have reproduced just how entrenched sexual assault, harassment, and rape culture are in every corner of social life, particularly in informal spaces and the private sphere, where legal frameworks are often beyond reach. Questions raised by Koivunen et al. (2018: 1) summarize this gap eloquently:

> What are the limits of feminist politics that draws first and foremost on a shared public victimhood, or survivorship? How much of this vulnerability

186   *Tigist Shewarega Hussen, and Tamara Shefer*

is shared, and by whom? Why is #MeToo having an impact only now, with wealthy and often white cis-women in Hollywood at the forefront of the movement, when the issue of sexual abuse and assault has been a key struggle in feminist, women of colour, and trans activisms for such a long time? What part does social media play in the successes and failures of activist efforts such as #MeToo, and how does it relate to broader media histories of addressing and representing painful issues and marginalised people?

Third, how does one measure the extent to which digital activism challenges the status quo in terms of rape culture and its political and collective impact? Since "hashtag narratives are driven by conflict, confrontation, and a large number of personal stories shared through hashtags and comments to co-produce a collective narrative of the movement" (Wolfe 2018: 3), the #MeToo movement has been criticized for simply accumulating individual narratives of sexual violence and amplifying the significance of emotionally charged stories of injury and vulnerability (Mendes et al. 2018; Koivunen et al. 2018). These rhythmic orchestrations of individualized stories position women as responsible for deconstructing sexual violence and are "inward-looking and part of a long-standing tradition that seeks to 'change the woman rather than change the world'" (Gill and Orgad 2018: 1317). This is particularly alarming because feminists have worked so hard to understand power and sexual violence and have strongly resisted the responsibility that is socially expected from the victim of the violence.

Fourth, we draw attention to the neoliberal capitalist logics that seem to be driving the #MeToo movement, an "uberization" of transnational digital feminist activism, given the rapid packaging of this model of activism as a global export to multiple contexts. Observing from the outside, "the themes of global reach, speed, immediacy, dialogue, visibility, engagement, contact, connection, collectivity and shared understanding all emerged as important for participants" in #MeToo (Mendes et al. 2018: 240). This is, of course, attractive to activists because of the global connectivity it provides.

Indeed, the mass distribution of stories of sexual harassment for public display and consumption allowed the movement to "go viral" on different social media platforms, using the precarious labour of activists, with no economic rewards for individuals who are connected to the movement. Of course, this is also primarily related to the fact that social activism and solidarity that focuses on social change has limited or no desire for personal or economic rewards. In relation to this, Mendes et al. (2018: 239) state that "the fact remains that it is very difficult (and contentious) to seek financial compensation from this type of work". Nevertheless, individuals and collective activists who are involved in feminist digital activism campaigning for #MeToo globally seem to be involved in a form of labour that is exploitative.

Furthermore, since the mapping of visibility goes hand in hand with sensational descriptions of victimization, injury, and pain (Koivunen et al. 2018), the larger the number of re-tweets and shares, the better the chance of becoming popular among #MeToo users and campaigners. This incentive also "open[s] space for a range of

#MeToo Through a Decolonial Feminist Lens 187

more nuanced engagements with 'sexualized' culture including seeing it as a neo-liberal capitalist phenomenon linked to consumerism and discourses of celebrity, choice, and empowerment" (Gill and Orgad 2018: 1316). Thus, it remains to be seen how sustainable the movement will be considering the amount of emotional, mental, and physical labour it demands.

Gentrification of Feminist Movements and Its Dangers

The critiques of #MeToo described earlier unlock significant concerns about conceptual frameworks that tend to be diluted in global and transnational feminist movements and the challenge to "respond in a unified voice to sexual violence" (Roy 2018: 2). Gill and Orgad (2018: 1314) argue that transnational solidarity "does not simply 'add in' new countries or cultures, but, more critically, offers ex-centric or decolonial perspectives that displace the hegemony of white, urban western theorizing". Technology and internet-enhanced movements seem to escape regional and national identity politics, and are able to access individual and collective attention and commitment, but when it comes to unravelling a deeper intersectional and postcolonial understanding of sexual violence and the representation of movements, the #MeToo movement remains rooted in and productive of irreconcilable power relations. Similarly, Milevska (2011: 53) argues that "even though it is clear that regions cannot function as the only relevant cultural identity concept, the regional context is relevant exactly because of the danger of essentialisation and the overburdening complexities and exclusions that prevail in the national context".

The perplexing proximity of #MeToo to individual voice and narratives, with the subtle erasure of differences in socio-economic and political context, culture, vulnerability, and identities, makes the movement susceptible to increased backlash. Raiva and Sariola (2018: 11) argue that "#MeToo appears *as though* it is a singularity and generates the affect of collective action, when these are actually manifestations of quite different political moments in quite distinct conditions". A significant challenge for feminists from the Global South is the difficulty of uncoupling local feminist movements from a "foreign" concept that has emerged from Western, Northern or Eurocentric influence, and from the way in which feminist discourse has operated in the service of global systems of privileging. Thus, homogenizing public expression and protest against sexual violence creates deep-seated anxieties that are embedded in economies of political recognition, exclusion, erasure, and invisibility of local feminist movements. In her article, "Decolonizing Feminism in the #MeToo Era", Ritty Lukose (2018: 36) writes:

Whether it is the category of "woman", notions such as "the personal is political", attention to a "politics of location", ideas of consent, privacy, patriarchy, power, subordination, exploitation, secularism, identity, sexuality, intersectionality, rights, agency, trauma, empowerment, and the very legal definition of sexual harassment, among others, these are all concepts that sit at the complex intersection between feminism as both a knowledge project and a political project.

The transition of the #MeToo "moment" to a globally trending feminist hashtag movement was achieved through the fusion of "social media into intimate lives, the explosion of self-representation in the articulation of sexual identities" (Gill and Orgad 2018: 1317). Unlike SlutWalk, FEMEN, #NakedProtest, and other feminist forms of activism that deploy collective and provocative uses of the body as a means of protest and mobilization, #MeToo uses individual stories of pain, violence, vulnerability, and injury.

In addition, according to Gill and Orgad (2018: 1317), the substance of #MeToo lies with the move from a "concern with 'sexualization' to a more critical and political register interested in how sex and power intersect, and the implications of this shift". While this argument is true, it is also not a unique discovery of the #MeToo movement. For instance, movements prior to #MeToo protested against this sexualization of Black women's bodies and engaged deeply with intersections of sex and power (Hussen 2018). Indeed, such movements also clearly took forward intersectional understandings of sexual and gender violence, nuances of which are often lacking in the dominant discourse on #MeToo. It is precisely such movements that have facilitated the popularity of the #MeToo movement, because "it follows a growing trend of the public's willingness to engage with resistance and challenges to sexism, patriarchy and other forms of oppression via feminist uptake of digital communication" (Mendes et al. 2018: 237). Yet the movements that made such a trend possible, particularly in global Southern contexts, have been discarded or obfuscated along the way.

Addressing the politics of location within transnational feminism, looking for deep-seated politics and aesthetic formations of regional feminist movements and organizations, is important to avoid reinstating historical and current geopolitical privileges and power relations. Such a project is also decolonial because it acknowledges how certain knowledges have been marginalized and devalued. Such decolonial and situated projects may help to contribute to a broader understanding of the predicaments of transnational feminist movements (Milevska 2011). Furthermore, Lukose (2018: 40) poses a question that pushes #MeToo and the transnational feminists invested in it to interrogate privileges:

> Will our very ideas and definitions of sexual harassment be transformed through a thorough interrogation and reckoning with how racism and sexism, among other vectors of difference and inequality, shape experiences of gendered and sexual violence across class lines?

Attempting to answer questions of privilege is enormously important, as is the centring of localized knowledges and "transversal dialogues, mutual learning practices and volatile but effective feminist coalitions" (Tlostanova et al. 2016: 211) that do not repeat the privilege of particular knowledges and locations. Specifically, even if an acknowledged reciprocal knowledge exchange takes place between movements in the Global North and South, there is still little attention given to the fact that movements from the Global North are often entwined in authoritative political and knowledge positions and relationships with the Global South.

#MeToo Through a Decolonial Feminist Lens 189

In principle, the localization of international movements requires the reshaping of existing local movements. Milevska (2011: 53) argues that, although the idea of "reshaping" is understood within the "notion of supplement . . . [that] aims to enhance the presence of something that is self-sufficient and therefore already complete", in unequal power dynamics, these acts are "overshadowed by the idea that a thing that has a supplement cannot be truly 'complete in itself'". As such, many African feminist advocacies (like advocacies in other parts of the world), protesting sexual violence against women, attempt to tag and put their countries on the map of the transnational feminist #MeToo solidarity movement. For instance, it became very popular with hashtag protests such as #MeTooEthiopia, #MeTooKenya, #MeTooSouthAfrica, #MeTooUganda, #MeTooSudan, etc. All these hashtags are politically powerful, and they critically point towards the crisis of sexual violence against women in these countries.

However, using a decolonial feminist perspective, or the coloniality of gender (Lugones 2010), a closer look at these hashtags shows a particular trend where #MeToo dominates rather than the image of African feminisms – and they are never intimately representative of African women's experience. Thus, attempts to explain violence in different contexts using one "universal" language, replacing all existing local languages of feminist protests, is an indication of the contradictory frameworks and awkward power relationship in transnational feminist movements. In turn, this symbolic act legitimizes #MeToo as the quintessential and authoritative definition of protest against sexual violence. Obviously, "positioned between local and global feminist tendencies, regional feminist knowledge is very often neglected and its potentialities remain unrecognized within the wider picture of transnationalism" (Milevska 2011: 52).

We, therefore, ask: What about existing African feminist movements in countries such as those foregrounded in hashtags like #MeTooEthiopia, #MeTooKenya, #MeTooSouthAfrica, #MeTooUganda, #MeTooSudan, etc.? Tweets like these often stream statistical facts of sexual violence in the mentioned countries (i.e. they line up numbers of cases of domestic violence, murders of women by boyfriends or male partners, etc., without any contextualization) using the sign of an internationally recognized movement. But confronted with such tweets we ask: How is #MeToo more concretely applicable to the local context, particularly in relation to the struggle against challenging the status quo? Related to this we further ask: How do we make sense of the temporality of feminist digital movements and their replacement by the next "new" digital trend? How can we rethink and destabilize the hegemonic power of Western/Northern feminism, "the dynamic interactions between fields of power such as the production of knowledge, geopolitical relations and intellectual, disciplinary and political locations" (Lukose 2018: 43), if we are not paying attention to diverse forms of feminist knowledge and activism in other contexts?

To this end, Lukose (2018: 47) contends that the "#MeToo era poses some interesting challenges for decolonizing feminism given that the universalizing horizon of feminism has been so centralized". As shown earlier, our own action of supplanting what we know and have worked hard for with #MeToo reveals the normative

190 *Tigist Shewarega Hussen, and Tamara Shefer*

impulse, particularly in digital activism, that leads to the destruction of such activist acts by effectively excluding other similar movements, erasing historical struggles of feminist activists, and weakening local feminist movement organizations.

As a result, critical feminist knowledge formation that pays attention to our context of specific struggle is diluted by the popular backlash claims of the "influence of Western ideology", which has long been a trope among anti-feminist discourse in South Africa (Narayan 2013). This is particularly evident in how #MeToo is represented and viewed as a feminist movement with global Northern roots and shape. This serves to bolster the stereotype of feminist activism as un-African, while also erasing local activism and resistance. These narratives force local feminist movements into a vicious cycle, required to defend our position against the patriarchal system that uses such opportunities to discredit our movement and feminist critique. On the other hand, it is imperative to talk back against the knowledge authority of Northern and Western feminism that excludes and "others" those in marginal geopolitical spaces. A final concern is that highlighting the high rates of sexual violence in African countries may contribute to an othering of global Southern communities and strengthen the perception of Northern, white innocence (Wekker 2016), an "outsourcing of patriarchy" from the Global North to the South (Grewal 2013; Boonzaier and Kessi 2018; Shefer 2016).

Conclusion

This chapter has reflected on the #MeToo movement and its deployment and uptake across transnational contexts with a focus on the Global South, in particular, South Africa. While it is impossible to measure the impact of #MeToo on local movements, or vice versa, the use of online activism to extend, strengthen, and facilitate on-the-ground activism in local movements is evident. This may, however, relate more to global shifts in communication than to the power of #MeToo specifically. There is also no doubt that the global presence of #MeToo brings more legitimacy to local online and material struggles against sexual violence. It is towards this somewhat ironic impact of #MeToo that our chapter is directed. Underneath the conversations in this chapter, there runs a current resistance to being forgotten, and a call for reciprocal knowledge transfer and solidarity across differences.

We read the movement through contemporary South African online (and material) activism, acknowledging the value of globalized online activism but also critically reflecting upon its failures and gaps, as well as the possible dangers. In the world of digital activism, #MeToo is a unique feminist movement, especially for having succeeded in maintaining its momentum beyond a year. Yet, from our perspective in the Global South, we question how the movement retains its energy and the political effect thereof.

We illustrate that, as much as #MeToo features intersectionality and transnational digital feminist activism, it also unintentionally overshadows and may undermine local feminist movements. For example, South Africans saw a wide range of feminist activism against sexual violence prior to #MeToo. Yet #MeToo is now widely represented as *the* defining feminist digital activism work globally. In

#MeToo Through a Decolonial Feminist Lens 191

this respect, we asked: "what does it mean to be part of a global movement when it demands the erasure of local historical activist work?"

While #MeToo has achieved some inclusion and engagement, arguably its energy and visibility remain dependent on famous and high-profile narratives to engage public interest and have an impact. We suggest that this may reflect and re-entrench global inequalities and un/privileges in which certain bodies and lives are more valued than others. In this way, rather than representing a global and intersectional challenge against sexual violence, the ever-present entanglements of race, geopolitical imbalances, poverty, etc. within the campaign may serve to re/ entrench and re/produce the privileging and centring of some and the dispensability and subalternity of others.

Finally, taking into consideration the historical eruptions of multiple feminist waves that resist neoliberalist ideologies and witness a reclaiming of identity and positionality by those positioned as powerless, we have questioned what seems to be the superficial recognition of a diversity of voices and subjective experience in the #MeToo campaign. This might leave feminist activists and scholars in the Global South with the inevitable burden of dis-identification with labels such as "influenced by Western feminist ideology and popular culture". The task of decolonial work that focuses on undoing the power dynamics and reclaiming political identity and collaborative ownership of feminist knowledge production and meaning-making similarly devolves to those in this position, leaving the larger terrain of knowledge untouched. In some ways, we recognize that this chapter may be repeating the same process.

Note

1 The pervasiveness of sexual and gender violence, what Pumla Gqola (2015) has more aptly described as "rape culture" has been a key concern in post-apartheid South Africa and the focus of proliferating research over the last few decades, especially by public health researchers and feminist scholars. Rape crisis organizations have long drawn upon the slogan that "one in three women" will be victims of sexual violence in their lifetime, and epidemiological researchers have bolstered these claims statistically. For example, some studies have found that physical intimate partner violence is reported by 25–40% of women (Jewkes et al. 2003, 2006), and 42% of men report having perpetrated intimate partner violence, while 28% report ever having raped a woman (Abrahams et al. 2006; Jewkes et al. 2009).

References

Abrahams, Naaemah, Rachel Jewkes, Ria Laubscher, and Margaret Hoffman. 2006. "Intimate Partner Violence: Prevalence and Risk Factors for Men in Cape Town, South Africa." *Violence and Victims* 21 (2): 247–64.

Bonilla, Yarimar, and Jonathan Rosa. 2015. "# Ferguson: Digital Protest, Hashtag Ethnography, and the Racial Politics of Social Media in the United States." *American Ethnologist* 42 (1): 4–17.

Boonzaier, Floretta. 2017. "The Life and Death of Anene Booysen: Colonial Discourse, Gender-Based Violence and Media Representations." *South African Journal of Psychology* 47 (4): 470–81.

Boonzaier, Floretta, and Shose Kess. 2018. "Challenging Representations: Participatory Research Engagements With Young People in Postcolonial Contexts." In *Engaging Youth in Activism, Research and Pedagogical Praxis: Transnational and Intersectional Perspectives on Gender, Sex, and Race*, edited by T. Shefer, J. Hearn, K. Ratele, and F. Boonzaier, 125–46. New York, NY: Routledge.

Castells, Manuel. 2015. *Networks of Outrage and Hope: Social Movements in the Internet Age*. Cambridge: Polity Press.

Disemelo, Katlego. 2019. "Performing the Queer Archive: Strategies of Self-Styling on Instagram." In *Acts of Transgression: Contemporary Live Art in South Africa*, edited by J. Pather and C. Boulle, 219–42. Johannesburg: Wits University Press.

Dosekun, Simidele. 2007. "Defending Feminism in Africa." *Postamble* 3 (1): 41–7.

Ferguson, Jennifer. 2017. "Jennifer Ferguson Journals #One night in PE." Accessed January 18, 2020. https://jenniferkestisferguson.blogspot.com/2017/10/metoo-one-night-in-pe. html?spref=fb.

Gill, Rosalind, and Shani Orgad. 2018. "The Shifting Terrain of Sex and Power: From the 'Sexualization of Culture' to #MeToo." *Sexualities* 21 (8): 1313–24.

Gouws, Amanda. 2016. "Young Women in the 'Decolonizing Project' in South Africa: From Subaltern to Intersectional Feminism." Paper presented at the Nordic Africa Days Conference 2016, Uppsala, September 23–25.

Gouws, Amanda. 2017. "Feminist Intersectionality and the Matrix of Domination in South Africa." *Agenda* 31 (1): 19–27.

Gouws, Amanda. 2018. "#EndRapeCulture Campaign in South Africa: Resisting Sexual Violence Through Protest and the Politics of Experience." *Politikon* 45 (1): 3–15. https:// doi.org/10.1080/02589346.2018.1418201.

Gqola, Pumla. 2015. *Rape: A South African Nightmare*. Auckland Park: MfBooks Joburg.

Grewal, Inderpal. 2013. "Outsourcing Patriarchy: Feminist Encounters, Transnational Mediations and the Crime of 'Honour Killings'." *International Feminist Journal of Politics* 15 (1): 1–19. https://doi.org/10.1080/14616742.2012.755352.

Hearn, Jeff. 2018. "You, Them, Us, We, Too? . . . Online – Offline, Individual – Collective, Forgotten – Remembered, Harassment – Violence." *European Journal of Women's Studies* 25 (2): 228–35.

Hussen, Tigist Shewarega. 2018. "ICTs, Social Media and Feminist Activism: #RapeMustFall, #NakedProtest, and #RUReferenceList Movement in South Africa." In *Engaging Youth in Activism, Research and Pedagogical Praxis: Transnational and Intersectional Perspectives on Gender, Sex, and Race*, edited by T. Shefer, J. Hearn, K. Ratele, and F. Boonzaier, 199–214. New York, NY and London: Routledge.

Jewkes, R., K. Dunkle, M. P. Koss, J. B. Levin, M. Nduna, N. Jama, and Y. Sikweyiya. 2006. "Rape Perpetration by Young, Rural South African Men: Prevalence, Patterns and Risk Factors." *Social Science & Medicine* 63: 2949–61. https://doi.org/10.1016/j. socscimed.2006.07.027.

Jewkes, R., Y. Sikweyiya, R. Morrell, and K. Dunkle. 2009. *Understanding Men's Health and Use of Violence: Interface of Rape and HIV in South Africa (Research Report)*. Pretoria: Medical Research Council.

Jewkes, R. K., J. B. Levin, and L. A. Penn-Kekana. 2003. "Gender Inequalities, Intimate Partner Violence and HIV Preventive Practices: Findings of a South African Cross-Sectional Study." *Social Science & Medicine* 56 (1): 125–34. https://doi.org/10.1016/ S0277-9536(02)00012-6.

Kessi, Shose, and Floretta Boonzaier. 2015. "All #Rhodes Lead to Transformation." *Mail & Guardian Online*, May 28. http://mg.co.za/article/2015-05-21-all-rhodes-lead-to-enlightenment.

#MeToo Through a Decolonial Feminist Lens 193

Koivunen, A., K. Kyrölä, and I. Ryberg. 2018. "Vulnerability as a Political Language." In *The Power of Vulnerability: Mobilising Affect in Feminist, Queer and Anti-racist Media Cultures*, edited by A. Koivunen, K. Kyrölä, and I. Ryberg, 1–26. Manchester: Manchester University Press.

Lugones, Maria. 2010. "Toward a Decolonial Feminism." *Hypatia* 25 (4): 742–59.

Lukose, Ritty. 2018. "Decolonizing Feminism in the #MeToo Era." *The Cambridge Journal of Anthropology* 36 (2): 34–52.

Mendes, K., J. Ringrose, and J. Keller. 2018. "#MeToo and the Promise and Pitfalls of Challenging Rape Culture Through Digital Feminist Activism." *European Journal of Women's Studies* 25 (2): 236–46.

Milevska, S. 2011. "Solidarity and Intersectionality: What Can Transnational Feminist Theory Learn from Regional Feminist Activism?" *Feminist Review* 98 (1_suppl): e52–e61.

Mohanty, Chandra Talpade. 1984. "Under Western Eyes: Feminist Scholarship and Colonial Discourses." *Boundary 2* 12 (3): 333–58.

Narayan, Uma. 2013. *Dislocating Cultures: Identities, Traditions, and Third World Feminism*. New York, NY and London: Routledge.

Nathaniel, Amity. 2019. "#MeToo Mishaps: Black Bodies, Bloody Grounds." *South Central Review* 36 (2): 52–67.

Omarjee, Nadira. 2018. *Reimagining the Dream: Decolonising Academia by Putting the Last First*. Leiden: African Studies Centre.

Onwuachi-Willig, A. 2018. "What About #UsToo: The Invisibility of Race in the #MeToo Movement." *The Yale Law Journal* 128. Accessed January 20, 2020. www.yalelawjournal.org/forum/what-about-ustoo.

Pather, Jay, and Catherine Boulle (eds.). 2019. *Acts of Transgression: Contemporary Live Art in South Africa*. Johannesburg: Wits University Press.

Raiva, M., and S. Sariola. 2018. "#MeToo & Feminist Activism in India." *EASST Review* 37 (3). Accessed January 23, 2020. https://easst.net/article/metoo-feminist-activism-in-india/.

Ratele, Kopano. 2013. "Of What Value Is Feminism to Black Men?" *Communication* 39 (2): 256–70. https://doi.org/10.1080/02500167.2013.804675.

Roy, Srila. 2018. "#MeToo Is a Crucial Moment to Revisit the History of Indian Feminism." *Economic & Political Weekly* 53 (42). Accessed January 20, 2020. www.epw.in/engage/article/metoo-crucial-moment-revisit-history-indian-feminism.

Shefer, Tamara. 2016. "Resisting the Binarism of Victim and Agent: Critical Reflections on 20 Years of Scholarship on Young Women and Heterosexual Practices in South African Contexts." *Global Public Health: An International Journal for Research, Policy and Practice* 11 (1–2): 211–23. https://doi.org/10.1080/17441692.2015.1029959

Shefer, Tamara. 2018. "Embodied Pedagogies: Performative Activism and Transgressive Pedagogies in the Sexual and Gender Justice Project in Higher Education in Contemporary South Africa." In *Socially Just Pedagogies in Higher Education: Critical Posthumanist and New Feminist Materialist Perspectives*, edited by V. Bozalek, R. Braidotti, T. Shefer, and M. Zembylas, 171–88. London: Bloomsbury.

Shefer, Tamara. 2019. "Activist Performance and Performative Activism Towards Intersectional Gender and Sexual Justice in Contemporary South Africa." *International Sociology* 34 (4): 418–34.

Spivak, Gayatri. 1988. "Can the Subaltern Speak?" In *Marxism and the Interpretation of Culture*, edited by C. Nelson and L. Grossberg, 271–313. Urbana, IL: University of Illinois Press.

Statistics South Africa. 2018. "General Household Survey." Accessed April 21, 2020. www.statssa.gov.za/publications/P0318/P03182018.pdf.

194 *Tigist Shewarega Hussen, and Tamara Shefer*

Tlostanova, Madina, Suruchi Thapar-Björkert, and Redi Koobak. 2016. "Border Thinking and Disidentification: Postcolonial and Postsocialist Feminist Dialogues." *Feminist Theory* 17 (2): 211–28. https://doi.org/10.1177/0141778918816946.

UCT the Trans Collective. 2016. "Tokenistic, Objectifying, Voyeuristic Inclusion Is at Least as Disempowering as Complete Exclusion." *Hola Africa Facebook Page*. www.facebook.com/HolaAfrica/posts/745161412287899.

Wekker, Gloria. 2016. *White Innocence: Paradoxes of Colonialism and Race*. London: Duke University Press.

Wolfe, Katherine. 2018. "Narrative Form and Agency in #MeToo." *Student Research Submissions*. 227. https://scholar.umw.edu/student_research/227.

Xaba, Wanelisa. 2017. "Challenging Fanon: A Black Radical Feminist Perspective on Violence and the Fees Must Fall Movement." *Agenda* 31 (3–4): 96104. https://doi.org/10.1080/10130950.2017.1392786.

Yuval-Davis, Nira. 1999. "What Is 'Transversal Politics'?" *Soundings* 12: 94–8.

Postscript

Reflection Upon the Making of This Chapter

Before we landed, happy but bruised, in this edited volume, this piece has gone through a lot. We as scholars have also gone through a lot. It feels important to reflect briefly upon the process of writing this chapter because we feel that it speaks to some of the continuing troubled practices of working as feminists across unequal geopolitical spaces. These range from presenting this chapter at an international conference, organized by the Nordic, feminist journal *NORA* in Iceland in 2019, where it was fully recognized and celebrated for its critical views and interventions, to the backdoor negotiations with the editors of a book focusing on #MeToo from a transnational feminist perspective. Overall, the journey of writing this chapter was messy in terms of understanding what was needed from editors whose primary response, in our opinion, was to undermine and dilute the post/decolonial feminist position that we deliberately took. Moreover, the practices of engagement reproduced many of the still-dominant logics of a patriarchal, colonial scholarship in which multiple lines of authority were evident.

We felt that not disclosing this experience or reflecting upon the process would contribute to the dismissal of the painful processes of power dynamics embedded in transnational efforts at working together that are still experienced by feminists from the Global South. We have learned and tussled with three wicked pedagogical problems within transnational feminist knowledge-making:

- The formulation of dialogue between Global South and Global North within the parameters of transnationalism impulsively recruits critical feminist voices from the Global South, and cheers their critique as an exotic revelation about what is known as deeply entrenched postcolonial violence. Global South feminist views are presented in the room as a radical voice that speaks against the power structures. Unfortunately, the act of offering this space to us is part of the performance of postcolonial engagement and lip service to the recognition of

#MeToo Through a Decolonial Feminist Lens   195

marginalities, but it seldom extends to the materiality of the critic and/or investment in "walking the talk".

- Based on our experience, the first point above was expressed in the resistance
to and rejection of the actual work, which was not at all different from the presentation we gave at the NORA conference. We were consistently told to reshape
this chapter in order to dilute the voice and make it digestible to the few white
feminist scholars and Global South scholars located in the Global North who are
on the rota of territoriality and gatekeeping of transnational feminist knowledge.
The process was prescriptive, we did not have room to authentically engage
with the critique, the words used were harsh and hierarchical, embedded in the
authority of the global Northern scholar and without any recognition of our
generosity in providing a perspective from where we are located.
- Another valuable, but painful, piece of learning, which was a giant awakening
for us, was how the thematic alignment of the edited book was prioritized over
the unique engagement with the topic by differently situated communities. In
this particular case, the intention was to illustrate the uptake and worthiness of
#MeToo, regardless of its shortcomings. Hence, we felt that it was difficult for
us to break free from the parameters introduced to us, which in fact constrained
us from making our key argument. Furthermore, the constant requirement for
the presentation of case studies or empirical work that presents narratives of
sexual violence against women did not sit comfortably in the light of the context
of the paper, which was criticizing how women's stories of their experiences of
sexual violence are used as capital to cultivate and sustain international feminist
movements such as #MeToo. It left us wondering: Why is feminist analytical
work on gender-based violence constantly expected to present horrific experiences of violent cases? And to what extent will such a focus reproduce a secu-
larization of violence against women and, in this case, the "outsourcing" of
violence to contexts in the Global South?

15 Translocality

A Decolonial Take on Feminist Strategies

Caroline Betemps

In this short chapter, I bring the categories of transnational feminisms and translocality into dialogue by telling stories of interconnectedness with no clear endings. For that purpose, I try, and probably fail, to intertwine stories about the place I am from, and the places where I live/d or have passed through. These stories invoke different dimensions of coloniality within feminist frames, quotidian dimensions, and, to some eyes, apparently disconnected dimensions, which have nonetheless spoken to me in their connectedness. This chapter aims to respond to the need to analyse global phenomena through a provincializing of the centre(s) (Sandoval 2000; Chakrabarty 2007), as one among several anti-colonial gestures. This also implies looking for "the interconnectedness of our colonial histories" (Mendoza 2017: 638).

One of the purposes of this book about *Pluriversal Conversations on Transnational Feminisms* is "to transgress methodological nationalisms" via different kinds of "conversations between [the] transnational, decolonial and intersectional feminisms" (Chapter 1, this volume) that we, the scholars participating in the project, embody. Hence, I will make use of one of the many transformational conversations that occurred during the encounters we experienced within this framework.

The South Atlantic Connections

I am sitting in the sun at the Company's Garden in Cape Town. I arrived here in South Africa just a few days ago; it is my first time on the African continent, and since my arrival I have not been able to stop making analogies with my country of origin, Brazil. It is very evident that the place where I was born and raised is, more or less, at the same longitude: Bagé is 31° South while Cape Town is 33° South. I can't stop thinking of this South–South connection, my mirror on the other side of the Atlantic. I see people walking by on the streets of the city centre of Cape Town, and it reminds me of the centres of many Brazilian cities: Salvador, Porto Alegre, São Paulo . . . I am also thinking about the fact that both sides of the Atlantic are deeply connected via modern colonial capitalism, which originated in invasion, trafficking, and genocide of the Indigenous societies, their territories, cultures, and philosophies.

DOI: 10.4324/9781003378761-18

Translocality: A Decolonial Take on Feminist Strategies   197

The Company's Garden, as I was told during a walking tour, was the beginning of what later became the city of Cape Town. European ships, mostly Dutch and British, needed fresh water supplies on their way to South Asia, and the crews often suffered from scurvy (a lack of vitamin C).[1] Therefore, the Dutch and British authorities built the first hospitals, and then a garden to provide fresh food for them. The Garden's vegetation includes trees that are characteristic of the Amazonian Forest, such as the *Seringueira* (rubber tree) and the *Butiá* (Yatay or Jelly palm) – trees that were part of my childhood landscape were brought here. Colonizers and their descendants enjoy moving beings and things around. I cannot think of a better place to observe how colonization functioned, and coloniality remains in place. We, white people, like to mark the beginnings and endings of things as though they were exterior to us, and as though we were not part of them, as the Indigenous thinker and writer Ailton Krenak articulated it in an interview with the Macuxi artist Jaider Esbell (Krenak and Esbell 2019). That is one of the tricks of whiteness and racial hegemony.

I am back walking the streets of Cape Town, where you can feel the tension in the air, in people's gaze. . . . People here (in South Africa) and there (in Brazil) look at you and don't look away as they do in many European countries, especially the Northern ones. I feel at home here, I am used to similar places where criminal violence is just the tip of the iceberg, beneath which there are so many other kinds of violence, deeper and less visible, such as systemic impoverishment, structural racism, and the denial of access to basic goods (food, energy, water, housing, healthcare, etc.), but not only . . . I grew up in a territory similar to this, where all these sources of life abound, but where modern/colonial capitalism has made them into objects of swindling and looting. In the words of Denise Ferreira da Silva, the "total violence" of colonization was the thing that made capitalism possible by "guaranteeing the expropriation of the productive capacity of the black and slave body" (2019: 92). In other, simpler, words, modern capitalism started in the colonies, not in Europe as we have been taught (Mendoza 2016).

And yet, despite how "at home" I feel in Cape Town, and how many similarities I can find between it and the spaces where I come from, I am a white person in *The Áfricas* (Ekine 2016: 27). This is a space colonized and still inhabited by white Europeans who stayed, and they are the ones who created and benefitted from Apartheid in the 20th century – as the owners of the good lands and the beachfront buildings in the 21st century. More than 500 years in 45.

A Question of Belonging

"Why are you dialoguing with US and European feminisms, and not with the African ones? A South–South dialogue would be much more interesting, besides leaving aside those well-known and hegemonic narratives", Tigist Shewarega Hussen from the University of the Western Cape (South Africa) asked me, when they learned about my research (Betemps in prep.). That night in 2016, we were walking, arm in arm, through the cold streets of Karlstad (Sweden), where we

198 *Caroline Betemps*

had attended an academic event and stayed overnight. Those moments of being together, which were repeated during every edition of the project that led to this book, gave us space for these kinds of actual encounters, where we brought our bodies and existences together and shared our worldviews and experiences.

My first answer to Tigist was that indeed it would be wonderful but that I did not feel comfortable, as a white person from Aba Yala, about analysing social movements from the African continent – a place where I had never been until then – and that my ignorance about its feminisms was, if not total, then very close to it. But a simple answer was not enough within the framework of those vulnerable and intimate conversations, and this recognition made me think about the fact that the colonial history of the country where I was born and raised was directly connected to the history of the African continent, and that I as a white person am related to that history on very particular terms. Not in terms of belonging, but of being held accountable.

I am a white person from a colonized country. This fact has many implications, and its analysis is not within the scope of this chapter. My kuir/queerness and sexual and gender dissidences, my low social class, my unstructured family, and even my own migrant body territory[2] (Cabnal 2010) are parts of me that interact with my whiteness, they do not just exist in parallel with it. My ancestors, five or six generations before me, were what Ferreira da Silva called "immigrants-turned-colonisers [settlers]" (2019: 174). They were members of the groups of Europeans who went to the Southern parts of Abya Yala, in my family's case to Brazil and Uruguay, at the end of the 19th century, to "populate" – that is, to colonize – these spaces, and were given small pieces of land or were put to work in commerce or providing services as cheap workers. This colonially facilitated migration had a dual purpose: on the one hand, it was intended as an eugenic move, as a way of whitening the population living there after three centuries of genocide, rape, and enslavement. On the other hand, with the official abolition of the slavery system (in 1888) – which never actually happened[3] – a cheap workforce was needed to maintain the mercantilist system and an economy based on the export of raw materials and the import of goods and services from Europe (Pochmann 2022).

Translocality as an Analytical Strategy

A term that could help us to understand the complex connections that the conversation with Tigist led me to think about is the geopolitical *tropos* of translocality (Álvarez 2009; Lima Costa 2012; Anthias 2013; Álvarez et al 2014). I understand translocality as a conceptual field in which positionalities are plastic, and its malleability is displayed accordingly in relation to context and temporality, space, and time. As suggested by Anthias:

> it points to the existence of contradictory and shifting social locations where one might be in a position of dominance and subordination simultaneously on the one hand or at different times or spaces on the other. This is not to

Translocality: A Decolonial Take on Feminist Strategies 199

deny that some individuals and groupings of individuals are not more unequal than others – indeed quite the opposite.

(2012: 108)

I find the concept of translocality appealing, in accordance with Brazilian feminist Sônia Álvarez, for whom this notion binds "geographies of power at different levels (local, national, global), of subjects (defined by gender or sex, 'race', ethnicity, social class, etc.) that constitute the self" (Laó-Montes 2007 in Álvarez 2009: 744). From her point of view, Abya Yala is a "cross-border and not territorially delimited cultural formation" (Álvarez 2009 in Lima Costa 2012: 49–50).

Álvarez and Lima Costa are both well-known authors within feminist studies in Brazil. They live or spend long periods of time in the United States. The moves and translations between these two different geopolitical spaces make up an important context for their methodological choices, which Álvarez proposes to expand to include a "hemispherical policy of the translocal dimension" that would also serve an understanding of the "heterogeneity of the *Latinidades* (Latin identities) inside the United States" (Álvarez 2009: 744).

In contrast to these authors, who analyse the axis (of coming and going) between the United States, where they are not white, and Brazil, where they are (Álvarez 2009: 745), the translocal dimension helps me in my research to understand feminist movements from Abya Yala, and connections between this continent and Europe. According to Anthias: "The translocal lens makes you aware of the context, of the meaning and of its contradictory positions, which can be productive when one starts elaborating theories" (Anthias 2012, 2013; in Falconí Trávez et al. 2014). It is in this sense that I find the concept of the translocal fruitful for exploring unexpected connections and ways to think about feminist resistances outside of the frame of nation-states.

Instead of the more established frame of transnational feminisms, a translocal lens allows me to work with categories that differ from those referring to conventional modern/colonial geopolitical divisions. The concept of the translocal helps me to overcome the analytical framework of nation-based thinking (Wimmer and Schiller 2003: 301–34). A translocal approach seems to me to be a more relatable choice for a researcher like me, who comes from an *ex*-colony, the Federative Republic of Brazil, which is still colonized, or at least ruled by colonial and imperial interests, and which was also dismantled and artificially rebuilt as a nation-state.

Moreover, in line with some decolonial feminist researchers, I am also critical vis-à-vis the genealogy of the theoretical framework of transnational feminisms insofar as it is a US-produced theory that shares a Cold War logic reframed in new words (Leela Fernandes 2013, in Tlostanova et al. 2019: 82). It is a framework that does not belong to "any discussion of decoloniality" (Tlostanova et al. 2019: 81–7) and does not attend to global dimensions of intertwined inequalities (Boatcă 2015). A liberal transnational perspective (Mohanty 2013: 971–2) mainly suggests a solidarity that does not take the coloniality of knowledge into account (Lander 2000) and reproduces the epistemic dominance of modern/colonial Europe.

200   *Caroline Betemps*

In contrast to a transnational approach, the particular cross-spatial framework of translocality corresponds with the thinking of Alexander and Mohanty, according to which:

> To talk about feminist praxis in global contexts would involve shifting the unit of analysis from local, regional and national culture to relations and processes across cultures. Grounding analyses in particular, local feminist praxis is necessary, but we also need to understand the local in relation to larger, cross-national processes. This would require a corresponding shift in the conception of political organizing and mobilization across borders. . . . [T]his critical application of feminist praxis in global contexts would substitute responsibility, accountability, engagement and solidarity.
>
> (1997: xix)

Approaching our common stories and interconnected differences through a translocal lens can be helpful for attempts to decolonize our feminist practices. Moreover, this framework can open up symbolic spaces where we can meet and act – spaces that are meaningful, even on a temporary basis, for both the political movements and the people with whom we are working towards forming *deep coalitions* (Lugones 2003). In this sense, I am using a translocal approach not as a recipe but as background music, a reading frame in space and time, one that is not all-encompassing. The translocal lens calls for an endeavour that attempts to seek the interconnectedness of our global histories via our local stories – not as a colonial narrative but as a rooted and relational conversation.

In my imagination, I continue the dialogue with Tigist today, although we are on different continents. I continue it as one among many conversations held with my colleagues on this project, with whom I have shared the not always easy intersections of our experiences, which are formed through our different locations and epistemic starting points, but also through vulnerable and intense attempts to reach out translocally.

Notes

1 For a more detailed description, see "The Dutch East India Company, scurvy and the victualling station at the Cape" by J. C. de Villiers (2006).
2 Lorena Cabnal understands the body as part of the territory it inhabits, and vice versa. She defines this relation as "territorio cuerpo-tierra" [body-land territory].
3 The Brazilian prison system is mainly Black or *pardo* [equivalent to *mixed race* in this context], while higher education institutions and political positions are mostly white. "Black genocide" is how anti-racist movements describe the current situation of state violence against the Black population. The number of Black and racialized people murdered by police in Brazil is more than five times higher than the corresponding numbers of deaths in the United States, according to the *Yearbook of the Brazilian Forum on Public Security* (Updated in May 2022) and to *The Washington Post* (Updated in May 2022). Every 23 minutes, a young Black cis male is executed by the police in Brazil.

References

Alexander, M. Jacqui, and Chandra Talpade Mohanty. 1997. "Introduction: Genealogies, Legacies, Movements." In *Feminist Genealogies, Colonial Legacies, Democratic Futures*, edited by M. Jacqui Alexander and Chandra Talpade Mohanty, XIII–XLII. New York, NY and London: Routledge.

Álvarez, Sônia. 2009. "Construindo uma política feminista translocal da tradução." *Revista Estudos Feministas* 17 (3): 743–53.

Alvarez, Sônia E., Claudia de Lima Costa, Norma Klahn, and Millie Thayer (eds.). 2014. *Translocalities/Translocalidades. Feminist Politics of Translation in the Latin/a Américas*. Durham, NC: Duke University Press.

Anthias, Floya. 2012. "Transnational Mobilities, Migration Research and Intersectionality." *Nordic Journal of Migration Research* 2: 102–10.

Anthias, Floya. 2013. "Social Categories, Embodied Practices, Intersectionality: Towards a Translocational Approach." In *Interdependencies of Social Categorisations*, edited by Daniela Célleri, Tobias Schwarz, and Bea Wittger, 27–41. Madrid: Iberoamericana.

Betemps, Caroline. in prep. *Decolonial Feminisms: Dialogues and Frictions Between the Global South and North*. Linköping: Linköping University Electronic Press.

Boatcă, Manuela. 2015. *Global Inequalities: Beyond Occidentalism*. Farnham: Ashgate.

Cabnal, Lorena. 2010. "Acercamiento a la construcción de la propuesta de pensamiento epistémico de las mujeres indígenas feministas comunitarias de Abya Yala." In *Feminismos diversos: el feminismo comunitario*, 11–25. Madrid: ACSUR Las-Segovias.

Chakrabarty, Dipesh. 2007. "Provincializing Europe in Global Times: Introduction." In *Provincializing Europe: Postcolonial Thought and Historical Difference* (2nd ed.), edited by Dipesh Chakrabarty, 3–26. Princeton, NJ: Princeton University Press.

Ekine, Sokari. 2016. "Beyond Anti-LGBTI Legislation: Criminalization and the Denial of Citizenship." In *Decolonizing Sexualities: Transnational Perspectives, Critical Interventions*, edited by Sandeep Bakshi, Suhraiya Jivraj, and Silvia Posocco, 19–31. Oxford: Counter Press.

Falconí Trávez, Diego, Santiago Castellanos, and María Amelia Viter (eds.). 2014. *Resentir lo queer en América Latina: diálogos desde/con el Sur*. Madrid: Egales.

Ferreira da Silva, Denise. 2019. *A Dívida Impagável*. São Paulo: Oficina de Imaginação Política e Living Commons. [English edition: *Unpayable Debt: Coloniality, Raciality, and Global Capitalism From a Black Feminist "Poethical" Perspective*. Berlin: Sternberg Press, 2022].

Krenak, Ailton, and Jaider Esbell. 2019. "Desafios para a decolonialidade" [Challenges for Decoloniality]. Interview accessible at www.youtube.com/watch?v=qFZki_sr6ws.

Lander, Edgardo (ed.). 2000. *La colonialidad del saber: eurocentrismo y ciencias sociales Perspectivas latinoamericanas*. Buenos Aires: CLACSO.

Lima Costa, Claudia de. 2012. "Feminismo e tradução cultural: sobre a colonialidade do gênero e a descolonização do saber." *Portuguese Cultural Studies* (4): 41–65.

Lugones, María. 2003. *Peregrinajes/Pilgrimages: Theorizing Coalition Against Multiple Oppressions*. New York, NY: Rowman & Littlefield Press.

Mendoza, Breny. 2016. "Coloniality of Gender and Power: From Postcoloniality to Decoloniality." In *The Oxford Handbook of Feminist Theory*, edited by Lisa Disch and Mary Hawkesworth, 100–20. New York, NY and Oxford: Oxford University Press.

Mendoza, Breny. 2017. "Colonial Connections." *Feminist Studies* 43 (3): 637–45.

202 *Caroline Betemps*

Mohanty, Chandra Talpade. 2013. "Transnational Feminist Crossings: On Neoliberalism and Radical Critique" (Intersectionality: Theorizing Power, Empowering Theory). *Signs* 38 (4): 967–91.

Pochmann, Marcio. 2022. *O neocolonialismo à espreita: Mudanças estruturais na sociedade brasileira*. São Paulo: Edições Sesc.

Sandoval, Chela. 2000. *Methodology of the Oppressed*. Minneapolis, MN and London: University of Minnesota Press.

Tlostanova, Madina, Suruchi Thapar-Björkert, and Redi Koobak. 2019. "The Postsocialist 'Missing Other' of Transnational Feminism?." *Feminist Review* 121 (1): 81–7.

Villiers, J. C. de. 2006. "The Dutch East India Company, Scurvy and the Victualling Station at the Cape." *SAMJ* 96 (2).

The Washington Post. 2022. "Report: Fatal Force." May 6. www.washingtonpost.com/graphics/investigations/police-shootings-database/.

Wimmer, Andreas, and Nina Glick Schiller. 2003. "Methodological Nationalism and Beyond: Nation-state Building, Migration and the Social Sciences." *Global Networks* 2.2 (4): 301–34.

16 Re-Routing the Sexual

A Regional and Relational Lens in Theorizing Sexuality in the Middle East (West Asia)

Adriana Qubaiova

Can the adoption of a regional perspective in theorizing gender and sexuality serve as a productive feminist tool for knowledge-making? In this chapter, I argue that regionalism offers a unique perspective on researching gender and sexuality; one that can remain feminist while working to circumvent the cycle of perpetual reference to Western and Northern centres, hence contributing to rearticulating feminist knowledge in a troubled field.

Theories of the transnational travel of ideas frequently suffer not only from a Northern and Western orientation but also from a recurring flattening of geopolitical situatedness and difference, often in favour of a universalizing sameness. Even when difference is acknowledged, it seldom escapes being defined in relation to the Northern and Western centres. In my work as a gender and sexuality scholar, I am acutely aware of the messy and often violent imposition of concepts such as sexuality or Queer Theory in postcolonial areas, including the Middle East (hereafter West Asia). At the same time, I see the potential in building Queer and feminist solidarities across the globe through the transnational flow of ideas, people, and agendas. Women, feminist activists, and scholars in the region are intimately familiar with the contradiction posed by transnationalism; they navigate a yearning for global sisterhood among the violent hierarchization imposed on them through the very claim of globality.

In what follows, I review how scholars have theorized this interaction as it specifically pertains to the study of sexuality in and about West Asia. I reveal how "stuck" the scholarship is in this contradiction and then suggest that we turn our attention towards a regional lens. Seeing through such a lens opens up the potential for theorizing gender and sexuality as a set of power relations configured among various actors, systems, and politics in West Asia, and *not only* through the centre–periphery route. By moving away from this dominant route, feminist and Queer scholarship can shed more light on the neighbouring context, on regional relations, and on relationality itself as a mode of analysis, hence creating a feminist alternative.

Understanding Gender and Sexuality Studies in Middle East Studies

Although I have begun using West Asia instead of the Middle East, I continue using Middle East Studies when referring to the field of area studies itself. Sexuality

DOI: 10.4324/9781003378761-19

204   *Adriana Qubaiova*

Studies in the field of Middle East Area Studies faces an irreconcilable tension today: How can scholars use a modern European category of analysis such as "sexuality", accompanied by Western-originating theories such as Queer Theory, to conceptualize the region's erotic practices? While some scholars have argued that one can indeed use and expand these conceptual toolkits in ways that make them relevant to Middle Eastern histories of desire (Babayan and Najmabadi 2008), others wondered what Queer Theory would look like "when it is not routed through Euro-American histories, sexualities, locations, or bodies" (Mikdashi and Puar 2016: 215), and whether it is indeed possible for Queer Theory to divest itself of its US origins.

This debate has pushed the field of Middle Eastern Sexuality Studies in two directions. The first is most prominently marked by the work of Joseph Massad, who posits that the study of sexuality in a previously colonized region is a continuation of colonial and imperial intervention (Massad 2007, 2015). How can a Western and Northern field and its concepts *not* travel through imperialist channels? If we look at the region today, many of its current political and socio-economic conditions are strongly tied to its subordinate relationship with US and EU imperialist politics. Imperialist militarized intervention is rampant, including, for example, the bloody and failed occupations of Iraq and Afghanistan, the war in Syria, heavily marked by Russian and American interventions, or the 2020 American "Deal of the Century" plan that lends impunity to Israel's ongoing illegal occupation of Palestine, to name just a few. Beyond militarized occupation, the region has also suffered the political undermining of democratic aspirations, most notably during the Arab Revolts of 2011, economic sanctions, and economic setbacks due to IMF and World Bank lending policies. And while transnational solidarity and assistance have also flourished, some are implicated in perpetuating the region's inferiority, including transnational NGOs and the humanitarian machine. Therefore, anyone navigating gender and sexual non-normativity in the region is primarily experiencing this regime of global economic and racial inequality first-hand.

It is thus no surprise that several scholars see fields such as Sexuality Studies, Queer Theory, or Gay and Lesbian Studies as yet another Western and Northern intervention into Southern and Eastern lives, and a continuation of the drawing of Orientalist depictions of the Other using gender, sexuality, and the erotic more broadly (Said 1978; Boone 2014). In this sense, scholars such as Massad would argue that even contemporary identification using the transnational categories of LGBT(IQ) is part of the "Gay International's" mission and "incitement to discourse", which results in creating "homosexuals, as well as gays and lesbians, where they did not [previously] exist" (2007: 163). With such a stance, Massad directly criticizes regional and local LGBT rights NGOs for taking part in perpetuating Western and Northern imperialist hetero- and homonormativity. By tracing the history of non-normative desire, he demonstrates that the very modern concept of sexuality relies on the unequal transnational travel of ideas, bodies, and politics (Massad 2007, 2015).

A second direction in the field supports the expansion in excavating and (re) writing the history of sexuality but rejects the Massadian depiction of sexuality's

Re-Routing the Sexual 205

unidirectional travel from West to East (Babayan and Najmabadi 2008). Rather, its supporters see Queer Theory as useful, if not essential, for informing the conceptualizing of contemporary non-normative desires, and even past ones such as sexual regulation in 19th-century Iran (Najmabadi 2008). In other words, this scholarship agrees that it is vital to first rewrite the history of erotic desire – an overlap with Massad and other historians, as well as with decolonial approaches to theorizing gender and sexuality (Lugones 2008) – but still insists on the relevance of Queer Theory and transnational Sexuality Studies more broadly to the conceptualization of this history (Traub 2008).

What these two directions have in common is that they frequently skip over the very people they are speaking about; the gender and sexually non-normative people who are navigating this conundrum first-hand today (Qubaiova 2019). This is partly because much of the scholarship on West Asian sexualities began approaching the debate from the fields of history and literary studies (El-Rouayheb 2005; Habib 2007; Mourad 2013; Hammad 2016). At the same time, engaging directly with people's daily lived realities through anthropological studies has been difficult due to the region's prolonged suffering from Western-led wars and illegal occupations, which not only limited access but also rendered life "overbearing" for local researchers, that is, characterized by "the weight of seemingly unmoving and non-negotiable circumstances and forces" (Kanafani and Sawaf 2017: 4). Today, emerging anthropological and ethnographic works are multiplying and answering this need, many of them written by local or regional researchers (Kaedbey 2014; Merabet 2014; Moussawi 2020). However, they remain few, and some apply Queer Theory without much interrogation of its US origins beyond a passing acknowledgement.

This debate continues to pose a difficult task for scholars of contemporary sexuality and activists alike, who are attempting to capture the reality of people's non-normative lives in the present, as they navigate the current manifestation of the above tension. As a feminist scholar from the region, I cannot ignore the relevance of Queer Theory and Sexuality Studies for analysing the region's contemporary politics and lived realities (Qubaiova 2019). After all, as Anna Tsing reminds us, in a world where the local and the global continuously interact with friction, the unequal contamination of ideas, bodies, and environments is inevitable (Tsing 2005, 2015). At the same time, the nascent field of Queer Sexuality Studies in West Asia must not ignore its deep attachment to the European and American theoretical frameworks that frequently force each conversation back to the Northern and Western centre, as Massad warns us. How, then, can we conceptualize sexuality without reaffirming imperialism and without denying the place of gender and sexual non-normativity in our lives? How might we move the debate in a productive direction while acknowledging the central tension within it?

This conundrum is not exactly new. Similar kinds of debates about the globality of feminism, or the place of a universal understanding of human rights, have been fleshed out between Western, postcolonial, and post-socialist scholars for decades (Mohanty 2003; Bakshi et al. 2016; Tlostanova et al. 2016). While feminist movements that claim to be global often hold White[1] and Western privilege at their

206 *Adriana Qubaiova*

centre, the transnational movement of feminist ideas and people has also enabled precious alliances that could exert pressure both locally and globally. Similarly, while the Global North has used the discourse of human rights (HR) to justify illegal occupation and war in the Global South, many across the Global South have adopted and redefined this discourse to seek legitimacy for their civil rights (Basu 2016), including, for example, the Lebanese Women's Right to Nationality and Full Citizenship campaign that argues for the right of Lebanese women to pass nationality to their spouses and children.

While ideas travel transnationally, there remains far too little interest in writing the sexual or the erotic outside of the frame of the West–North to East–South route. In fact, such a suggestion is often treated as unimaginable. For example, during the numerous times that I presented my study on alternative motherhood practices among sexually non-normative Syrian refugee men in Beirut, I was always met with the same question: "how is their practice of motherhood related to Black queer house-ballroom kinship cultures in New York?" The short answer is: "it isn't". The long answer forces me to refer back to the US as a centre of knowledge production, acknowledge the Queer house-ballroom cultures in New York (even though periph-eral within the US context, they are treated as universalizable in the context of Queer kinship), and emphasize that my study is grounded in local and regional Arab kinship structures. From the point of view of a feminist regional lens, the main ques-tion here should be: Why should we assume that a Syrian refugee in Lebanon has more in common with Black and Latino house-ballroom cultural practices of Queer kinship in the Bronx, than with concepts of kinship and practices of motherhood in Homs, Aleppo, Damascus, or Beirut? The naturalization of this assumption not only reflects the dominance of West–North travel to the South–East but also dem-onstrates that even creating new concepts or attempting new routes is unthinkable within the academy without a reference back to the centre that would, ultimately, enrich knowledge about the centre itself and not the periphery. The subaltern can speak, but not without permission, redirection, and translation (Spivak 1988).

There remains little theorization of how diverse members of the region affect each other, how they interact, and what role this interaction plays in establishing gender and sexual norms and non-normativities. How is it, for example, that the reclamation of Queer from a slur to a theory is assumed to have more resonance in Arabic-speaking communities than the regional travel of derogatory Arabic terms such as *Shaz* or *Luti*? How can a regional lens rectify this absence and multiply the routes of knowledge travel?

Regionalism

I propose regionalism as a useful feminist analytical perspective that promises a richer understanding of gender, sexuality, and the erotic more broadly, as concepts shaped by inter-regional relations. Regionalism can remain feminist when we con-stantly acknowledge power inequality, when we break down limited conceptual binaries, and when we prioritize voices from the region itself and do not re-route them through the centre's channels.

Regionalism, however, has a border problem. Scholars of sexuality and regionalism have attempted to answer this critique by relying on "queering" for border disruption. For example, Chiang and Wong argue that: "the critical promise of queer regionalism lies precisely in its refusal to frame scalar units in a pre-defined way. Indeed, the elasticity in both the regional and the queer defies unifying and coherent scalar units" (2016: 4). If regionalism is imagined as a halfway point between the global and the local, then it does little to dismantle the operating scalar units. Additionally, relying on "queering" as the sole strategy for challenging borders not only traps "queer" into meaning only "disruptive" – a reductionist function of Queer Theory – but also still forces us into the same problematic of using Western and Northern tools uncritically. We must be more imaginative. This is why I imagine a regional lens to function together with the principle of relationality. Approaching sexuality through this lens means analysing social phenomena and practices *in relation* to contextual events within the region itself. It means shifting the scales of transnationalism from a perspective that privileges Western and Northern centrism and the unidirectional flow of ideas, *and* also scaling up from a decolonial perspective that argues for excavating a pure local origin in local history.

I further argue that reading relationally, reading regionally, offers new insights into defining the sexual through the feminist principle of breaking persistent knowledge-making binaries between the West and North, on the one hand, and the rest on the other. Moreover, regionalism insists on the relevance of the broader neighbouring context in which phenomena such as sexual acts, practices, and activism take place, and offers a complication to the story of the sexual itself, extending it beyond being only a field stuck in a debate between transnational imposition and local authenticity.

In the next section, I demonstrate how to employ a regional lens. First, I argue for the simple analytical outcome that is accomplished by renaming the Middle East as West Asia. Second, I show how inter-relational knowledge can offer new insights into gender regimes by analysing the gendered symbolism in the Treaty of Brotherhood between Syria and Lebanon. Finally, I end with suggestions on how to rewrite the history of sexual activism through offsetting the dominant interpretive frames.

What's in a Name? From Middle East to West Asia

Scholars of Middle East Studies are acutely aware of the field's problematic name. One major issue is that the name continues to position the people in relation to Europe and ties them to a geographical space on the periphery. As many have noted, the region's name is connected to the Cold War era, during which states were divided in accordance with their political positions and strategic importance. After 1989 and the collapse of the Soviet Union, the region became a primary site of Western intervention, increasingly so in the aftermath of the 9/11 attacks and the subsequent US-led War on Terror. These developments saw area studies become "an intelligence-gathering force for consolidating US power" (Arondekar and Patel 2016: 152), while also becoming a central field from which to critique imperialist

208　*Adriana Qubaiova*

politics (Naber 2013). Because of this legacy, the name communicates the continuation of colonial epistemological violence through contemporary imperialism; a process that decolonial thinkers refer to as the coloniality of power (Quijano 2000).

Another problem posed by the name is disagreement over whom is included. While some scholars see the Middle East as including only Arabic-speaking nation-states, others include Iran, Israel, and Turkey. Likewise, scholars often add Egypt due to its proximity to regional conditions, despite being geographically located in North Africa. In other instances, countries as far away as Afghanistan and Pakistan are included. Still, some choose to focus on Arab ethnicity as the region's main defining marker, choosing a term such as "Arab-majority" countries, while openly acknowledging that the name erases ethnic diversity (Deeb and Winegar 2012). While scholars are careful to define whom they include in their use of the "Middle East", politicians and the media in general have misused the term's wide applicability to consolidate their depiction of a hostile region that requires intervention. In such public discourse, Arab, Muslim, Sikh, and Kurd all became synonymous categories. Thus, instead of serving as a way to emphasize our shared history and experiences, the term is repeatedly misused to collapse ethnic and racial diversity in the service of racism. This dynamic is once again enabled by the term's function in modern imperialist history.

As noted earlier, in my work I have begun using West Asia instead of the Middle East (see, for example, Ninan Koshy quoted in Spivak 2003: 1), but I continue using Middle East Studies when referring to the field of area studies itself. This simple replacement is an attempt to disrupt the taken-for-granted name and expose the imperialist relations that continue to dominate its meaning. The sense of unfamiliarity and interruption that West Asia may cause the reader to experience is purposeful. It is a hiccough, a kind of jolt that forces us to re-imagine in relation to whom, or to where, is the region middle and/or east to? And what does West Asia mean? While undermining the region's problematic name, West Asia also opens up a new set of conversations with North, South, and East Asia, rather than serving as a route to Europe or the United States. Given some shared histories of language, colonialism, and modern capitalist imperialism, there is ample room to rethink the region through its relations to its geographically proximate neighbours. While not a perfect replacement, the analytical promise here is that such a term can provide a route to shake up some of the fundamental structures of knowledge. For example, Arondekar and Patel (2016) ask: What would the concept of race look like if it was not viewed solely through "structures of representation that foreground the Atlantic model" in the history of the transatlantic slave trade? (2016: 157). West Asia today is heavily reliant on East Asian migrant labour that is premised on gendered regimes of colourism and racial difference. While few academics remain committed to exploring this structure, a critical and theoretical account of racialization *between* these regions is hard to find. How might we better understand the function of race as an identity marker, and racism as a structure of inequality, if we consider it as one fundamental relation of labour and migration between West and East Asia? This does not mean throwing out the functioning definitions of race that are based on the transatlantic model; rather, it means focusing our analytical lens elsewhere into our homes and neighbouring contexts.

Conceptualizing the Sexual Differently

I now proceed to give an example from my primary research site in Lebanon. Definitions of the sexual in Lebanon are intimately tied to regional power dynamics and political events, including geopolitical relationships with Syria, Palestine, Israel, Iran, Saudi Arabia, and others. Relations with Syria in particular have tangible effects on the lives of people in Lebanon. Gendered narratives depicting the political relationship between Syria and Lebanon have frequently oscillated between images of the "Arab brother" and the threatening, invading "foreign other". The feminist anthropologist Suad Joseph has argued that privileging the conjugal relationship as the main symbol of citizenship is an inadequate approach for theorizing state relations and citizenship itself in this context (Joseph 1999, 2000). Instead, Joseph claims that "natal relationships often have been seen to compete with husband/wife relationships" and are frequently perceived as more powerful in the determining of social relations (Joseph 2000: 117). If we take natal relationships such as brotherhood seriously and examine their symbolic function in state discourse, then Joseph's analysis indicates that we can draw different conclusions about the very definitions of the sexual.

For example, in 1991, Syria and Lebanon signed the treaty of "Brotherhood, Cooperation, and Coordination", detailing the nature of their "special brotherly tie" (United Nations 1992). The treaty's text offers an astute depiction of this tenacious duality between Brother and Other. On the one hand, the treaty refers to the two states as "brothers" and their relationship as "fraternal" three times on the first page, citing "roots of kinship, history, common affiliation, joint destiny and shared interests" as the maternal origins of this Arab fraternity, without explicitly making reference to the mother – the Arab Umma (nation).[2] In a move typical of modern nationalist discourses, the treaty employs pan-Arabist rhetoric and draws an imagined continuum between Syrian and Lebanese pre-colonial Arab unity and a future "joint destiny" to underscore a naturalized movement forward towards progress (United Nations 1992). The brotherhood metaphor is thus useful in normalizing quite serious political and military conflicts between the two nations – which includes the Syrian occupation of Lebanon from the end of the civil war until 2005 – as nothing more than predictable and inevitable brotherly quarrels, that is, fights that do not threaten the very basis of the relationship, its past or its future.

Notably absent from this richly gendered and familial imagery are references to sexuality, rendering it an imagined homosocial relation. Moreover, this relationship is not portrayed as a happy marriage – as the word choice of "shared destiny" might seem to suggest – but rather as a natural result of pre-existing and unchangeable familial ties. In other words, "(biological) brothers will be brothers" in spite of any conflict, and the conflict will be a quarrel but not depicted as a rape, as is common in depictions of the Israeli occupation of Lebanon and Palestine, for example, or other US interventions in West Asia. Therefore, even though the unequal power relationship is revealed and acknowledged, it is neutralized by the absence of a sexual dimension in its portrayal and justified through using the idea of a natural hierarchy between an older sibling and a younger one. At the same time, however,

210 *Adriana Qubaiova*

neutralization through familial hierarchies erases incest and familial rape from the realm of family relations. This erasure is not coincidental; rather, it is intentional in acknowledging only specific definitions of violence and maintaining the family as the principle structural unit.[3]

This type of regional-relational analysis pushes us to take inter-regional power dynamics seriously as key to our understandings of gender and sexuality. By tying conceptions of normativity to ideas of kinship, homosociality, and the non-sexual, it is easy to see how conceptions of non-normativity could then include notions of foreignness and the sexual, and hence how the sexually non-normative becomes an area of punishment locally (Amar 2013). Indeed, in the same treaty described earlier, once the text begins to address security issues, direct references to brotherhood are dropped, and a language of internal and external state threat is adopted instead, in a form that clearly reveals the unequal positions of both states towards each other. While there is no explicit mention of sexualization, the effect is to associate the Other (in this case Syrians in Lebanon) with unwelcome invaders. A regional-relational lens would hence shed more light on the building of the concepts of normativity and non-normativity and the ways in which these notions shape the very definitions of gender and sexuality.

Re-Writing the Story of LGBT Activism Through a Regional Lens

As briefly explored in the introduction, scholars such as Joseph Massad view the creation of LGBT organizations in West Asia as part of the Gay International's imperialist politics. While one might think that this is only the view of one academic, it has been met with much reaction from regional activists. Lebanese activists in particular have responded to this position using various arguments. For example, Ghassan Makarem, one of the co-founders of the first LGBT rights organization in Lebanon, HELEM, argued that LGBT activists are not "Agents of the West" or mindless imitators of Western politics (Makarem 2009). Anonymous members of a Lebanese queer women's group also addressed this debate in a collection of stories titled *Bareed Mista3jil*. They argued that the transnational term "queer" represents their politics more accurately than "LGBT" acronyms, and that homosexuality in the region can be found in much 7th-century erotic poetry, hence proving its local existence across time and not its imposition by the West (Meem 2009). Both activist responses continue to inform the debate over the sexual as one between an impositional imperialist West and a local authentic practice that I reviewed earlier.

However, we can complicate this debate if we consider the story of LGBT activism as not simply part of the Gay International or as only an extension of 7th-century erotic sensibilities. The impulse to formally organize into a group advocating for sexual freedoms in Beirut was triggered by two critical regional events. The first was the perceived increase in repression in Lebanon, which, according to my interlocutors, included a proposal at the governmental level that would further broaden Lebanon's anti-homosexuality law to include homosexual love relations and not only the act of penetration. Such a law would effectively have moved beyond

Re-Routing the Sexual 211

penalizing an "act" to penalizing a sexual orientation or practice, and hence punishing a type of person. Second, the Queen Boat raid in Cairo in 2001, in which over 50 Egyptian men were arrested and tried in military court, was perceived as a very threatening precedent for various leftist activists in Beirut (Makarem 2011). These two events pushed activists to create a new group specifically for non-normative sexual politics and to begin organizing regionally.

Additional regional events contributed to HELEM's and other activist groups' growth and public engagement with sexuality as a political issue. For example, during the US military occupation of Iraq from 2003 onwards, a wave of organized murder campaigns against feminine men in the country led many to flee and seek refuge in Lebanon, pushing the activists to engage transnational humanitarian funding to which they have access to assist them (HRW 2009). Likewise, frequent moral panics in the United Arab Emirates, Qatar, and elsewhere around so-called masculinized women, or boyat (from "boy"), were debated in queer women's activist circles to reach a better understanding of the phenomenon and its (in) applicability to the Lebanese context. Therefore, such regional events and relations with neighbouring countries profoundly inform the politics of gender and sexuality through (re)defining (non-)normativity, the role of armed conflict in perpetuating violence against gender and sexual difference, and the postcolonial state's role in defining internal others (Amar 2013). Hence, it is clear that adopting a regional framework of analysis that centralizes regional relations can greatly enrich our understanding of the reproduction of gendered non-normative sexualities and their politics in West Asia. Chiefly, it can tell a different story about desire than only the debate between imperial imposition and local authenticity. Instead, a new story emerges about gender and sexual non-normativity becoming an area of state intervention and punishment, and about a cross-regional activist response.

Conclusion

My analysis pushes us towards a more systemic exploration of the role of the regional scale as a central tenet for informing gender and sexuality, in West Asia and beyond. Adding the third pillar of "the regional" helps us to complicate the boundaries between the local and the global, and the story of the imperialist and transnational travel of concepts and politics. A regional perspective is more effective in revealing the permeability of these conceptual boundaries, while also moving us away from seeing their interaction as only vertical or horizontal. Rather, we can imagine the regional as a three-dimensional wave, vibrating across the horizontal while also shifting up and down the vertical. Therefore, what I have proposed is that, instead of analysing sexual politics and gender relations in West Asia as solely an interaction between imperialist channels of transfer from the North and the West to the South and the East, or as new arrivals on a map of porous transnational analysis that still refers back to the empire in order to make sense of itself, or even as pure manifestations of local and trans-historical sexuality, we should aim our analytical gaze elsewhere. Rather than focusing on the Gay International in writing about sexuality politics in Lebanon and West Asia, we should examine regional

212 *Adriana Qubaiova*

events that inform contemporary lived realities. For example, we should be looking at emerging regional conversations in spaces such as Nadwe; a semi-above-ground annual feminist and "Queer" conference and a series of events that brings together activists from West Asia and North Africa to build a joint cross-regional politics. These conversations from and about the people navigating the politics of gender and sexuality can offer a very different perspective and challenge the concepts with which we work in academia.

Notes

1 I capitalize White to situate Whiteness as a racial category in an unequal racial system of power that privileges White over Black. Drawing attention to the category through capitalization removes its neutral appearance as simply an ahistorical colour. See Appiah (2020) for a summary of this debate.
2 The slippage between "brotherhood" and "fraternity" is unnoticed due to the word's shared Arabic root; however, it is informative insofar as it is read alongside the absent reference to the Umma, as it denotes a homosocial bond.
3 I thank my colleagues from the STINT workshop at the University of Western Cape for alerting me to this point.

References

Amar, Paul. 2013. *The Security Archipelago: Human-Security States, Sexuality Politics, and the End of Neoliberalism*. Durham, NC: Duke University Press.
Appiah, Kwame A. 2020. "The Case for Capitalizing the B in Black." *The Atlantic*, June 18. www.theatlantic.com/ideas/archive/2020/06/time-to-capitalize-blackand-white/613159/.
Arondekar, Anjali, and Geeta Patel. 2016. "Area Impossible: Notes Toward an Introduction." *GLQ: A Journal of Lesbian and Gay Studies* 22 (2): 151–71.
Babayan, Kathryn, and Afsaneh Najmabadi (eds.). 2008. *Islamicate Sexualities: Translations Across Temporal Geographies of Desire*. Cambridge, MA and London: Harvard University Press.
Bakshi, Sandeep, Suhraiya Jivraj, and Silvia Posocco (eds.). 2016. *Decolonizing Sexualities: Transnational Perspectives, Critical Interventions*. Oxford: Counterpress.
Basu, Soumita. 2016. "The Global South Writes 1325 (Too)." *International Political Science Review* 37 (3): 362–74.
Boone, Joseph A. 2014. *The Homoerotics of Orientalism*. New York, NY: Columbia University Press.
Chiang, Howard, and Alvin K. Wong. 2016. "Queering the Transnational Turn: Regionalism and Queer Asia." *Gender, Place & Culture: A Journal of Feminist Geography* 23 (11): 1–14.
Deeb, Lara, and Jessica Winegar. 2012. "Anthropology of Arab-Majority Societies." *Annual Review of Anthropology* 41: 537–58.
El-Rouayheb, Khaled. 2005. *Before Homosexuality in the Arab-Islamic World, 1500–1800*. Chicago, IL and London: University of Chicago Press.
Habib, Samar. 2007. *Female Homosexuality in the Middle East: Histories and Representations* (1st ed.). New York, NY and London: Routledge.
Hammad, Hanan. 2016. *Industrial Sexuality: Gender, Urbanization, and Social Transformation in Egypt*. Austin, TX: University of Texas Press.

HRW. 2009. "'They Want Us Exterminated': Murder, Torture, Sexual Orientation and Gender in Iraq." *HRW.* www.hrw.org/report/2009/08/17/they-want-us-exterminated/murder-torture-sexual-orientation-and-gender-iraq.

Joseph, Suad. 1999. *Intimate Selving in Arab Families: Gender, Self and Identity.* Syracuse, NY: Syracuse University Press.

Joseph, Suad. 2000. "Civic Myths, Citizenship, and Gender in Lebanon." In *Gender and Citizenship in the Middle East,* edited by Suad Joseph, 107–36. Syracuse, NY: Syracuse University Press.

Kaedbey, Dima. 2014. "Building Theory Across Struggles: Queer Feminist Thought From Lebanon." Doctoral Dissertation, Ohio State University, OhioLINK Electronic Theses and Dissertations Center. http://rave.ohiolink.edu/etdc/view?acc_num=osu 1405945625.

Kanafani, Samar, and Zina Sawaf. 2017. "Being, Doing and Knowing the Field: Reflections on Ethnographic Practice in the Arab Region." *Contemporary Levant* 2 (1): 3–11.

Lugones, Maria. 2008. "The Coloniality of Gender." *Worlds and Knowledges Otherwise* 2 (2): 1–17.

Makarem, Ghassan. 2009. "We Are Not Agents of the West." *Reset DOC Dialogues on Civilization* (blog), December 14. www.resetdoc.org/story/we-are-not-agents-of-the-west/.

Makarem, Ghassan. 2011. "The Story of Helem." *Journal of Middle East Women's Studies* 7 (3): 98–112.

Massad, Joseph A. 2007. *Desiring Arabs.* Chicago, IL and London: University of Chicago Press.

Massad, Joseph A. 2015. *Islam in Liberalism.* Chicago, IL and London: University of Chicago Press.

Meem. 2009. *Bareed Mista3jil.* Beirut: Meem.

Merabet, Sofian. 2014. *Queer Beirut.* Austin, TX: University of Texas Press.

Mikdashi, Maya, and Jasbir K. Puar. 2016. "Queer Theory and Permanent War." *GLQ: A Journal of Lesbian and Gay Studies* 22 (2): 215–22.

Mohanty, Chandra T. 2003. *Feminism Without Borders: Decolonizing Theory, Practicing Solidarity.* Durham, NC and London: Duke University Press.

Mourad, Sara. 2013. "Queering the Mother Tongue." *International Journal of Communication* 7: 2533–46.

Moussawi, Ghassan. 2020. *Disruptive Situations: Fractal Orientalism and Queer Strategies in Beirut* (1st ed.). Philadelphia, PA: Temple University Press.

Naber, Nadine. 2013. "Transnational Anti-Imperialism and Middle East Women's Studies." *Jadaliyya – 2013."* جدلية. www.jadaliyya.com/Details/28909.

Najmabadi, Afsaneh. 2008. "Types, Acts, or What? Regulation of Sexuality in Nineteenth-Century Iran." In *Islamicate Sexualities: Translations Across Temporal Geographies of Desire,* edited by Kathryn Babayan and Afsaneh Najmabadi, 275–96. Cambridge, MA and London: Harvard University Press.

Qubaiova, Adriana. 2019. *Cross-Bracing Sexualities: Hedging 'Queer'/Sexual Non-Normativity in Beirut.* Budapest: Central European University. https://sierra.ceu.edu/record=b1421476.

Quijano, Aníbal. 2000. "Coloniality of Power and Eurocentrism in Latin America." *International Sociology* 15 (2): 215–32.

Said, Edward W. 1978. *Orientalism.* New York, NY: Pantheon Books.

Spivak, Gayatri Chakravorty. 1988. *Can the Subaltern Speak?* Basingstoke: Macmillan.

Spivak, Gayatri Chakravorty. 2003. *Other Asians.* Malden, MA: Blackwell Publishing.

214 *Adriana Qubaiova*

Tlostanova, Madina V., Suruchi Thapar-Bjorkert, and Redi Koobak. 2016. "Border Thinking and Disidentification: Postcolonial and Postsocialist Feminist Dialogues." *Feminist Theory* 17 (2): 211–28.

Traub, Valerie. 2008. "The Past Is a Foreign Country? The Times and Spaces of Islamicate Sexuality Studies." In *Islamicate Sexualities: Translations Across Temporal Geographies of Desire*, edited by Kathryn Babayan and Afsaneh Najmabadi, 1–40. Cambridge, MA and London: Harvard University Press.

Tsing, Anna Lowenhaupt. 2005. *Friction: An Ethnography of Global Connection*. Princeton, NJ: Princeton University Press.

Tsing, Anna Lowenhaupt. 2015. *The Mushroom at the End of the World: On the Possibility of Life in Capitalist Ruins*. Princeton, NJ: Princeton University Press.

United Nations. 1992. "Treaty of Brotherhood, Cooperation, and Coordination Between the Syrian Republic and the Lebanese Republic". *United Nations – Treaty Series*, 154–57. https://peacemaker.un.org/lebanon-syria-brotherhood-treaty91

17 Beautiful Diversity?

Diversity Rhetoric, Ethnicized Visions, and Nesting Post-Soviet Hegemonies in the Multimedia Project *The Ethnic Origins of Beauty*

Dinara Yangeldina

The multimedia project *The Ethnic Origins of Beauty* (EOB, Ivanova 2023) aims to represent the ethnic diversity of the entire world through women's beauty. This trilingual project with global ambition is coordinated by Russian photographer and photojournalist Natalia Ivanova and is comprised of portraits and video interviews with young women "representing" different ethnicities. It has a social media presence on YouTube,[1] Instagram,[2] Facebook,[3] and VK,[4] as well its own website.[5] I first came across EOB in 2016 and was lured by its decolonial promises, while being perplexed by its contradictions.[6] This chapter aims to unpack these entanglements by looking at how ethno-cultural diversity functions within EOB. I argue that, to fully grasp its operation, one needs to unpack EOB on two interrelated planes. First, it is necessary to deal with the global rhetoric of diversity and explain its visual workings. Second, firmly grounding EOB's diversity in the "ethnicized vision of the world" (Hutchings and Tolz 2015) rooted in the tensions of post-Soviet Russian multi-ethnicity allows one to simultaneously contextualize it, de-centre its global aspirations, and pay attention to post-soviet hegemonies.

These tensions comprise the legacies of early Soviet "chronic ethnophilia" (Slezkine 1994) and the affirmative action measures realized through the USSR's indigenization policies (Martin 2001): the promotion and support of ethnic identities, languages and local elites, the construction of ethnoterritorial units and the creation of nations. Promoting ethnonational identities was seen as a stepping-stone within the programme that Hirsch called "state-sponsored evolutionism" (2005). This was an effort to build a common Soviet identity held together by the Russian language and culture as the lingua franca of the USSR through merging "the family of nations" into the Soviet people (Zamyatin 2018). While early Bolshevik anti-imperialist, internationalist, and anti-racist policy was critical of this "great Russian chauvinism", from the 1930s the hierarchy of nationalities/ethnicities,[7] with ethnic Russians on top, became salient. Soviet policy revealed contradictory tendencies: looking at nationalities/ethnicities in culturalist, non-biological, and historicist terms but also primordializing them through ascriptive nationality/ethnicity. This was an official category in Soviet

DOI: 10.4324/9781003378761-20

216   *Dinara Yangeldina*

passports and from 1938 it was "inherited" from one's parents (Baiburin 2012). Recent research dedicated to the everyday racism within the USSR has complicated the officially proclaimed rhetoric of "the friendship of peoples" (Law 2012; Matusevich 2020; Sahadeo 2007). Post-Soviet Russia has inherited Soviet models of governing diverse populations, characterized as an "ethnicized vision of the world" (Hutchings and Tolz 2015: 23). It retained the Soviet model of "institutionalized and territorialized ethnicity" (Ibid., 2015: 24), albeit all official mention of nationality/ethnicity in passports was abandoned in 1997. Contemporary Russia is fraught with differential tensions between the remains of inherited ethno-territorial federalism and a symbolic recognition of ethnic diversity, and more or less exclusive attempts to construct a civic/ethnic "Russian nation" tied to linguistic, cultural, or ethnic Russianness (Shevel 2011). It is this tension that I aim to unpack by zooming in closer on the global/local hegemonies within EOB's diversity rhetoric.

Through the critical investigation of EOB, this chapter will contribute to the ongoing dialogue between postcolonial and postsocialist feminisms. Several scholars have argued that transnational feminism failed to include postsocialist women in its conversations (Suchland 2011; Tlostanova et al. 2019). Within such dialogues, racialized positionalities are often connected to the Global South and "women of colour", while modes of East European alterity, racializations, and aspirations to whiteness and Europeanness remain unexamined (Tlostanova et al. 2019: 83). This chapter has two broad critical goals: first, to nuance the imaginary of transnational feminisms by explicitly including post-socialist differences into the conversations on racialization and ethnicity and, second, to critically examine the relations of power within post-Soviet constructions of diversity exemplified by EOB. Building upon critical diversity studies, I begin by demonstrating how EOB as a global diversity project depoliticizes and flattens diversity through the usage of mosaic imagery in the project's photography. I then focus on the gender dimensions of ethnic symbolization in EOB and its controversial effects. Afterwards, I locate EOB within the context of post-Soviet diversity. Through examining the archive of the first batch of partially translated EOB interviews[8] conducted in Russian in 2014 in Moscow, I foreground discussions about racialization, language politics, and the place of ethnic Russianness in order to demonstrate the workings of post-soviet hegemonies.

Global circuits of value inform the messy origins of EOB. As its author, Russian photojournalist Natalia Ivanova, who lives and works in France,[9] stated in one interview, the idea of ethnic diversity as a resource and inspiration for EOB came to her while she was in Paris and witnessed diversity there. Post-Soviet diversity and Russia's multi-ethnicity became translated into a valuable commodity within a global valuation of difference through filming the first interviews in Moscow. In 2014, EOB received an acknowledgement from UNESCO, which hosted an exhibition introducing the project to the public at its Paris headquarters as a celebration of International Women's Day.

Unpacking the Global Diversity Rhetoric of EOB

Making ethnicity its primary focus of attention, EOB sees its significance as educating the public and facilitating inter-ethnic cohesion and peacekeeping. Ivanova describes EOB as a:

> non-profit, artistic, documentary and research project about the ethnic diversity of mankind, presented through the beauty of women of all ethnic groups of the world. The aim of this project is to show the real scale of ethnocultural diversity in a full, systematic and creative way; to illustrate each and every distinctive ethnicity, however small it is, and whatever its political status.[10]

Additionally, EOB stresses its contribution to the "heritage of mankind" through the creation of an "interactive collection of ethnic diversity of humanity".[11] The criteria for participating in the project include an age limit (18–35), gender (cis-women), attractiveness (defined on the website as "photogenic beauty", and on Instagram as "natural beauty face"),[12] having a "pure" ethnic background for a minimum of three generations (having both parents of the same ethnicity/nationality for three generations), and an awareness and knowledge of one's ethnic roots and culture. EOB is presented as a non-commercial project without a stable source of funding or external sponsors. The scouting of potential participants takes place mostly through social media, as well as youth and diaspora organizations.

EOB employs several visual strategies (interview videos, photos, photo collages, backstage photos/videos) to represent ethno-cultural diversity. I examine the forms of visuality produced by these strategies. Building upon visual culture scholar Gillian Rose's writing on visual methodologies (2016), I look at the power relations articulated through EOB and at the social effects of its visuality. What understandings of ethnicity and gender does it offer? What roles does it make available and what kind of seeing does it invite? How can looking at an image itself and at the modes of its production enhance the analysis of EOB?

One of EOB's visual strategies is to use mosaics to signal diversity, and this often features in its promotional videos. Scholars working within critical diversity studies have highlighted the increasingly positive value assigned to workplace diversity by a range of organizations (Swan 2010; Ahmed 2012). The language of diversity is widely used and commitments to diversity are publicly advertised and used by companies and brands for self-promotion. EOB fits this trend, along with several other artistic projects focusing on human diversity, such as the Humanae project and The Atlas of Beauty project.[13] Critical diversity studies scholar Elaine Swan (2010) analyses a photograph of a mosaic as a diversity image and looks at how difference and sameness are played out through it. Examining interpretations of racial difference through such images, Swan argues that a mosaic "inscribes difference within a sameness grid and commodifies it" (2010: 77). The mosaic metaphor and images are used by organizations both to celebrate diversity through the valuing of difference and to reproduce views of cultures as static and self-contained entities (Swan 2010: 82). Building on the work of Rose and Swan, I read the mosaic image

218 *Dinara Yangeldina*

employed by EOB (see Figure 17.1) to argue that, through its usage, difference is both recognized and also flattened out and pacified.

At first glance, EOB's use of a mosaic composed of portraits does represent diversity – indicated through different skin tones, face shapes, and eye and hair colour. Yet, simultaneously, everyone looks strangely the same in the pictures. There is a concerted effort to stress sameness in beauty through juxtaposition in the mosaic. The same editing principle has been applied to each individual face, and this produces a uniform look. All the women presented have similar makeup and long hair groomed in the same way to extend and fade into the background. Long, straight, or straightened hair functions here as a marker of beauty and femininity (this is probably what is meant by the "natural beauty" requirement). Yet a shift in skin and hair tones to fairer and lighter ones towards the upper right-hand corner

Figure 17.1 Mosaic from the project "The Ethnic Origins of Beauty", © Natalia Ivanova.
Source: Reprinted with permission from Natalia Ivanova.[14]

Beautiful Diversity? 219

can be read as reinstating Northern European beauty standards, positioning straight hair and "whiteness" "at the top" as superior.

Photos of women typifying different ethnicities are displayed as exhibits, presented for consumption by the implied viewer, who can take up a bird's-eye position to gain an overview. If the mosaic images portraying workplace diversity symbolize a happy and productive diversity (Swan 2010: 90), then the diversity displayed by EOB is a "beautiful diversity", whereby beauty becomes a strategy of containment (Giroux in Rose 2016). (Hetero)normative visions of beauty make the portrayal of ethnic diversity non-threatening and downplay any potential political meanings. Paradoxically, while Natalia Ivanova, in an interview about EOB, claims to be tired of fashion/advertising industry clichés, which make the models look homogeneous, the choices made while producing the EOB portraits reinforce the visual effect of sameness in beauty.[15]

EOB also claims to be an educational project spreading knowledge about human ethnic diversity. Experts and ethnologists are invited to author short introductory notes about the various ethnicities, which are then displayed in the description box under the videos.[16] Reliance on expert knowledge seems to contribute towards generating greater scientific credibility and legitimacy for the whole enterprise. Following Rose's suggestion that we should question the types of seeing that the visual imagery invites, I argue that the mosaic imagery of EOB encourages the implied viewer to engage in quasi-anthropological comparisons of "pure" types by presenting each woman's face as typical of a larger ethnic group. The portraiture recalls images of taxonomies of ethnic/racial classification, where "pure" types are juxtaposed against one another in a comparative table. Such visual racial comparativism was a hallmark of the scientific racialism of the 18th and 19th centuries (Keevak 2011). EOB's visuality thus encourages racialist readings. Such readings are performed in the comments' section under the videos on YouTube.[17] One commenter wonders: "Where does such mongoloidness come from in a Circassian? They are supposed to be autochthonous inhabitants of the Caucasus", while another reflects: "She is a beautiful girl, without doubt, but high cheekbones and mongoloid facial features are atypical for Circassians". Video viewers conduct battles over participants' eye shapes and bone structure, and discuss whether their facial features are typical or atypical for a particular ethnicity. For some commentators, the allegedly atypical faces of EOB participants are read as testifying to an "impure" background and suggestions of suspicious intermixing in the past. Thus, EOB's excessive focus on physical appearance and beauty provokes anxieties about the authenticity of ethnic representation.

EOB's preoccupation with beauty and physical appearance may encourage racialist readings. Natalia Ivanova, for example, argues that each ethnic group has characteristic "ethno-physiological" features.[18] This statement hints at the permeability of the boundaries between "race" and ethnicity. The representational choice that requires EOB participants to have the "same ethnicity for three generations" biologizes culture and ethnicity, presenting it as an inborn and ancestral trait, something that cannot be chosen and remains static across generations. Three works as a

220 *Dinara Yangeldina*

magical number here. The "three-generations rule" ensures an alleged typicality of ethnic representation, not "contaminated" by admixtures. Each ethnic collectivity is in turn represented by a group of three women, suggesting the saturation/representativity of such a sample.

Another set of images, found under the subsection "art" on the EOB website, has an even more disturbing feel. We see nine independent images (eight of them are presented in Figure 17.2), each of which is a composite of "sliced" images of the faces of several participants merged together into one face – three using jigsaw patterns, three horizontally and vertically aligned swatches, two other rectangular and triangular swatches, and the last one using swatches with blended contours. The intended meaning of "beauty in diversity" is overshadowed by the uncanny feeling that these images produce. The dissection of individual pictures into slices to be fitted into one portrait produces a dismembered effect, as though the faces were mutilated (see Figure 17.2).

These collages again emphasize sameness, displaying how effortlessly different pieces can be fitted together into one picture of an always-beautiful face. Yet a sense of interchangeability comes along with such effortlessness since any piece can be combined with any other to generate multiple combinations of beautiful faces. It looks as though the only mixing allowed within EOB's logic is an artistic mixing generated through the merging of sliced faces into a collage. How can we think EOB's preoccupation with origins and authenticity together with gender?

Figure 17.2 Art collage from the project "The Ethnic Origins of Beauty" © Natalia Ivanova.
Source: Reprinted with permission from Natalia Ivanova.

Ethnic Symbolization and Gender in EOB

Each EOB video presenting an interviewee opens with an ethnic folk song playing in the background. In most of the videos, the women are prompted to speak about either ethnic cuisine or customs. In the recently published teasers for upcoming videos, this tendency is even more intensified: interviewees are presented while putting on national costumes, trying on jewellery and accessories, sometimes singing or dancing, and occasionally talking. Most of the EOB videos finish by asking participants to say something in their mother tongue. As has been critically demonstrated in feminist scholarship on gender and nation, women often play a special role in the functioning of ethnic and national collectivities: they become the symbols of their people and stand for their roots and spirit (Yuval-Davis 1993: 627). Women are expected to play the role of "intergenerational transmitters of cultural traditions, customs, songs, cuisine, and, of course, the mother tongue" (Yuval-Davis 1993: 627). EOB is deeply rooted in such gendered thinking along the lines of fixed ethnic symbolisms. It not only reinforces associations of womanhood with normative visions of beauty but also firmly links it with domesticity, reproductive labour, and the transmission of culture.

Ethnic symbolization in EOB works on several levels, the most striking of which is that the titles of the video interviews do not mention the names of the interviewees. Instead, the titles, displayed on the screen while traditional music are being played, foreground only ethnonyms, emphasizing group belonging ("Buryat", "Tatar", "Bashkir", etc.). Through such framing, the possibility of looking at participants as individuals, who might have vastly divergent ideas about what ethnic belonging means to them, is foreclosed. This framing reinforces the project's taxonomical ethos, implying unity, homogeneity, and coherence within an "ethnic type". The mode of questioning employed during the interviews sustains this ethos further; questions such as "When did you realize that you are Tatar?" or "How does the fact that you are Kalmyk manifest in your daily life?", frame these women, first and foremost, as symbols of ethnic collectivities, speaking on behalf of their entire community. "What characterizes Bashkirs?" or "What is typical for Kalmyks?" is another set of questions that participants are asked in the interviews. EOB thus embraces what Brubaker called "groupism": a tendency to reify ethnic/racial groups "as if they were internally homogenous, externally bounded groups, even unitary collective actors with common purposes" (2004: 8). Moreover, the construction of members of an ethnic collectivity as having a certain number of immutable traits may be viewed as characteristic of racist discourses and politics (Law 2012: 19).

Women's behaviour, including their sexual behaviour, is used as a signifier for ethnic and cultural boundaries, foregrounding the importance of "women's culturally 'appropriate behavior'" (Yuval-Davis 1993: 627). Yuval-Davis argues that the stress on "culturally appropriate" behaviour gains specific significance for multicultural societies and that women often symbolize national and collective "honour" (1993: 627). As a close examination of the comment threads on EOB's YouTube channel demonstrates, some videos provoke heated reactions from viewers, who express sentiments of both pride and scepticism. Statements are made that evaluate

222   *Dinara Yangeldina*

the physical appearance/beauty of interviewees and approving/disapproving of them as potential candidates for marriage. Comments such as "Proud daughter of our nation", "Most beautiful amongst all others", "This one I would have married", and "Nice girl, very modest" are common. The evaluative comments about the physical appearance of interviewees suggest that, for some viewers, EOB also approximates a digital ethnic beauty pageant offering an array of videos for the consumption and evaluation of an eroticized ethnic Other.

The mode of visuality produced by EOB is deeply gendered, which begs the question: Who is not seen and why? Would people of other genders, ages and abilities have told the stories differently? Stories that might be less pleasant to hear, closer to traumatic events from the past or more politicized accounts of the present? Indeed, as Natalia Ivanova claims in the interview:

> So even if we take a very handsome young man and make him look directly into your eyes without smiling, agree with me that the image would have a different energy to it. No matter how handsome the man is, he is first of all, a warrior and his nature is manliness. We prioritize a sense of peace coming from each portrait, not a provocation.[19]

If masculinity is viewed as always threatening, then selecting young photogenic cis-women to represent the ethno-diversity of humankind works as the least confrontational strategy, where youth, femininity, and (hetero)normative beauty provide a fragile pass for the ethnic other to access the realm of the "representable". In the context of racism and xenophobia in present-day Russia, which is especially harsh towards men from the Caucasus and Central Asia, who often become victims of police harassment, a project dedicated to young men would have hardly gained similar popularity.

Despite its essentializing rhetoric, EOB's interviewees often lead a diasporic existence, studying or working in Moscow or large cities in other countries, and thus also having experiences of living abroad. Such a translocal, transnational existence complicates the authenticity claims of the project, exposing life trajectories that are less linear than the apparent ideal. As I will show in the next section, through the analysis of several interview excerpts, it is the experience of migration that often leads to the emergence of ethnic identification. In this and other ways, the interview narratives challenge the logic of representing ethnicities as primordial, static entities. This ambiguity is not always met with enthusiasm by the audience, however. It is not unusual to find commentaries to the videos posted by viewers, who criticize interviewees' life choices or reprimand them for not representing their ethnic collectivities properly through statements such as "Another one from Moscow, she is completely Russified now"; "You live in Moscow, you have a Russian name, you talk like a Russian"; and "To truly represent our ethnicity/nationality, the authors need to go to the regions and not pick someone who lives in Europe". Thus, the central representational claim of EOB can never be fulfilled in practice, since there will always be commentators for whom the interviewee is not authentic or representative enough. EOB participants are thus torn between a

Beautiful Diversity? 223

number of objectifying gazes: from quasi-anthropological racialist comparisons to diasporic gendered policing to sexualized consumption.

Disrupting Diversity

At this point, the reader might wonder: Is there anything in EOB worth salvaging? What was inspiring about it in the first place? I suggest that a change of scale might answer this question. Scaling down from the global to the regional, or localizing EOB's diversity, opens up a space for its politicization. Through the analysis of several video interviews conducted in Russian,[20] I explore three possible sites of such politicization in EOB's interviews: experiences of racialization, place of ethnic Russianness, and language politics.

The theme of racialization and navigating life in Moscow as a migrant surfaced in several EOB interviews. Moscow is a megacity with a remarkable concentration of resources, attracting internal migration within Russia as well as migration flows from South Caucasus and Central Asia. Moving to a big city from a national republic/village/small city is often cited by the participants of EOB as a foundational moment for the realization of difference. The process of moving is often the first thing they mention when they are asked the ubiquitous question: "When did you first realize that you are Circassian/Bashkir/Tatar etc.?" Interviewees speak about being categorized as others through racialization. This process of othering is insensitive towards complex "origins" and exposes the constructed nature of racialization: no matter whether you were born in Pamir, Buryatia, or Nartkala, you become "churka"[21] in Moscow.

In the following video interview with Adissa,[22] she is asked: "When was it that you first realized especially clearly that you are Buryat?" Adissa replies that it was upon her first move to Moscow in 2003, when there were very few people around who looked like her and she attracted too much attention, including negative attention and manifestations of a xenophobic Russian nationalism. She mentions that even now these problems have not disappeared entirely and that during her school-years it was especially difficult, she did not have any friends and felt homesick. In trying to answer the initial question about self-identification, she concludes: "I think it was then when I realized that I am . . .". She does not finish the sentence and starts crying and one second later the scene is cut. This moment dramatically challenges the logic of beautiful and happy diversity espoused by EOB.

Another challenge to the ideal of comfortable narratives is represented by the interview with Svetlana,[23] a Circassian actress, who currently lives in Moscow. Svetlana narrates an event that happened to her in Moscow during the rehearsals for a theatre project. She was talking about her family members with a young theatre director, routinely mentioning their names: Karina, Fatima, Alim, when he suddenly asked her: "How come you have so many *chernojopye* [black-assed] people as your acquaintances?" The original compound word "*chernojopye*" is used as a harsh racist slur within Russia to refer to people from Central Asia, the Caucasus, and other ethnic groups. This slur underlines the peculiarity of Russian racialization patterns, whereby blackness is attached not to skin colour but to phenotypical traits such as hair and facial structures or cultural belonging, names, and religion. Svetlana answered: "You know, I'm '*chernojopaya*' too, that's why". Ashamed, he apologized. Svetlana passionately narrates her answer to him, which was: "You know, it doesn't really hurt my pride". Svetlana's border positioning is peculiar: her Slavic/Russian-sounding name allows her to pass as unmarked/ethnic Russian in this context. Her interlocutor, therefore, felt free to utilize racist slurs to refer to the people she was mentioning, thinking she would relate to the joke. When she challenged him, her conversation partner apologized, ashamed, whereas Svetlana reclaimed the slur and explains that she had "enough dignity . . . not to react to provocations".

For some EOB interviewees, Moscow, where people migrate for better employment prospects, is characterized by ruthless competition and an intense speed of life. Therefore, another theme emerging from these interviews is the need to find a way of navigating this reality from an in-between position: not losing oneself or one's dignity, but at the same time remaining open to new experiences. Later, Svetlana, who moved to Moscow from Nartkala, Diana, who was born in Moscow, and Karina, who grew up in Cherkessk, narrate their experiences:

> My father used to tell me from my childhood: Sveta, "napa"! That is to say: don't lose face. Never lose face. So, this word, this spirit, it's like a faith, I carried it across my nine years in Moscow . . . where there are many people, many ethnicities, a huge mixture and there are no points of reference. So, for me, this is a type of force which together with faith allows me not to abandon my key principles. There are things I will never do. No matter how aggravating my circumstances are, or how many times I'm told that I have to switch from the Oriental culture to the Western one, find a compromise with oneself, otherwise it's impossible.[24]

> That's why it can be very hard to come to Russia, especially Moscow, and not forget yourself, not lose yourself, not follow a common way . . . My parents were born in Kusary, they have an absolutely different mentality, a different understanding of the world, a different cosmos. And we, who were born here, we are caught between two fires. So, from one side it's our parents with their traditions, their worldview, and from the other side it's Moscow, your peers, most of them Russians, other nationalities. And all the time you must navigate between your past, your roots and at the same time stay tuned, communicative, finding common language with other nations.[25]

> At first, the behaviour of my peers in Moscow seemed very strange to me. They behaved very differently. I wasn't used to it. There are many ethnic Russians living in Cherkessk, you could even say that most people who live there are Russians. But all the Russians there behave exactly like us.[26]

In the last of these quotes, Karina defies the value-laden temporalities assigned to spaces: provincial and backward regions/republics versus progressive metropolitan centres. She demonstrates the presence of a transcultural exchange flowing both

Beautiful Diversity? 225

ways: not only in Moscow, where newcomers accommodate themselves to new norms, but also in Cherkessk, where contact with locals affects the norms and values of the ethnically Russian population. However, normally, Moscow serves as a signifier of "advanced time" when juxtaposed with the regions. This is visible in the narrative of Alina, who decided to return to Nalchik after spending four years in Moscow, and describes how it was read by people around her as an incomprehensible step and as downward mobility:

> It was a turning point. I said I wanted to be closer to my roots, wanted to get back to my homeland. It was after school. I went back to Nalchik, entered a university there. No one appreciated this move. "How is it possible, you graduated from a school in Moscow!" My teachers were telling me: "Alina, why are you doing this, why do you want to go there?" And in fact, no one was waiting for me in Nalchik either, because when I got there I was told: "Girl, what on Earth are you doing here? Why did you come back here?" It offended me a bit, I was striving so hard to get there, and no one was waiting for me.[27]

De-centring Russianness?

Scaling down and situating EOB in the context of post-Soviet multi-ethnicity enables a better grasp of its contradictions. One of these is the enthusiastic embrace of EOB by non-Russian viewers, who see participation in it as a source of pride. EOB is eagerly discussed on YouTube and widely covered by diasporic media. This desire to be seen, to be represented, and to "represent" must be understood through the prism of the persistent patterns of lack of recognition of non-Russians as equal citizens within the Russian Federation, which can result in daily manifestations of racism and xenophobia. Non-Russian participants in EOB jokingly narrate experiences of being read as foreigners in their own country: the names of the national republics are perceived within Russia itself as distant and Oriental (when marked with "-stan"-ending). The appeal of EOB for minoritized groups rests on the fact that it centres "ethnicity", "no matter how small it is"[28], and not "nation" in its representational regime. This can be important to many stateless peoples scattered across several states or those who have been subsumed into larger nations and have very few outlets for expression.

Russian ethnicity is included as just one ethnicity among others in EOB, and three interviews[29] were filmed with ethnically Russian women. Suddenly, ethnic Russianness as the unquestioned norm (within Russia) becomes visible, located, and ethnicized. This is unusual in the sense that, within Russia, it is often only non-Russians who function as ethnically marked subjects. However, EOB may not be doing enough to de-centre Russianness by presenting it as just one ethnicity among many. But it is possible to repoliticize EOB through taking into consideration the ongoing politics of dismantling ethnic federalism and the contradictory projects of Russia's nation-building, including Russian language hegemony over non-Russian languages.

EOB promotes itself by posting video interviews with celebrity supporters of the project on its YouTube channel. One of these videos features the well-known

226 *Dinara Yangeldina*

Russian model Inna Zobova. I include a quote from her interview to open up a discussion about the place of Russianness within the EOB:

> I was born in Moscow and I grew up in Moscow. I lived there until the age of 17. Later, I started my international career. I lived in New York, Paris and for a little while in Japan. I was lucky to travel around the world and discover the beauty of its variety. I could think about it and realize how ethnically Russian I am inside in my mentality. I realized I was ethnic Russian very early. When I was a young girl, I stayed at the Russian mission in Cambodia. We went to the local market one day. Young women approached me there and touched my hair and skin. I couldn't understand what they wanted. Later, I was told that they thought I was covered with light powder, they thought my skin wasn't naturally white . . . This made me ask myself numerous questions that led to the roots of my personal identification. Later, in 1994, I represented Russia in the beauty pageant Miss Universe, in which 79 or 82 nationalities participated. I saw such a huge number of people who carry different genetic material and as a consequence different mentalities and physical features. And it was great! I think the mystery of the Russian soul is that we are rationally uncontrollable. We have our own inner laws, our own system of values, our own notions. That's why it is difficult for us to fit in the particular system of rules.[30]

In this excerpt, Zobova narrates how she first became aware of her ethnic Russianness in the foreign context of Cambodia. Russianness is understood here both as "whiteness" and also as a mindset informed by biologically determinist thinking linking it to genes. A different "genetic material" is reflected not only in physical features but also in mentality, which is framed as common and shared by all members of one nationality. At the same time, Zobova reproduces the narrative of the mysterious Russian soul, which does not want to be governed by law or reason. However, the fact that Zobova represented Russia at the 1994 Miss Universe beauty pageant is important for the politics of representation and the constitutive tension between competing visions of Russia. The question of who can and who cannot claim the title of Miss Russia and thus represent the country further at the Miss World and Miss Universe pageants has been a matter of contestation. In 2013, Elmira Abdrazakova won the title of Miss Russia and represented Russia at the 2013 Miss World and Miss Universe pageants. She was subjected to intense online harassment for her non-Slavic name and Tatar ethnicity and to claims that she could not legitimately represent Russia. A similar story emerged with the 2021 Eurovision song contest, when ethnically Tadjik singer Manizha Sangin was subjected to a xenophobic hate campaign for her "Russian Woman" song.

EOB's way of representing Russian ethnicity as simply "one among many in Russia" erases history and omits any mention of Russian-majority cultural hegemony. For example, one EOB interviewee who answered the question about when she realized she was ethnically Russian said that it was never something she thought about since she was simply born with it.[31] This answer contrasts with the experiences of racialization that non-Russian interviewees encountered in

Moscow, where they were forced to "realize" their alterity. The hierarchical difference implied in this contrast is not taken into account in EOB. Ethnic Russianness itself is presented in fixed, essentialist terms, as though it were not possible to become Russian through religious conversion to Orthodox Christianity, mixed marriages, cultural assimilation, or identity change.

EOB uses the Russian language as an interview medium for the interviewees from post-Soviet space, building both upon the legacy of using Russian as the lingua franca of the USSR and today's status of Russian as the official language of the Russian Federation. Non-Russian languages are relegated to the brief moment at the end of each video when interviewees are asked to sing or say something in their mother tongue. Thus, the "exotic" mother tongue becomes just another spice, embellishing the video instead of taking up central space as a medium of narration. The minimal space that non-Russian languages receive within EOB mirrors the second-rate status of non-Russian languages in today's Russian Federation. The Russian constitution guarantees them the right to be protected and preserved, but this is rarely so in practice. Throughout the 2000s, a range of measures was implemented, gradually reducing the status and sphere of use of non-Russian languages (Suleymanova 2020: 3–4), including the liquidation of the regional component in school education (Shnirelman 2009: 132) and the use of Russian as the only language for state exams, which are obligatory for entering universities. In summer 2017, the "rhetoric about discrimination" against Russian speakers in the national republics of Russia was used to limit the public usage of non-Russian languages (Zamyatin 2018: 48), revealing the "assimilationist objectives" and monolingual language ideology of Russia (Zamyatin 2018). This assault on non-Russian languages culminated in 2018, when the state languages of the republics of the Russian Federation lost their status as obligatory subjects in schools, while the number of hours dedicated to studying them also dropped significantly. Such change has officially positioned non-Russian languages as second-rate languages in Russia and further facilitated the long-term and ongoing processes of their marginalization. From July 2020, the Russian constitution has been amended to claim a "special role" for ethnic Russians as "state-forming people" in the formation of Russia, thereby reinforcing the dismantling of federalism and symbolically framing the non-Russian peoples of Russia as second-rate citizens.[32]

Through creating linkages between gender, culture, and language, EOB contributes to the depoliticization of the language question. If it is only the women who are responsible for the transmission of ethnic culture, can anything be demanded from the state? Recent assaults on the obligatory learning of non-Russian languages in the republics of the Russian Federation have demonstrated the instrumentalization of the discourse of the family as the main site for the preservation of language and culture. Within the discourse of the opponents of the obligatory school teaching of non-Russian languages in the republics of Russia, the family is represented as having the primary responsibility as a site for learning and maintaining such languages. This kind of discourse creates the illusion that minoritized languages can survive within families alone, without the need to broaden the sphere of their usage and introduce them at all levels of the education system.

228 *Dinara Yangeldina*

Concern about the preservation of languages features persistently in the EOB interviews with non-Russian women, but it is not incorporated at all into the diversity agenda of the EOB. The erasure of languages is brought up by Baira[33] and Evgeniya,[34] who express their concerns that the Kalmyk language is disappearing and fewer and fewer people in Kalmykia can speak it. Rushaniya[35] expresses similar concerns about the Bashkir language. Karina[36] is anxious that not only will the Abazin language die out soon but that the Abazin people themselves, whose estimated population in Russia is only around 40,000 people, will also vanish. Minority languages are not simply disappearing but are being displaced by the higher-status Russian language, a phenomenon that linguists call language shift or language assimilation.

Snezhana[37] reflects upon her experiences of growing up in Chuvashia and mentions the feeling of disgust "towards one's own culture" and the non-prestigious status of the Chuvash language, which is associated with rurality. She recollects the feeling of shame that she experienced while growing up, linked to this marginalization of the Chuvash language: being ashamed of speaking Chuvash. Snezhana stresses that, while it is unpleasant to speak about these memories now, her attitude towards the Chuvash language was widely shared at the time by her peers. However, Snezhana rethought her stance later on in life when she moved out of Chuvashia to study and later travelled to other countries: it became possible for her to problematize her previous attitudes towards the Chuvash language. This example makes visible how an ethno-spatial divide becomes loaded with a value-laden temporality. Speaking the Chuvash language in this scheme is a marker of belonging to a village, a signifier of rural backwardness, while the Russian language stands for urban modernity and progress. The attitude of disgust felt towards the Chuvash language can be grasped by means of the concept that Tlostanova describes as the self-orientalization of multiple colonized subjects (2012). This works through the internalization of externally imposed values and standards: local languages become erased partly through state policies but partly also through the desire on the part of minorities to modernize and distance themselves from the perceived backwardness of ethnic languages.

Concluding Remarks

As I have demonstrated in this chapter, EOB works by presenting ethnicities as fixed and homogenized entities, reinforcing folklore-related difference, and inviting racialist readings. Through its gendered symbolism, EOB's vision of global diversity acquires conservative meanings. Diversity is pacified and stripped of politics. To repoliticize EOB is to localize it. I have argued that much can be gained from rooting EOB in the experiences of post-Soviet multi-ethnicity. Positioning it against the context of withering federalism and Russian nation-building projects, I have positioned racialization, ethnic hierarchies, and language politics as three sites of contention that disrupt the logic of beautiful diversity. Paying critical attention to local hegemonies allows us to examine, in Tlostanova's words "the ex-Second world as a diverse, contradictory, non-homogenous semi-alterity with its unique intersectionality" (2014: 169).

Notes

1 Accessed February 28, 2023. www.youtube.com/channel/UCSi9LpPZR7CUZMJ knep7-QQ.
2 Accessed February 28, 2023. www.instagram.com/lesoriginesdelabeaute.
3 www.facebook.com/Les-origines-de-la-beaut%C3%A9-444900195589145/
4 Accessed February 28, 2023. https://vk.com/club53212025.
5 Accessed February 28, 2023. www.lesoriginesdelabeaute.com/en/page_47806.html.
6 The idea for this article came in 2016; most of it was written by 2019 and edited by 2020. Due to the delays related to the COVID-19 pandemic and the publication process, this chapter will only appear in print in 2023. Many things have changed since that, and I acknowledge these limitations through this endnote.
7 I use the formulation nationality/ethnicity to preserve the meaning of *natsionalnost* as used in Russian, which is different from its English equivalent.
8 Accessed February 28, 2023 www.youtube.com/playlist?list=PLmJ5j8aF-M5OrnxFP_ wwOF4tbbf4lF2JS.
9 Natalia Ivanova is a political science graduate of the prestigious International Relations Institute in Moscow, Russia (MGIMO). Later she moved to Paris, France, and graduated there from SPEOS Institute of Photography as a photojournalist. She also worked as a photo correspondent for the government-owned Russian news agency TASS at its bureau in Paris.
10 Accessed February 28, 2023. http://lesoriginesdelabeaute.com/en/page_47806.html.
11 Ibid.
12 Accessed February 28, 2023. www.instagram.com/p/BtjBGchg4Ju/.
13 The website of the Humanae project is https://angelicadass.com/photography/humanae/. Accessed February 28, 2023. The Website of The Atlas of Beauty project is https://theatlasofbeauty.com. Accessed February 28, 2023. The Humanae project is run by Spain-based Brazilian photographer Angélica Dass. It represents human diversity through a PANTONE® guide taxonomy of human skin-colour shades. The Atlas of Beauty project is run by Romanian photographer Mihaela Noroc and is composed of portraits showing "the diversity of our planet through portraits of women" (Facebook page www.facebook.com/MihaelaNorocPhoto. Accessed February 28, 2023). EOB thus shares the taxonomic mode of representation with the Humanae project, and the focus on gender and beauty with *The Atlas of Beauty*. However, the declared aims of the Humanae project seem to be different in that it aims to destabilize existing racial categorizations. The extent to which this can be achieved by using tools such as skin-colour taxonomies inherited from epistemologies of scientific racialism is a separate question.
14 I would like to thank Natalia Ivanova, the author of the project "The Ethnic Origins Of Beauty", for her kind permission to reprint two images from the project in this chapter (Figures 17.1 and 17.2). Although the chapter was ready by 2020, I contacted Natalia about permission to use the images in 2023. Her kind response made me aware of the ethical dilemmas of research and the limits of feminist critique. I acknowledge the labour that Natalia has put into the project and apologize in advance if my feminist take on the project may at times, seem unjust.
15 Accessed February 28, 2023. http://gradus.pro/natal-ya-ivanova-yazy-k-krasoty-dostupen-i-ponyaten-bol-shinstvu-lyudej/.
16 Ibid.
17 Comments on the video: www.youtube.com/watch?v=FU-XHL5WMPM. Accessed February 28, 2023.
18 Accessed February 28, 2023. http://gradus.pro/natal-ya-ivanova-yazy-k-krasoty-dostupen-i-ponyaten-bol-shinstvu-lyudej/.
19 Ibid.
20 Translations from Russian are my own; most of these videos are not translated into English.

230 *Dinara Yangeldina*

21 A racialized slur symbolizing ethnic others from Central Asia or the Caucasus or anyone with non-Slavic features; it literally translates as small pieces of wood for the stove.
22 www.youtube.com/watch?v=JEVvqGaueHo; this video is now (February 28, 2023) listed as private but was publicly available when I carried out the research for this chapter in 2019.
23 Accessed February 28, 2023. www.youtube.com/watch?v=FU-XHL5WMPM.
24 Accessed February 28, 2023. www.youtube.com/watch?v=FU-XHL5WMPM.
25 Accessed February 28, 2023. www.youtube.com/watch?v=xzP8XqKNDKk.
26 Accessed February 28, 2023. www.youtube.com/watch?v=QW5oykLJ6uo.
27 Accessed February 28, 2023. www.youtube.com/watch?v=fP8elnPRwaw.
28 Accessed February 28, 2023. http://gradus.pro/natal-ya-ivanova-yazy-k-krasoty-dostupen-i-ponyaten-bol-shinstvu-lyudej/.
29 Two interviews and one teaser.
30 Accessed February 28, 2023. www.youtube.com/watch?v=z8kmvGmxjaY.
31 Accessed February 28, 2023. www.youtube.com/watch?v=MMRTs-JMAz4.
32 As well as ignoring the histories of statehood that the non-Russian peoples of Russia had.
33 Accessed February 28, 2023. www.youtube.com/watch?v=6OtDDibLw4s.
34 Accessed February 28, 2023. www.youtube.com/watch?v=W7SHiWZo1Co.
35 www.youtube.com/watch?v=1iU_CiP8VgU; this video is now (February 28, 2023) listed as private but was publicly available when I carried out the research for this chapter in 2019.
36 Accessed February 28, 2023. www.youtube.com/watch?v=QW5oykLJ6uo.
37 Accessed February 28, 2023. www.youtube.com/watch?v=-hNihCGxPNs.

References

Ahmed, Sara. 2012. *On Being Included: Racism and Diversity in Institutional Life*. Durham, NC: Duke University Press.

Baiburin, Albert. 2012. "'The Wrong Nationality': Ascribed Identity in the 1930s Soviet Union." In *Russian Cultural Anthropology After the Collapse of Communism*, edited by Albert Baiburin, Catriona Kelly, and Nikolai Vakhtin, 59–76. London: Routledge.

Brubaker, Rogers. 2004. *Ethnicity Without Groups*. Cambridge, MA: Harvard University Press.

Hirsch, Francine. 2005. *Empire of Nations: Ethnographic Knowledge and the Making of the Soviet Union: Culture and Society After Socialism*. Ithaca, NY: Cornell University Press.

Hutchings, Stephen, and Vera Tolz. 2015. *Nation, Ethnicity and Race on Russian Television: Mediating Post-Soviet Difference*. London: Routledge.

Ivanova, Natalia. 2023. "The Ethnic Origin of Beauty." Accessed February 28, 2023. http://lesoriginesdelabeaute.com/en/page_47806.html.

Keevak, Michael. 2011. *Becoming Yellow: A Short History of Racial Thinking*. Cambridge, MA: Princeton University Press.

Law, Ian. 2012. *Red Racisms: Racism in Communist and Post-Communist Contexts*. London: Palgrave Macmillan.

Martin, Terry Dean. 2001. *The Affirmative Action Empire: Nations and Nationalism in the Soviet Union, 1923–1939*. Ithaca, NY: Cornell University Press.

Matusevich, Maxim. 2020. "Soviet Anti-racism and Its Discontents: The Cold War Years." In *Alternative Globalizations: Eastern Europe and the Postcolonial World*, edited by James Mark, Artemy M. Kalinovsky, and Steffi Marung, 229–50. Bloomington, IN: Indiana University Press.

Rose, Gillian. 2016. *Visual Methodologies: An Introduction to Researching With Visual Materials*. London: SAGE.

Sahadeo, Jeff. 2007. "Druzhba Narodov or Second-Class Citizenship? Soviet Asian Migrants in a Post-Colonial World." *Central Asian Survey* 26 (4): 559–79.

Shevel, Oxana. 2011. "Russian Nation-Building From Yel'tsin to Medvedev: Ethnic, Civic or Purposefully Ambiguous?" *Europe-Asia Studies* 63 (2): 179–202.

Shnirelman, Victor. 2009. "Stigmatized by History or by Historians? The Peoples of Russia in School History Textbooks." *History and Memory* 21 (2): 110–49.

Slezkine, Yuri. 1994. "The USSR as a Communal Apartment, or How a Socialist State Promoted Ethnic Particularism." *Slavic Review* 53 (2): 414–52.

Suchland, Jennifer. 2011. "Is Postsocialism Transnational?" *Signs* 36 (4): 837–62.

Suleymanova, Dilyara. 2020. *Pedagogies of Culture: Schooling and Identity in Post-Soviet Tatarstan, Russia*. Cham: Springer Nature.

Swan, Elaine. 2010. "Commodity Diversity: Smiling Faces as a Strategy of Containment." *Organization* 17 (1): 77–100.

Tlostanova, Madina. 2012. "Postsocialist ≠ Postcolonial? On Post-Soviet Imaginary and Global Coloniality." *Journal of Postcolonial Writing* 48 (2): 130–42.

Tlostanova, Madina. 2014. "Why the Post-Socialist Cannot Speak: On Caucasian Blacks, Imperial Difference and Decolonial Horizons." In *Postcoloniality-Decoloniality-Black Critique. Joints and Fissures*, edited by Sabine Broeck and Carsten Junker, 159–73. Frankfurt and New York, NY: Campus Verlag.

Tlostanova, Madina, Suruchi Thapar-Björkert, and Redi Koobak. 2019. "The Postsocialist 'Missing Other' of Transnational Feminism?." *Feminist Review* 121 (1): 81–7.

Yuval-Davis, Nira. 1993. "Gender and Nation." *Ethnic and Racial Studies* 16 (4): 621–32.

Zamyatin, Konstantin. 2018. "A Russian-Speaking Nation?: The Promotion of the Russian Language and Its Significance for Ongoing Efforts at the Russian Nation-Building." In *The Politics of Multilingualism: Europeanisation, Globalisation and Linguistic Governance*, edited by Peter A. Kraus and François Grin, 39–64. Amsterdam: John Benjamins Publishing Company.

18 Reducing Costs While Optimizing Health?

A Transnational Feminist Engagement
With Personalized Medicine

Maria Temmes

During the 21st century, terms such as "personalized medicine", "precision medicine", and "P4 systems medicine" have framed the hopes for emerging new biomedical techniques and the possibilities they hold. These involve transforming healthcare practices to be more effective, preventative and, thus, better value for money. While each term has different connotations in relation to healthcare futures (see Erikainen and Chan 2019), they all share aspirations to increase the opportunities for individuals to participate in their own treatment planning and disease prevention. At the heart of preventative strategies in personalized medicine is an individual who participates actively and takes care of their own health with the help of diagnostic tools, health coaches, and medication made available either nationally or commercially (Hood 2013). This, in effect, also means that the organization of healthcare is increasingly visualized in relation to individuals' responsibility for their own health (Erikainen and Chan 2019: 322). I use the term "personalized medicine" as an umbrella term that includes both existing plans for healthcare organizations and future visions in which individuals' actions are the basis of preventative strategies aiming to optimize wellness and avoid disease. In this chapter, I critically analyse how personalized medicine, when described on a global scale, is viewed as an effective, cost-cutting, and more equitable approach to healthcare.

Previous research has criticized descriptions of personalized medicine as a "holistic" approach to wellness because it medicalizes health and does not pay enough attention to social understandings of health in relation to, for example, gendered, racial, or class inequalities in society (e.g. Temmes 2018; Vogt et al. 2016). However, there is less analysis of how global visions become embedded in future visions of personalized medicine. While researchers have noted that personalized medicine needs to be critically analysed in relation to both the existing organization of healthcare and social behaviour (e.g. Erikainen and Chan 2019; Vogt and Green 2020), research focusing on countries labelled as "developing", "Low-to-Middle-Income" (LMIC) or as part of "the Global South" tends to direct its analyses towards the existing problems in healthcare organization, rather than examining the goals of personalized medicine (e.g. Haque et al. 2020; Chong et al. 2018). What remains unexplored is how the envisioned benefits of cost-cutting and more effective treatment would shape healthcare practices globally: Whose money

DOI: 10.4324/9781003378761-21

Reducing Costs While Optimizing Health? 233

is saved and how? How is the subsequent treatment/prevention organized? To what extent would such a new approach take existing social inequalities into account?

With the help of feminist postcolonial and medical anthropology research, this chapter reads against these "developed/developing" country dichotomies to argue that a global approach to personalized medicine needs to take into account the ways in which personalized medicine initiatives can further exacerbate health disparities globally. A close examination of the current organization of healthcare in Finland and Bangladesh helps to show how the goal of cost-effectiveness can increasingly turn healthcare planning towards the privatization of medical care and individual responsibility for disease prevention, even in very different geopolitical contexts and/or where the local organization of medical care is different.

Forming a Transnational Approach to Personalized Medicine

Personalized medicine is often applauded as a cost-effective option for future healthcare organizations because it could reduce the need for medical care. For example, in their 2015 briefing on personalized medicine, the European Union (EU) urged all member states to modify their research and healthcare systems to better incorporate big-data approaches to medicine. As stated in the European Council report, personalized medicine should be seen as a novel approach to medical care, which to a certain extent has always been personalized, because it:

> refers to a medical model using characterisation of individuals' phenotypes and genotypes (e.g. molecular profiling, medical imaging, lifestyle data) for tailoring the right therapeutic strategy for the right person at the right time, and/or to determine the predisposition to disease and/or to deliver timely and targeted prevention.
>
> (European Council 2015)

In other words, increased individual data collection, both biological and behavioural, could enable new insights into the emergence and development of disease that can be used when designing both treatment and prevention. Importantly, personalized medicine is seen as essential not only because it can help to develop medical care but also because it can help to form *sustainable* healthcare systems (ibid.). This is considered crucial because healthcare expenditure has escalated across the EU during the past decade (Pastorino et al. 2021).

Making healthcare systems more sustainable entails broader changes in healthcare management, shifting the focus increasingly towards preventative actions and early treatment, or to put it differently: "optimizing the wellness of individuals and avoiding disease" (Hood 2013: 1). Personalized medicine is marketed as an approach that will not only bridge the gap between basic research and treatment but also transform the understanding and organization of healthcare altogether – and save money in the process. While researchers have critically analysed this formulation in North American/European contexts (e.g. Vogt and Green 2020), there has been less consideration of how narratives of cost-effectiveness are employed when

234   *Maria Temmes*

discussing the possibilities of implementing a personalized medicine approach globally.

Arguments for the global implementation of personalized medicine stress that it can generate both savings and equitable healthcare. Hood goes as far as to suggest that P4 medicine – predictive, preventive, personalized, and participatory future medicine:

> will be able to reduce sharply the escalating costs of health care to the point where we will be able to export it to the developing world, leading to a democratization of health care, a concept unimaginable five years ago.
>
> (Hood 2013: 13)

This vision from 2013 not only assumes that personalized medicine will be something that is *exported* by *us*, neglecting to account for how countries such as Thailand had already formulated a biotechnology policy in 2004 (Chong et al. 2018: 3), but also portrays this implementation as a process of *democratization*. Even if we accept Hood's approach as overly optimistic, we can see similar aims expressed, for example, in the visions of the International Consortium of Personalized Medicine, launched by the EU, to become "global leaders in personalised medicine research" and "investigate the benefits of personalised medicine to citizens and healthcare systems" (ICPerMed n.d.). Expressed in both sources is the idea of knowhow, organized and led in the United States and Europe, which can benefit healthcare systems globally.

This geopolitical dichotomy is echoed, although less optimistically, in research studying healthcare systems outside European and North American contexts. For example, Alyass, Turcotte, and Meyre warn that, if not properly executed, "[p]ersonalized medicine will further increase [health funding] disparities and many low and middle-income countries may miss the train of personalized medicine" (2015: 2). They argue that the increase in disparities between countries can be prevented by also investing in high-throughput technologies, which are crucial for personalized medicine, in LMICs (10). Similarly, Chong, Allotey, and Chaiyakunparuk note in their examination of the existing implementation of personalized medicine in Southeast Asia that "the current [personalized medicine] distribution has the potential to widen existing health disparities" (2018: 1). However, they still maintain that personalized medicine, if correctly incorporated, can benefit Southeast Asia through its "efficacy, safety, cost-effectiveness, analytical validity, clinical validity, and clinical utility" (2018: 12). Thus, while these two accounts critically assess the establishment of personalized medicine in existing contexts in LMICs, they still frame its promise through the geopolitical dichotomy between countries where personalized medicine can currently be actualized, benefitting people across society, and countries that do not currently have the infrastructure for developing personalized medicine but could benefit from it.

Portraying the development of medical care in reference to the dichotomies of "developed/developing countries", "High Income Countries (HICs)/LMICs" or

"North/South", conceals the ways in which the introduction of personalized medicine can also differentially influence countries listed on the same side of this division, as well as different groups of people within them. As Mohanty stresses:

> "North/South" is used to distinguish between affluent, privileged nations and communities, and economically and politically marginalized nations and communities, as is "Western/non-Western". While these terms are meant to loosely distinguish the northern and southern hemispheres, affluent and marginal nations and communities obviously do not line up neatly within this geographical frame.
>
> (2003: 226)

This critical approach is essential when considering the possible changes brought by personalized medicine initiatives because national healthcare is organized in different ways globally and the rights and opportunities for people to access healthcare are similarly diverse within countries. For example, Finland and the United States are both listed among the "developed economies" in the UN's 2020 country classification. However, the foundation of these countries' healthcare organization is different. In Finland, healthcare primarily relies on public funding (Saltman and Teperi 2016: 308). In the United States, medical care is commercialized, relying mostly on private health insurance which is inaccessible to many (Kirch and Vernon 2009). Without considering these differences, it is impossible to analyse, for example, patients' access to new, expensive, precision drugs – a key development in personalized medicine. Following Mohanty's approach, the full analysis thus requires considering quality of life as a criterion "for distinguishing between social minorities and majorities" (2003: 227). Viewed in this way, the focus on the division between the Global North/South overshadows the divisions between the "One-Third/Two-Thirds Worlds", which Mohanty uses to highlight differences in people's socioeconomic status to illustrate how people living in the same country may not have the same quality of life (ibid.).

While it is essential to consider local differences when analysing the implementation of personalized medicine strategies, a transnational feminist analysis must also simultaneously ask how global power relations, shaped in accordance with the capitalist market, affect local practices. Framing the implementation of personalized medicine as a "global assemblage", following Ong and Collier's definition (2007), helps to link the global and local. As a term, global assemblage aims to focus the analysis on considering how:

> Global forms are able to assimilate themselves to new environments, to code heterogeneous contexts and objects in terms that are amenable to control and valuation. At the same time, the conditions of possibility of this movement are complex. Global forms are limited or delimited by specific technical infrastructures, administrative apparatuses, or value regimes.
>
> (2007: 11)

236   *Maria Temmes*

Global assemblage theory highlights that, while particular localities form in distinct ways, they do so in relation to global changes. The surrogacy market is a fitting example. While gestational surrogacy is either prohibited or very expensive in countries like the United States, wealthy customers can afford to outsource it to countries with cheaper prices and fewer legal protections for surrogates. The global surrogacy market is thus "structured by racial, class and economic inequalities" (Twine 2011: x). Applying this lens to personalized medicine would entail considering how it might create life-enhancing possibilities for some while for others it might mean increasing exploitation as a source of the data needed for research, or further limitations on available healthcare.

I will next analyse some possible outcomes of personalized medicine in Finland and Bangladesh. This is a challenging task because such medicine is still largely described as a *future* plan. While in Finland personalized medicine terminology is central to the national "health sector growth strategy" (STMa n.d.), in Bangladesh it has gained attention in medical publications (e.g. Haque et al. 2020) but not as a national initiative. The Bangladeshi healthcare system should not be equated with any other countries classified by the UN as "developing economies", just as Finland and the United States are not comparable even though framed as "developed economies". In addition, due to their differences, a comparison between Finland and Bangladesh could easily reduce to reinforcing the analytical division between the Global North and South. Therefore, instead, I will show how global market logic frames the possible outcomes of personalized medicine in relation to existing healthcare in each locality. I start by examining the establishment of biobanks.

Public Health and Biovalue: Biobanks and Economics

One of the main challenges for personalized medicine is the amount of new infrastructure needed to establish it in the first place. For instance, biobanks that contain "human biospecimens – such as tissue, blood, urine – and information pertaining to the donors: demography and lifestyle, history of present illness, treatment and clinical outcomes" (Parodi 2015: 15) are central to personalized medicine, which relies on big data. What has changed in recent years, due to the increasing emphasis on big-data approaches in biomedicine, is that biological, clinical, and environmental data are collected not only for the study of particular diseases but also for uses that are as yet unknown. As Leonelli states:

> [w]e are not witnessing the birth of a data-driven method but rather the rise of a data-centric approach to science, within which efforts to mobilize, integrate, and visualize data are valued as contributions to discovery in their own right and not as a mere by-product of efforts to create and test scientific theories.
>
> (2016: 1–2)

There is an increasing emphasis on accounting for biological and environmental factors in disease emergence due to the growing awareness that "most genetic

Reducing Costs While Optimizing Health? 237

diseases are caused by a complex interplay of many factors, both genetic and environmental" (Fobelets and Nys 2009: 20). While biobanks are central to personalized medicine, they require extensive funding and political support to set up, meaning that biobank infrastructures in Finland and Bangladesh are very different.

In Finland, an active governmental strategy supports genomic research. There are ten operational biobanks, some of them collecting samples nationwide, others regionally. Most of them are collaborative projects between hospital districts and universities (BBMRI n.d.). Moreover, governmental strategy is to further centralize biobank activities in Finland through its vision of "Biobank Finland" and to establish a Genome Centre to support public biobank activities (Tarkkala et al. 2019: 145–6).

In Bangladesh, there have been two attempts to establish biobanks: the first connected to an international study on pregnancy-related outcomes in developing countries, established in 2014 (AMANHI et al. 2017), while the second is the Biobank of Bangladesh (BBB), a collaborative project between Dhaka University and Birdem General Hospital, begun in 2016. The latter not only aimed to study multiple complex diseases, such as diabetes and hypertension, but also operated for six months because its funding was largely based on an agreement between the existing leaders of institutions, and leadership changes in both led to unclear legal and financial responsibilities, bringing the operation to a premature end (interview with Dr Jesmin, one of the biobank's founders conducted together with Ashfeen Aribea on 6 February 2020).

Analyses of global biobanking are often based on the developed/developing world dichotomy. Scholars highlight that the uneven global distribution of biobanks contributes to the failure to study diseases that mostly affect the poorest countries in the world (Sgaier et al. 2007; Rudan et al. 2011). The establishment of biobanks in the Global South, the argument goes, could support a deeper understanding of these diseases, and consequently aid in the development of medicines and diagnostic tools, thus helping to tackle global health inequalities. The need for biobanks in the Global South is connected both to the need to study diseases that mostly affect the poorest countries and to examine possible "genetic and environmental variations that contribute to complex chronic diseases" (Sgaier et al. 2007: 1074) that exist all over the world. For example, BBB was planning to focus on diseases that are common in Bangladesh but also globally.

An analysis of the global distribution of biobanks can sometimes illustrates the power relations embedded in global biomedical research; for example, how poorer countries have been sites of "parachute research" – where biological samples are collected but not stored, leading to research findings having only a small local impact (Wonkam et al. 2011: 123). However, a more detailed local analysis is needed to fully assess the multitude of ways in which transnational power relations can shape biomedical research on diseases, the establishment of biobanks, and the translation of biomedical research into healthcare practices. A central element in this transformation is biovalue.

Biovalue as a term highlights the economic possibilities envisioned in the collection, usage, and selling of biological data. While most Finnish biobanks are

238   *Maria Temmes*

publicly owned and BBB was established in collaboration with Dhaka University, any appearance of a clear line between public and private entities in biobanking is an illusion. The public health benefits connected to biobanks cannot be separated from pharmaceutical companies' interest in successfully producing and selling precision drugs. As Robert Mitchell and Catherine Waldby state: "national biobanks almost invariably present the path from biobank to public good as one that leads through the commercial creation of profitable drugs and diagnostic tools" (Mitchell and Waldby 2010: 34–5). In other words, the described public benefits of national biobanks stem not only from the extended possibilities for basic research to identify patient subgroups but also from pharmaceutical companies using the collected data to create and sell precision drugs tailored for these groups.

Expectations of biovalue influence biobanking activities in both Finland and Bangladesh. While the current situation of BBB makes it impossible to know whether its research focus could have been extended to neglected diseases, the preliminary focus on diseases such as hypertension and diabetes does support the view that biobank activities are largely directed towards diseases with (international) market opportunities. As Lykke has shown in the case of liver cancer, global biomedical research has focused on studying diseases with a profitable drugs market in the West, while neglecting other diseases (Lykke 2019: 117). This does not mean that Finnish biobanks would necessarily be more attuned to solving national health problems but that the operational logic of biobanks is connected to their perceived economic value. As Tarkkala, Helén, and Snell highlight: "visions of advances in medical science and care have been eclipsed by expectations of business opportunities and commercial collaborations with Big Pharma and international investors" (2019: 149). Profit-driven drug development makes the developed/developing country distinction questionable because it undermines the argument that the increase in (national) biobanks in the Global South would lead to greater pharmaceutical investment in diseases affecting the poorest people in the world. Furthermore, even though biobanking infrastructures might help to create precision drugs for neglected diseases, market logic also influences the prices of drugs, raising the question: Who can afford them?

Precision Drugs and Equitable Healthcare: An Impossible Equation?

New precision drugs, developed for specific patient sub-groups, are often sold at high prices (Gronde et al. 2017). Hence, if one wishes to consider the actual impact that personalized medicine could have on treatment options, it is imperative that the analysis includes a consideration of availability and access to treatment. A closer look into the organization of healthcare in Finland and Bangladesh reveals local differences in access to healthcare, an understanding of which is necessary in order to further analyse how the argument for the sustainability of healthcare can shape both contexts.

Presently in Finland, the progress in precision treatments can be connected to ideas of better public healthcare. This is because 75 percent of medical care is

Reducing Costs While Optimizing Health? 239

publicly funded and citizens' access to treatment is supported by social insurance. What is more, healthcare provision in Finland is decentralized, managed by the municipalities to ensure equal access to healthcare in this sparsely populated country (Saltman and Teperi 2016: 305–6). Medication is also fully or partly covered: it is freely dispensed in public hospitals, while prescription drugs are partly paid by social insurance within an annual personal expenditure limit, currently set at around 600 € (KELA, n.d.). While current estimates show that this limit already prevents full access to medication for people on lower incomes (Keskimäki et al. 2019), the new precision drugs, when provided under social insurance coverage, would at least not worsen the situation.

However, increasing demands for sustainability within the medical sector have emerged to counter the combined effects of stalled economic growth, an ageing population and the demands for accessible, high-quality care (Saltman and Teperi 2016: 304–5). These include, for example, plans to rationalize pharmacotherapy in order to balance the personal and social costs and benefits of particular treatments (STMb, n.d.). Increasing precision drug prices has been publicized as problematic for the equity of future healthcare in Finland because social insurance does not cover new drugs that lack proper evidence backing their effectiveness in relation to their cost, so patients can only access these treatments if they pay for them themselves.

Furthermore, the pricing of new drugs is ambiguous as countries try to negotiate better drug prices or sign confidential risk-sharing agreements with pharmaceutical companies that agree to co-pay if the expected results are not achieved (YLE, n.d.). In such agreements, as seen in relation to the different prices for COVID-19 vaccinations in the EU and South Africa (Dyer 2021), entities such as the EU have stronger negotiating power, further distorting global access to drugs. The overarching market logic of biomedical research, then, directs attention not only towards which diseases are currently studied but also towards how new treatment options can be accessed in the future and who can afford them.

In Bangladesh, healthcare is provided by the public sector, private sector, NGOs, and donor agencies. As Khan et al. (2017) state, this division of healthcare organization perpetuates inequitable healthcare access because most of the curative treatment is focused on private hospitals, which rely heavily on patients' out-of-pocket payments, while the state and NGOs, guided by international donor organizations, focus more on preventative actions and basic care directed especially towards poorer people (2017: 360). Furthermore, M. A. Mannan (2013) argues that many people, especially poor people living in rural areas, have difficulties travelling to access care even though it is publicly organized. According to Mannan, poor women in rural areas in particular are in a disadvantageous situation due to the social stigma connected to visiting a male doctor without a chaperone, and rural areas lack female practitioners (2013: 28–36). Many richer patients also travel abroad if a particular treatment is not available in Bangladesh (Ali and Medhekar 2018). Therefore, in reality, public healthcare is unequally available based on wealth, location, social class, position, and gender. Interestingly, Khan et al. suggest that one solution to the problem would be to make the private sector more

240   *Maria Temmes*

accessible (2017: 364). Privatization in itself is not seen as a problem. While this could be a reflection of the state's lack of resources to take over the organization of curative healthcare in Bangladesh, it also resonates with widespread arguments supporting the "need" for privatization.

In discussions about sustainable healthcare systems, arguments supporting the "need" for further privatization are often made. As Prainsack states: "[t]oday's health entrepreneurism is situated within a political economy whose dominant discourse considers it possible to combine social benefit and capitalism" (Prainsack 2017: 107). Arguments for the democratization of healthcare in the personalized medicine literature have to be assessed with this relation in mind. In Finland, ideas about the effective organization of the healthcare system often include plans for further privatization. While privatization can be used as a tool by state-led healthcare organizations – for example, by municipalities buying services from private hospitals so that they do not have to organize services such as elderly care themselves (Saltman and Teperi 2016: 306) – research also suggests that private hospitals favour patients who are easier to treat, whereas people with multiple co-morbidities are often treated in public hospitals (Tynkkynen and Vrangbæk 2018). Thus, one challenge to the cost-effectiveness of privatization has been that it could leave the most difficult, and expensive, medical cases for public care.

Combined with the possibility of increasing out-of-pocket costs due to new precision drugs, the extent to which personalized medicine initiatives could merge economic savings and health equity in Finland is questionable. In Bangladesh, high out-of-pocket payments are already a reality and, thus, it is doubtful that new precision drugs would be within the reach of most citizens. Therefore, in relation to new treatment options, the argument for cost-effectiveness does not seem to coincide with increasing equity. To be fair, the sustainability of personalized medicine is often more closely linked to the possibility of preventing diseases rather than treating them with precision drugs. Still, the analysis of cost-effectiveness in relation to precision treatments helps to explain why preventative treatment strategies might also fail to lead to more democratized healthcare practices, instead emphasizing individual responsibility for disease prevention.

Preventative Healthcare and Social Inequalities: Narrating Responsibilities

While disease prevention has been at the heart of the biopolitics of public health planning since its inception, with guidelines on how to eat well and exercise more, it is hoped that molecular-level information will further intensify personalized guidelines on how to prevent disease. As Hood describes these preventative actions:

> in 10 years each patient will be surrounded by a virtual cloud of billions of data points, and we will have the tools to reduce this enormous data dimensionality into simple hypotheses about how to optimize wellness and avoid disease for each individual.

(Hood 2013: 1)

His vision is based on the idea that "[b]iology can be defined as an informational science" (2013: 4) and that it is possible to measure different types of risk, including environmental influences, in the emergence of different diseases. For example, in Finland, the pilot programme "KardioKompassi" aims to further individualize the existing cardiovascular disease risk assessment by adding genomic data to the calculations, which could better reveal the risk factors, including in younger people. While the actual guidelines given by doctors could be very similar to those under the old model (e.g. stop smoking, exercise more), the assumption is that more personalized *genomic* risk information could further motivate people to act on these suggestions. In other diseases, preventative medication could also be considered (Temmes 2018: 76–7). In preventative measures such as these, the cost-effectiveness logic of personalized medicine entails that helping individuals to take better care of their bodies will reduce future medical costs (Erikainen and Chan 2019: 322–3). It is important to note that this increasingly shifts the responsibility for health maintenance to the individual and, by so doing, also conceptualizes good health as based upon measurable information.

When considering the extent to which personalized medicine initiatives would change existing preventative healthcare measures, it is essential to consider how existing models approach health inequalities. This includes not only access to healthcare but also environmental factors, such as pollution. While these "social determinants of health" are increasingly emphasized by the World Health Organization, Yates-Doerr argues that this "framework may uphold and even exacerbate conditions of inequality by prioritizing and targeting a form of health that has been predetermined by distant experts" (2020: 379–80).

For example, measuring height has become a standardized tool in assessing health inequity, connecting shortness with malnutrition. However, Yates-Doerr's research in Guatemala shows that, in practice, height is not very strictly monitored in medical exams, but the negative notions connected to shortness still end up reinforcing existing social stereotypes by linking shortness and poverty, further stigmatizing short people, for example, in workplaces. Thus, she highlights the need for a materialist-semiotic approach when assessing local public health interventions, because medical procedures may have unexpected consequences that cannot be expressed as biological information (2020: 387–9). Furthermore, when thinking about the possibilities of taking local specificities into account in public health initiatives, it is important to remember that preventative actions in many poor countries, such as Bangladesh, are organized and financed by international donor agencies, and this has also strongly influenced the organization of preventative actions. A good example of this would be the emphasis on maternal health.

As Lock and Nguyen (2010) highlight, maternal health has become a focus in preventative global public health initiatives because pregnant women are often easily accessible for data collection. The data are then used to justify different public health measures, decided by donor organizations, in both developing countries and poor areas of developed countries (2010: 27). As Yates-Doerr notes, focusing on early-life interventions is seen as a way of achieving the best results within a limited budget with "impressive 'downstream' effects, impacting everything from

242   *Maria Temmes*

cognitive processes to chronic health" (2020: 391). Importantly, other research-ers have argued that the increasing attention given to the study of environmental influences on the embryonic stages of human life is linked to increasing social control over maternal bodies. This increasing control has also strengthened exist-ing social inequalities because mothers most "at risk" are defined according to racialized and socioeconomic stereotypes (Mansfield and Guthman 2015). In other words, the establishment of these prevention strategies relies on existing social inequalities, marking poor and racialized women in particular as preferable sites for intervention.

These examples also provide insights into the possible organization of preventa-tive measures in a future of personalized medicine because they show, first, how the cost-effective model is operating in preventative public health strategies and, second, how this directs attention towards individual bodies rather than social responsibilities. Studies in medical anthropology show why health and wellness cannot be understood solely as measurable biological information and that consid-erations of cost-effectiveness can direct attention and medical control especially towards bodies that are already in a socially unequal position. Social inequalities or environmental pollution are not necessarily things over which an individual can have any influence, and framing them as such removes the responsibility from governments. This is not an issue that only affects "the Global South". As Lykke shows, environmental pollution is connected to higher breast cancer rates in three distinct areas in the United States (2019: 120–1).

In order to fully assess the extent to which new biotechnologies could support equitable healthcare, studies on personalized medicine, in both its current forms and future applications, need to stop drawing stark geopolitical dichotomies when discussing personalized medicine in LMICs. They also need to extend the theoreti-cal critical analysis, made in relation to European and North American contexts, to account for different types of healthcare organization globally. Following Mohan-ty's words: "specifying difference allows us to theorize universal concerns more fully" (Mohanty 2003: 226).

In this chapter, my concern has been directed especially towards the logic of the cost-effectiveness of personalized medicine, not because saving money would necessarily be a negative aim but because "cost-effectiveness" has become a man-tra, used to justify changes without asking whose money is being saved or what benefits it brings to society. If the answer to these questions directs healthcare planning further away from poorer communities globally, or increasingly limits the willingness of governments to listen to what problems are actually faced by poorer communities, then it certainly is not a road towards increased equity.

Conclusion

In this chapter, I have taken a critical approach to statements that personalized medicine could herald the democratization of global healthcare by showing how the arguments relating to cost-effectiveness can shape personalized medicine ini-tiatives in various contexts. I have argued that, while the comparison between the

Reducing Costs While Optimizing Health? 243

Bangladeshi and Finnish contexts revealed vast differences in opportunities for biomedical research and public access to healthcare, both contexts reveal the market logic behind personalized medicine initiatives. I have argued that a transnational feminist engagement with personalized medicine, while taking into account local differences, should challenge universalizing narratives that frame personalized medicine as a cost-effective option that could bring increased equity to healthcare.

Acknowledgements

I would like to thank Nina Lykke, Kharnita Mohamed, and Petra Bakos for their insightful feedback, which helped to strengthen this chapter. I also thank Elepa Popa and Dejan Lukić for their helpful comments.

References

Ali, M. M., and A. Medhekar. 2018. "Healthcare Quality of Bangladesh and Outbound Medical Travel to Thailand." *Ekonomika regiona* (Economy of Region) 14 (2): 575–88.

Alyass, Akram, Michelle Turcotte, and David Meyre. 2015. "From Big Data Analysis to Personalized Medicine for All: Challenges and Opportunities." *BMC Medical Genomics* 8: 33.

AMANHI, Abdullah H. Baqui, Rasheda Khanam, Mohammad Sayedur Rahman, Aziz Ahmed, Hasna Hena Rahman, Mamun Ibne Moin, Salahuddin Ahmed, Fyezah Jehan, Imran Nisar, Atiya Hussain, Muhammad Ilyas, Aneeta Hotwani, Muhammad Sajid, Shahida Qureshi, Anita Zaidi, Sunil Sazawal, Said M. Ali, Saikat Deb, Mohammed Hamad Juma, Usha Dhingra, Arup Dutta, Shaali Makame Ame, Caroline Hayward, Igor Rudan, Mike Zangenberg, Donna Russell, Sachiyo Yoshida, Ozren Polašek, Alexander Manu, and Rajiv Bahl. 2017. "Understanding Biological Mechanisms Underlying Adverse Birth Outcomes in Developing Countries: Protocol for a Prospective Cohort (AMANHI Biobanking) Study." *Journal of Global Health* 7 (2): 021202. https://pubmed.ncbi.nlm.nih.gov/29163938/

BBMRI. n.d. "Finnish Biobanks." Accessed January 10, 2020. www.bbmri.fi/bbmri-network/finnish-biobanks/.

Chong, Huey Yi, Pascale A. Allotey, and Nathorn Chaiyakunapruk. 2018. "Current Landscape of Personalized Medicine Adoption and Implementation in Southeast Asia." *BMC Medical Genomic* 11. https://doi.org/10.1186/s12920-018-0420-4

Dyer, Owen. 2021. "Covid-19: Country Are Learning What Others Paid for Vaccination." *BMJ* 327. https://doi.org/10.1136/bmj.n281

Erikainen, Sonja, and Sarah Chan. 2019. "Contested Futures: Envisioning 'Personalized,' 'Stratified,' and 'Precision' Medicine." *New Genetics and Society* 38 (3): 308–30.

European Council. 2015. "Conclusion on Personalised Medicine for Patients." *Official Journal of the European Union C* 421.

Fobelets, Geraldine, and Herman Nys. 2009. "Evolution in Research Biobanks and Its Legal Consequences." In *New Challenges for Biobanks: Ethics, Law and Governance*, edited by Kris Dierickx and Pascal Borry, 19–30. Antwerp, Oxford, and Portland: Intersentia.

Gronde, Toon van der, Carin A. Uyl-de Groot, and Toine Pieters. 2017. "Addressing the Challenge of High-Priced Prescription Drugs in the Era of Precision Medicine: A Systematic Review of Drug Life Cycles, Therapeutic Drug Markets and Regulatory Frameworks." *PLoS ONE* 12 (8): 1–34.

244 *Maria Temmes*

Haque, Mainul, Tariqul Islam, Massimo Sartelli, Adnan Abdullah, and Sameer Dhingra. 2020. "Prospects and Challenges of Precision Medicine in Lower- and Middle-Income Countries: A Brief Overview." *Bangladesh Journal of Medical Science* 19 (1): 32–47.

Hood, Leroy. 2013. "Systems Biology and P4 Medicine: Past, Present, and Future." *Rambam Maimonides Medical Journal* 4 (2): 1–15.

ICPerMed. n.d. "Vision Statement." Accessed April 29, 2021. www.icpermed.eu/en/icpermed-vision-statement.php.

KELA. n.d. "Reimbursements for Medicine Expenses." Accessed April 29, 2021. www.kela.fi/web/en/medicine-expenses.

Keskimäki, Imo, Liina-Kaisa Tynkkynen, Eeva Reissell, Meri Koivusalo, Vesa Syrjä, Lauri Vuorenkoski, Bernd Rechel, and Marina Karanikolos. 2019. "Finland: Health System Review." *Health Systems in Transition* 21 (2): 1–166.

Khan, Jahangir A.M., Sayem Ahmed, Mary MacLennan, Abdur Razzaque Sarker, Marufa Sultana, and Hafizur Rahman. 2017. "Benefit Incidence Analysis of Healthcare in Bangladesh: Equity Matters for Universal Health Coverage." *Health Policy and Planning* 32: 359–65.

Kirch, Darrell G., and David J. Vernon. 2009. "The Ethical Foundation of American Medicine." *JAMA* 301 (14): 1482–4.

Leonelli, Sabina. 2016. *Data-Centric Biology: A Philosophical Study*. Chicago, IL: University of Chicago Press.

Lock, Margaret, and Vinh-Kim Nguyen. 2010. *An Anthropology of Biomedicine*. Malden, MA and Oxford: Wiley Blackwell.

Lykke, Nina. 2019. "Making Life and Letting Die: Cancerous Bodies Between Anthropocene Necropolitics and Chthulucene Kinship." *Environmental Humanities* 11 (1): 108–36.

Mannan, M. A. 2013. "Access to Public Health Facilities in Bangladesh: A Study on Facility Utilisation and Burden of Treatment." *Bangladesh Development Studies* XXXVI (4): 25–80.

Mansfield, Becky, and Julie Guthman. 2015. "Epigenetic Life: Biological Plasticity, Abnormality, and New Configurations of Race and Reproduction." *Cultural Geographies* 22 (1): 3–20.

Mitchell, Robert, and Catherine Waldby. 2010. "National Biobanks: Clinical Labor, Risk Production, and the Creation of Biovalue." *Science, Technology, & Human Values* 35 (3): 330–55.

Mohanty, Chandra Talpade. 2003. *Feminism Without Borders: Decolonizing Theory, Practicing Solidarity*. Durham, NC and London: Duke University Press.

Ong, Aihwa, and Stephen J. Collier. 2007. *Global Assemblages*. Malden, MA, Oxford and Victoria: Blackwell.

Parodi, Barbara. 2015. "Biobanks: A Definition." In *Ethics, Law and Governance of Biobanking: National, European and International Approaches*, edited by Deborah Mascalzoni, 15–20. New York, NY and London: Springer.

Pastorino, Roberta, Claudia Loreti, Silvia Giovannini, Walter Ricciardi, Luca Padua, and Stefania Boccia. 2021. "Challenges of Prevention for a Sustainable Personalized Medicine." *Journal of Personalized Medicine* 11: 311. https://doi.org/10.3390/jpm11040311

Prainsack, Barbara. 2017. *Personalized Medicine*. New York, NY: New York University Press.

Rudan, Igor, Ana Marušić, and Harry Campbell. 2011. "Developing Biobanks in Developing Countries." *Journal of Global Health* 1 (1): 2–4.

Saltman, Richard B., and Juha Teperi. 2016. "Health Reform in Finland: Current Proposals and Unresolved Challenges." *Health Economics, Policy and Law* 11 (February): 303–19.

Sgaier, S. K., P. Jha, P. Mony, A. Kurpad, V. Lakshmi, R. Kumar, and N. K. Ganguly. 2007. "Biobanks in Developing Countries: Needs and Feasibility." *Science* 318 (5853): 1074–5.

STMa. n.d. "Personalised Medicine Creates Preconditions for More Effective Treatment." Accessed April 29, 2021. https://stm.fi/en/personalized-medicine.

STMb. n.d. "Rational Pharmacotherapy." Accessed April 29, 2021. https://stm.fi/en/rational-pharmacotherapy.

Tarkkala, Heta, Ilpo Helén, and Karoliina Snell. 2019. "From Health to Wealth: The Future of Personalized Medicine in the Making." *Futures* 109 (May): 142–52.

Temmes, Maria. 2018. "A Feminist Engagement With Systems Medicine." PhD Dissertation, Central European University.

Twine, France Winddance. 2011. *Outsourcing the Womb: Race, Class, and Gestational Surrogacy in a Global Market*. New York, NY: Routledge.

Tynkkynen, Liina-Kaisa, and Karsten Vrangbæk. 2018. "Comparing Public and Private Providers: A Scoping Review of Hospital Services in Europe." *BMC Health Services Research* 18: 141. https://doi.org/10.1186/s12913-018-2953-9

Vogt, Henrik, and Sara Green. 2020. "Personalised Medicine: Problems of Translation Into the Human Domain." In *De-Sequencing: Identity Work With Genes*, edited By Dana Mahr and Martina von Arx, 19–48. Singapore: Palgrave Macmillan.

Vogt, Henrik, Bjørn Hoffmann, and Linn Getz. 2016. "The New Holism: P4 Systems Medicine and the Medicalization of Health and Life Itself." *Medical Health Care and Philosophy* 19: 307–23.

Wonkam, Ambroise, Marcel Azabji Kenfack, Walinjom F. T. Muna, and Odile Ouwe-Missi-Oukem-Boyer. 2011. "Ethics of Human Genetic Studies in Sub-Saharan Africa: The Case of Cameroon through a Bibliometric Analysis." *Developing World Bioethics* 11 (3): 120–7.

Yates-Doerr, Emily. 2020. "Reworking the Social Determinants of Health: Responding to Material-Semiotic Indeterminacy in Public Health Interventions." *Medical Anthropology Quarterly* 34 (3): 378–97.

YLE. n.d. "Suomi maksaa superkalliista lääkkeistä ylihintaa – Asiantuntija: Kymmeniä miljoonia euroja olisi helposti säästettävissä." Accessed April 29, 2021. https://yle.fi/uutiset/3-10452404.

19 The Meanings of Chronopolitics and Temporal Awareness in Feminist Ethnographic Research

Christine M. Jacobsen, and Marry-Anne Karlsen

This chapter reflects on the meanings of geopolitical location and positioning in ethnographic feminist research by foregrounding the role of time. Critics have firmly established the need to develop greater awareness of how knowledge production is situated within an uneven geopolitical terrain, structured by borders between nation-states as well as divisions between (the Global) North and (the Global) South, East, and West (e.g. Tlostanova et al. 2016). Chronopolitics, the politics of time, is deeply entangled with geopolitics. Questions of location and positioning thus have a temporal as well as a spatial dimension. In this chapter, we argue for greater temporal awareness in feminist ethnographic research. We reflect on how our own temporal positioning as anthropologists and feminist researchers is relationally constituted in the encounters with our interlocutors within nationalist, racialized, and gendered power structures.

A question that has received much critical attention is the role of temporal distancing in processes of othering, what Fabian referred to as a "denial of coevalness" in his landmark publication *Time and the Other* (1983). Fabian identified "denial of coevalness" as a persistent and systematic tendency in anthropological research to position "those who are observed" in a different time from "the Time of the observer". This, he argued, turned the relation "between the West and its Other, between anthropology and its object" into a question not only of (cultural) difference but of "distance in space *and* Time" (1983: 147). Fabian's critique of temporal othering and his foregrounding of "an active sharing of time" as a requisite for establishing relations of coevalness in research has since been applied to new domains, and further developed and challenged, not least by feminist scholars.[1]

What it means to share time is not always clear, however. It can refer to physical "simultaneity" as well as typological "contemporaneity". Fabian's notion of coevalness further connotes a common, active "occupation" or sharing of time (1983: 31), or what he calls "intersubjective Time". In this sense, coevalness is something that must be "created" (Fabian 1983: 34). Feminist scholars have conceptualized the creation of coevalness as "a political act" (Sharma 2014), or as "a stance of recognition and respect in situations of mutual implication" (Massey 2005: 70). This "act" or "stance" is also necessarily informed by background conceptualizations of space and time. In this chapter, we explore how the critique of temporal othering and calls for a "sharing of time" sit alongside calls by feminist scholars to

DOI: 10.4324/9781003378761-22

The Meanings of Chronopolitics and Temporal Awareness 247

conceptualize time as multiple and relational (Massey 2005; Bastian 2011; Sharma 2014; Browne 2014). What challenges do questions of temporal sharedness and multiplicity pose for thinking about temporal locations and positionings in ethnographic feminist research? What are the implications for crafting conceptual and analytical frameworks and "tools"?

We draw upon approaches to time as multiple and relational, as developed by feminist scholars such as Bastian (2011, 2013) and Sharma (2014). To Bastian (2013: 112), the call to share time can be seen as "a call to recognize more clearly the way that a community's co-temporality is always multiple and never absolutely synchronous". However, Bastian (2011) also recognizes that merely claiming that there are "multiple times" does not get us very far because it does not address the question of how different times and temporalities coexist, interrelate, and conflict with one another. Stressing the power relations involved, Sharma (2014: 149) argues that: "As a political act, temporally aware coevalness means recognizing one's own place within the landscape of uneven time as a relational temporal position".

Other scholars have been more sceptical about the usefulness of the concept of coevalness, insofar as it may also be seen as a time discipline (Thompson 1967), which in some cases is violently imposed. Bevernage (2016: 355–6), for example, provocatively suggests that the best way to dismantle the abusive politics of spatiotemporal distancing is not to establish the Other as coeval through locating them in the "same time" as the researcher, but instead to radically question the construction of hegemonic contemporaneity as a natural and undeniable "given".

Our aim is not to assess the conceptual dilemmas or usefulness of coevalness as such, but – based on insights from these discussions – to highlight some dilemmas related to temporal sharedness and difference that we encountered in our research among irregularized migrants[2] in Norway and France. In order to do so, we draw attention to two different dimensions of time. First, we address the question of "sharing present time" as a "micropolitics of temporal coordination", and, second, we discuss the relationship of "sharing present time" to the question of pastness and futurity. Analysing two ethnographic vignettes from our fieldwork, we explore how we are positioned in the always already hierarchical and relational multiplicity of temporalities. In conclusion, we argue that a critique of temporal othering needs to be combined with awareness of how uneven and shifting temporal relations shape the production of knowledge; in our case, through ethnographic practice and anthropological writing.

Point of Departure

Our point of departure for thinking about these questions is a reflection on the dilemmas we encountered as researchers during the project *Waiting for an Uncertain Future: The Temporalities of Irregular Migration* (WAIT).[3] As part of this project, we conducted long-term ethnographic fieldwork among irregularized migrants in Marseille (Jacobsen) and Oslo (Karlsen). Migration is a pertinent site for exploring the entanglement of spatial and temporal co-ordinates of othering in feminist ethnographic research. Massey (2005) has argued that migration from

248   *Christine M. Jacobsen, and Marry-Anne Karlsen*

the Global South to Europe and the USA involves the arrival not merely of people who are perceived as "from the spatial margins", but also of people who, through temporal distancing, are perceived as "from the past" – as coming from traditional and/or pre-modern societies. Adapting Fabian's terminology, Massey (2005: 70) further claimed that the eradication of spatial and temporal distance through migration may be seen as an "assertion of coevalness" (cf. also Harney 2014) insofar as it reasserts the coexisting multiplicity that Massey saw modernity as having repressed through the convening of spatial heterogeneity into a temporal sequence.

However, given that coevalness must be actively created, it seems hasty to assume it to be asserted through migration, let alone that the reassertion of coexisting (spatial) multiplicity should transform the relationship between "anthropology and its object" (Fabian 1983: 147). Migration can have consequences for this relationship though, and for how researchers are positioned in relation to their interlocutors. De Genova (2016) has pointed out that, in anthropological studies of migration, the mobile subject is no longer the anthropologist, but the people whom anthropologists study. This has implications for the traditional anthropological axiom of taking "the native's point of view". While migrants continue to be construed as attached to spatially different "native cultures", this reversal also involves another form of "nativism" – that of the anthropologist as native. According to De Genova (2016: 230), "To conduct research related to the migrant non-citizens of a given nation-state from the unexamined standpoint of its citizens clearly would involve [an] uncritical ethnocentrism". Thus, in order to apprehend the critical perspectives and lived experiences of migrants, De Genova calls for a systematic effort to formulate an anthropology of migration that includes the researcher's privileged relation to the state as a "native" and citizen as part of the analysis.[4]

While De Genova focused on how researchers and irregularized migrants are positioned differently within the space of the nation-state, other migration scholars have suggested moving beyond a stark insider/outsider division and focusing instead on contextual and hybrid positionalities (e.g. Carling et al. 2014). Factors such as ethnicity, language, gender, and other markers may constitute a more dynamic interplay between researcher characteristics and particular social contexts. Researchers may also be part of migrant communities and (in rare cases such as that of WAIT-project researcher Shahram Khosravi) may themselves have been in situations of irregularity or in other less privileged relations to the state (Khosravi 2010). While contributions of this kind suggest important avenues for reflecting on positionality and situated knowledge production, there is a need to further probe the temporal implications of such (re)positioning. In this chapter, we suggest that an ethnographic practice which is mindful of the researchers' own subjectivity and positionality needs to recognize how chronopolitics is implicated in creating the difference between "migrant" and "citizen"

In the WAIT project, we started from ethnographies of the lived experience of irregularized migrants who find themselves in conditions of prolonged waiting due to their legal status: at border crossings, in refugee camps and detention centres, and within the urban fabric. The project investigated how waiting is produced through law and the social organization of time, as well as the practices through which migrants encounter, incorporate, and resist conditions of prolonged waiting. One recurring concern during the project was the epistemological and ethical challenges of studying migration through the prism of waiting (Jacobsen and Karlsen 2020). Waiting is not a neutral concept but is deeply entangled with modern conceptions of linear time and progress. Notions of waiting often rest on gendered, sexual, classed, or racialized norms concerning particular lifecycle expectations, or expectations of productivity and development. A challenge in the WAIT project thus became how to acknowledge migrants' experiences of having their lives put on hold without re-inscribing gendered, sexual, classed, and racialized norms. Further concerns related to the extent to which waiting as a temporal lens risked naturalizing migration-related differences and nation-state borders (Rozakou 2020; Drangsland 2020). Does the focus on "waiting" produce temporal others, and if so, in what ways? How can we analyse waiting without reinforcing the unexamined standpoint of the researcher?

Fabian (1983, 2014) was interested in the denial of coevalness that occurred in the move from ethnographic practice to anthropological discourse. Whereas he saw ethnographic practice as rooted in inter-subjectivity and shared time, it was through the writing up and analysis of these encounters that the denial of coeval-ness was produced, in that the referent(s) of the research was/were positioned in a different time from that of the present of the anthropologist as author. By shar-ing two ethnographic excerpts from Oslo (Karlsen), and Marseille (Jacobsen), we will complexify notions of shared time by presenting it as both a question of what it means to share time in ethnographic practice and what it means to produce an anthropological discourse that recognizes the multiplicity and relationality of time.

Using edited fieldnote excerpts to investigate the possibility of "shared time" is problematic in the sense that the communication that took place during fieldwork is already mediated by the text, whose present is different from that of the encoun-ters. What we are analysing here is thus not so much the actual encounters as our recollection of those encounters through the use of ethnographic fieldnotes written immediately after the situations, and our subsequent reworking of those notes to fit the format of a book chapter. In the moment of writing, the question of sharing time is both past and present. While reflecting upon fieldwork during writing is a retrospective process, new technologies of communication and travel have com-plicated this temporal sequencing, making "the field" temporally ever-present in a new way (Dalsgaard and Nielsen 2013) as we have continued to communicate with our interlocutors far beyond the spatial and temporal frames of our initial fieldwork. The "temporal awareness" for which we argue thus requires reflection on "shared time" during both the fieldwork encounter and the subsequent writing up of that encounter in the authors' present.

Case 1: Tramspotting in Oslo

This Case Draws on Marry-Anne's Fieldnotes

Ruth and I were sitting together at the tram stop, occupying the only seats. The stop was quite crowded, and more people were constantly arriving. It was rush hour,

250   *Christine M. Jacobsen, and Marry-Anne Karlsen*

and the tram was almost 20 minutes late due to traffic congestion. When it finally arrived, it was already quite full. Unlike the other people at the stop, we did not try to squeeze on. Two minutes later a new tram arrived, half full, but we did not board. As soon as it drove off, a third tram arrived, and this one was empty. Ruth and I shared a laugh about all the people who had squeezed into the first tram, who could have had a seat if they had had the patience to wait a few minutes. However, Ruth and I were not going anywhere. We were sitting, mainly quietly, at the stop, watching the three trams pass by again on their return trip, at a similar pace, the first one full, the second half full, and the third empty.

Ruth was a woman in her fifties, born in Ethiopia and living in Norway without legal residence. I was a majoritized[5] Norwegian citizen in my late thirties doing research for my postdoctoral project. We had met earlier that day at the weekly meeting of Mennesker i Limbo (People in Limbo), an organization for and run by irregularized migrants, which organized a mixture of political and social activities. Sitting at the tram stop, Ruth and I were waiting for a place that serves free meals to migrants once a week to open. The meals were served in the basement of a church near the stop. During my fieldwork, I participated in the two activities (meeting and free meal) most weeks. So did Ruth. However, there were a few hours between the meeting ending and the place that serves free meals opening, so Ruth was letting me hang out with her.

Before sitting down at the tram stop, we had been walking around the city, visiting a few shops and shopping malls, looking at clothes on sale, without buying anything. Walking around, we mainly engaged in small talk about the weather and the things we saw. At one point, Ruth started chiding me for not having kids yet. "You mustn't wait", she kept telling me, expressing concern that I was too focused on my career. She dismissed my concern regarding a suitable partner, noting that I had "a [Norwegian] passport, and a job – why are you waiting? It will be too late soon". Her chiding surprised me a bit, but questions of children and family were of course issues that I had previously prodded her about.

I had first met Ruth in 2012 when I was doing fieldwork for my PhD thesis on access to healthcare. At that time, Ruth had already been living in Norway for nearly a decade without legal residence. She had no children, nor any family in Norway. During her first few years in Norway, she had been able to find regular work. She had been issued a temporary work permit when she first applied for asylum. When her application was rejected, she kept receiving a tax card and continued to work. In 2010, however, the authorities discovered that tax cards had been issued to irregularized migrants due to a system error and immediately stopped the practice. Since then, Ruth had not been able to work and had lost her apartment. While she could generally sleep at a friend's place, her days were often spent walking around the city.

After we had walked around for about two hours, I tried to invite Ruth for a cup of tea or coffee, so that we could sit down inside somewhere. It was a cold day, just a few degrees Celsius above zero. The rain, which had previously been a drizzle, was becoming heavier. "We get coffee at the place [that serves the free meal]. No need to spend your money", she responded, before suggesting that we

The Meanings of Chronopolitics and Temporal Awareness   251

sit down at the tram stop which had a roof protecting us against the rain. After a while, I was starting to feel a bit bored and restless, but Ruth looked tranquil and I tried to copy her.

Case 2: Queueing in Marseille

This Case Draws on Christine's Field Notes

Ania, a recently divorced woman from Niger in her early thirties, her one-year-old daughter Hannah, and I were waiting outside the Préfecture in the chilly morning air. After leaving her abusive husband, Ania had lost her legal right to remain in France. Due to a medical condition, she had been issued a temporary residence permit while she underwent surgery. Now that she was recovering, she was applying for a less precarious residency status, which would allow her to work and thus pay her rent and provide for Hannah. The line to the front desk moved quickly once the Préfecture opened. We got ticket number 418. Seated in the waiting area upstairs, we attentively followed the numbers being called. After more than an hour, number 400 appeared on the display. At 411, our eyes met in the shared knowledge that it would soon be our turn. Then, there was a long pause, before the display suddenly jumped to 420. "What's happening?" Ania asked anxiously. "I have no idea, maybe we should ask", I replied. "Maybe", Ania confirmed. "Do you want me to do it?", I asked. "Yes, please", Ania replied. I went over to the door where the 400 numbers were received. A sign said, "Please wait until your number or name is called". When the door opened for the people with ticket number 420 to exit, I squeezed in and confronted a row of caseworkers behind glass windows. I approached the caseworker at counter 6, asking "What happened to 418?" "We had to do 420 first", she explained, "but we will start again at 411 now".

There was again a long wait before the numbers on the display started moving. Hannah was crying now. At 417, we got ready to enter. Then, it happened again, the display jumped to number 419. Increasingly frustrated, I popped my head in through the door and inquired: "What happened to 418?" "Some papers are lacking", the caseworker answered curtly. How can it take hours to move papers from the ground floor to the first floor? I thought, but did not say it out loud.

Another hour passed, and we were exhausted from the wait by the time I impatiently latched onto an employee passing by, demanding why it was taking so long for them to call 418. She went to inquire and came back to explain that they were waiting for a signature, but it would soon be our turn. After a few minutes, the display showed 418 and we rushed to the counter. "Bonjour", we politely ventured. "Luckily, not everyone is as annoying as you Madame", the caseworker replied sourly, giving me a hostile stare. "I'm sorry", I mumbled "but . . ." Ania, worried that this might go the wrong way, whispered: "Just leave it". Ania's anxiety and my own tension were now palpable. It felt almost like a miracle when the caseworker handed Ania the paper.

On our way out, Ania showed me a sign informing visitors that you can be denied access, fined, or arrested if you speak discourteously to caseworkers. "It's

252   *Christine M. Jacobsen, and Marry-Anne Karlsen*

because of your skin colour that I let you ask why they skipped our number, you being white and all", Ania shared with me. "She would have treated me way worse". Outside, we stopped to give the paper a closer look and discovered that it was not the residence card that had been issued, only a receipt, this time valid for a year. She would have to come back to get the actual card. Ania did not seem to mind too much though. "It says here that I can work", she exclaimed happily. For a moment, we remained in this optimistic mode. We bought groceries and went back to my place to cook lunch. When it was time for Ania and Hannah to go home, however, the anxious look returned to Ania's eyes. In a week, the temporary housing she had been given after her surgery would expire, and she would have to find a new solution for Hannah and herself.

Discussion

The Micropolitics of Temporal Coordination

To what extent can the ethnographic examples of "waiting together" described earlier be unpacked as an active "occupation" or "sharing" of "present time"? One of the first challenges that we encountered when examining the question of whether we had created a "shared time" with our interlocutors was the following: While we as researchers may occupy the same social space and experience at a common location in (calendar) time (e.g. autumn 2017) with our interlocutors, we are, in these same situations, also "calibrated" to different "temporal itineraries", to use Sharma's (2014) terminology. "Recalibration", she contends, is about the micropolitics of temporal coordination and social control between multiple temporalities (Sharma 2014: 7). Expectations about recalibrating time permeate the social fabric differently for distinct populations (Sharma 2014: 18). While waiting is a prominent feature of everyday modern life, to the extent that its familiarity and pervasiveness have meant that it is difficult to pin down analytically, the request to recalibrate by "waiting", configured within a broader regime of migration control, is ubiquitous for irregularized migrants and asylum seekers (Jacobsen 2020).

What we can perhaps see most clearly in Christine and Ania's case is how the concrete waiting situation at the Préfecture was to Christine a "situational" form of waiting, while Ania's waiting also had an "existential" dimension. Ania's future depended on the decision of the Préfecture, and to some extent on the discretion of the caseworker, on whether to include her in the futures offered by France and other European nation-states to their residents. While Christine was not a French citizen, the Schengen agreement of 1985, to which Norway became a signatory in 1996, secured her free movement between European countries. The same agreement fortified the external borders of Europe and reduced Ania's prospects of travelling to and legally staying in France, despite her being born in what was during colonial rule a part of "French territory" in "French West Africa".

The geopolitical bordering of Europe has consequences for positioning in terms of citizenship and racialization (Mezzadra and Neilson 2013). As Fassin (2010) argues, the external borders of the French nation-state are deeply interlinked with

The Meanings of Chronopolitics and Temporal Awareness   253

internal borders produced by colonialization and racialization. While neither Christine nor Ania was a French citizen, Christine, unlike Ania and other people from former French territories, is not perceived as a (racialized) migrant. In Christine's excerpt, Ania pointed out the risks associated with impatience for racialized bodies who lack legal status, and whose impatience may be perceived and sanctioned as "uncourteous" behaviour. The way in which Christine and Ania were differently racialized (as European and white and as African and Black) created different subject positions across which the ability to display impatience or voice protest, and the expectation of fair treatment and affects were differentially distributed. Thus, even though their "waiting" may be perceived as a "shared" experience, their socio-economic and racial positioning differently condition the affective experience of waiting and the ability to curtail boredom, display impatience, voice protest, or demand fair treatment.

Marry-Anne's excerpt draws further attention to how waiting occurs within a larger web of relations and meaning, with significance for whose time and tempos are made to matter. While the busy tram stop could be said to exemplify the acceleration of everyday life under global capitalism, it is also a social space constituted by different temporal itineraries. For example, Ruth and Marry-Anne were not part of the five o'clock rush of people commuting home from work. They were adjusting to the timing and tempo of civil society organizations that support irregularized migrants. Nonetheless, they were still required to relate to the ways in which expectations of a faster life contribute to privileging certain populations and temporal practices and disavowing others (see Sharma 2014). Ruth was showing Marry-Anne how to "blend in" within a city landscape in which even the temporal architecture of waiting (built environments, commodities, and services, technologies) privileges a certain kind of subject's time. For irregularized migrants such as Ruth, reducing visibility in public places is one of their survival strategies. Yet trends within urban development, including the proliferation of semi-public spaces (e.g. shopping centres), and attempts to regulate and remove specific groups from public space (e.g. the general ban on outdoor sleeping in Oslo, the collective removal of drug addicts from the area around Oslo Central Station, benches designed to discourage long-term occupancy) affect a person's exposure in the city across a range of social differences such as age, gender, and race. Marry-Anne's suggestion to make the "waiting time" more comfortable inside a café also displays how the experience of waiting can be conditioned, both materially and affectively, by socio-economic status.

In both the waiting situations discussed, there was also another temporal dimension to the ethnographers' positionality, in that the situations provided good fieldwork opportunities for participant observation. Marry-Anne was not simply "killing time" until she could go to the place serving free meals; rather, she was doing research, for which she was being paid. Feminist ethnographers have long problematized the conflicting interests and emotions integral to participant observation, as it involves both affective engagement (i.e. participation) and more detached calculation (i.e. observation) (Stacey 1988; Karlsen 2015). This split has a temporal dimension, because researchers are required to be emphatically present in the field,

254   *Christine M. Jacobsen, and Marry-Anne Karlsen*

while thinking about the future point of writing up (Rooke 2010). Marry-Anne and Ruth's case thus draws attention to the way in which they are unevenly positioned within the power relations shaping a temporal order oriented around being productive. Although Marry-Anne attempted to synchronize her body clock to Ruth's and that of the civil society organizations supporting irregularized migrants, it was not primarily their temporal expectations to which she was adjusting, but those of neoliberal academia.

How Ruth and Marry-Anne are unevenly positioned in the research encounter can also be seen in the courtesy that Ruth showed Marry-Anne when she declined the offer of coffee, even though she was in fact doing Marry-Anne a favour by letting her hang out with her. The greater value often accorded to Marry-Anne's and Christine's time during fieldwork felt deeply paradoxical to them but must be seen in light of the fact that they as researchers were freer to enter and leave the system of relationships of which the "field" was constituted (see Stacey 1988).

The Uneven Pasts and Futures of Waiting

To be co-temporaneous, to actively occupy or share time, concerns more than just the question of the tempo and duration of time. Fabian argued in *Time and the Other* (1983: 92) that, in order to be knowingly in each other's present, we must somehow be able to share each other's past (see also Fabian 2014). Sharing each other's pasts does not mean that they need to be identical, according to Birth (2008), but that sufficient common knowledge about the past is shared to make communication in the present intelligible. Marry-Anne and Christine both knew Ruth and Ania from previous fieldwork at the times when the situations described earlier occurred. Multiple conversations and time spent together had thus, to some extent, facilitated the shared temporal frameworks necessary for intersubjective communication. However, there were also many aspects of Ruth's and Ania's pasts to which we had access only through their narratives, notably the pasts they shared with people in the communities from which they had migrated, and with other migrants crossing borders. But occupying a shared present is not only conditioned by pasts, but it may also involve horizon(s) of expectation (Bevernage 2016) and the question of futures (Birth 2008).

The question of creating a shared past and future concerns not only the ethnographic encounter but also its translation into an ethnographic account. One way of establishing shared time when analysing our excerpts would be to focus on shared future horizons of uncertainty, as suggested by Ramsay (2019). Under neoliberal conditions, temporal uncertainty is not an exceptional condition for irregularized migrants – it is a condition that many migrants and citizens share. Prolonged and existential forms of waiting, what Vigh (2008) calls "chronic waiting", has been seen, for example, as a constitutive practice of globalization and as central to the postcolonial experience as such (Bayart 2007; Jeffrey 2010). Work on precarity and austerity further suggests that existential waiting has spread to previously more privileged groups and regions, including academics (e.g. Loher and Strasser 2019). At the time of writing, the COVID-19 pandemic, and the economic crisis triggered

The Meanings of Chronopolitics and Temporal Awareness   255

by efforts to combat it, has further generalized the experience of an uncertain future to ever broader segments of the global population.

Using this framework to examine our own positionality, we could point out, for example, that, while Christine was a full-time professor in a permanent position during fieldwork, Marry-Anne was in a temporary position whose opportunities for continued work beyond the WAIT project were uncertain. Marry-Anne's position could thus also be read as waiting for an uncertain future. However, while the increasing neoliberalization of academia is contributing to a state of unpredictability, academic jobs in the Norwegian context still come with relatively decent wages, access to social security and healthcare, and a planning horizon of two to four years. It also comes with the expectation of, and also the opportunity for, mobility. Ruth and Ania, on the other hand, were denied access to the formal labour market and lived with the constant spectre of being deported. These two cases thus illustrate the need to couple a focus on the shared insecurity created by neoliberal restructuring with a careful analysis of the temporal specificities of different modes of precarity, and how these are configured differently at the intersections of class, gender, sexualities, citizenship, and racialization.

While conceptualizations of shared existential waiting can destabilize neat partitions between citizens and migrants, applying a shared temporal framework of neoliberal restructuring to our cases reveals that the tendency to generalize about the temporality of "modernity" or "neoliberalism" and its embodied effects risks obscuring important differences. The challenge from a feminist perspective, according to Browne (2014), is to conceptualize shared time without falling back on presumptions of a higher historico-temporal totality or oneness, and to make sense of multiple temporalities while also addressing the workings of global capitalism.

Here, we suggest that feminist ethnographic research needs to reflect upon how chronopolitics is implicated in reinforcing the difference between "migrant" and "citizen", and how temporal difference affects the ethnographic encounter. In some nativist anti-immigration discourses, the future of Marry-Anne and Christine (as citizens) is relationally constituted in opposition to that of migrants. This configures, for example, the relationship between social reproduction and futurity differently for Ruth and Marry-Anne. As the case shows, both Marry-Anne and Ruth, as "childless women" of a certain age, were affected by gendered expectations of a successful life course. However, in nativist and anti-immigration discourses in both Norway and France, migrants' reproductivity is sometimes construed as a "threat" to the future of natives, whereas low reproductive numbers among majority (particularly affluent and educated) women is cast as a problem for the future of the nation.

Towards a Greater Temporal Awareness in Feminist Ethnographic Analysis

In the epilogue to his article on spatio-temporal distancing and temporal heterogeneity, Bevernage (2016: 355) gives an example that is directly relevant to the cases presented earlier. Analysing a situation in which he translates a refusal letter to an asylum seeker, which effectively irregularizes her by making her presence

256 *Christine M. Jacobsen, and Marry-Anne Karlsen*

on European territory illegal, Bevernage argues that, while they were physically simultaneous, they were not coeval. This, he argues, was not so much due to different past experiences but rather to the radically different expectations they were allowed to have. This radical difference in expectations (to get a degree, a job, a pension) is an effect of how the nation constructs hegemonic contemporaneity by excluding large numbers of people. While we agree with Bevernage about the need to stress the constituted nature of contemporaneity, our aim has been to highlight the dilemmas that questions of temporal sharedness and difference raise for feminist ethnographic research. In analysing our ethnographic cases, we have argued for a greater awareness of how multiple and uneven temporal relations shape the production of knowledge.

In our opinion, feminist ethnographic research must acknowledge differential temporal situatedness, the multiple experiences, and the lines of time and of history that operate within the present. A call to recognize the multiplicity and relationality of times in the present does not in and of itself decentre forms of normative temporalities that create hierarchies, however. Recognizing and reflecting upon the interdependence of differentially lived time, and how time, like space, is an always-already intersecting form of social difference, is hardly a new feminist tool (thinking technology or approach, to use the terminology of this volume). However, we believe that it can inspire further reflections on the meanings of geopolitical and chronopolitical locations and positionings in ethnographic feminist research.

Notes

1 Tlostanova et al. (2016), for example, have reflected on how transnational feminist discourses sometimes reproduce othering, in representing not only the Global South but also the East, as "lagging behind" in relation to Western progress narratives.
2 Irregular migration is generally understood as border-crossings and/or dwelling within state borders without authorization from the state. When speaking of migrants, we use the term "irregularized" to foreground how hardening regimes of migration control produce those whose mobility is not authorized by sovereign states as "irregular".
3 The project was funded by the Research Council of Norway and included four ethnographic studies in Oslo, Stockholm, Marseille, and Hamburg, as well as an interdisciplinary theoretical exploration of waiting and temporality in irregular migration.
4 Anthropologists who occupy different positions in relation to their interlocutors have offered nuanced ways of thinking about locatedness and positionality, such as, for instance, Abu-Lughod's (1991) "halfie", Narayan's (1993) "native", or concepts such as "citizen anthropologist" (Cheater 1987) and "insider anthropology" (Cerroni-Long 1995).
5 In migration research, the concept of "majoritized" is used to signal that majority and minority groups are always relationally constituted. Here, we use the concept of majoritized to signal that a particular individual (in this case Marry-Anne) is constructed as representing and belonging to a majority ethnic group due to specific attributes related to aspects including ethnicity, race, and religion.

References

Abu-Lughod, Lila. 1991. "Writing Against Culture." In *Recapturing Anthropology: Working in the Present*, edited by Richard Fox, 137–62. Santa Fe, NM: School of American Research Press.

The Meanings of Chronopolitics and Temporal Awareness 257

Bastian, Michelle. 2011. "The Contradictory Simultaneity of Being With Others: Exploring Concepts of Time and Community in the Work of Gloria Anzaldúa." *Feminist Review* 97 (1): 151–67.

Bastian, Michelle. 2013. "Political Apologies and the Question of a 'Shared Time' in the Australian Context." *Feminist Theory* 17 (2): 211–28. https://doi.org/10.1177/0263276413486679

Bayart, Jean-Francois. 2007. *Global Subjects: A Political Critique of Globalization.* Cambridge: Polity Press.

Bevernage, Berber. 2016. "Tales of Pastness and Contemporaneity: On the Politics of Time in History and Anthropology." *Rethinking History* 20 (3): 352–74. https://doi.org/10.1080/13642529.2016.1192257.

Birth, Kevin. 2008. "The Creation of Coevalness and the Danger of Homochronism." *Journal of The Royal Anthropological Institute* 14 (1): 3–20.

Browne, Victoria. 2014. *Feminism, Time, and Nonlinear History.* Basingstoke and New York, NY: Palgrave Macmillan.

Carling, Jørgen, Marta Bivand Erdal, and Rojan Tordhol Ezzati. 2014. "Beyond the Insider – Outsider Divide in Migration Research." *Migration Studies* 2 (1): 36–54.

Cerroni-Long, Liza. 1995. "Introduction: Insider or Native Anthropology." Special Issue: Insider Anthropology. *NAPA Bulletin* 16 (1): 1–16.

Cheater, Angela P. 1987. "The Anthropologist as Citizen: The Diffracted Self?." In *Anthropology at Home*, edited by Anthony Jackson, 164–79. London: Tavistock.

Dalsgaard, Steffen, and Morten Nielsen. 2013. "Introduction: Time and the Field." *Social Analysis* 57 (1): 1–19.

De Genova, Nicholas P. 2016. "The 'Native's Point of View' in the Anthropology of Migration." *Anthropological Theory* 16 (2–3): 227–40.

Drangsland, Kari Anne. 2020. "Mo's Challenge: Waiting and the Question of Methodological Nationalism." In *Waiting and the Temporalities of Irregular Migration*, edited by Christine M. Jacobsen, Marry-Anne Karlsen, and Shahram Khosravi, 75–96. London and New York, NY: Routledge.

Fabian, Johannes. 1983. *Time and the Other.* New York, NY: Columbia University Press.

Fabian, Johannes. 2014. "Ethnography and Intersubjectivity: Loose Ends." *Hau: Journal of Ethnographic Theory* 4 (1): 199–209.

Fassin, Didier. 2010. "Introduction." In *Les Nouvelles frontières de la société française*, edited by Didier Fassin, 1–24. Paris: La Découverte.

Harney, Nicholas. 2014. "Temporalities of Migration and Reflexive Ethnography." *Mondi Migranti* (3): 47–62.

Jacobsen, Christine M. 2020. "They Said 'Wait, Wait' – and I Waited': The Power-Chronographies of Waiting for Asylum in Marseille, France." In *Waiting and the Temporalities of Irregular Migration*, edited by Christine M. Jacobsen, Marry-Anne Karlsen, and Shahram Khosravi, 40–57. London and New York, NY: Routledge.

Jacobsen, Christine M., and Marry-Anne Karlsen. 2020. "Introduction: Unpacking the Temporalities of Irregular Migration." In *Waiting and the Temporalities of Irregular Migration*, 1–19. London and New York, NY: Routledge.

Jeffrey, Craig. 2010. "Timepass: Youth, Class, and Time Among Unemployed Young Men in India." *American Ethnologist* 37 (3): 465–81. https://doi.org/10.1111/j.1548-1425.2010.01266.x

Karlsen, Marry-Anne. 2015. "Precarious Inclusion: Irregular Migration, Practices of Care, and State B/ordering in Norway." PhD Thesis, University of Bergen.

Khosravi, Shahram. 2010. *"Illegal" Traveller: An Auto-Ethnography of Borders*. Basingstoke and New York, NY: Palgrave Macmillan.

Loher, David, and Sabine Strasser. 2019. "Politics of Precarity: Neoliberal Academia under Austerity Measures and Authoritarian Threat." *Social Anthropology* 27 (2): 5–14. https://doi.org/10.1111/1469-8676.12697.

Massey, Doreen. 2005. *For Space*. Thousand Oaks, CA: SAGE.

Mezzadra, Sandro, and Brett Neilson. 2013. *Border as Method, or the Multiplication of Labor*. Durham, NC: Duke University Press.

Narayan, Kirin. 1993. "How Native Is a 'Native' Anthropologist?." *American Anthropologist* 95 (3): 671–86.

Ramsay, Georgina. 2019. "Time and the Other in Crisis: How Anthropology Makes Its Displaced Object." *Anthropological Theory* 6 (2): 139–52.

Rooke, Alison. 2010. "Queer in the Field: On Emotions, Temporality, and Performativity in Ethnography." In *Queer Methods and Methodologies: Intersecting Queer Theories and Social Science Research*, edited by Kathe Browne and Cathereene Jean Nash, 25–40. Burlington, VT: Ashgate.

Rozakou, Katarina. 2020. "Accelerated Time: Waiting and Hasting during the 'Long Summer of Migration'." In *Waiting and the Temporalities of Irregular Migration*, edited by Christine M. Jacobsen, Marry-Anne Karlsen, and Shahram Khosravi, 23–40. London and New York, NY: Routledge.

Sharma, Sarah. 2014. *In the Meantime: Temporality and Cultural Politics*. Durham, NC: Duke University Press.

Stacey, Judith. 1988. "Can There Be a Feminist Ethnography?." *Women's Studies International Forum* 11 (1): 21–7.

Thompson, Edward P. 1967. "Time, Work-Discipline, and Industrial Capitalism." *Past & Present* 38: 56–97.

Tlostanova, Madina, Suruchi Thapar-Björkert, and Redi Koobak. 2016. "Border Thinking and Disidentification: Postcolonial and Postsocialist Feminist Dialogues." *Feminist Theory* 17 (2): 221–8.

Vigh, Henrik. 2008. "Crisis and Chronicity: Anthropological Perspectives on Continuous Conflict and Decline." *Ethnos* 73 (1): 5–24.

20 Disrupting the Colonial Gaze

Towards Alternative Sexual Justice Engagements With Young People in South Africa

Tamara Shefer

Some years ago, I presented my work at a Nordic conference, together with a group of South African and Finnish colleagues. We were sharing research on young people and intersectional gender and sexual equality that was part of a collaborative research project between us (Hearn et al. 2015). When we finished our presentation, the questions and comments primarily focused on South Africa and Africa, and most of the respondents asked about sexual violence, crime, homophobia, and other injustices. Many of the questions were about the extent, nature, and roots of the violence, implying it was specific to South African or global Southern contexts, and all of the questions were directed at the South Africans, locating the Finnish context as "innocent" and a Northern "civilized" nation-state. We found ourselves deeply implicated in the othering gaze of Northern authority and innocence over Southern unruliness and disorder. This chapter discusses my sharpened awareness to how transnational scholarship, notwithstanding good intentions, may add to dominant and damaging stories about gender and sexuality across contexts of inequality and difference.

This chapter draws on the proliferating body of work on sexual practices, particularly those of young people in the post-apartheid South African context. My intention is to think critically about the ideological and political impact of such research. I argue that the way this body of work has been deployed reiterates and reinstates lines of power, authority, and privilege endemic in colonialist, patriarchal scholarly traditions, while bolstering the very racist, heteronormative, and other epistemological violences we had hoped to challenge. I discuss the lens of transnational engagements and how we can do critical transnational post,[1] decolonial feminist research better through an interrogation of contemporary research on young people's sexual practices in South Africa.

The last few decades of research in South African contexts powerfully speaks to transnational research, highlighting the dangers and pitfalls of gender research across diverse contexts in light of continuing multi-layered inequalities between different parts of the world (Shefer and Hearn 2022; Shefer et al. 2015; Ishengoma 2016). Research on young people's sexualities in South Africa has over the last few decades been spurred on by the international "industry" of HIV reproductive health research and global emphases on HIV and gender-based violence (GBV). Much of this research, while underpinned by apparent well-meaning global justice and

DOI: 10.4324/9781003378761-23

260   *Tamara Shefer*

public health goals, has tended to be uncritically located within global politics and existing inequalities. This has had problematic effects, both in the methodologies employed and in how such research is taken up the public domain. I argue here that the bulk of this research, and the policies and practices it fuels, has the unintended consequence of reproducing the normative binarisms and consequent violences it was intended to challenge. I attempt to illustrate how transnational[2] (and transethnic/class/race within particular nation-states) practices of research, and the politics of knowledge and global relations of power and privilege that they are located in, are deeply implicated in these problematic practices.

This chapter unpacks the failures and embeddedness of much of the research on young sexualities in South Africa in an exploitative and epistemologically violent politics of knowledge. I argue that it is not only a lack of rigorous attention and reflexivity but also neglect of a political ethics of care (Tronto 1993, 2013) and relational ontology (Barad 2007) that undermines efforts to achieve an ethical, just, non-extractive, and non-representational transnational intersectional feminist research praxis. I find Haraway's (2016) call to "stay with the trouble" and Sedgwick's (2003) notion of "reparative reading" particularly helpful in highlighting how the problematic practices and political effects outlined here are embedded in a larger imperative to re-think how we make knowledge. This chapter concludes with some possibilities for a more hopeful transnational feminist engagement; one that engages a feminist ethics and politics of care and relationality, inspired by the "troubling" knowledges emerging from the fruitful entanglements of decolonial, feminist, and queer art, activism, and scholarship.

Global Surveillance: Northern Innocence, Privilege, and Patronage

Since the early 1990s, as South Africa emerged out of apartheid, HIV as a global and local challenges became a national imperative, alongside building a democratic state. Consequently, significant international focus and funds were directed at Southern Africa and other global Southern contexts. In South Africa, the wave of funding and invitations for collaborative research was welcome, especially in light of the apartheid era isolation. As a result, a wide range of research was initiated focusing on sexual practices in South Africa, primarily through the lens of HIV and GBV (Vetten 2018). Given that the epidemic was identified at this point as predominantly heterosexual with highest rates among young people, much of the emphasis was on young people in poor communities and other "risk groups", such as sex workers and migrants (Campbell 2000; Dunkle et al. 2007; Varga 1997). A range of research projects were initiated by Northern scholars, often with funding from North America or Europe and frequently drawing on local scholars and fieldworkers.

Numerous problematics are evident within this form of transnational collaboration. For example, it repeats a colonial model of existing privilege, power, and resources, underpinned by and resulting in the promotion and reproduction of this very inequality. Thus, a Northern scholar engaging in Southern research immediately represents and reinserts Northern privilege and power, building and re-reifying

Disrupting the Colonial Gaze 261

privileged geopolitical knowledges at both an individual career level and a more symbolic level, underlining whose knowledge counts. While some South African scholars have benefited from this scholarship and the influx of funding to support research, many Northern scholars have grown their careers through the representation of Southern knowledge, reproducing a colonial model of the Global South as fieldwork and the Global North as academic authority.

A form of global surveillance is also enmeshed in such scholarship and its implementation in policy and practice. Much of the scholarship was and is located in colonial habits of extraction, perpetuating regulation of the majority by spaces of power and privilege, resulting in the deployment of authoritative knowledge towards disciplinary and policing frameworks in South Africa. Such research has therefore been used in the reproduction of global Northern, Western privileging, superiority, and "innocence" (Wekker 2016). It becomes evident that South African research on young people's sexualities is enmeshed with a transnational global "civilizing" project characterized by (post)colonial exploitative relations between resourced and subjugated parts of the world. The intense focus on poor, Black, and young South Africans and the knee-jerk association with violence fuels a narrative in which sexual violence, patriarchy, and heteronormativity are exported from "civilized", "gender just" countries, what Grewal (2013) calls "outsourcing" patriarchy, to those already historically subjugated and othered. Such discursive practices, and the global and local imaginary, are fodder for racist, colonial tropes of African sexualities that have been unpacked in analyses of local and global responses to HIV/AIDS and African sexualities in general (Jungar and Oinas 2004; Patton 1997; Tamale 2011).

Further, the international concerns related to homophobic violence and "hate crimes" that are prominent in research and the public and popular gaze on South Africa are threaded through with homonationalist (Puar 2007) and femonationalist (Farris 2017) discourses. This interrogative surveillance extends the civilized, developed, and authoritative position of white, Western, Northern societies (Jungar and Peltonen 2015, 2016; Peltonen and Jungar 2018). Feminist postcolonial scholars have also illustrated how such dynamics operate within global Northern countries in relation to migrants and ethnic minorities (Farahani and Thapar-Björkert 2019; Keskinen 2012, 2014). Thus, research on gender inequality and violence may be used to perpetuate notions of global Northern, Western, and white civility, advancement, and supremacy, while "othering" patriarchy and gender violences to those nations and communities already in subjugated geopolitical and ideological locations. HIV and the resultant surveillance of sexualities in global Southern contexts has thus shored up the colonial "othering" and denigrating tropes of Black bodies and sexualities, conflating HIV, gender and sexual injustice, and violence and illness with Black bodies (Flint and Hewitt 2015; Settler and Engh 2015).

At a global level, such research has cast those in more privileged nation-states as civilizing benefactors who face no troubles or injustices of their own but are "generously" directing their efforts at the troubled "others". This assumption also speaks to what Joan Tronto (2013) has called "privileged irresponsibility" in which those in privileged, majority, or dominant (geo)political positions fail to

262   *Tamara Shefer*

acknowledge the exercise of power, thus maintaining their taken for granted positions of privilege, even when engaging in practices of care. As Tronto argues that the burden of care globally falls on those who are locally and globally subjugated at political, material, and ideological levels, so too in the research terrain, privileged researchers do not acknowledge how the "troubles" of the Global South are entangled with the privileges of the Global North. Researchers, already privileged by their geopolitical, class, race, or gender location, rationalize their work through a narrative that frequently reinforces the very othering they hope to challenge. This is of course not a new argument. Spivak's (1988: 296) ground-breaking chapter, including her famous remark about "white men saving brown women from brown men" as key to colonial power dynamics, remains salient regarding contemporary research conducted at transnational and transcultural local levels directed at HIV and young people's sexualities. In particular, the continued relations of patronage, which Tronto (2013) argues are a key component of privileged irresponsibility, mask unequal power and the exploitative appropriation of the lives and resources of peoples and parts of the world that remain subjugated and denigrated.

The practices of othering and devaluation that are reinforced by this scholarship are located "uncritically within the framework and horizon of the nation state, neither discussing the globally uneven relations between nation states nor reflecting on changed meanings of nation states and their borders in an era of transnational capital, intensive transnational migration, etc." (Lykke et al., this volume). An ethics of relationality, an acknowledgement of the entanglements of peoples and nations, of the privileges of some and the subjugation and marginalization of others, is deeply lacking in dominant practices of research which remain oblivious to the damages they do and the symbolic (and sometimes actual) violence that is set in motion.

Reproduction of Raced, Classed, and Heteronormative Moralities

Another key concern is the ways in which mainstream research on gender and sexuality in South Africa has reinstated stereotypical gender and sexual binaries. The reproduction of such normative discourses is also ensnared in transnational and local "othering". It is increasingly evident that intersectional gender binarisms are reflected in research, policies, and practices, so that femininity, in particular, poor, Black, African young femininity, is constructed as always vulnerable and violable (Boonzaier 2017; Boonzaier and Kessi 2018; Gqola 2015; Helman 2018; Shefer 2016), and masculinity, particularly poor, Black, African, young masculinity, as inherently predatory and violating (Bhana and Pattman 2009; Ratele 2014).

For many local feminist scholars and activists, the imperative to address HIV was a potentially positive moment to bring the feminist critique of heterosexuality to a more mainstream public forum. Thus, acknowledgement that the intersectional gendered dynamic of HIV infection in South Africa had to be key to both prevention and mitigation efforts was an opportunity to challenge normative gender and sexual practices and the violences that these engender. However, it has become increasingly evident that research may be re-entrenching dominant

Disrupting the Colonial Gaze 263

discourses around gender and sexuality, preserving the binarisms of gender and heteronormativity within public terrains, such as sexuality education at school or in public advocacy directed at challenging HIV and gender inequalities (Shefer 2016; Bhana 2016). Research, policy, and practice regarding young people's sexualities have tended to not only assume but also, in many cases, actively reinforce gender binarisms and heteronormative gender performance in sexual intimacies.

Enmeshed in the reiteration of gender binarisms embedded in research and practice is the presentation of women as asexual victims to male hypersexual desires. African feminist researchers, such as McFadden (1992, 2003), have noted how HIV/AIDS responses in Africa have further constrained women's sexual agency and positive discourse on women's desire and pleasure. A punitive voice on young people's sexuality has been further entrenched through HIV prevention methods, particularly evident in current sexuality education at school, where a gender binary and heteronormative approach to teaching HIV/AIDS and sexuality has been well documented (Macleod 2009; Ngabaza and Shefer 2019; Bhana et al. 2019). While sexuality education has been promoted as a way of challenging gender and sexual injustice in democratic South Africa, normative gender and sexual practices are reinscribed in the curriculum (Bhana 2014, 2016).

Similarly, a growing body of research on sexuality education within the life orientation programme in South African schools has shown how HIV has been deployed as governmentality over gender normativity and dominant moralities (arguably imposed by Northern, Western, middle-class framings) related to young people's sexualities (Kruger et al. 2015; Shefer et al. 2015). The reproduction and rationalization of gender binarisms are reinforced through the dominant narrative of danger, disease, and damage, where young women are set up as responsible for their own and their male partners' well-being (Macleod et al. 2015; Ngabaza and Shefer 2019) and for ensuring a "respectable femininity" (Van Wyk 2015).

However, the opposite research inclination is equally problematic. Feminist scholars have interrogated attempts at flagging women as agentic no matter their material and discursive subjugations, and how the binarism of agency versus victimhood itself continues to repeat transnational dynamics of patronage and dominant group privilege (Campbell and Mannell 2016; Hemmings and Kabesh 2013; Mahmood 2001). Jungar and Oinas (2011: 255) unpack how both asserting women's agency and claiming their victimhood re-inscribes the privilege and authority of the researcher who has the power to name.

Heteronormativity and the hegemonic heterosexual nuclear family have also been key within contemporary public health research and educational interventions directed at young people (McEwan 2018). Much of the research and practice directed at young people is underpinned by and focused on re-animating heterosex as normative. Research tends to focus on heterosexual gender binary practices without explicitly acknowledging this, thereby erasing diverse sexual and gender desires and practices. Heteronormative and homophobic discourse and practices in school and higher education remain commonplace (Bhana 2014; Hames 2007; Msibi 2012). This is seen in young people's reports on how HIV and sexuality education are "taught", in the assumption of heterosex as normative and idealized, and of normative nuclear families as the only imaginable sexual and intimacy outcome for young people (Ngabaza and Shefer 2019).

As mentioned, gender stereotypes in literature and its public effects are also enmeshed with racist and classist discourses, further challenges for transnational feminist projects. A popular advertisement, see one version of this reproduced here, cautioning against transactional sex, posted in public spaces in the 2000s as part of the larger HIV/AIDS mass educational campaign, provided an example of this unitary gendered, raced, and classed picture (Brouard and Crewe 2013; Shefer and Strebel 2013). This advert warned young poor women against transactional relationships with older, better resourced men. Notably, billboards were only located in poor Black communities and represented a young, poor, Black woman in a markedly submissive, vulnerable pose in relation to a well-dressed, predatory, older Black man.

One frightening example of the impact of gender scholarship on the racist and sexist public imaginary was international and local response to the publication of a research project in South Africa that found that one in three men admitted to rape (Jewkes et al. 2010). Responses on a blog linked to an international posting of this research (Tay 2010) illustrate the manipulative way in which the research findings

Figure 20.1 An example of billboards placed in predominantly poor Black communities as part of HIV public education in South Africa, © Guy Harling 2012.

Source: Reprinted with permission from Guy Harling.

Disrupting the Colonial Gaze   265

are deployed towards racist and global "othering" ends, while also belittling feminist research:

> You can always tell feminist statistics – they paint "men" with a broad brush, but somehow never manage to get around to analyzing the racial makeup of the "men" in question . . .
> . . . Perhaps they also can not face up to the reality that the best defense of women is with a white male patriarchal system. Like apartheid.

These are two crude examples, but it is increasingly clear that both scholarship and pedagogical efforts to address gender inequalities tend to be embedded in and/ or in/advertently reproduce or bolster racist and classist tropes as enmeshed with gender stereotypes.

Reconceptualizing Gender and Sexual Justice Scholarship Within a Larger Transversal, Transnational Decolonial Feminism

The repetition in research on young people's sexual practices in South African contexts of power relations, privileges, and problematic political effects is powerfully enmeshed with normative colonial and masculinist scholarly practices in global and local contexts. Key to disrupting the "troubling" dynamics of research and related practice is a deeper engagement with reconceptualizing academic "business as usual". This means a cautious reflexivity about how we do our scholarship and how it could get taken up in the public imaginary. This practice of conscious and cautious thoughtfulness means going beyond reflexivity (Lenz Taguchi 2010) and empathy (Hemmings 2012) to an ethics of care and relationality, to foreground our entanglements with each other across and beyond nation-states.

This means imagining and experimenting with ways to do scholarly work that challenge the epistemic violence of scholarship on sexuality and gender, and to reflect "on the ways in which this system can be interrupted through a self-conscious and deliberate set of pedagogies, methodologies, and tactics" (Nagar 2013: 3). In research on young people's sexual practices in a global Southern context, this means seeking ways to disrupt the authority and logic of surveillance and "othering" that is built into normative logics and practices of research.

One terrain for such an interruption is dialogue and collaborations between scholars, activists, and artists. This seems a particularly fruitful avenue, especially since it may serve to destabilize the dominant colonial, patriarchal logics of the academy in which bodies, affect, and relationality are denigrated and excluded in a long commitment to mind, rationality, and individualism. In this respect, scholars could work in dialogue with alternative forms of scholarship and practice that cross and deconstruct boundaries of discipline, nation-state, and mobilities.

In 2015, a South African artist, Sithembile Msezane, performed an embodied installation as the Rhodes statue was removed from its place of dominance on the University of Cape Town campus. Msezane performed an African Bird, modelled on the beautiful soapstone statues that were stolen (or coercively sold) from

266   *Tamara Shefer*

Great Zimbabwe by white colonialists like Rhodes[3]. As Buikema (2017: 147, see also 2021)[4] argued, Msezane's performance "inserts both academy and art into an activist performance, creating an image which *forever links the de-colonization movement's critique of imperialism and patriarchy in an innovative and thought provoking way*" (my emphasis). An artist–activist–scholar, challenging the erasure of African women in both art and political imaginaries (Msezani 2017), had created a pedagogical and scholarly intervention that extended understandings of intersectionality and coloniality. Far more poignantly than words on a page, Msezane's installation exposed the entanglements of coloniality, its exploitation and appropriation of culture, land, and animals, and patriarchal power relations. As I have suggested elsewhere (Shefer 2018: 175):

> Msezane draws attention to intersectional inequalities and violences of the past. She performs the ascendance of an African woman in the form of a Zimbabwe bird stolen from Great Zimbabwe, historically a place of power and strength. Not only is a symbolic challenge to patriarchal (post)colonization and the university as vehicle articulated, but so too is a symbolic disruption of the civilising and violent humanist scholarly project achieved.

Msezane's installation is one of many artistic and performative interventions in contemporary South Africa emerging in the wave of student and civil society activism that raised intersectional sexual and gender justice concerns within a decolonial project. Such artistic installations or activist engagements offer a productive space for re-thinking contemporary feminist scholarship. Decolonial, feminist, and queer activism have proliferated in the wake of student resistance to continued inequalities and exclusions at South African universities, widely known as the #fallist movement (Kessi and Boonzaier 2015; Gouws 2016, 2017; Omarjee 2018; Xaba 2017).

There are many further novel and creative intersectional gender justice moments, actions, and movements, with many drawing on performative, artistic modes of engagement (Pather and Boulle 2019; Shefer 2018, 2019). For example, local queer art activists such as FAKA and Nigel Patel[5] generate online and public transgressions of heteronormativity through proud, pleasurable, and joyful performances as gender non-binary Black people (see Malcomess 2019 and Disemelo 2019 for more). These widely available performances of Black queer desire, pleasure, and relationality can challenge raced expectations of queerness (such as the notion of homosexuality as unAfrican) while troubling sexual and gender binarisms, thus contributing to a "queer archive" (Disemelo 2019: 221). Such engagements offer resources for critical transnational intersectional feminist scholarship on gender and sexuality as well as productive, inspiring, and ethical ways of challenging hegemonic epistemic violence in higher education. Embodied, participatory, and creative modalities in our pedagogical practices in the academy will also enable us to reimagine bodies, affect and materiality in the clinical, cold and civilizing academy where so many feel unsafe, non-belonging, exclusion, and violation. They may also provide everyday utopian moments (Cooper 2014) and

Disrupting the Colonial Gaze   267

micro- and macro-resistances to enable alternative imaginaries of intersectional gender and sexual justice and equality.

Scholarship that embraces and models the overlaps of art, activism and research also transgresses disembodied and dis-affected/ive scholarship, in which the mind and rationality dominate. Such embodied, affective scholarly projects and situated knowledges resist representational research, foregrounding relational ontology, recognition, and an ethics of care, both materially and symbolically. Using activist-performance and performative-activism in our pedagogies and research is a powerful way of transgressing the rigid normativities and violences of the academy and the colonial and patriarchal repetitions of our scholarship. Haraway (2016: 1) reminds us to *not only* stay with the trouble but to actively "make trouble, to stir up potent response to devastating events" while also creating safe spaces "to settle troubled waters and rebuild quiet places". This further highlights the value of activisms, performances, moments and spaces of creativity, agency, and energy that work with "troubles" and open up new imaginaries. Occasions that "make trouble" are rich resources of "new" tools for sexual and gender justice scholarship in transnational contexts. A critical transnational feminism that engages different scholarship and avoids the violences of young people's sexualities research has much to gain from collaborations with current performative, artistic activism in South Africa. These should not be used merely as "data" to enhance individual careers in the neoliberal capitalist economy of higher education but should be acknowledged as powerful leading scholarship gender and sexual justice, and as both making new knowledge and constituting new tools in transnational, intersectional feminist scholarship. These positive and hopeful "corrections" of colonial, patriarchal, and heteronormative injustices also destabilize the othering lens on South African young sexualities elaborated earlier.

Key when rethinking our scholarship through relationality and an ethics of care is dislodging habits of colonial thinking and knowledge-making that feminists are *not* innocent of. Contemporary scholarship has been directed by what Sedgwick (2003) called a *paranoid reading* which has privileged a particular academic critique, a combative masculinist militarized engagement of seeking power. This chapter argues for the importance of "reparative readings" in rethinking "tools" of transnational feminist scholarship to enable the generation and acknowledgement of multiplicity, resistance, the disruption of normative logics, and creativity. I have shown that much current research and practice have scarcely acknowledged or studied resistances and counter-hegemonic practices in contemporary contexts, rather reproducing problematizing and pathologizing speculatory lenses where certain bodies, identities, practices, and desires are under scrutiny and need to be controlled, regulated, or erased. Sedgwick (2003) has argued that the dominance of deconstructive readings in critical scholarship may have silenced alternative readings. Sedgwick's call for reparative readings suggests appreciation of the "motives and positionalities" of reparation in our work which "undertakes a different range of affects, ambitions, and risks" (Sedgwick 2003: 150).

Working across the divide underpinning the (post)colonial, neoliberal academy, in which body and affect have been othered and erased within normative practices

268   *Tamara Shefer*

of pedagogy and research, I propose working across multiple locations of knowledge-making that resist binarisms and their repetitive privileging of rationality over emotion/affect, the mind over embodied knowledges, intellectual over art and activist insights, research over pedagogy, etc. It also means disrupting normative scholarship, enacted through a combative, individualist project of seeking power, and authority in a brutal bounded "occupied territory" (Kamler and Thomson 2006: 29). Feminist scholars, most of whom are in privileged positions across classed, raced, geopolitical, and other inequalities, may repeat the very violences they seek to subvert even when engaging in theoretical critique. It is challenging to avoid habits of privilege and status and un/intended repetitions of the academic canonical practices. Locating critical transnational intersectional feminism in the larger framework of an ethical, relational, and reparative reconceptualizing of scholarship is crucial. It is imperative that critical reflexivity disturbs the seeming inevitability of co-optation of our scholarship for oppressive and violent ends. Simultaneously, we need to continue working towards research and pedagogical practice that destabilizes academic authorities and works with diverse knowledges to create alternative and ethical imaginaries of critical, feminist, queer, decolonial scholarship that aims for intersectional, transnational gender and sexual justice. This means disrupting normative forms of research and pedagogy and other forms of scholarship in the academy "to listen . . . and hear . . . and work together on building and producing new knowledge" (Tlostanova, this volume).

Notes

1   I use post- and decolonial to acknowledge that both traditions inform this chapter. This chapter does not unpack their differences, elaborated on by Madina Tlostanova in this edition, but I do not conflate these bodies of work, realizing that they have different histories, geopolitical locations, vocabularies, and emphases, and acknowledging the significant ways in which they speak to a critique of coloniality and/or a project of resisting and transforming societies and institutions that actively destabilizes the logic and practice of coloniality. Where I use decolonial alone, I take Tlostanova's clarification of the "postcolonial condition more as an objective given, a geopolitical and geo-historical situation of many people coming from the former colonies", while the "decolonial stance is one step further in the sense that it involves a conscious choice of how to interpret reality and how to act upon it". The latter is how decolonial feminism has been taken up in current South African contexts as a way of rejecting colonial, patriarchal institutionalized practices and forms of knowing through drawing on local and situated knowledges and traditions.
2   I use transnational here to refer to any collaborative or non-collaborative research that takes place between nation-state borders, acknowledging the wide variety in the dynamics of such transnational research, with some conducted ethically and democratically with sensitivity to power inequalities and the contexts of canonical colonialist research which could count as transnational. Much of the research in South Africa in the context of HIV/AIDS has tended to be financed by Northern funders, sometimes without any local partners, but usually with southern partners in an unequal partnership and lacking an intersectional postcolonial lens. Where non-comparative research is conducted to gain deeper understandings through reading each other's research together, transnational feminist collaborations are evident but also face dangers.

Disrupting the Colonial Gaze   269

3 Accessed March 20, 2020. www.theguardian.com/artanddesign/2015/may/15/sethembile-msezane-cecil-rhodes-statue-cape-town-south-africa. Also see www.sethembile-msezane.com/projects/ for more of Msezane's work. Accessed December 4, 2017.
4 This quote appears in Buikema's (2017) book in Dutch, recently translated into English as cited (Buikema 2021).
5 Find FAKA at www.siyakaka.com and "I Rise" by Nigel Patel, www.youtube.com/watch?v=Ojr8wEdAt6o. Accessed March 20, 2020.

References

Barad, Karen. 2007. *Meeting the Universe Halfway: Quantum Physics and the Entanglement of Matter and Meaning*. Durham, NC: Duke University Press.

Bhana, Deevia. 2014. *Under Pressure: The Regulation of Sexualities in South African Secondary Schools*. Johannesburg: MaThoko's Books.

Bhana, Deevia. 2016. *Childhood Sexuality and AIDS Education: The Price of Innocence*. New York, NY: Routledge.

Bhana, Deevia, Mary Crewe, and Peter Aggleton. 2019. "Sex, Sexuality and Education in South Africa." *Sex Education* 19 (4): 361–70.

Bhana, Deevia, and Rob Pattman. 2009. "Researching South African Youth, Gender and Sexuality within the Context of HIV/AIDS." *Development* 52 (1): 68–74.

Boonzaier, Floretta. 2017. "The Life and Death of Anene Booysen: Colonial Discourse, Gender-Based Violence and Media Representations." *South African Journal of Psychology* 47 (4): 470–81.

Boonzaier, Floretta, and Shose Kessi. 2018. "Challenging Representations: Participatory Research Engagements With Young People in Postcolonial Contexts." In *Engaging Youth in Activism, Research and Pedagogical Praxis: Transnational and Intersectional Perspectives on Gender, Sex, and Race*, edited by T. Shefer, J. Hearn, K. Ratele, and F. Boonzaier, 125–46. New York, NY and London: Routledge.

Brouard, Pierre, and Mary Crewe. 2013. "Sweetening the Deal? Sugar Daddies, Sugar Mummies, Sugar Babies and HIV in Contemporary South Africa." *Agenda* 26 (4): 48–56.

Buikema, Rosemarie. 2017. *Revoltes in de Cultuurkritiek*. Amsterdam: Amsterdam University Press.

Buikema, Rosemarie. 2021. *Revolts in Cultural Critique*. London: Rowman & Littlefield.

Campbell, Catherine. 2000. "Selling Sex in the Time of AIDS: The Psycho-Social Context of Condom Use by Sex Workers on a Southern African Mine." *Social Science & Medicine* 50: 479–94.

Campbell, Catherine, and Jeneviève Mannell. 2016. "Conceptualising the Agency of Highly Marginalised Women: Intimate Partner Violence in Extreme Settings." *Global Public Health* 11 (1–2): 1–16.

Cooper, Davina. 2014. *Everyday Utopias: The Conceptual Life of Promising Spaces*. Durham, NC and London: Duke University Press.

Disemelo, Katlego. 2019. "Performing the Queer Archive: Strategies of Self-Styling on Instagram." In *Acts of Transgression: Contemporary Live Art in South Africa*, edited by J. Pather and C. Boulle, 219–42. Johannesburg: Wits University Press.

Dunkle, K. L., R. K. Jewkes, M. Nduna, N. Jama, J. Levin, Y. Sikweyiya, and M. P. Koss. 2007. "Transactional Sex with Casual and Main Partners among Young South African Men in the Rural Eastern Cape: Prevalence, Predictors, and Associations with Gender-Based Violence." *Social Science & Medicine* 65: 1235–48.

270   *Tamara Shefer*

Farahani, Fataneh, and Suruchi Thapar-Björkert. 2019. "Postcolonial Masculinities: Diverse, Shifting and in Flux." In *Routledge International Handbook of Masculinity Studies*, edited by L. Gottzén, U. Mellström, and T. Shefer, 92–102. London: Routledge.

Farris, Sara. 2017. *In the Name of Women's Rights: The Rise of Femonationalism*. Durham, NC: Duke University Press.

Flint, Adrian, and Vernon Hewitt. 2015. "Colonial Tropes and HIV/AIDS in Africa: Sex, Disease and Race." *Commonwealth and Comparative Politics* 53 (3): 294–314.

Gouws, Amanda. 2016. "Young Women in the 'Decolonizing Project' in South Africa: From Subaltern to Intersectional Feminism." Paper presented at the Nordic Africa Days Conference, Uppsala, September 23–25.

Gouws, Amanda. 2017. "Feminist Intersectionality and the Matrix of Domination in South Africa." *Agenda* 31 (1): 19–27.

Gqola, Pumla. 2015. *Rape: A South African Nightmare*. Auckland Park: MfBooks Joburg.

Grewal, Inderpal. 2013. "Outsourcing Patriarchy: Feminist Encounters, Transnational Mediations and the Crime of 'Honour Killings'." *International Feminist Journal of Politics* 15 (1): 1–19.

Hames, Mary. 2007. "Sexual Identity and Transformation at a South African University." *Social Dynamics* 33 (1): 52–77.

Haraway, Donna J. 2016. *Staying with the Trouble: Making Kin in the Chthulucene*. Durham, NC: Duke University Press.

Hearn, Jeff, Kopano Ratele, and Tamara Shefer (eds.). 2015. "Special Issue: Men, Masculinities and Young People: North-South Dialogues." *NORMA: The International Journal for Masculinity Studies* 10 (2).

Helman, Rebecca. 2018. "Mapping the Unrapeability of White and Black Womxn." *Agenda* 32 (4): 10–21. https://doi.org/10.1080/10130950.2018.1533302.

Hemmings, Clare. 2012. "Affective Solidarity: Feminist Reflexivity and Political Transformation." *Feminist Theory* 13 (2): 147–61.

Hemmings, Clare, and Amal Treacher Kabesh. 2013. "The Feminist Subject of Agency: Recognition and Affect in Encounters With 'the Other'." In *Gender, Agency, and Coercion*, edited by S. Madhok, A. Phillips, and K. Wilson, 29–46. London: Palgrave Macmillan.

Ishengoma, J. M. 2016. "North-South Research Collaborations and Their Impact on Capacity Building: A Southern Perspective." In *North-South Knowledge Networks: Towards Equitable Collaboration Between Academics, Donors and Universities*, edited by T. Halvorsen and J. Nossum, 149–86. Cape Town: African Minds.

Jewkes, R. K., K. Dunkle, M. Nduna, and N. Shai. 2010. "Intimate Partner Violence, Relationship Power Inequality, and Incidence of HIV Infection in Young Women in South Africa: A Cohort Study." *Lancet* 376 (9734): 41–8. https://doi.org/10.1016/S0140-6736(10)60548-X.

Jungar, Katarina, and Elina Oinas. 2004. "Preventing HIV? Medical Discourses and Invisible Women." In *Re-Thinking Sexualities in Africa*, edited by S. Arnfred, 97–114. Uppsala: Nordic Africa Institute.

Jungar, Katarina, and Elina Oinas. 2011. "Beyond Agency and Victimisation: Re-Reading HIV and AIDS in African Contexts." *Social Dynamics* 37 (2): 248–62.

Jungar, Katarina, and Salla Peltonen. 2015. " 'Saving Muslim Queer Women From Muslim Hetero-Patriarchy' in LGBTI: Savior Narratives in Youth Work in Finland." *NORMA* 10 (2): 136–49.

Jungar, Katarina, and Salla Peltonen. 2016. "Acts of Homonationalism: Mapping Africa in the Swedish Media." *Sexualities* 20 (5–6): 715–36.

Disrupting the Colonial Gaze   271

Kamler, Barbara, and Pat Thomson. 2006. *Helping Doctoral Students Write: Pedagogies for Supervision*. London: Routledge.

Keskinen, Suvi. 2012. "Limits to Speech? The Racialised Politics of Gendered Violence in Denmark and Finland." *Journal of Intercultural Studies* 33 (3): 261–74.

Keskinen, Suvi. 2014. "Re-Constructing the Peaceful Nation: Negotiating Meanings of Whiteness, Immigration and Islam in Media and Politics after a Shopping Mall Shooting." *Social Identities: Journal for the Study of Race, Nation and Culture* 20 (6): 471–85.

Kessi, Shose, and Floretta Boonzaier. 2015. "All #Rhodes Lead to Transformation." *Mail & Guardian Online*, May 28. http://mg.co.za/article/2015-05-21-all-rhodes-lead-to-enlightenment.

Kruger, Lou-Marie, Tamara Shefer, and Antoinette Oakes. 2015. "'I Could Have Done Everything and Why Not?': Young Women's Complex Constructions of Sexual Agency in the Context of Sexualities Education in Life Orientation in South African Schools." *Perspectives in Education* 33 (2): 30–43.

Lenz Taguchi, Hillevi. 2010. "Images of Thinking in Feminist Materialism: Ontological Divergences and the Production of Research Subjectivities." *International Journal of Qualitative Studies in Education* 23 (5): 525–42.

Macleod, Catriona. 2009. "Danger and Disease in Sex Education: The Saturation of 'Adolescence' With Colonialist Assumptions." *Journal of Health Management* 11 (2): 375–89.

Macleod, Catriona, Dale Moodley, and Lisa Saville-Young. 2015. "Sexual Socialisation in Life Orientation Manuals Versus Popular Music: Responsibilisation Versus Pleasure, Tension and Complexity." *Perspectives in Education* 33 (2): 90–107.

Mahmood, Saba. 2001. "Feminist Theory, Embodiment, and the Docile Agent: Some Reflections on the Egyptian Islamic Revival." *Cultural Anthropology* 16 (2): 202–36.

Malcomess, Bettina. 2019. "Don't Get It Twisted: Queer Performativity and the Emptying out of Gesture." In *Acts of Transgression: Contemporary Live Art in South Africa*, edited by J. Pather and C. Boulle, 193–218. Johannesburg: Wits University Press.

McEwan, Hayley. 2018. "The U.S. Pro-Family Movement and Sexual Politics in Africa." Unpublished Doctoral Dissertation, University of Witwaterstrand, Johannesburg.

McFadden, Patricia. 1992. "Sex, Sexuality and the Problems of AIDS in Africa." In *Gender in Southern Africa: Conceptual and Theoretical Issues*, edited by R. Meena, 157–95. Harare: SAPES.

McFadden, Patricia. 2003. "Sexual Pleasure as Feminist Choice." *Feminist Africa* 2: 50–60.

Msezani, Sithembile. 2017. "Artist Statement, Kwasuka Sukela: Re-Imagined Bodies of a (South African) 1990s Born Woman." Master of Arts (Fine Arts) Exhibition, University of Cape Town.

Msibi, Thabo. 2012. "'I'm Used to It Now': Experiences of Homophobia Among Queer Youth in South African Township Schools." *Gender and Education* 24 (5): 515–33.

Nagar, Richa. 2013. "Storytelling and Co-Authorship in Feminist Alliance Work: Reflections from a Journey." *Gender, Place & Culture* 20 (1): 1–18. https://doi.org/10.1080/09 66369X.2012.731383.

Ngabaza, Sisa, and Tamara Shefer. 2019. "Sexuality Education in South African Schools: Deconstructing the Dominant Response to Young People's Sexualities in Contemporary Schooling Contexts." *Sex Education* 19 (4): 422–35.

Omarjee, Nadira. 2018. *Reimagining the Dream: Decolonising Academia by Putting the Last First*. Leiden: African Studies Centre.

Pather, Jay, and Catherine Boulle (eds.). 2019. *Acts of Transgression: Contemporary Live Art in South Africa*. Johannesburg: Wits University Press.

272 Tamara Shefer

Patton, Cynthia. 1997. "Inventing 'African AIDS'." In *The Gender/Sexuality Reader: Culture, History, Political Economy*, edited by R. Lancaster and M. di Leornado, 387–405. New York, NY: Routledge.

Peltonen, Salla, and Katarina Jungar. 2018. "The Ascendency of Whiteness: On Understanding Racialized Queerness in LGBTQI Refugee Work." In *Engaging Youth in Activism, Research and Pedagogical Praxis: Transnational and Intersectional Perspectives on Gender, Sex, and Race*, edited by T. Shefer, J. Hearn, K. Ratele, and F. Boonzaier, 57–75. New York, NY: Routledge.

Puar, Jasbir. 2007. *Terrorist Assemblages: Homonationalism in Queer Times*. Durham, NC: Duke University Press.

Ratele, Kopano. 2014. "Currents Against Gender Transformation of South African Men: Relocating Marginality to the Centre of Research and Theory of Masculinities." *NORMA: International Journal for Masculinity Studies* 9 (1): 30–44.

Sedgwick, Eve Kosofsky. 2003. *Touching Feeling: Affect, Pedagogy, Performativity*. Durham, NC and London: Duke University Press.

Settler, Federico, and Mari Haugu Engh. 2015. "The Black Body in Colonial and Postcolonial Public Discourse in South Africa." *Alternation* 14: 126–48.

Shefer, Tamara. 2016. "Resisting the Binarism of Victim and Agent: Critical Reflections on 20 Years of Scholarship on Young Women and Heterosexual Practices in South African Contexts." *Global Public Health: An International Journal for Research, Policy and Practice* 11 (1–2): 211–23. https://doi.org/10.1080/17441692.2015.1029959.

Shefer, Tamara. 2018. "Embodied Pedagogies: Performative Activism and Transgressive Pedagogies in the Sexual and Gender Justice Project in Higher Education in Contemporary South Africa." In *Socially Just Pedagogies in Higher Education: Critical Posthumanist and New Feminist Materialist Perspectives*, edited by V. Bozalek, R. Braidotti, T. Shefer, and M. Zembylas, 171–88. London: Bloomsbury.

Shefer, Tamara. 2019. "Activist Performance and Performative Activism Towards Intersectional Gender and Sexual Justice in Contemporary South Africa." *International Sociology* 34 (4): 418–34.

Shefer, Tamara, and Jeff Hearn. 2022. *Knowledge, Power and Young Sexualities: A Transnational Feminist Engagement*. London and New York, NY: Routledge.

Shefer, Tamara, Jeff Hearn, and Kopano Ratele. 2015. "North-South Dialogues: Reflecting on Working Transnationally on Young Men, Masculinities and Gender Justice." *NORMA: International Journal for Masculinity Studies* 10 (2): 164–78.

Shefer, Tamara, Catriona Macleod, and Jean Baxen, eds. 2015. "Special Issue: Life Orientation Sexuality Education and Gendered Norms, Justice and Transformation." *Perspectives in Education* 33 (2).

Shefer, Tamara, and Anna Strebel. 2013. "Deconstructing the 'Sugar Daddy': A Critical Review of the Constructions of Men in Intergenerational Sexual Relationships in South Africa." *AGENDA* 26 (4): 57–63.

Spivak, Gayatri. 1988. "Can the Subaltern Speak?." In *Marxism and the Interpretation of Culture*, edited by Cary Nelson and Lawrence Grossberg, 271–313. Urbana, IL: University of Illinois Press.

Tamale, Sylvia. 2011. "Researching and Theorising Sexualities in Africa." In *African Sexualities: A Reader*, edited by S. Tamale, 11–36. Cape Town: Pambazuka Press.

Tay, N. 2010. "More Than 1 in 3 South African Men Say They've Committed Rape, New Survey Says." *Los Angeles Times*, November 26. https://www.amren.com/news/2010/11/more_than_1_in/. Accessed 19 June 2023.

Tronto, Joan. 1993. *Moral Boundaries: A Political Argument for an Ethic of Care*. New York, NY: Routledge.

Tronto, Joan. 2013. *Caring Democracy: Markets, Equality, and Justice*. New York, NY: New York University Press.

Van Wyk, Sherinne. 2015. " 'It's Hard to Be a Girl': Adolescent Girls' Experiences of Girlhood in Three Low-Income Communities in South Africa." Unpublished PhD Dissertation, University of Stellenbosch, South Africa.

Varga, C. A. 1997. "The Condom Conundrum: Barriers to Condom Use Among Commercial Sex Workers in Durban, South Africa." *African Journal of Reproductive Health* 1 (1): 74–88.

Vetten, Lisa. 2018. "Preventing Rape in South Africa Since 1976." Paper presented at Wellsexuality: Youth and Contemporary Notions of Sexuality in South Africa. WISER, University of Witwatersrand, 8–9 March.

Wekker, Gloria. 2016. *White Innocence: Paradoxes of Colonialism and Race*. Durham, NC and London: Duke University Press.

Xaba, Wanelisa. 2017. "Challenging Fanon: A Black Radical Feminist Perspective on Violence and the Fees Must Fall Movement." *Agenda* 31 (3–4): 96104. https://doi.org/10.1080/10130950.2017.1392786.

21 Studying Happiness in Postcolonial and Post-Apartheid South Africa

Theoretical and Methodological Considerations

Carmine Rustin

What is happiness? Are Black women happy? Can poor women be happy? These are some of the questions that intrigued me when studying gender equality and happiness. These questions become more pertinent when considering my locatedness in South Africa, a country haunted by colonialism and apartheid. In this chapter, I reflect on how to study happiness among women within a postcolonial, post-apartheid context, where women occupy different positionalities across race and class. How does one take these complexities into account in the methodologies employed? And which methods does one employ to best study intersectionalities of gender, race, class, and happiness?

This chapter builds on a larger study on gender equality and happiness among South African women in which I draw on survey data and qualitative research to study happiness. I consider the value that these methods may have for contemporary feminist research across transnational contexts. This chapter is structured in four parts. First, I provide a brief overview of the theoretical framing of the study. Second, I reflect upon particular conceptualizations of happiness (as mainly constructed in the Global North) and consider how the meanings of these conceptualizations change, when becoming informed by empirical research undertaken with a group of women in the Global South. Here, I draw on data from my study – from the focus group conversations and the in-depth qualitative interviews which I carried out. Third, I discuss the value of survey methodologies for the shaping of understandings of happiness from an intersectional and postcolonial perspective. Lastly, I reflect upon the ways in which my findings speak to contemporary theoretical and methodological frameworks.

Theoretical Framing

South Africa is shaped by its colonial and apartheid past. The ravages of slavery, colonialism, and apartheid, which were all underpinned by and extended patriarchal power, continue to have an impact on our lives today. Postcolonial and postcolonial feminist theories thus provide a foundational theoretical framework for this study.

DOI: 10.4324/9781003378761-24

Studying Happiness in Post-Apartheid South Africa 275

An intersectional lens further lends itself to my study. As it has been widely argued in global contexts, women are not a homogenous group. Black feminists, including Audre Lorde (1984), bell hooks (1981), Kimberlé Crenshaw (1989, 1991), and Patricia Hill Collins (1990), have long argued that the struggles of Black women are not the same as those of white women or Black men. The struggles of Black women have been rendered invisible, as gender injustices have been addressed from the perspective of white women, and race injustices from the perspective of Black men. The term intersectionality, introduced by Crenshaw (1989, 1991), takes the complexities and multiple oppressions of (Black) women into account. Intersectionality emerged as both a critique and a conceptual lens to challenge dominant discourses primarily within the Global Northern white feminist movement. In my investigation of gender equality and happiness, it has been imperative for me to use an intersectional approach and to look at other social identities and structurations such as race and class. The study foregrounds intersections of gender, race, class, and age together with other social categorizations, and, therefore, a feminist postcolonial framework, with a focus on intersectionality, was an ideal framework.

Postcolonial feminists and Black feminists, in particular, have criticized Western, white feminisms for assuming that all women face the same kind of oppression, and that women constitute a unitary group. Postcolonial feminist scholar Chandra Mohanty has critiqued the work of Western feminist scholars, arguing that a number of their writings continue to ignore the heterogeneity of women in the "third world", portraying women as a "composite, singular 'third-world woman'" (Mohanty 1988).

Taking the history of slavery, colonialism, and apartheid thoroughly into account, postcolonial feminists in South African contexts have argued that gender (in)equality and gender related injustice cannot be considered without addressing women's (men's and gender non-conforming persons') multiple forms of oppression and power. Hence, models of gender equality within a postcolonial feminist framework consider the intersections of gender with race, class, age, culture, nationality, and other social categorizations. Postcolonial feminist perspectives further imply that, to study women and happiness, it is not enough to think about gender; we need to address the colonial experiences of gender, as it shapes women's notions and experiences of (in)equality and (un)happiness.

Conceptualizations of Happiness

So what is happiness? As one of the participants in my study noted, happiness could mean different things to different people (Rustin 2018). Happiness scholars, mostly situated in the Global North, have however conceptualized and studied happiness, based on two main conceptualizations, that is, hedonic happiness and eudaimonic happiness (Kashdan et al. 2008; Ryan and Deci 2001).

Hedonic happiness is also referred to as subjective well-being (Diener 1984) and is further seen as comprising two aspects: affect and cognition (Frey and

276   *Carmine Rustin*

Stutzer 2002; Helliwell et al. 2012). In this context, affect refers to positive or negative emotions while cognition is related to rational thought (Frey and Stutzer 2002). Traditionally, happiness on the level of cognition (the evaluative aspect) is measured by an "overall evaluation of one's life" or life satisfaction (Sachs 2012: 6). Eudaimonic happiness, on the other hand, refers to psychological well-being (Ryff 1989), which includes mental health, meaning (in daily life, life events, and inter-personal relations), self-actualization, and personal growth.

Following many Happiness Studies scholars, I took my point of departure in the first of these two conceptualizations: happiness related to subjective well-being. As a working definition for the study, I defined happiness as the "overall enjoyment of your life as-a-whole" (Veenhoven 2004).

Given feminist critiques of Happiness Studies and conventional conceptualization of happiness (Ahmed 2007/8, 2010), one of the objectives of my overall study was to see how women in South Africa define happiness in their lives and in the lives of others and how this is linked with gender equality. The women in my study were not involved in Happiness Studies scholarship, and, therefore, I thought that their perspectives – as laypersons – would be an important contribution to the field. It would reflect the lived experiences and knowledge of women and foreground South African women's voices. This approach would challenge not only the notion of "who are the knowers" and "who can construct knowledge" but also the locatedness of those who are seen as the producers of knowledge.

In order to ensure that women's voices would be heard, and that the research would ultimately be about making a difference in the lives of women, I found it necessary to employ a method that would be appropriate for this purpose and to build on research questions which focused on women's constructions of happiness. Against this background, I deemed qualitative in-depth interviewing, as well as focus groups to be the most appropriate methods for conducting this part of the research.

I conducted 11 individual interviews with women whom I considered key informants. These women were recruited from a number of institutions including universities, the Commission for Gender Equality (a constitutional body set up to monitor the gender-related activities of the government), a non-governmental organization and a teacher's union. The women were identified as relevant interviewees because of their professional gender expertise. In addition, three focus groups were organized with women who were supposed to share their everyday lived experiences, and who were not professionally involved in work related to gender issues or happiness.

The focus group method was considered to be an appropriate technique to use in this part of the overall study as it allowed me to take into consideration the personal, racial, gender, socio-political, and cultural contexts of the participants, while the individual interviews made it possible to shed light on individually unique perspectives (Fontana and Frey 1994).

The focus groups were comprised as follows. Group 1 was a group of teachers at a primary school. I sought the assistance of the principal at the school to invite the women to the discussions. Group 2 comprised a group of women from the surrounding community who were assisting at the school in a support role. Group 3 was a group of older women, who were part of a women's group at a church, which I attend. The data were rich in documenting the diverse experiences of women across different raced, class, and age backgrounds.

Feminist interviewing techniques provided the tools by which I could investigate the meanings which my research participants attributed to happiness not only including but also beyond the normative conceptualizations thereof. Using my skills as an interviewer, I explored with participants deeper and fuller meanings of happiness in their lives. One of the things that stood out was that happiness was not *(only)* about individual perspectives but also tied to the collective.

Participants articulated their take on happiness through a relational perspective, and an ethics of care, which take happiness beyond the normative framings, steeped in colonial and patriarchal logics. For them, happiness was not only an individual thing but also linked to improving the lives of others, contributing to and involving themselves in the lives of others in order to make a difference for the better. This relational understanding of well-being as entangled with others was clearly expressed by two participants, Sandra and Candice:

Sandra: Happiness to me also means that yes I need to feel good about myself, but also need to feel good about what I'm doing to better and improve the lives of others because in the end it will make me happy, that's the type of person I am. My happiness is like throwing a stone in the river and it has spread out, one light has to light up the world, then I'm internally happy.

Candice: So well-being in my life is for me to be fine, and to have good relations with friends and family, but also to know that women and South African citizens, in particular, are at this space where our constitution and what we fought for is benefiting their lives, like "a better life for all".

The well-being of others, referring not only to individuals but also to the collective other, as in society or communities, stood out as an important element, when the participants described what happiness meant to them. Happiness was for the participants defined by the inter-connections between people/communities, by the well-being of the collective as well as by feelings of solidarity with others (often marginalized groups) in terms of achieving a common goal. For the participants, happiness was shaped not only by values such as individual and personal achievement but also by values related to the collective well-being of others, to assisting in and having an impact on the lives of others, as well as to social and community engagement and to collective action taken by communities/groups.

The findings of my study reveal the complexity of what happiness is for women in South Africa in their everyday lives. Participants spoke about happiness in a eudaimonic sense (referring to psychological well-being) as well as in a hedonic sense (referring to subjective well-being, including affect as well as life satisfaction) (Rustin 2018). Notwithstanding, for the participants happiness is simultaneously

278   *Carmine Rustin*

about social processes and about the everyday (and past) struggles against injustices, and the (resultant) betterment of the lives of women.

It is, however, noteworthy that conceptualizations of happiness as inter-connectedness with others were first and foremost articulated in some of the 11 interviews with key informants. There could be many reasons for this. It could, for example, have something to do with the nature of the key informants' work. My key informants were, in different ways, involved in activist work, the work of non-governmental organizations or in academia, concerned with gender issues. They were in active practice, or through scholarly work, involved in making a difference in the lives of others. So I assume that their situatedness, in knowledge production and practical work around issues of (in)equality, made them link happiness to well-being tied to others. Basically, happiness was for these participants related to activism and politics for social change

While not asked specifically, I think that many of the key informants would identify as feminists. One participant, however, clearly stated that she did not consider herself a feminist, but it is also noteworthy that this participant works is an organization set up under the auspices of the Constitution of South Africa with the mandate to promote gender equality. I am thus making the assumption that, as feminists, these interviewees are concerned with the lives of others – and more precisely, with making a difference in the lives of others. Or in other words, it resonates with their feminist commitments that they link their own happiness to that of others

The feminist qualitative methods, on which this part of my work was based, provided the necessary tools to challenge normative conceptualizations of happiness. The idea that this kind of methods can be used to critically challenge normativities is supported by Cieslik (2015: 424), who argued that "qualitative and biographical research that explores happiness as a social process involving struggle and negotiation in everyday life" is needed. The method that I employed, further takes the geo-political location of the participants firmly into account. The initial working definition of happiness in the study, as well as the interview questions were posed to the research participants in an open manner. While expressing my view of happiness through the working definition, the open-ended interview format was, at the same time, apt for inviting participants to explore their own articulations of happiness. I started the interview like this:

> Happiness is defined by scholars as the "overall enjoyment of your life as-a-whole". Keeping this definition in mind, how would you define happiness in your life? Are you happy? What does happiness mean to you?

Against the backdrop of the qualitative methods employed and the open-ended manner in which the interview questions we are asked, I shall argue that I take the geo-political location of the participants into account. My method allows the situated knowledge of the participants, firmly rooted in their South African realities and everyday experiences, to be explored. When participants articulate this situated perspective, normative conceptualizations of happiness, emerging from

Studying Happiness in Post-Apartheid South Africa 279

Global North contexts, can be challenged and disrupted. But the normative conceptualizations of happiness can also be reproduced and maintained, and in my study, normative conceptualizations of happiness were actually *both* reproduced and maintained *and* challenged. This finding underscores the complexity of happiness as experienced in everyday life.

Intersections: Happiness, Race, Gender, Class

Next to subjective experiences of happiness, I was also interested in the intersections of gender, race, and class in women's constructions of happiness and gender equality in South Africa, and to address this objective, I found a quantitative methodology most appropriate. Quantitative methods would allow me to extract the necessary comparative data for women across diverse backgrounds, taking the various complexities and categories of women's positionality into consideration (McCall 2005). I was mindful of some feminist scholars' critique of quantitative research, in particular, its positivist epistemological and ontological stance that can contribute to a fixating of normative categories as essentially given. But in agreement with other feminist scholars (Einstein 2012; Hesse-Biber 2010; McCall 2005) who argue that quantitative research can shed critical light on social structurations and patterns of inequality, and also be fruitfully combined with qualitative, in-depth studies of subjectivities, I chose to opt for quantitative methods that would allow me to investigate specific research questions regarding the bigger social patterns of (un)happiness among different groups of women in South Africa – questions which would not necessarily be answered by another method. I shall also once more note that the quantitative part of my study, too, was firmly rooted within a feminist epistemological, ontological, and methodological framework which sought to address injustices and discriminations that women faced, and to do so by including women's perspectives.

Given the financial implications of a large survey, I drew on data from Wave 6 of the *World Values Survey* for South Africa (Ingelhart et al. 2014). The *World Values Survey* is a global research project which is carried out in nearly 100 countries. It is a representative survey and measures people's opinions, values, and beliefs in relation to a number of topics including happiness understood as subjective well-being (in terms of satisfaction with life).

Happiness-as-Life-Satisfaction

In this section, I report the survey's findings related to whether women in South Africa are happy or not and how happiness (satisfaction with life) intersects with race and class. Overall, the survey results indicate that women are somewhat satisfied with their lives, with a mean score of 6.66 (standard deviation (SD) = 2.27). A score closer to 10 indicates complete satisfaction with one's life. The score thus indicates that the women were somewhat satisfied with their lives as a whole.

Given that I was interested in the complexities of women's positionalities, and the intersections between various social markers and happiness, I used

280   *Carmine Rustin*

cross-tabulations as a statistical method to showcase this relationship. The findings show that race and happiness as well as class and happiness intersect in interesting ways. When one further looks at race and class together with its intersections with happiness, it becomes clear how positions of (historically past) privilege continue to benefit certain groups of women today.

When considering race,[1] we see that white women reported higher levels of satisfaction when compared to women of diverse race groups. While not completely satisfied with their lives as a whole, white women indicated that they are somewhat satisfied, leaning towards completely satisfied with their lives as a whole. The mean scores for Black and coloured women indicate that they are fairly or somewhat satisfied with their lives as a whole. Indian women were the least satisfied of the groups, being somewhat dissatisfied with their lives.

Regarding women's positionality in terms of class[2] and happiness issues, upper-class women report higher degrees of happiness-as-life-satisfaction, with the scores indicating that they are completely satisfied with their lives. It should, however, be noted that the sample size for the upper class was quite small (N = 15). Upper-middle-class women report being somewhat satisfied, with scores leaning strongly towards completely satisfied with life. Women who identified as lower class report being the least satisfied with life, with a mean score of 5.98 (SD = 2.36), indicating that they are somewhat dissatisfied with life as a whole.

As the above results indicate women's positionality in respect to race and class matters when looking how satisfied they are with their lives. The findings show that it is important to consider the intersections of race and class and their associations with life satisfaction.

White upper-class and white upper-middle-class women were most satisfied with their lives when compared to other groups. Indian women who identified as lower class were least satisfied with their lives when compared with others, reporting that they were somewhat dissatisfied with their lives. White women who identified as lower class were also somewhat dissatisfied with their lives, as were coloured women. Lower-class Black women were relatively more satisfied with their lives than coloured, white or Indian women of the same social class.

When we consider the findings of happiness across race and class, we see that it reflects the heterogeneity of women and the importance of an intersectional approach to the understanding of happiness. As Crenshaw (1989, 1991), Hill Collins (1990), hooks (1981), and others have shown, an intersectional approach is critical in understanding the multiple oppressions that Black women have faced and is critical in rendering visible their oppressions and how their oppressions intersect. An intersectional framework further shows how white women have benefitted from their locatedness as white persons but also from their class position, thus enjoying privileged positions on multiple fronts. The findings of this study thus reflect the privileged position of rich, white women indicating that they have benefitted from colonialism and the policies of apartheid, and that they continue to enjoy high levels of satisfaction with life.

Poor Indian and coloured women indicated that they were somewhat dissatisfied with their lives. An intersectional approach is once again useful in understanding

Studying Happiness in Post-Apartheid South Africa   281

the subordinations that Indian and coloured women have faced on the basis of not only race and class but also colonization (Herr 2014). It is surprising to note that Indian and coloured women were more dissatisfied than Black women. A possible explanation is that Indian and coloured women might have expected that their material conditions would change post-1994, and it may not have worked out like that. The findings also point to the importance of redistribution and recognition as means to ensure gender justice (Fraser 2005, 2007). While economic redress is important, it cannot be done within a vacuum and without looking at race. It is to be assumed that not only improving the poor's material conditions in general but also specifically targeting Indian, coloured, and Black poor in relation to injustices based on race will lead to a raise of their levels of happiness (Møller 2007).

The results for lower-class white and Black women are also interesting. Black women as compared to white women (of the lower class) showed higher levels of satisfaction with life. Given the intersection of race and class, as well as the South African history of apartheid and colonialism, one might well have expected that Black women would be most dissatisfied with life. Both Black and white women's position can, however, best be explained using Social Comparison Theory (Festinger 1954). This theory argues that individuals would compare themselves to others, and their lives to the lives of others around them. I would thus argue that when lower class white women compare themselves to others, and I would suggest that they would compare themselves to other white women (the majority of whom are employed and not poor), they feel dissatisfied with their lives. Black women would also compare themselves to other Black women, the majority of whom are poor and unemployed (Statistics South Africa 2014) and would thus see that their lives are comparable with other Black persons. They would thus be less dissatisfied with their lives as a whole.

Reflections: Methodologies, Methods, Location

What are the lessons that I learnt by employing quantitative survey data as well as qualitative methodologies? Einstein (2012) argues that when employing different methodologies and methods in feminist research, it is important to ensure that the methodological principles of the different disciplines and fields of study involved are adhered to. Turning to the survey and to ensure that I adhered to adequate discipline- or field-related principles, I worked with a seasoned academic, who had the necessary skills and expertise in analysing statistics and quantitative data. The rules relating to statistical analysis were followed. Where both of us were unsure about the application of specific techniques, we consulted (multiple) colleagues for assistance.

As I drew on existing survey data, I cannot attest to whether or not a feminist epistemology informed the survey research (from the construction of the questions to the collection of the data, among others). In contrast, what I can attest to is that feminist epistemologies informed my approach to the data. When focusing on happiness and drawing on these survey data, my purpose was to address injustices and discriminations (Bennett 2008; Fonow and Cook 2005) – and to do this from the

282   Carmine Rustin

perspectives of women, who are best placed to address the meaning of these matters for themselves.

The survey drew on a representative sample of 1,486 women. This allowed for the findings to be generalized to a broader population, within certain parameters. I considered such a large sample to be a strength of the study, and the fact that the survey recognized the heterogeneity of women in South African society meant that it could contribute meaningfully to an understanding of heterogenous social patterns of different groups of South African women's (un)happiness in relation to life satisfaction. It is important to choose methods that will adequately reflect and address the complexities of the research question, as argued, for example, by Einstein (2012). Given my intersectional approach and the complexities of my study of the interplay between gender and other social categorizations such as race and class, I drew on statistical techniques, such as correlations and cross-tabulations, which would best highlight the intersections. As can be seen from the results discussed earlier, and given South Africa's history of coloniality and apartheid, the statistical techniques that I used exposed inequalities that continue to shape the lives of South African women across difference. One example, as shown earlier, is that white women in the upper middle class, the lower middle class, and the working class show higher levels of life satisfaction than women of other racial groups within the particular class and that poor women reported being the least satisfied with their lives. The statistical techniques employed were thus effective in allowing me to study the complexities of gender, race, and class in interplay with each other.

So, what lessons would I draw from this study for further feminist studies of happiness?

Against the background of my study, I would argue that it is necessary to critically contextualize research questions, taking geography, politics, and culture into account within the domain of Happiness Studies. Happiness Studies have been criticized by some feminist scholars. Ahmed (2010), for example, argues that discourses on happiness are used to justify oppression, particularly the oppression of women. Ahmed pinpoints that many feminist, Black, and queer scholars have criticized the ways in which social norms are publicly portrayed as social goods the pursuit of which is supposed to make one happy. Happiness, one can argue, is also used to ensure that women in particular are made to stick to certain social norms, no matter how oppressive, and that these social norms at the same time is cast as representing what is considered to be "good". We should thus acknowledge the importance of Ahmed's caution against these popular – and oppressive – discourses on happiness, which may serve to obfuscate the material conditions of women's lives. Notwithstanding, the struggle for happier lives should be seen as a feminist struggle. Not, as Ahmed argues, because a popular and academic construction of happiness may serve discursively to justify oppression, but rather because struggles against oppression are also struggles for conditions which should make happier lives possible. In this struggle for happiness, the feminist "killjoy" (a term used by Ahmed (2010) is a necessity). As I have shown in my study, the employment of methods that enable a consideration of the everyday experiences and narratives of women can lead to a disruption of a notion of happiness, focused

Studying Happiness in Post-Apartheid South Africa 283

mainly on the individual. Happiness Studies in the Global North tend to portray happiness as something that is achieved by the individual and that is within the control of the individual. However, a postcolonial feminist framing of happiness as it emerges from my study transforms the notion into something that is relational and puts care central. Happiness becomes linked to activism and to the challenging of the structural injustices that persist in postcolonial and post-apartheid societies. Happiness is thus not only about what the individual can or cannot do but also about the accomplishments of the collective and the collective struggles against injustices.

My study has been firmly located within South Africa, the Global South. It is grounded in the belief that the complexities of colonialism and apartheid should not be ignored when one considers the research questions, epistemologies, and methodologies which are meant to inform and guide a certain research project. Taking the geo-political conditions into account provide an essential guide to the theoretical underpinnings as well as to the methodological approach of research projects such as the one I have described here.

Precisely because South Africa is a postcolonial and post-apartheid society, a feminist intersectional and critical postcolonial approach is imperative. The diversities of women's knowledge and experiences across raced, and classed backgrounds necessitate the use of methods which can take these differences and complexities into account. This is clearly demonstrated by the findings of this study.

A further important consideration, when it comes to the study of happiness from feminist perspectives, concerns the agency of the research participants. The qualitative interviewing techniques foreground the agency of the participants. Upon reflection, this stood out clearly in the interviews with the key informants as well as in the focus group conversations. However, one cannot reflect upon the agency of research participants within the groups without considering the power dynamics and group inter-relations and the skills of the interviewer. These factors may have allowed some participants to be more vocal and outspoken in the conversations while others might have been more reticent in terms of expressing their views.

Conclusion

The methodologies and methods employed in this study have made a contribution to scholarship in a number of ways. First, I have explored how quantitative feminist research can be put to use together with and brought into conversation with qualitative feminist methodologies. Quantitative research was able to highlight social patterns of interplay between happiness and categorizations such as gender, race, and class, and in this way it was also clearly foregrounded why an intersectional approach to the study of happiness is important. Given the scale of the quantitative research, it is possible, within certain parameters, to generalize the findings. Second, the findings from the qualitative research speak to the nuances and complexity of happiness, which the quantitative study does not and is not intended to do. The qualitative part of the study clearly highlights the everyday struggles and joys in women's lives, and how they navigate these, while shaping an alternative notion of

284   *Carmine Rustin*

happiness. Normative, quantitative studies on happiness do provide the scope neither for such an alternative articulation nor for complexities to become visible, as far as subjective levels of experience are concerned. To delve into these complexities was therefore a task for the qualitative part to accomplish. Furthermore, the qualitative study took women's locatedness into account underscoring the importance of geo-politics in the understandings of happiness. In summation, the combined qualitative and quantitative methodologies and methods utilized have been put to use in aiding feminist research as well as critically suggesting new paths for Happiness Studies.

Acknowledgements

Special thanks to Anna Strebel for her comments and guidance, Tamara Shefer for her considered input, and Kopano Ratele for initial suggestions on how to approach this chapter. I'm also appreciative of the comments that the STINT participants at the Montfleur meeting made on the draft chapter.

Funding

The Andrew W. Mellon funded New Imaginaries for an intersectional, queer feminist project on gender and sexual justice (Grant G-31700714) supported this work.

Disclosure statement

I have no conflict of interest in the publication of this chapter.

Notes

1 While I consider race to be a social construction with material effects, I employ the categories constructed under apartheid of Black, coloured, Indian, and white (Population Registration Act 30 of 1950, RSA). I do this because the survey data follow the same categorizations and as I used these categories in the qualitative part of my study. Most importantly, I do this as racial inequalities continue to shape the lives of South African women.
2 The WVS survey used the categories upper, upper middle, lower middle, working, and lower class. I have retained these categories in my analysis but acknowledge that these are problematic.

References

Ahmed, Sara. 2007. "Multiculturalism and the Promise of Happiness." *New Formations* 63: 121–37. www.mcgill.ca/igsf/files/igsf/Ahmed1_multiculturalism.pdf.
Ahmed, Sarah. 2010. *The Promise of Happiness*. Durham, NC and London: Duke University Press.
Bennett, Jane. 2008. "Editorial: Researching for Life: Paradigms and Power." http://agi.ac.za/sites/agi.ac.za/files/editorial-_researching_for_life-_paradigms_and_power-_jane_bennett_0.pdf.

Cieslik, Mark. 2015. "'Not Smiling but Frowning': Sociology and the 'Problem of Happiness'." *Sociology* 49 (3): 422–37.

Crenshaw, Kimberle. 1989. "Demarginalizing the Intersection of Race and Sex: A Black Feminist Critique of Antidiscrimination Doctrine, Feminist Theory and Antiracist Politics." *University of Chicago Legal Forum* 139: 139–67.

Crenshaw, Kimberle. 1991. "Mapping the Margins: Intersectionality, Identity Politics, and Violence against Women of Color." *Stanford Law Review* 43 (6): 1241–99.

Diener, Ed. 1984. "Subjective Well-being." *Psychological Bulletin* 95: 542–75.

Einstein, Gillian. 2012. "Situated Neuroscience: Exploring Biologies of Diversity." In *Neurofeminism: Issues at the Intersection of Feminist Theory and Cognitive Science*, edited by Robyn Bluhm, Anna Jaap Jacobson, and Heidi Lene Maibom, 145–74. Basingstoke: Palgrave Macmillan.

Festinger, Leon. 1954. "A Theory of Social Comparison Processes." *Human Relations* 7: 117–40.

Fonow, Mary Margaret, and Judith A. Cook. 2005. "Feminist Methodology: New Applications in the Academy and Public Policy." *Signs* 30 (4): 2211–36.

Fontana, Andrea, and James H. Frey. 1994. "Interviewing: The Art of Science." In *Handbook of Qualitative Research* (1st ed.), edited by Norman K. Denzin and Yvonna S. Lincoln, 361–77. Thousand Oaks, CA: SAGE.

Fraser, Nancy. 2005. "Reframing Justice in a Globalizing World." *New Left Review* 36: 69–88.

Fraser, Nancy. 2007. "Feminist Politics in the Age of Recognition: A Two-Dimensional Approach to Gender Justice." *Studies in Social Justice* 1 (1): 23–35.

Frey, Bruno S., and Alois Stutzer. 2002. *Happiness and Economics: How the Economy and Institutions Affect Human Well-Being*. New Brunswick, NJ: Princeton University Press.

Helliwell, John, Richard Layard, and Jeffrey Sachs. 2012. "World Happiness Report." http://issuu.com/earthinstitute/docs/world-happiness-report.

Herr, Ranjoo Seodu. 2014. "Reclaiming Third World Feminism: Or Why Transnational Feminism Needs Third World Feminism." *Meridians: Feminism, Race, Transnationalism* 12 (1): 1–30.

Hesse-Biber, Sharlene Naggy. 2010. "Feminist Approaches to Mixed Methods Research: Linking Theory to Praxis." In *Sage Handbook of Mixed Methods in Social and Behavioral Research* (2nd ed.), edited by Abbas Tashakkori and Charles Teddlie, 169–92. Thousand Oaks, CA: SAGE.

Hill Collins, Patricia. 1990. *Black Feminist Thought: Knowledge, Consciousness, and the Politics of Empowerment*. New York, NY: Routledge, Chapman and Hall.

hooks, bell. 1981. *Ain't I a Woman: Black Women and Feminism*. Boston, MA: South End Press.

Ingelhart, Ronald, Haerpfer Christian, Moreno Alejandro, Welzel Christian, Kizilova Kseniya, Diez-Medrano Jaime, Lagos Marta, Norris Pippa, Ponarin Eduard, and Puranen Bi. (eds.). 2014. *World Values Survey: Round Six – Country-Pooled Datafile*. Madrid: JD Systems Institute. www.worldvaluessurvey.org/WVSDocumentationWV6.jsp.

Kashdan, Todd B., Robert Biswas-Diener, and Laura A. King. 2008. "Reconsidering Happiness: The Costs of Distinguishing between Hedonics and Eudaimonia." *The Journal of Positive Psychology* 3 (4): 219–33.

Lorde, Audre. 1984. *Sister Outsider*. Berkeley, CA: Crossing Press.

McCall, Leslie. 2005. "The Complexity of Intersectionality." *Signs: Journal of Women in Culture and Society* 30 (3): 1771–800.

Mohanty, Chandra. 1988. "Under Western Eyes: Feminist Scholarship and Colonial Discourses." *Feminist Review* 30: 61–88.

Møller, Valerie. 2007. "Quality of Life in South Africa: The First Ten Years of Democracy." *Social Indicators Research* 81: 181–201.

Population Registration Act 30 of 1950 (RSA).

Rustin, Carmine. 2018. "Gender Equality and Happiness Among South African Women." PhD Dissertation, University of the Western Cape, South Africa.

Ryan, Richard M., and Edward L. Deci. 2001. "On Happiness and Human Potentials: A Review of Research on Hedonic and Eudaimonic Well-Being." *Annual Review of Psychology* 52: 141–66.

Ryff, Carol D. 1989. "Happiness Is Everything, Or Is It? Explorations on the Meaning of Psychological Well-Being." *Journal of Personality and Social Psychology* 57: 1069–81.

Sachs, Jeffrey. 2012. "Introduction." In *World Happiness Report*, edited by John Helliwell, Richard Layard, and Jeffrey Sachs, 2–9. www.earth.columbia.edu/sitefiles/file/Sachs%20 Writing/2012/World%20Happiness%20Report.pdf.

Statistics South Africa. 2014. "Vulnerable Groups Indicator Report: 2014." www.statssa. gov.za/publications/Report-03-19-02/Report-03-19-022014.pdf.

Veenhoven, Ruut. 2004. "Happiness as an Aim in Public Policy: The Great Happiness Principle." In *Positive Psychology in Practice*, edited by P. Alex Linley and Stephen Joseph, 658–78. Hoboken, NJ: John Wiley and Sons.

22 Decolonization, the University, and Transnational Solidarities

A Conversation

Swati Arora, Redi Koobak, and Nina Lykke

Swati Arora works at Queen Mary University of London. Redi Koobak and Nina Lykke interviewed her about her transnational journey into feminism and decolonial thinking. We follow Swati's trajectory from her time as a student at the University of Delhi; her participation in the college's theatre society, The Players; her tenure as a postdoctoral fellow in Cape Town, South Africa, at a time where the #RhodesMust-Fall and #FeesMustFall protests were widespread; and when the #MeToo and Black Lives Matter movements took off internationally. The conversation includes Swati's coming to London for a job on a fixed-term contract, and later joining Queen Mary as Lecturer in Performance and Global South Studies. Before the interview, Swati shared chapters from her forthcoming book on art and performance in Delhi at the interface of the urban and the political with the two interviewers, Redi and Nina. We also read the Manifesto that Swati wrote to call for decentring Theatre and Performance Studies (Arora 2021a), and her essay on The Mothertongue Project's South African adaptation of Walk which was first performed in Delhi by the Indian performer and playwright Maya Rao (Arora 2020). Here, Swati engages with the "trickster" feminist and decolonial practice of translation as transgression. In the interview, we asked Swati to share her reflections on key issues of Pluriversal Conversations on Transnational Feminisms. The conversation pivoted around the Decolonize the University movement, transnational feminisms, building feminist solidarities across borders, and translation as dialogue.

Theatre, Performance, and Transnational Feminism

Redi: Could we start with your journey into feminism and Feminist Studies?

Swati: I have never thought about this in concrete terms . . . but Sara Ahmed comes to mind. I remember finding her blog, feministkilljoys (Ahmed 2023), at some point during my PhD and retrospectively thinking: these are the words I was looking for all this time. Ahmed says that the words and concepts that make sense of the embodied experiences of sexism and racism come to you in retrospect. When you are living the violence or feel that something is wrong . . . in that moment, you do not necessarily know how to name the thing that has happened. But as we read and grow and come to understand the insidious nature of violence,

288 *Swati Arora, Redi Koobak, and Nina Lykke*

these concepts come to us retrospectively. Looking back, it was very much my introduction to the world of theatre in Delhi that radicalized me. As a lonely child in school who found refuge in reading, English Literature was the obvious choice when it came to choosing a subject for my undergraduate degree. We read a lot of texts that were mostly by dead white men – there was Chaucer and Shakespeare and Milton, but there also happened to be Virginia Woolf. I remember reading *Mrs Dalloway* (1925) and *A Room of One's* Own (1929) and relating quite deeply with these texts. In retrospect, I wish I was taught Uma Chakravarti (2003) and Sharmila Rege (2006) but a programme like English Literature has very colonial roots in India; out of all the modules across three years – around 16 I think – we had maybe two or three on translated works in English and one on Postcolonial Literature.

At the same time, I joined the theatre society of my college as an extracurricular thing that you do on the side. It is called The Players, at Kirori Mal College in Delhi. It was there that I met people from all walks of life – from outside Delhi, from different class, caste, and linguistic backgrounds. After our lectures finished for the day, we met in the auditorium to read and discuss plays. During inter-college festival season on campus, we rehearsed till late into the night. As the first child, as the eldest daughter, I had to fight with my parents to make this happen. I come from a fairly humble background where women do not aspire for big things – my mother is a homemaker who quit her full-time job as a teacher to raise kids, fairly common for her generation. But then I had to make it clear that this was not going to be my life trajectory. When we had a performance coming up, I had to convince my parents that I am not partying, that I am not doing anything illegal, that they could come and see me in the auditorium if they wanted. Post rehearsals, a male friend would have to drop me back home – this is pre-Uber era, and I did not have money for taxi anyway – on their motorbike (it was rare for students to have a car), which created another kind of problem. Apparently, neighbours were unhappy because not only was I coming home late, with a man, but with a different man each time! We would giggle about this with my friends but I can imagine how this traumatized my parents. I guess just breaking the bubble of my middle-class upbringing, meeting people, and reading texts outside of the formal education made me realize that what I had been feeling all along can be explained by what feminism has to offer. The more I read, the more I understood the multiple meanings of feminism and how it is always a journey of constant unlearning and learning.

Redi: You moved from India to the UK, and you have also been in South Africa for some time, doing a postdoc. What are your thoughts on these different experiences? What shifted along the road? How do these different experiences come together around feminism? How do they perhaps resonate with transnational forms of feminism?

Decolonization, the University and Transnational Solidarities   289

Swati: The first time I left India, I went to Germany, to the Technical University of Dresden, as a research student in 2009. The same year, I won an Erasmus Mundus scholarship to do an MA in Performance at the Universities of Amsterdam and Warwick. I went on to a PhD at Exeter, supported by UK-India Education Research Initiative funding. Performance Studies offered methods and concepts that Literature did not. I witnessed a different style of pedagogy that focused on embodied learning and also a more formal introduction to feminism. I remember reading Chandra Talpade Mohanty (2013) for the first time and her observations around how feminism is taught at institutions in the Global North: she writes about how the topic of feminism is placed towards the end of the 12-week term within introductory modules on critical theory, and how feminist concepts from the Global South are relegated to an even shorter timeframe. The module might aim to do a survey, but minoritized voices are placed in the very last weeks. By then, students are tired, and they have already decided the topic of their essays, and no one is really interested in learning anything new in the very last week. Through the formal teaching of feminism at the university, I began to understand how my lived experience of feminism in India was very different to how feminism was taught in the Global North – my lived reality was a footnote in the UK classroom. But also, looking around and realizing that there are only a handful of us in academia in the Global North – it was this constant feeling of being invisible.

Nina: How was your postdoctoral stay in South Africa?

Swati: I finished my PhD in the UK and faced the reality of UK's hostile environment. My UK visa was about to expire, so I applied to academic positions elsewhere. Because of visa rules, my partner and I had to live separately on different continents for two years. It was hell. And what is really heart-breaking is that the majority of people in the UK have no idea how migrants navigate the violence of borders. I often think about how I have managed to do what I do, with the passport that I have . . .

I joined the Centre for Humanities Research and subsequently, the Centre for Women's and Gender Studies at the University of Western Cape (UWC), South Africa, and that was absolutely amazing. After the #RhodesMustfall and #FeesMustFall movements[1], academic spaces in South Africa were, and still are, undergoing upheaval. This is not to romanticize anything because these Fallist movements have been critiqued for excluding Black queer voices. I spent a lot of time with academics, activists, artists, organizers who continue to do a lot of work at the grassroots level. A few of them had rented a venue that functioned as a hub – a space for community gatherings where film screenings, talks, live music, and performances are organized. With a few other comrades, I organized a film screening and discussion on the rising Hindutva politics in India[2]. We screened Nakul Sawhney's

290   *Swati Arora, Redi Koobak, and Nina Lykke*

Muzaffarnagar Baaqi Hai (2015) and people were shocked to see how dangerous the political situation is in India, a fact which continues to be completely ignored by mainstream media everywhere.

Being a part of the South African university system reminded me of my time at Delhi University where education, in its true sense, was not just limited to the classroom – one learnt through activism, meeting, and talking to people who are committed to organizing. This was, of course, before privatization took over and before public universities were captured by the current government.

I was so fortunate to have been invited to participate in a conference on the #MeToo movement in India and South Africa at The University of Witwaterstrand where it was made abundantly clear in the presentations that #MeToo retains its position as a hegemonic, universal, international wave of resistance against gendered and sexualized violence, while overlooking histories of localized struggles in the Global South (see Arora 2022). Many scholars have now pointed out #MeToo's erasures of Black, queer, Trans, and Dalit voices, and how African American women's rights activist Tarana Burke's launching of the phrase "MeToo" on the digital social networking platform MySpace in 2006 did not receive the same attention as white Hollywood actress Alyssa Milano's coining of #MeToo in 2017 (see Hussen and Shefer, this volume; Arora 2021b).

Decolonization and the Academy

Nina: What was your PhD about?

Swati: It was on street theatre and urban space in Delhi. I looked at a number of examples across feminist, Marxist, and ritual theatre practices to examine their engagements with spatial structures in the city and explored how the affective, material, and discursive aspects of urban space get negotiated through performance.

Nina: You also wrote a Manifesto (Arora 2021a) about decentring Theatre and Performance Studies. Could you say more about it?

Swati: As far as the history of disciplines and departments go, Performance Studies as an area of study is fairly recent. It is only in the 1980s that the first Performance Studies department was established at New York University. Even today, the number of departments across the world is limited, most of them in North America and the UK. In India, we have a handful of departments that focus on Performance: in Delhi, Hyderabad, and, very recently, in Kolkata. Until more recently, Jawaharlal Nehru University (JNU), Delhi, was the only university to have one dedicated department to focus on discursive aspects of theatre and performance. There are institutions in Delhi, Kerala, Manipur that focus

Decolonization, the University and Transnational Solidarities 291

on the practical aspects of theatre, but, as a legitimate theoretical mode of enquiry, the subject has not acquired much attention, funding, or value across India, even though there is no dearth of cultural practices that centre embodiedness and orality.

My Manifesto (2021a) was a response to what Decolonize the University demanded and came from my lived experience of being part of the UK academia with its hostile institutional and border policies. I wrote it at the start of the pandemic, at a time of so much grief. Academics were made redundant, job adverts retracted, and I was convinced that I had no future in academia or in the UK. Every day, I would see horrific images of killings and lynchings of Muslims and Dalits by Hindu mobs on the streets in India – minoritized communities were being mercilessly beaten to death because they were suspected of eating beef or for an inter-faith marriage. We all saw the murder of George Floyd in May 2020 and how it intensified the Black Lives Matter movement. Police violence against minoritized communities was becoming commonplace in India but there was no outrage or mobilization at the same scale.

Then I saw a call for a special issue on decentring Theatre and Performance Studies and I just sat down to write something. I did not know what shape the writing would take. I was just really tired of everything around me and the shallow promises and statements released by institutions in the aftermath of George Floyd's murder, tired of the whiteness of my discipline. Even today, there is only one Black professor in Theatre and Performance in the entire UK. The Manifesto is very much a result of the moment in which it was written – the world was in crisis, the UK academia was in crisis, COVID had hit the world, and we were under lockdown. I am not sure how much has structurally changed since then, but I have since received several emails and words of support about the Manifesto. Graduate students from Black and Global Majority backgrounds across the world have written to thank me and say that they feel seen in my writing. I did not expect it to be received so well, and for it to resonate do deeply with so many people, and I am really grateful that it happened.

Conversations on racism and inclusivity are certainly happening. Students are really tired of being fed white, patriarchal, racist, ableist reading lists. My place of work, Queen Mary University of London, has an active student body that continues to be active in Decolonize the University. Sixty percent of students at Queen Mary are first-generation students, 30 percent students have working-class parents, a majority of our students are Black or from Global Majority backgrounds and they have been outspoken about their impatience with the canon. They are saying that enough is enough and their refusal is resolute. To see them articulate their dissent with such confidence is beautiful. This is very much a product of the moment and I am glad I am alive to see this.

292   *Swati Arora, Redi Koobak, and Nina Lykke*

Revolution Is in the Classroom!

'The learning process is something you can incite, literally incite, like a riot. And then, just possibly, hopefully, it goes home, or on'.

– Audre Lorde, *Sister Outsider: Essays and Speeches* (1984)

Nina: Since you wrote the Manifesto, you have become a permanent member of staff at Queen Mary. Now that you have become part of the "we" of Performance Studies, how do you see yourself contributing to the call for decolonization after this shift of position?

Swati: This reminds me of a memory: when I applied to English Literature at Kirori Mal College in Delhi, I was interviewed as part of the selection process. I remember being asked the reason for studying Literature. I said that it is because I want to teach at the university. I was maybe 16 at the time, and I did not really go there having thought about my life plan. My parents were very unhappy with my choice – they wanted me to become a doctor, a "real" doctor (laughs). After all these years, I think that memory has motivated me towards making the world a more inclusive space. I feel like this is what gives my life a purpose. It feels awkward saying it like that . . . The kind of dystopia we are living in, the world needs a complete overhaul, a revolution. And I believe that revolution is in the classroom. If I can prevent one student in the classroom from behaving in a racist manner or being transphobic, perhaps I have succeeded a little? In my brief time in the UK academia, I have realized that you cannot do much about institutions because they are way more powerful than you; what you can do is just engage with students in the classroom. That is what I am committed to and passionate about. So many first-generation students have come to me during my office hours to share how much they have appreciated my presence in an otherwise really white institution. If I can make students feel truly seen and heard, I must be doing something right.

Redi: So much of what you are saying resonates with me: pedagogy in the classroom as the site of revolution. I wholeheartedly believe in that as well, and that is very much true for Gender Studies as well.

Nina: What you are saying made me think of a wonderful quote from a song by the poet Faiz Ahmed Faiz which was sung as part of the current street protests in India, that you analyse in the chapter you shared with us from your forthcoming book: "When the enormous mountains of tyranny and oppression will be blown away like cotton".[3] It is quite common to think about institutions as being so grounded that they will stay forever. But, no, they will not. They will blow away. Like cotton. And this is what seems to happen in the revolutionary classroom. What you do in the classroom is part of this soft power that makes real changes.

Decolonization, the University and Transnational Solidarities 293

Swati: Thank you for giving us all hope, Nina. Perhaps my weariness comes from the denial of racism in the UK. When the murder of George Floyd led to a resurgence of the Black Lives Matter movement, a lot of organizations released official statements of solidarity but the underlying belief is still that anti-Black violence happens "elsewhere". We are all aware of the Windrush scandal[4] that is ongoing and people from the Caribbeans are forcefully being deported as we speak. These violent policies are an effect of the very long Tory government rule in the UK and their hostile, racist immigration policies. There have been massive cuts to public funding, and the universities are very much agents of neoliberalism and xenophobia. Students do not get taught the histories of British colonialism in their school textbooks, so it is all the more crucial they get to know about these facts at the undergraduate level. But the government does not want this to happen; they do not want students to develop any kind of critical thinking. In 2022, entire Humanities departments have been closed and their staff made redundant. The University and College Union have been fighting against the massive cuts and restructuring for the last five years, and the fight to save the Humanities is ongoing.

Redi: I felt a deep resonance with what you were saying about teaching. But I also see in your story of coming to feminism and becoming more radical than the context where you were brought up that the informal education outside the classroom was really important for you. But you still also have a belief in changing the university system from within? I guess otherwise you would not persist on staying there, writing the Manifesto, demanding a change from the university, and I also guess that you somehow believe that change may be possible because the student body has changed. Is the student body not different in some sense, because of the changing context that the different decolonization movements and Black Lives Matter, and all of that, have generated? The students come to the classroom wanting to get more knowledge. But today they also already come equipped with certain kinds of knowledge from outside the classroom. I have been thinking a lot about the impact of the current social movements on our pedagogies, and how we think about our fields. Just to take #MeToo as an example of something that I have been working with myself, #MeToo as a gateway to Gender Studies. It is impossible for our students not to know about #MeToo. It is ubiquitous, it is everywhere. So, they already come equipped with a certain knowledge that has become part of Gender Studies. In this sense, it is different from I guess even a decade ago, when students came not having that kind of knowledge about this sort of social media enhanced movements. The same applies to Black Lives Matter and Decolonize the University. The students come with certain knowledges, and then a sense of "we can change the fields" somehow come to the fore, right? I am curious to know if this perhaps resonates with your experiences, and I would also like to hear your reflections on what still keeps you in the space of the university, when there are all these amazing things happening outside the university structures. In your Manifesto, you are talking about creating your own reading lists, creating your own communities, which, of course, does not necessarily need to happen within the university. What are your thoughts on all this?

Swati: Thank you, this is a brilliant question! It really hits the nerve of the Decolonize the University movement – if the institutions are colonial and patriarchal, why bother with them anyway?

Redi: Why do you not just give them up?

Swati: (laughter) Steal from them! I was talking to a friend the other day about this too, that I am so glad and so grateful that I got my first few years of university education in Delhi. I am so glad that I did not go to the UK for my first degree, not least because I had neither money nor support! I spent the formative years of my life at a public university where the annual fee was next to nothing, and where the meaning of education was different. We did not consider ourselves to be consumers. Today, things are very different in India, and everywhere really. Cuts to public funding have turned education into a commodity whose worth is measured in how much salary you make once you graduate. Increasing student fees also means only upper-class, upper-caste people can afford to go to the university. For so many of us, university education remains a way to cross class barriers. For lots of working-class students who come from small cities and towns, and not from urban centres, a degree is a gateway to a stable job which their parents did not have access to.

What I am trying to say is that you *can* find community at the university, and that there is something about being in this space called the university that can be empowering and life-changing. But it does not necessarily have to be through what happens *inside* the classroom. For instance, we have had a series of industrial strike actions against increasing workloads, lack of permanent contracts, and pension cuts in the UK. It is during these strikes, at the picket line, when I got to have proper conversations with colleagues whom I otherwise do not get to see. Standing outside the university, being in community with comrades, holding placards, we spoke about the occupation of Hong Kong, and about ongoing Hindutva violence against Muslim and Dalit students in India. That was a powerful experience of coming together because we shared the belief of making the world a better place for all. I am never not thinking with Stephano Harney and Fred Moten who, in *The Undercommons* (2013), advocate for a strategic use of resources available at university spaces. Steal from them, they say. Use the library for reading widely, distribute what you can, organize reading groups!

Decolonization, the University and Transnational Solidarities 295

Convergences of Students' Movements and Social Movements in India

Nina: In the chapter from your book, which we read, you talk about convergence of students' movements and social movements in India. Could you elaborate on that?

Swati: Student protests against rising fees, illegal arrests of students from minoritized communities and oppressed castes, and infiltration of right-wing ideologues in positions of power at the universities have been going on in India for a few years now. Rohith Vemula, a Dalit scholar at the University of Hyderabad, was driven to suicide because the university administration stopped his scholarship as a punishment for his activism. This incident further mobilized student movements in other cities Delhi, Mumbai, and Pune. Umar Khalid, a Muslim student activist from JNU, has been in jail for years. The process of writing the chapter that I shared with you – the one on the Shaheen Bagh[5] protest in Delhi – was my way of making sense of what was happening in India in 2020. The Indian government introduced Citizenship Amendment Act and National Citizen Register to criminalize Muslim citizens and Shaheen Bagh became a powerful symbol of resistance, a movement that spread across India, inviting solidarity from not just the Dalit student movement but from people across ages, castes, and classes. Muslim women who were active during the Shaheen Bagh protests were in jail for the longest time. One of them, Safoora Ali, was pregnant at the time and it took multiple court hearings for her to be granted bail.

I think that the students' movements and social movements have always spoken to each other. India stands at a very, very dangerous moment in history. What we are witnessing is a complete breakdown of law to perpetuate violence against Muslims and Dalits. There is no space for dissent against this terror. What worries me is that the media does not talk about it the way it mentioned the horrors of Trump in the USA or Erdogan in Turkey.

Nina: I think it somehow came through in the European media, I read. I think the quasi-fascism of the Indian government was exposed through the ways in which Prime Minister Modi handled the COVID crisis, imposing a sudden lockdown with no support for the vulnerable and the marginalized, so that people were literally just thrown out on the road.

Swati: In April 2021, when the second COVID wave hit Delhi and other cities, the situation was catastrophic. There were neither vaccines nor oxygen nor enough hospitals, not even space to say proper goodbye to those who did not survive. Funeral pyres were set in parks and parking lots because the graveyards were full. But neither the pandemic nor the lockdown stopped the government from spending millions on the construction of the Central Vista, which is going to be the new seat of the government in central Delhi.

The irony is that this hard-line version of Hindutva and xenophobia is being legitimized under the garb of decolonization. A complete restructuring of New Delhi, which was built as the capital city of the British empire, is being undertaken in the name of reclaiming "tradition". Decolonization does not mean ethno-nationalism – a potential trap Fanon anticipated in *The Wretched of the Earth* (1963) – but that is what is being sold on the television in India.

My book talks about this: how nationalism legitimizes itself through the capture of public spaces – whether it is building a Central Vista in New Delhi or changing street names or intending to destroy the Mughal Taj Mahal, one of the seven wonders of the world! – and how performance subverts that process, if at all.

Nina: Could you elaborate on the ways in which you see the role of art, poetry, and performance as crucial in relation to activism?

Swati: Because of their embodied nature, art, performance, and poetry have always been an integral part of the resistance culture in India. Not just against the ruling Bharatiya Janata Party, but against the British rule in late 19th and early 20th centuries as well as against Congress Party's autocracy in 1970s and 1980s, when the women's movement in India intensified. Even then, street theatre was used quite extensively. After the horrific Delhi rape case occurred in 2012, artists across India used performances to express their anger and rage, but that rage is absent if there is a similar incident involving a Dalit woman. This is something I talk about in my book. The #MeToo movement, celebrated globally, was met with a challenge for similar erasures which I have written about (Arora 2021b). So, coming back to answer your question about the role of arts and performance, I think if the right-wing Hindu government captures university spaces and media, arts, and performance is all we have left as tools of resistance.

Transnational Feminisms, Transversal Politics, and Translation as Dialogue

> How do we organize around our differences, neither denying them nor blowing them up out of proportion? The first step is an effort of will on your part. Try to remember, to keep certain facts in your mind.
>
> – Audre Lorde, *I am Your Sister: Black Women Organising Across Sexualities* (1985)

Redi: In your research on the performance *Walk* (Arora 2020), translations between different, postcolonial contexts – South Africa and India – play an important role. I am curious to hear more about your reflections on translations, and the relation to transnationalism. Translations have

Decolonization, the University and Transnational Solidarities 297

been a lot on my mind lately and thinking about the travel of concepts between different contexts: how concepts shift when they cross borders, and how movements shift when they cross borders. I guess, this is the eternal question in Feminist Studies about the local/global relation. There is a lot of this "that is about a US context, but it does not apply to us". There is also a lot of miscommunications, and misunderstandings circulating because so much knowledge shaping happens in translation, and things get lost in translation. So, I am wondering how you are navigating these conundrums and tensions. You are working in multiple contexts, multiple cultural contexts, multiple linguistic contexts. You are presenting your analyses mostly, I guess, within Western academic contexts, but I am also curious to know if you are doing any work on this within an Indian context, and if your work might be sometimes translated to other languages than English? It is a big question. Feel free to pick to up any thread of this that speaks to you.

Swati: I find Walter Benjamin's idea of translation quite helpful (2002), and this is what I use in my essay as well (Arora 2020). He talks of translation as a carrying over, and not just linguistically, from one context to another. The act of translation itself as a dialogue – not just replicating, but actually extending the conversation when bringing it to a different context. Let me take an example from when the Black Lives Matter protests intensified in 2020, and statements on solidarity and anti-racism were released by organizations in the UK. I am categorized as a "woman of colour" in the UK context and clubbed under the BAME acronym, which includes people from Black Asian and Minority Ethnic backgrounds. This acronym was useful during the 1960s and 1970s when Conservative governments' racist policies needed a united opposition; clubbing minority communities made sense in order to fight for funding and rights. But this naming ignores the fact that violence against Black people is not the same as violence against Asians. It also obscures other aspects of South Asian identity, for instance, caste. Similarly, in the USA, BIPOC is the widely used acronym, which stands for Black Indigenous and People of Colour. Again, the question of caste gets overlooked and it also excludes the fact that anti-Black violence is singular.

So, if we consider the question of translation or lack thereof, these calls for global solidarity and anti-racism were blindly regurgitated in India without any kind of introspection from *savarna* Hindus about violence against Dalits and a very deeply entrenched anti-Black racism in the Indian society. Everyone wanted to support Black Lives Matter, but without any acknowledgement of caste violence in our own contexts. This identification with BAME or BIPOC is so strong that multiple marginalizations within South Asian communities continue to get overlooked.

I am thinking of my time in South Africa and how I was read on the streets in Cape Town. Histories of Trans-Atlantic slavery are perhaps

298   *Swati Arora, Redi Koobak, and Nina Lykke*

more commonly known but not many people are aware of the histories of slavery across the Indian Ocean. There is a long history of indentured slave trade between the Southern and Western parts of India and the south-eastern coasts of Africa – South Africa, Mozambique, Tanzania, Zanzibar have a huge South Asian population. I am sure people in Cape Town could tell by my body language that I am not a local. Every time I would meet an Indian immigrant in South Africa, they would ask my surname. They were not satisfied with just my first name, as the last name reveals one's caste. As an Indian woman in South Africa, they wanted to place me: When did I come there? Where are my parents? Could I be the child of . . . indentured slave labourers? Immediately, that history of slavery between India and South Africa was transcribed on my body and people were reading me through that lens.

It is crucial to pay attention to the multiple colonialities within the Global South. *Savarna* privilege and Dalit violence are deeply entrenched in India, and it is so absolutely horrific that Rohith Vemula had to commit suicide to bring these concerns to the fore. Which is why it is important to unpack what Decolonize the University demands from specific local contexts, rather than simply mirroring its concerns elsewhere.

Nina: What you are stressing here is so important: the existence of these deep internal differences in social justice movements such as Decolonize the University. The movements are somehow cut through by a lot of internal differences. To overcome this requires transversality, transversal politics (Yuval-Davis 1997) where people carefully acknowledge both their differences, and what they might have in common. What you said about translation as dialogue is really important for developing a true transversal transnational feminist and decolonial politics and solidarity. So, could you elaborate on the ways in which you understand the (im) possible task of navigating transnational solidarity, using the tool of translation as dialogue?

Swati: For my postdoc in South Africa —where Decolonize the University began—I was grateful to have been based at UWC, an institution built as a product of apartheid. My experience of the movement would have been very different if I was at University of Cape Town, for instance, which is historically a predominantly white university. With students and colleagues at UWC, there were intense discussions on *savarna* privilege of someone like me and the value of deep solidarities between Black and Dalit women. These were important conversations because it is crucial to recognize these differences without flattening them. In that context, the role of caste was acknowledged as well as inscribed because of the histories of immigration of labour diaspora between India and South Africa. Conversely, in the UK, for instance, minoritized brown bodies get clubbed under BAME, which erases the reality of caste violence.

Decolonization, the University and Transnational Solidarities 299

Your question of translation as dialogue and transversal politics makes me think of how the spaces and the city translated me in Cape Town, as opposed to how I am translated by people in London, and to how, because of my cultural capital, I get translated in Delhi. It is complex and complicated and perhaps just being mindful of these different positionalities helps me navigate them, and to keep the dialogue on translations open.

Redi: Perhaps, you have a final word on translation as dialogue, related to your very exciting research on the two versions of the performance *Walk*, and the subtle translations between an Indian and a South African context?

Swati: The feminist performer Maya Rao has been making street plays on women's rights issues in India since the 1970s. In 2012, she created the performance *Walk* in response to the horrific Delhi gang rape incident. The performance travelled nationally and internationally. It expresses the desire of women to inhabit public spaces at all times without fear: to sleep in the park, to be able to walk at night. Sara Matchett, from the South African ensemble. The Mother Tongue Project saw Rao's performance on YouTube, and reached out to Rao, asking her if they could collaborate. That is how *Walk: South Africa* came about.

Speaking of translations and transnational feminism, I focus on the process of making the South African iteration of *Walk*. Sara's version took shape as a result of a process of improvisation with a group of artists and took a very different form. Her collaboration with Black, queer, non-binary artists, what in South Africa is classified as "coloured" people, through workshops and discussions, highlights a pluriversal depiction of access to public spaces in contemporary South Africa, where legacies of spatial segregation of apartheid are very much apparent today. During my research, I spoke to one of the co-founders of The Mother Tongue Project, Rehana Abrahams. She mentioned that her own experience of navigating public spaces in Cape Town reminds her of Black women who work as domestic helpers – they travel from townships in remote areas to centre of the city for work, they walk in and through white neighbourhoods which are otherwise unwelcoming of their presence. So, a simple act of walking in those spaces reminds Black women of the historical injustices. *Walk: South Africa* is a beautiful example of translation as carrying over, translation as dialogue, while also emphasizing that situatedness is absolutely crucial when thinking about resistance and multiple marginalities.

Notes

1 #RhodesMustFall and #FeesMustFall were student movements that took shape in 2015 in South Africa to decolonize higher education in the country and make it accessible to

300 *Swati Arora, Redi Koobak, and Nina Lykke*

students from disadvantaged backgrounds. In March 2015, staff and students at the University of Cape Town collectively mobilized for the removal of the statue of Cecil John Rhodes, a British imperalist, from its campus. Following a wave of protests and sit-ins, the UCT administration took down the statue a month later. Later that year, #FeesMustFall movement gained momentum when the University of Witswatersrand decided to raise student fees and became the largest student protest since the end of apartheid in 1994.

2 Hindutva is an extremist form of Hinduism, taking the form of right-wing ethno-nationalism, and increasingly becoming widespread in contemporary India under the ruling Bharatiya Janata Party.

3 A poem by the Pakistani revolutionary and communist poet Faiz Ahmed Faiz, *Hum Dekhenge* (we shall bear witness), became the anthem of nationwide protests against the unconstitutional and Islamophobic Citizenship Amendment Act (CAA), National Population Register (NPR), and National Register of Citizens (NRC) introduced by the Indian government. It was originally written as a challenge and a response to the autocratic regime of Zia-ul-Haq, who had staged a military coup against the then Pakistani Prime Minister Zulfikar Ali Bhutto in 1977, sentencing him to death, and leading the country towards an Islamist dictatorship. After Faiz died in 1984, the noted singer Iqbal Bano defied Zia's restrictions on cultural expression and sang his poem to an ecstatic crowd in Lahore in 1985. Bano paid a huge price for her courage and was banned from doing public performance thereafter. Faiz's lyrics found an insurgent appeal against the divisive regime of the current Hindutva government.

4 The "Windrush" generation are people who arrived in the UK from the Caribbean islands between 1948 and 1973 – named after the "HMT Empire Windrush" ship that carried the first largest group of people in 1948. At the time, the Caribbean was part of the British commonwealth and those who came to the UK automatically became British citizens. But, since 2017, the UK government has, repeatedly, forcibly and illegally, deported members of this generation, dividing families.

5 Shaheen Bagh became the epicentre of nationwide protests when the unconstitutional and anti-Muslim Citizenship Amendment Act (CAA), National Population Register (NPR), and National Register of Citizens (NRC)were passed by the Parliament. Beginning in December 2019 and led by grannies of Shaheen Bagh, this peaceful sit-in went on for almost three months and inspired similar protests in various cities across India like Bangalore and Kolkata as well as at Turkman Gate, Inderlok, and Seelampur in peripheral corners of Delhi.

References

Ahmed, Sara. 2023. "Feministkilljoys." Accessed January 20, 2023. https://feministkilljoys.com/.

Arora, Swati. 2020. "Walk in India and South Africa: Notes Towards a Decolonial and Transnational Feminist Politics." Translation and performance in the age of global asymmetries, Part 2, Special Issue. *South African Theatre Journal* 33 (1): 14–33.

Arora, Swati. 2021a. "A Manifesto to Decentre Theatre and Performance Studies." *Studies in Theatre and Performance* 41 (1): 12–20.

Arora, Swati. 2021b. "Dissident Solidarities: Power, Pedagogy, Care." In *Performing #MeToo: How Not to Look Away*, edited by Judith Rudakoff, 141–58. Bristol: Intellect.

Arora, Swati. 2022. "Fugitive Aesthetics: Performing Refusal in Four Acts." In *Injury and Intimacy: In the Wake of #MeToo in India and South Africa*, edited by Nicky Falkof, Shilpa Phadke, and Srila Roy, 309–36. Manchester: Manchester University Press.

Benjamin, Walter. 2002. "The Task of the Translator." In *Walter Benjamin: Selected Writings Volume I 1913–1926*, edited by Marcus Bullock and Michael W. Jennings, 253–63. Cambridge, MA and London: Belknap Press of Harvard University Press.

Chakravarti, Uma. 2003. *Gendering Caste: Through a Feminist Lens*. Kolkata: Stree.

Fanon, Franz. 1963. *The Wretched of the Earth*. Trans. Contance Farrington. New York, NY: Grove Press.

Harney, Stefano, and Fred Moten. 2013. *The Undercommons: Fugitive Planning and Black Study*. New York, NY: Minor Compositions.

Lorde, Audre. 1984. *Sister Outsider: Essays and Speeches*. Trumansburg, NY: Crossing Press.

Lorde, Audre. 1985. *I am Your Sister: Black Women Organising across Sexualities*. New York NY: Kitchen Table, Women of Color Press.

Mohanty, Chandra Talpade. 2013. "'Under Western Eyes' Revisited: Feminist Solidarity Through Anticapitalist Struggles." In *Feminist Theory Reader*, edited by Carole R. McCann and Seung-Kyung Kim, 536–52. New York, NY and Abingdon: Routledge.

Nira Yuval-Davis. 1997. *Gender and Nation*. London: SAGE.

Rege, Sharmila. 2006. *Writing Caste/Writing Gender: Narrating Dalit Women's Testimonies*. Delhi: Zubaan.

Woolf, Virginia. 1925. *Mrs. Dalloway*. London: Hogarth Press.

Woolf, Virginia. 1929. *A Room of One's Own*. London: Hogarth Press.

Index

able-bodiedness, self-definition 181
Abrahams, Rehana 299
Abuela Lala 158
abuse, witness 104
academia: area studies, emergence 8;
austerity politics, effects 45;
entanglement 44; exit 162–3;
funding, importance 4; neoliberal
academia, adjustment 254;
neoliberal academia (change),
trickster tools (usage) 4;
neoliberalization 255; positions,
privilege/precariousness 1; publish
or perish attitude 77; recalibration
2; UK academia, problems 291;
writing, impact 80–1
academic expectations 77
academic experiment, repetition
(avoidance) 160
academic formats 18
academic precarity 39
academic setting 79–80
academic writing, orientation 81
academy, decolonization (relationship)
290–1
Accra: community members, concerns
74; experiences, description
75; NGOized context 72; sexual
rights 73
activism: father, impact 107–8; LGBT
activism 210–11; online activism
173, 181, 190; spiritual activism
105–7; transnational digital
feminist activism, featuring 190–1
activist-performance, usage 267
affect: absence 49–50; collective action,
affect (generation) 187; core affect
92; distribution, unevenness 54;
embodied collective action, affect/

intimacy 184–5; engagements
15; focus 47; generative
power 27; mobilization 20, 29;
othering 267–8; rage, affect 54;
reimagining 266; role/meanings 30;
understanding 50; usage 27–9
affected pedagogues 30, 77
affected writing 29, 46; approach 52;
discomfort 50; focus 20; myriad
tongues/multiple emotions 20, 27
affective approach, limitations 55–6
affective pedagogies 30, 77
affectivity 29; corpo-affectivity 107;
focus 47; importance 31;
understanding 50
affirmative subjectivity, empowerment 95
Africa, colonial notions 53
African countries, Imperialist Capitalist
Colonial relations 110
African diaspora 111
African feminism 103–7; decolonial
perspectives 115–16; practice
105; white women feminism,
contrast 113
African feminist life, living (decolonial
perspectives) 31, 103
African National Congress 63
African people: colonial notions 53;
construction 48
Áfricas, The 197
age/generation, socio-cultural
categorisation 50–1
ageism, Serbian government display 140
agency: idea 187; knowledge, boundaries
(blurring) 144
Ahmed, Sara 112
AIDS, mass educational campaign 264
aliveness, sense 79–80
alliances, building 126

Index

alter-epistemes, shaping 14
alter-methodologies 14
alternative sexual justice 259
alter-ontologies, shaping 14
Álvarez, Sônia 199
Alzheimer's patient, treatment situation 66
Amerindian concepts, use 125
Amin, Idi 103, 108
analysis, natural unit 6
ancestor, transition 35
ancestral knowledges 162–6; follower 156
And Words Collide from a Place
    (Kawesa) 103
anthropological discourse 249
anthropology/anthropologists, role 169–70
anti-racism 112–13, 116; US-centred/US-
    based anti-racism 112–13
anti-racist feminist activist, becoming
    109–11
anti-racist feminist groups, stories 83
Anzaldúa, Gloria 12, 106, 114, 122,
    130, 141
apartheid: complexity 283; emotions,
    shutdown 65; history 275, 281–2;
    legacies 47; ravages 274; spatial
    legacy 53
Appadurai, Arjun 139
Arab brother, images 209
Arab Revolts (2011) 204
area studies 8–9, 203; intelligence-
    gathering force 207–8; Middle East
    Area Studies 204; postsocialist
    rethinkings 8; queering 175
Arora, Swati 1, 121, 173, 177
Ashcroft, Bill 143
#AsiGanaChile 50
askew arrivals 2–5
assemblage 95–8; concept 90–1, 96;
    global assemblage aim 235;
    global assemblage theory 236;
    layers, connection 98; research,
    relationship 98–9
assimilationist objectives 227
asylum seekers, migration control 252
austerity politics, effects 45
austerity work 254
Australian Feminist Studies 159, 167
autophenomenographic storytelling,
    importance 31
autophenomenography: method 31, 103;
    workshop, hot moment
    (impact) 83
awkward engagement, zones 72

Baartman, Sara: autopsy 48; body display
    48; "Hottentot Venus" label 47;
    re-robing 53; scientific depictions
    48–9; sculpture 49–50
Bakos, Petra 1, 27, 77, 121; workshop 13
Bangladesh: biobank infrastructures
    237; biobanking activities 238;
    capitalist biopolitics 178;
    healthcare 233, 236, 238–41;
    personalized medicine
    175–6, 236
Bareed Mista3jil 210
"beauty in diversity" 220
becoming-assemblage 96
becoming-imperceptible:
    description 95; deterritorialization,
    relationship 95
becoming-stratum 96
Behar, Ruth 60
being: geopolitics/corpopolitics 132–3;
    indigenous decolonial methods
    135–6
belonging, question 197–8
Benjamin, Walter 297
Bergen workshop 82
Berlin Wall, fall 140
Bester, Willie 49
Betemps, Caroline 174, 196
Bhabha, Homi 141
Bharatiya Janata Party, ruling 296
Bible, perception 116
bidirectional exchange 145
Biko, Steve 60
Biobank Finland, vision 237
biobanking activities, biovalue expectations
    (impact) 238
Biobank of Bangladesh (BBB) 237
biobanks: economics, relationship
    236–8; establishment 236–7;
    establishment, analysis 176; global
    distribution, unevenness 237;
    operational biobanks, presence
    237; operational logic, perceived
    economic value (connection) 238;
    public health benefits, connection
    238; public ownership (Finland)
    237–8
biological data, collection/usage/sale
    237–8
biological information, expression 241
biomedical coloniality 136
biomedical research, establishment
    (analysis) 176

304 *Index*

biovalue: expectations, influence 238; public health, relationship 236–8; term, usage 237–8
Biskaabiiyang 135–6
Black Asian and Minority Ethnic (BAME) 297
Black feminism (Black Feminism): Americanization 113; decolonial feminism, difference 116; differentiation 31; magazine coverage 111
Black Indigenous and People of Colour (BIPOC) 297
Black Lives Matter movement, resurgence 293, 297
Black Masks/White Sins (Kawesa) 103
blackness: intersectional approach 181; white perspective, misunderstanding 109
Black-normative society, existence 108–9
Black queer voices, exclusion 289–90
Black theorizing, geopolitical locations (usage) 112–15
Black women: death 27, 33; death, intersection 35; death rates, causes (research) 35; life satisfaction 281; self-determination, battle 36; transition 36
Black womxn, sexual violence 52
Bloch, Ernst 144
body/brain matter, logic 100–1
body, information 92
body politics of knowledge 106
Boesak, Allan 63
Booksmart people 33–5
Booysen, Anene (rape/murder) 48
border-crossing feminist co-writing process, materialization 156–62
borderland: hermeneutics 130; place, vagueness 134
Borderlands (Anzaldúa) 141, 142
borderline 147
borders: disruption, queering reliance 207; existence, usage 133–4; loss 97; love letters, writing 155; opening 140; positioning 134; reinforcement 140–1; security, relationship 139–40; site marking 141
border thinking 140–4, 146; disidentification, relationship 144; exteriority, epistemology 141; feminist border thinking 122, 141–2, 150; pluriversal approaches,

link 122–3; transnational perspective, connection 142; usage 133–4; utopian potentiality 144
boundary-making/boundary-transgressing projects 9
Braidotti, Rosi 6, 90
brain: activity 91–2; distributed state 93
Briggs, Laura 142
British colonialism, histories 293
"Brotherhood, Cooperation, and Coordination" treaty 209
Budapest writing workshop 87; failure 83–4
Buganda Kingdom, white people (arrival) 114–15
Burke, Tarana 183–4, 290
burnt child, attention 66–7

cancer/death, mourning 161
Cape Town workshop 78–80, 85; body, focus 80; enjoyment 87
capitalism: perception 116; power relations 62
capitalist biopolitics (Finland/Bangladesh) 178
capitalist imperialism, shared history 208
Cartesian Western philosophical worldview 106
CASE *see* South African Community Agency for Social Enquiry
Castro-Gómez, Santiago 7, 133
Chakravarti, Uma 288
change, dynamism 95
Chapman, Anne 157–60, 169–70; work, prominence 162
Chief Oracle, impact 34–5
child care, release (emotional pain) 67
Chile País de Poetas 164
"Chinese way of life" 147
chronic ethnophilia 215
chronic waiting 254–5
chronopolitical locations, meaning 256
chronopolitics: discussion 252–4; impact, recognition 248; meanings 176, 246; migrant/citizen (difference reinforcement), chronopolitics (impact) 255; questions, departure point 248–50; self-reflexive study 176
chronotopical coordinates 145
cis-heterosexual, sexual violence stories 185
cis-women, harassment 185

Citizenship Amendment Act 295
citizenship, geopolitical bordering (impact) 252–3
class: consciousness 41–3, 45; intersections 279; self-definition 181; socio-cultural categorisation 50–1
classed moralities, reproduction 262–5
classroom, revolution 292–4
closeness, absence 147
coalitional journey 130
Coatlicue state (La herencia de Coatlicue) 130, 134, 136
coevalness 176, 246; assertion 248; creation 246; denial 246, 249; meaning, awareness 247; usefulness 247
Cold War 207–8; impact 8; logic 199; war/violence (geopolitics) 144
collective: embodied collective action, affect/intimacy 184–5; empowerment 95
collective action, affect (generation) 187
colonial capitalism 196
colonial gaze, disruption 49–50, 259
colonial injustices, corrections 267
colonialism: British colonialism, histories 293; complexity 283; historical effects, erasure 6; histories, thinking approaches 9; history 275, 281; impact 135; legacies 47; ravages 274; shared history 208; South Africa 274; white people, power 114
coloniality 40; biomedical coloniality 136; dimensions, differences 196; entanglements, exposure 266; placement 197; South Africa history 282; understanding 266; undoing 126
coloniality of gender 189
coloniality of knowledge 7, 125, 129, 199
coloniality of power 208
coloured women, life dissatisfaction 280–1
colourism, gendered regimes 208
Commission Gender Equality 276
communication, possibility 88
community (communities): construction 53; finding 294; loss 78–9; members, concerns (Accra) 74
Company's Garden 196–7
Concise Chinese-English Dictionary for Lovers, A (Xiaolu) 122, 146, 149, 151

condom, usage 54
consciousness: mode, tearing 134–5; preservation 145; shift 105–6
consent, idea 187
Constitution of South Africa, impact 278
constraining normativities, analysis 50–1
contemporaneity 246–7
contextualization 189
contextual positionalities 248
continental ontology, immobilizing locality 136
contours, loss 97
core affect 92
corpo-affectivity 107
corpopolitical contexts 7
corpopolitics of being 132–3
corpopolitics of knowledge 132–3
co-teacher experience 80
co-temporality 247
COVID-19 pandemic: impact 107, 139–40, 254–5, 291, 295; uncertainty, sense 3; vaccinations, prices (differences) 239
co-writing/co-publishing 123
co-writing process, meaning 166
creative imagination exercise 79
creative practices 164; importance 162
creative writing: ethico-political opening 166–9; formats 18; methodologies 82; methods 87; modalities 77; practices 162–6; usage 28; workshops 13, 20, 30
Crenshaw, Kimberlé 10, 275, 280
Critical Transnational Feminist Praxis (Lock Swarr/Nagar) 11
cultural ensemble, individual version 151
cultural identity concept 187
cultural standing 72
cultural traditions, intergenerational transmitters 221
culture: arrangements, changes 72; emotions, relationship 62
Cuvier, Georges 47

dance, impact 79
Dancing on Our Turtle's Back (Simpson) 135
data-driven method, birth 236
"Deal of the Century" 204
decolonial analysis 11
decolonial analytical tool 129–31
decolonial corpopolitics 132–3

306 *Index*

decolonial feminisms 2; Black feminism, difference 116; focus 31; materialization, absence 4; pluriversal conversations 6–8; transversal transnational decolonial feminism, gender/sexual justice scholarship (reconceptualization) 265–8
decolonial feminist lens, usage 181
decolonial groups, stories 83
decolonial hermeneutics 127–9
decolonial intersectional feminist approach, articulation 50–1
decolonial intersectional feminist engagement 46
decoloniality 10–12, 17; conceptual framework 14; discussion 199; focus 177; grounding 127; heteronormative male versions, internal critique 126; impact 133; opening 27; pluriversal context 115; writing 38
decolonial love, hermeneutics (preparation) 131
decolonial methodological imperatives 67–9
decolonial methodologies, possibility 125
decolonial perspectives 103, 115–16
decolonial pluritopic hermeneutics 129
decolonial pluriversality 133
decolonial queer feminism 129–30
decolonial strategies 115
decolonial thinking, examples 130–1
decolonisation, struggle 181
decolonization 287; academy, relationship 290–1; impossibility 11; movement 293; occurrence 16; pluriversal activity, relationship 11
de-colonization movement critique 266
Decolonize the University 294, 298; response (My Manifesto) 291
Decolonizing Methodologies (Tuhiwai Smith) 13
deconstruction, vulnerability (impact) 74
deep coalitions 126; formation 200
deeply entrenched postcolonial violence 194–5
defamiliarization 14, 127
defamiliarizing: move 126–7; tool 134
Deleuze Dictionary, The (Stagoll) 95
Deleuze, Gilles 30, 90; philosophy 91
Delhi rape case (2012) 296
delinking position (Mignolo) 129–30

Derrida, Jacques 127
de Silva, Ferreira 198
deterritorialization 99; becoming-imperceptible, relationship 95
developed/developing countries: dichotomies 233–5; dichotomy/ahistorical conception 9; distinctions, profit-driven drug development (impact) 238
developed economies, country classifications 235
Dhaka University, Birdem General Hospital (collaboration) 237
dialectical method 128–9
dialogical dialogue 128
dialogic critiques, production 12
dialogue: praxis 129; translation, relationship 287, 296–9
diasporic media 225
diasporic trickster identifications 134
diatopical hermeneutics 128–30
"dictionary," symbolic role 148
différance, notion (Derrida) 127
differentiation, axes 30
digital images, intermediacy 144
dis/ability, socio-cultural categorisation 50–1
disciplines: critique 131–2; remaking 131–2
discomfort, pedagogies 83
discourses, logic 100–1
disease: avoidance 240; prevention, molecular-level information (impact) 240–1
disidentification, border thinking (relationship) 144
dismembered effect 220
diversity: disruption 223–5; ethnocultural diversity 217; global diversity rhetoric, unpacking 217–20; rhetoric 215
Doležel, Lubomir 145, 150
domestic worker leader, diary extract 64–5
domestic workers, mistreatment 65–6
double consciousness 134
downward mobility 225
dreamspaces, knowledge (derivation) 168
drug addicts, collective removal 253
duboisean double consciousness 134

early-life interventions, focus 241–2
East/West, dichotomy/ahistorical conception 9

Index 307

economics, biobanks (relationship) 236–8
Eco, Umberto 148
education level 72
ego-politics 141
embarrassment, feelings 65–6
embeddedness 91–4
embedded subjectivity/identity 91
embodied collective action, affect/intimacy 184–5
embodied logos, presence/self-evidence 127
embodied subjectivity/identity 91
embodiment 91–4
emergent methodologies 12–18, 20, 27
emotional bonds: acknowledgement, absence 63–4; recognition 66
emotional journeys, acknowledgment 68
emotional knowledge 67–8
emotional reactions, verbal acknowledgment 68
emotional status, scanning 80
emotional vulnerability 73
emotions: accounting, impact 66–7; basis 92; discourse, relationship 61–2; eruption 84–5; evocation 67–8; habitual processes, challenges 151; multiple emotions 27; reified objects, relationship 62; revisiting 29, 60; shutdown 65
empathy, imperialistic possibility 68
employer, complaints/problems 64
empowerment, idea 187
enclosure, mechanism 184
end-state, approach 96
English language, semiotic channel (equivalence) 150
Ensayos, usage 164
EOB see Ethnic Origins of Beauty
epistemes: alter-epistemes, shaping 14; visibility 7
epistemic togetherness 121, 125
epistemological borders, multiplicity 122–3
epistemology (epistemologies): change, request 141; production 90
equitable healthcare 176; generation 234; precision drugs, connection 238–40; support 242
Esbell, Jaider 197
ethico-political opening 166–9
ethics: creation 166; myriad tongues/ multiple emotions 20, 27
ethnic hierarchies, identification 175

ethnicity (ethnicities): representation 222–3; socio-cultural categorisation 50–1
ethnicized visions 215
Ethnic Origins of Beauty, The (EOB) (multimedia project) 175, 215; art collage 220; description 217; diversity 223–4; ethnic symbolization 221–3; gender, examination 221–3; global diversity rhetoric, unpacking 217–20; mosaic 218; politicization 223
ethnic Russianness 216, 223
ethnic Russians, state-forming people 227
ethnic symbolism 221
ethnic symbolization 221–3
ethnocentrism 248
ethnocultural diversity 217
ethno-physiological features 219–20
eudaimonic happiness 275–6
Eurocentric positionality 133
Euromodern sameness 121–2, 125
Europe: geopolitical bordering, consequences 252–3; Imperialist Capitalist Colonial relations 110
European modernity, displacement 141
European Union (EU), medicine (big-data approaches) 233
event, participant/co-owner (experience) 63
executive attention 93
existential waiting 254–5
experiences: differences, perspective 288–9; logic 100–1
experiential reality, reflection 145
expert knowledge, reliance 219
exteriority, epistemology 141
external matter: impact 97; interactions 93–4; logic 100–1
external sensations 92
extinction, Selk'nam history (anthropological canon) 159–60

fabulation 169
facilitator-led writing workshops 87
Faiz, Faiz Ahmed 292
FAKA 266
"family of nations" 215
family tradition, opposition 149
farming narrative 181
feeling/sensing/thinking transnationalism, opening 27
#FeesMustFall 287, 289

308　*Index*

FEMEN 188
feminism 140–4; African feminism
　　105–7; decolonial feminisms,
　　pluriversal conversations 6–8;
　　decolonial feminist lens, usage
　　181; decolonial queer feminism
　　129–30; Indigenous feminism,
　　hybridic cultural formations
　　143; intersectional feminisms
　　6–8; knowledge/political project
　　intersection 187; locational
　　feminism, constitutive components
　　143; mother, relationship 116;
　　transnational feminisms 1, 6–9,
　　11–12; transversal transnational
　　decolonial feminism, gender/
　　sexual justice scholarship
　　(reconceptualization) 265–8;
　　understanding, origins/locations
　　(impact) 142–3; *see also* Black
　　feminism (Black Feminism);
　　postsocialist feminisms
feminism in the singular, reinstitution 142
feminist: anti-racist feminist activist,
　　becoming 109–11; becoming,
　　grandmother (impact) 103–5
feminist activism, struggle 186
feminist border thinking 122, 141–2, 150
feminist convictions 77
feminist ethnographic analysis, temporal
　　awareness (approach) 255–6
feminist ethnographic research 255–6;
　　chronopolitics, involvement 176;
　　chronopolitics/temporal awareness,
　　meanings 246; multi-sited queer
　　feminist ethnographic research
　　72; othering, spatial/temporal co-
　　ordinates (entanglement) 247–8
feminist interviewing techniques 277
feminist killjoy, impact 282–3
feminist knowledge: production 141–2;
　　transnational feminist knowledge,
　　territoriality/gatekeeping (rota) 195
feminist movements: gentrification, danger
　　187–90; perception 104
feminist praxis, global contexts 200
feminist qualitative methods 278
feminist research, experience (focus) 78
feminist scholars, network (creation) 86–7
feminist stages, decolonial examination 196
Feminist Studies, question 297
feminist utopia 144–6
Ferguson, Jennifer 182

fictional text: impact 148–9; ontological
　　sovereignty, violation 150–1;
　　world-constructing text,
　　equivalence 145–6
fictional worlds, ontological sovereignty
　　145
fiction/non-fiction/theory, merger 86–7
field diary: entry, police encounter
　　remembrance 63; migrant workers,
　　interviews 65; notes 29, 60; revisit
　　62–7; slavery notes 64–5
Finland: biobank infrastructures 237;
　　biobanking activities 238;
　　biobanks, public ownership
　　237–8; capitalist biopolitics 178;
　　healthcare 238; personalized
　　medicine 175–6, 236
first/third world, dichotomy/ahistorical
　　conception 9
Floyd, George (murder) aftermath 291–3
fourth wall, destruction 126–7
framing, writing (relationship) 85–6
freedom, theft 64–5
Friedman, Susan 143
friendship, birth 160–1
friendship group, joining 74
functional equivalence (homology) 130–1
future concerns, creation (question) 254–5

Gadamer, Hans-George 127
Ganguly, Debjani 144–5, 148
gender: binarism, preservation 263;
　　binarisms, reiteration 263;
　　coloniality 189; consciousness
　　41–3, 45; equity 142–3;
　　examination 221–3; (in)equality,
　　consideration 275; intersections
　　279; justice, ensuring 281; justice
　　scholarship, reconceptualization
　　265–8; Middle East studies,
　　understanding 203–6; oppression
　　103; pondering 97; references
　　149; relations, analysis 211–12;
　　scholarship, epistemic violence
　　265; self-definition 181; social
　　categorizations, study/interplay
　　282; socio-cultural categorisation
　　50–1
gender-based violence (GBV) 176,
　　259–60; feminist analytical work,
　　perspective 195
gender-based violence (South Africa) 47
gendered power relations 104

Index 309

gendered violence, experiences (shaping) 188
gender equality 274; marketization 183
gender nonconforming subjects, harassment 185
gender non-normativity: acceptance 205; story, emergence 211
gender normativity: governmentality, impact 263; navigation 204
Gender Studies: Centres, project emergence 13
Gender Studies, field-defining 10
genocide 196
genomic risk information, usage 241
genotypes, characterisation 233
gentrification of feminist movements, danger 187–90
geography of reason 13; shift 141; Western geography of reason, perspective shift 13–14
geography of reasoning 125; shift 132–3
geopolitical bordering 252–3
geopolitical dichotomies 242
geopolitical knowledge, building/re-reifying 260–1
geopolitical locations 99, 278; meaning 256; reflections 89; stress 92
geopolitical positioning 82
geopolitical situatedness, epistemic implications 21, 173–8
geopolitics: entanglement 246
geopolitics of being 132–3
geopolitics of knowledge 106, 132–3
geopolitics of reason 106
geopolitics of situated knowledge production, scrutiny 173
geopolitics of war/violence 144
Ghana: queer stories 73–4; queer women, relationship (experience) 75–6; "We Are Scared," Vimeo posting 73
global assemblage: aim 235; theory 236
global capitalism 255
global diversity rhetoric, unpacking 217–20
Global East-Global West Axes 30
global forms, self-assimilation 235
Global Fund watchdog 73
globalization, processes 72
Global North: decentring, regionalism (impact) 175; privileges 262; women, sexual violence stories 185
Global North/Global South: axes, usage 5, 30; change communities/coalitions 136; dichotomy/ahistorical conception 9
global othering ends, research findings 264–5
Global South: Global North, dialogue formulation 194–5; localized struggles 290
Global Southern contexts, sexualities (surveillance) 261
global surveillance 261
GLQ: A Journal of Lesbian and Gay Studies 8
"God-Trick" 6
"going national," absence 6
goodbye ceremony, heart-shaped leaf (usage) 35–6
Gordon, Lewis 131–2
Grandmother, The 33–4
great Russian chauvinism 215–16
Great Zimbabwe, African woman (ascendence) 266
Grewal, Inderpal 9
Grosz, Elizabeth 96
groupism 221
Guattari, Felix 30, 90; philosophy 91
Guo, Xiaolu 122, 146
Gusinde, Martin 170

happiness: conceptualizations 275–9; conceptualizations, inter-connectedness 278; eudaimonic happiness 275–6; hedonic happiness 275–6; intersections 279; meaning 277; methodologies/methods/location 281–3; parameter, importance 177; race/class, intersection 279; scholarly definition 278; study, theoretical/methodological considerations 274
happiness-as-life-satisfaction 279–81
Happiness Studies 282
harassment: facing 185; sexual harassment, legal definition 187
Haraway, Donna 6, 89
hard borders, return 140
Harney, Stephano 294
Hartman, Saidiya 169
hashtag activism 184
hashtag narratives 186
health: care, democratization 234; optimization 232; public health, biovalue (relationship) 236–8; responsibilities, narration 240–2; social determinants 241

310 *Index*

healthcare: equitable healthcare, precision drugs (connection) 238–40; preventative healthcare, social inequalities (connection) 240–2
heartbreak stories, sharing 75
hedonic happiness 275–6
hegemonic contemporaneity, construction (question) 247
hegemonic epistemic violence, challenge 266–7
hegemonic heterosexual nuclear family, importance 263–4
hegemonic language politics, identification 175
hegemonic power structures, overlap 12
hegemonic rape narratives, power 55–6
Heidegger, Martin 141
HELEM 210–11
Helman, Rebecca 15, 46
hemispherical policy, translocal dimension 199
"heritage of mankind," contribution 217
hermeneutical privilege 129
hermeneutical procedures, complication 129
hermeneutics 127; borderland hermeneutics 130; decolonial hermeneutics 127–9; decolonial love, hermeneutics (preparation) 131; decolonial pluritopic hermeneutics 129; diatopical hermeneutics 129–30; multispatial hermeneutics 127; pluritopical hermeneutics, ethical dimension 129; pluriversal hermeneutics 7, 14
hermeneutics of love, understanding 131
heterogenous contexts/objects, coding 235
heteronormative discourse/practices 263–4
heteronormative injustices, corrections 267
heteronormative moralities, reproduction 262–5
heteronormativity: binarism, preservation 263; exportation 261; importance 263–4; online/public transgressions, generation 266–7; perpetuation 204; reproduction 185
hierarchies, question (posing) 87
hierarchization 203
High Income Countries (HICs), dichotomies 234–5
Hignonet, Margaret R. 141
Hill Collins, Patricia 275, 280
Hindutva violence, discussion 294

historico-temporal totality 255
history, self-evident peak 7
HIV: intersectional gendered dynamic 262–3; mass educational campaign 264; perspective 260; prevention 111; public education billboard (South Africa) *264*; reproductive health research/global emphases 176–7
homeomorphic equivalence 128–9
homonormativity, perpetuation 204
homophobic discourse/practices 263–4
homophobic violence 261
Hong Kong, occupation (discussion) 294
hooks, bell 16, 113, 275, 280
"Hot Moments in Teaching and Learning" 83
household chores, problems 64
hubris of zero point 133
human biospecimens, presence 236
humankind, ethno-diversity (representation) 222
human rights (HR), discourse 206
humiliation, feelings 65–6
Hussen, Tigist Shewarega 173, 181, 197
hybrid positionalities 248
hyperconnectivity 144

ideas, transnational travel 203
identity 89; concept, problematization 91; marker 208
idioculture, concept (Attridge) 151–2
immigrants-turned-colonisers 198
imperceptibility 95–6; impact 97–8; lived imperceptibility 96–8; lived imperceptibility, research (relationship) 98–9
imperialism: capitalist imperialism, shared history 208; de-colonization movement 266; historical effects, erasure 6; power relations 62; reaffirmation 205
Imperialist Capitalist Colonial relations 110
in-between space 143
Indian women, life dissatisfaction 280–1
India, student movements/social movements convergence 295–6
indigenization policies 215
indigenous-centred alter-methodologies 14
indigenous-centred feminist methodologies 122
indigenous-centred methodologies 122; conversation 155

Index 311

Indigenous cultural issues 156
Indigenous feminism, hybridic cultural
formations 143
Indigenous feminisms, issue 19
Indigenous methodologies, perception 166
individual, creative avenues (opening) 79
information: bidirectional mediation,
allowance 149; usage 165
information technology, hyperconnectivity
144
injury, descriptions 186–7
inquiry, decolonial mode ("*La Facultad*")
133–5
interceptibility: concepts 90–1; logics 95;
subjectivity, relationship 91
interconnections, living nexus replacement
95
inter-ethnic cohesion, facilitation 217
internal/external sensations, logic 100–1
internal sensations 92
International Consortium of Personalized
Medicine 234
international movements, localization 189
inter-regional power dynamics 210
inter-relational knowledge 207
intersectional(ity) (intersectionality) 10–11,
14, 132–3; Black woman (death)
33; conversation, continuation
17; development/description
50–1; enunciator, identification
133; extended understandings
266; featuring 190–1; idea 187;
incorporation 173–4; opening 27;
term, usage 275; understanding 266
intersectional approach (blackness) 181
intersectional feminisms 10, 21, 196;
pluriversal conversations 6–8;
transnational intersectional feminist
research 89, 99–101
intersectional feminist approach, absence
185
intersectional feminist engagement 29, 46
intersectional gender binarism, perspective
262
intersectional groups, stories 83
intersectional inequalities/violences,
attention 266
intersections 10, 279; configuration 255;
consequence 27–8; discursive
intersections 136; examination
177; feminisms, intersections 173;
foregrounding 275; gendered/
sexualized/classed intersections

51; sex/power 188; social marker/
happiness, intersections 279–80
inter-subjective relations 132
inter-subjectivity 249
interviews: annoyance 68–9; questions,
participant emotions/feelings
(incorporation) 68
intimacy, absence 147
intimate relationships, entanglement 44
intrepid journeys 21, 173–8
introspective access, gaining (impossibility)
98–9
invading foreign other, impact 209
inventive writing, act 151
irregularized migrants 176, 178, 250;
civil society organization
support 253–4; lived experience,
ethnographies (usage) 248–9;
long-term ethnographic fieldwork
247–8; migration control 252;
positioning, focus 248; research
247; tax cards, issuance 250
Ivanova, Natalia 216, 222
"I Will Meet You at Twilight" 30, 89, 101

Jacobsen, Christine M. 176, 246; field
notes, usage 251–2
Jawaharlal, Nehru University (JNU),
impact 290–1
Jordaan, Danny 182
Jordan, June 28
Joy of Reading, The 86
Just, Edyta 89
justice-to-come, commitment 122–3

Kant, Immanuel 131–2
Kaplan, Caren 9
KardioKompassi (programme) 241
Karlsen, Marry-Anne 176, 246; fieldnotes,
usage 249–51
Karokynká (Tierra del Fuego) 155
Kaupapa research 135
Kawesa, Victoria 19, 103; father, political
murder 107–8
Khoisan people, presence 162
Khosravi, Shahram 248
Kirori Mal College 292; The Players 288
knowing, indigenous decolonial methods
135–6
knowledge: ancestral knowledges 162–6;
body politics 106; coloniality 7,
125, 129, 199; combination 90;
corpopolitics 132–3; geopolitics

312   *Index*

106, 132–3; material knowledge 163; principles, border thinking (relationship) 141; project, political project (intersection) 187; theo-politics/ego-politics 141; transnational feminist knowledge, territoriality/gatekeeping (rota) 195
knowledge-generation mechanism 134–5
knowledge-making, colonial logics (repetition) 183
knowledge-shaping process 121
Koobak, Redi 1, 27, 41, 77, 103, 121, 141, 177, 287; workshop 13
Koshy, Ninan 208
kuir 198
kuir/queerness 198

"La Facultad" (decolonial mode of inquiry/re-existence route) 133–5
language: preservation, concern 228; shared histories 208
lead meditation, usage (proposal) 80
Lebanon, anti-homosexuality 210–11
legal residence, absence 250
legitimate rage 54
LGBT activism story (re-writing), regional lens (usage) 210–11
LGBT organizations, creation 210
LGBT rights 175, 210
Liberty Square, blood (presence) 33
life: as-a-whole, enjoyment 276; dissatisfaction 280–1; embryonic stages, environmental influences 242; evaluation 276; experiences, sharing 68; interconnectedness/reciprocity 106; satisfaction 280; theft 64–5; "Western" life, replicas 148
literary transduction: argument 122–3; concept 140, 146; feminist tool 139
literary translation 146
literary workshops, participation 164
literature, power 144–6
lived experience, ethnographies 248–9
lived imperceptibility 96–8; research, relationship 98–9
local activism, erasure 190
local feminist praxis, necessity 200
localized knowledges, centring 188
locational feminism: accounting 122; concept 142; constitutive components 143; term, introduction 142; transduction, relationship 146

locational, understanding 143
location-in-movement 141
location, politics 5–6, 187
Lock Swarr, Amanda 11
Lorde, Audre 125, 275, 292, 296
Los atravesados 134
love: decolonial analytical tool 129–31; decolonial love, hermeneutics (preparation) 131; hermeneutics, understanding 131
love letters, writing 155
lower-class white women, life satisfaction 281
Low-to-Middle Income (LMIC): focus 232–4; personalized medicine, discussion 242
Lugones, Maria 125
Lukić, Jasmina 139
Lukose, Ritty 187
Lykke, Nina 1, 19, 77, 121–2, 155, 173, 177, 287

macro-level tools 126
Madre Tierra (Molina) 164
Makarem, Ghassan 210
Manifesto, The 290–2
manliness, nature 222
Mannan, M.A. 239
"Man, the One God" 6
Marambio, Camila 122, 155
marginalities, recognition 194–5
Marseille, queueing 251–2
masculinist dominance 185
Massad, Joseph 210
mastery, dismantling 126
Matchett, Sara 299
material borders, multiplicity 122–3
material concreteness 167
material coordinates 145
materialist subjectivities, connections 99–100
material knowledge 163
matter 91–4
McKittrick, Katherine 12
Mcwatts, Susheela 15, 60
meaning-making processes 90–4; connections 99–100; logic 94, 100–1; probabilities 94; result, logic 100
mechanistic science, secular worldview 167
medication, coverage 239
medicine *see* personalized medicine
memories, logic 100–1

Mennesker i Limbo (People in Limbo), meeting 250
mental activity 91–4; connections 99–100; logic 94
mental health, self-definition 181
Mernissi, Fatema 88
method-centrism, questioning 131–2
methodological considerations 121–3
methodological nationalism 7; counteracting 121; disruption 20; humanities/social sciences, embedding 12; transcendence 9; transgressing 18, 196; traps 5–6
methodology (methodologies) 20; alter-methodologies 14; consideration 121–3; decolonial methodologies, possibility 125; defamiliarizing move 126–7; indigenous-centred methodologies, conversation 155; research methodologies, decolonising 65; *see also* autophenomenography; border thinking; emergent methodologies; feminist ethnographic research; postdisciplinary methodologies; postqualitative methodologies; qualitative methodologies; quantitative research; transduction; vulnerability as method
Methodology of the Oppressed (Sandoval) 13, 130–1
#MeToo 173, 287, 296; decolonial feminist lens, usage 181; displacements 178; impact 186; legitimization 189; protests 188; sexual gendered violence understanding 185; voice narratives, proximity 187; white cis-women, involvement 186
#MeTooEthiopia 189
#MeTooKenya 189
#MeToo moment: building 183–7; transition 188; virality 183
#MeTooSouthAfrica 189
#MeTooSudan 189
#MeTooUganda 189
micro-level tools 126
micropolitics (temporal coordination) 247, 252–4
Middle East 8, 174, 203; name, usage 208
Middle East Area Studies 204
Middle Eastern Sexuality Studies 204
Middle East (West Asia) sexuality (theorizing), regional/relational lens (usage) 203

Middle East Studies: gender, understanding 203–6; nomenclature, problem 207–8; sexuality studies, understanding 203–6
middle-passage epistemologies 31
Mignolo, Walter 7, 141; knowledge, geopolitics/body politics 106–7
migrant/citizen (difference reinforcement), chronopolitics (impact) 255
migrant domestic worker leader, diary extract 65
migrant workers, interviews 65
migration: consequences 248; control 252
Milano, Alyssa 183–4, 290
Million Ways To Die, A (symposium) 35
Miss Universe, Russia (representation) 226
Mitchell, Robert 238
mobilization, conception 200
modernity: temporality 255; undoing 126; Western hegemonic discourse 106–7; Western invention, entanglement (border positioning) 134
Mohamed, Kharnita 1, 27, 37, 77, 122, 155, 173, 275; workshop 13
Mohanty, Chandra 175–6, 275
Mohanty, Chandra Talpade 289
molecular-level information, impact 240–1
Molina Vargas, Hema'ny 122, 155–6; writing, observation 159
monolingual language ideology (Russia) 227
Moraga, Cherry 12
moral indignation, fuel 131
moralities, reproduction 262–5
morning after pill, offering 54
mosaics, usage 217
Motala, Mohamed 66
Moten, Fred 294
Mothadi, Lawen 111
motherhood: alternative motherhood practices 206; entanglement 44
Mother Tongue Project, The 299
mother tongue, socio-cultural categorisation 50–1
mourning, politics 166
Mrs Dalloway (Woolf) 95–7, 289
Mrwetyana, Uyinene (rape/murder) 53
Msezane, Sithembile 265–6
multimedia project, post-Soviet hegemonies (nesting) 215
multimodal information, usage 93
multiple emotions 27
multi-sited queer feminist ethnographic research 72

314 Index

multispatial hermeneutics 127
Musée de L'Homme: Bester sculpture, exhibit 49; exhibit, Qureshi analysis 47–8
Muslim, citizens, criminalization 295
mutual learning practices 188
Muzaffarnagar Baaqi Hai (movie) 290
muzungu zungu 114

Nagar, Richa 11
Naidoo, Pralini 1, 20–1
#NakedProtest 182, 188
narrative: emotions, evocation 67–8; wounds, opening 63–4
National Citizen Register 295
national identity, recognition/ reinforcement 143
nationalism, power relations 62
nationality, socio-cultural categorisation 50–1
national ontology, immobilizing locality 136
nation-state, space 248
nativism 248
"natural beauty" requirement 218–29
nature-cultural subjectivity 94; connections 99–100
navel-gazing 12
neoliberal academia: adjustment 254; change, trickster tools (usage) 4
neoliberal academic notions 86–7
neoliberalism, temporality 255
neuroscience 90
"New Tools in Transnational Feminisms" (working title) 2–4, 17
Nomvula, interview 54
non-exclusive duality 134
non-governmental organizations (NGOs), relationship (unease) 29
non-hierarchical im-parative approaches, usage 128–9
non-homogenous semi-alterity 228
non-normativity, conceptions (impact) 210
non-representational transnational intersectional feminist research praxis 260
non-Russian languages: second-rate status 227
non-Russian languages, Russian language hegemony 225
NORA (journal) 194
NORA conference 195
normativity, conceptions (connections) 210

(non-)normativity, (re)defining 211
Northern heteronormativity/ homonormativity, perpetuation 204
Northern innocence 260–2
North/South: dichotomies 235; term, usage 235
Notes Toward a Politics of Location (Rich) 5
novel, genre 144–5
novelistic genre, introduction 144

object hierarchy, decoloniality (impact) 133
objective truth 52
objectivity, illusion 48
obruni 72; feeling 74
Obuntu Bulamu 104–8; practice 31, 105; teaching 108; *see also* Ubuntu
Offensiv (Marxist group) 110
Olivares Molina, Fernanda 155
oneness 255
One-Third/Two-Thirds Worlds 175, 235
online activism 173, 181, 190
online classroom, writing exercises 79
onto-episteic changes 27
ontological sovereignty, violation 150–1
ontologies 166–9
open categories 141–2
open-ended interview format, usage 278
operational biobanks, presence 237
oppression: Global North/South perspective 110; impact 181; resistance 104; structural dimensions, awareness 110; systems, feminist/queer understanding 181
oppressive barriers 105
Oslo Central Station, drug addicts (removal) 253
Oslo, tramspotting 249–51
othering: ends, research findings 264–5; patriarchy 261
otherness, production 151
others: subjugation/marginalization 262; well-being 277
"Other, The" stories, #MeToo moments (building) 183–7
out-of-pocket costs, increase 240

P4 *see* predictive, preventive, personalized and participatory
pain: descriptions 186–7; expression 163
pan-Arabist rhetoric 209
Panikkar, Raimundo 127–9
paranoid reading, privilege 267

Patel, Nigel 266
patriarchal injustices, corrections 267
patriarchy: de-colonization movement 266;
exportation 261; outsourcing 261
patronage 260–2
Pavel, Thomas 145
peacekeeping, facilitation 217
pedagogical psychology, impact 80–1
pedagogy 28; embodied pedagogy 30;
importance 292; normative
practices 267–8; style, difference
289; thoughts/reflection 77–8, 87;
transnational commitments 177
peer-to-peer learning 82
Performance Studies 177–8, 287, 292;
decentring 290–1; department,
establishment 290; methods/
concepts, offering 289
performance, transnational feminism
(relationship) 287–90
performative-activism, usage 267
personal identification, roots 226
personalized guidelines, molecular-level
information (impact) 240–1
personalized medicine 175–6; biobanks,
importance 237; cost-effectiveness
logic 241; future 242; global
approach, implementation
(possibilities) 233–4; healthcare,
democratization (arguments) 240;
impact 238; initiatives 240–1;
outcomes 236; studies 242;
transnational approach, formation
233–6; transnational feminist
engagement 232
personal stories, sharing 68–9
perspectives, shift 81
phenotypes, characterisation 233
photogenic beauty 217
physical closeness/touch, overload 80
physical environment, brain/body
embeddedness 92
physical simultaneity 246–7
physical status, scanning 80
Pierre, Jemima 72
Players, The (Kirori Mal College) 288
pluritopical hermeneutics, ethical
dimension 129
pluriversal, access depiction 299
pluriversal activity 177; decolonization,
relationship 11
pluriversal approaches 18, 122; relearning
11

pluriversal categories 141–2
pluriversal concept 106
pluriversal context 115
pluriversal conversations 1, 6–8, 14, 27,
196, 287
pluriversal critique 133
pluriversal dialogues 178
pluriversal hermeneutics 7, 14
pluriversality 115; author composition,
characterization 18–19; call
141; commitment 77; concept 7;
connection 106–7; critique 133;
decolonial attempt 132; decolonial
pluriversality 133; discussion 106;
implications 173
pluriversal landscapes 2
pluriversal research, unfolding 12–13
pluriversal, term (usage) 6–7
pluriverse, notions 7
poetic co-writing 123, 155
poetry, work (display) 165
point-to-point connections 96
police, encounter/fear 62–3
political action, materiality 184
political organizing, conception 200
political recognition, economies 187
political responsibility 131
political subjectivity 184–5
political technology 131
politics: austerity politics, effects 45;
chronopolitics 246, 248–50;
micropolitics (temporal
coordination) 247; sexual politics,
analysis 211–12; time, politics 246;
transversal politics 296–9
politics of location 5–6, 187
portals of possibility 121
positionality 253–4; sharing 68
possible worlds 144–6
post-Apartheid period, sexual practices
(research) 176
post-Apartheid South Africa 275–83;
context 259; displacements 178;
happiness study 177; happiness
study, theoretical/methodological
considerations 274; happiness
study, theoretical/methodological
considerations, theoretical framing
274–5; living, contradictions 155
postcolonial areas, sexuality/Queer Theory
(concept imposition) 203
postcolonial engagement, performance
194–5

316 *Index*

postcolonial feminist framework 275
postcolonial methodological imperatives
  67–9
postcolonial South Africa, happiness
  study (theoretical/methodological
  considerations) 274; theoretical
  framing 275–6
postcolonial violence 194–5
postdisciplinarity 12–18; radical
  postdisciplinarity 13
postdisciplinary methdologies 12–18
postqualitative methodologies 14, 17
post-rape 53
postsocialist difference 175
postsocialist feminisms 216
postsocialist studies 8
post-Soviet hegemonies, nesting 215
post-study reflexivity 61–2
potentiality 151
power: affect, generative power 27;
  arrangements, changes 72;
  asymmetries 135; coloniality
  208; differentials, analysis 50–1;
  dynamics 86–7; embedding 182;
  gendered power relations 104;
  geographies 199; relationality 73;
  relations 89, 187; relations, impact
  94; sex, intersections 188
practices, logic 100–1
praxis, instability 12
precarity: academic precarity 39; awareness
  42; confidence 38; entanglement
  44; experiences 28, 43; modes,
  temporal specificities 255;
  pedagogies 28, 37; problem 44–5;
  scenes 28, 41; work 254
precision drugs, equitable healthcare
  (connection) 238–40
precision medicine 232
predictive, preventive, personalized and
  participatory (P4): medicine,
  impact 234; systems medicine 232
present time, sharing 247
pre-slavery, fantasy 114
pre-understanding (horizon) 128
preventative actions, description 240
preventative healthcare, social inequalities
  (connection) 240–2
prior experience, representations 92–3
privacy, idea 187
privatization, need 240
privilege 260–2; acknowledgment 68;
  impact 181

professionalism, breakdown 75
profit-driven drug development, impact 238
psychological reunification/re-
  identification, process 135–6
psychological well-being 277–8
public health: benefits, biobanks
  (connection) 238
public health, biovalue (relationship)
  236–8

qualitative methodologies 281
quantitative research, feminist scholar
  critique 279
quantitative survey data, usage 281
Qubaiova, Adriana 174, 203
Queen Mary University 291
queer archive, contributions 266
queering: reflections 175; reliance 207;
  texts/histories, experience 159
queerness 198; raced expectations 266–7
queer relationship 72–3
Queer Sexuality Studies 205
queer subjects of colour, harassment 185
Queer Theory: appearance, question
  204; application 205; concept,
  imposition 203; emanation 174;
  reductionist function 207; relevance
  174–5, 205; usefulness 205; US
  origins, divestment 204
queer vulnerability/heartbreak 74–6
queer woman, welcoming 74
queer women, relationship (experience)
  75–6
Qureshi, Sadiah 47

race: consciousness 41–3, 45; intersections
  279; socio-cultural categorisation
  50–1
raced moralities, reproduction 262–5
racial difference 208
racial hegemony, tricks 197
racialization: geopolitical bordering, impact
  252–3; identification 175
racism 107, 216; anti-racism 112–13,
  116; context 222; experiences
  31, 287; focus 116; historical
  background 111; histories 9, 29;
  impact 110, 112, 188; intersection
  51; manifestations 225; navigation
  110–11; power relations 62;
  reflections 82–3; Scandanavian
  labour market 43; service 208;
  sexualized racism, discourses 50;

Index 317

structural/institutionalized racism 111, 197; US-centred/US-based racism 112–13
racist othering ends, research findings 264–5
radical immanence 95
rage, affect 54
Rao, Maya 299
rape: collective attention/rage 54; healthcare centre visit, nurse reaction 52; hegemonic rape narratives, power 55–6; impact 52–4; logistics 55; post-rape 53; real rape, appearance (dominant narrative) 55; research, ethical complexity 51–2; writing, discomfort 47–9
#RapeMustFall 182
ratiodicea, manifestation 132
Razack, Sherene 73, 75
realities, epistemological/ontological underpinnings 68
real rape, appearance (dominant narrative) 55
reason, geography 13–14; shift 141
reasoning, geography 125; shift 132–3
recalibration, defining 252
reductionist function 207
re-existence, route (*"La Facultad"*) 133–5
refuturing 136
Rege, Sharmila 288
regionalism 206–7; impact 175; perspective 203
regional lens: LGBT activism story (re-writing), regional lens (usage) 210–11; usage 203
regional-relational analysis, usage 210
relational experiential epistemic togetherness 125
relational-experiential rationality, principle 132
relationality, materialization 87
relational lens, usage 203
relational self-construction 73–4
relational subjectivities, connections 99–100
relational temporal position 247
relationships: formation 74; in-depth commitment 161
reorientation, vulnerability (impact) 74
reparation, motives/positionalities (appreciation) 267–8
reparative reading 268; notion 260

"Report from the Bahamas 1982" (Jordan) 28
(re)positioning, plications 248
representation, crisis 11–12
Research and Indigenous Peoples (Gordon/Tlostanova) 13
researcher/researched: duality, breakdown 75–6; power, relationality 73
researcher/research subjects, differentiation axes 100
research methodologies, decolonising 65
research, normative practices 267–8
research, transnational commitments 177
resentment, display (absence) 67
residency status, precariousness 251
resistance: erasure 190; negative part 114
resistant terrain 130
"respectable femininity," ensuring 263
resurgence, process 135–6
rethinking process 167
Revista Paula 160
revolution in the classroom 292–4
#RhodesMustFall 50, 287, 289
Rich, Adrienne 5
rights, idea 187
risk factors, revealing 241
romance, concept (questioning) 149–50
Ronen, Ruth 145
Room of One's Own, A (Woolf) 288
Roots (TV series) 111
roots, closeness 225
Rose, Gillian 217
#RoyalMustFall 50
#RUReferenceList 182
Russia: mentality, difference 224; monolingual language ideology 227
Russian chauvinism 215
Russianness: de-centring 225–8; ethnicity/mentality 226; ethnic Russianness 216, 223; privileging 175; Russian nation, connection 216; whiteness, relationship 226
Rustin, Carmine 177, 274

Said, Edward 145
Sandoval, Chela 13, 114, 125
Sangin, Manizha 226
Sawhney, Nakul 289–90
Scandinavian labour market, racism 43
Scattered Hegemonies (Grewal/Kaplan) 9
schemata, order 96
Schengen agreement 252
Schengen Treaty 140

318 *Index*

Scheper-Hughes, Nancy 62
school, sexuality education 263
scientific theories, creation/testing 236
secular rationality 169
self: evanescence, point 95; habitat, fusion 95
self-confidence 165
self-conscious parallelism, presupposition 129
self-determination, encouragement 136
selfless behaviour 67
selflessness 67
self-promotion, brands (usage) 217
self-reflexive critiques, production 12
Selk'nam: ally 122, 155; ancestry 155; cause 122, 155–6, 162; culture 157–60, 166; elder, recording 158; extinction 159–60, 162; language 168–9; people 155–7, 160; philosophy 167; study 170
Selk'nam Corporation of Chile 158
semiotic channel: access 149; English language, equivalence 150; usage 146
sense, counter-universe 130
sensory input 92–3
sexism: experiences 287; history 29; impact 188; intersection 51; power relations 62
sex/power, intersections 188
Sexton, Anne (poem, usage) 84
sexual: conceptualization, difference 209–10; re-routing 203
sexual abuse/assault 186
sexual gendered violence, understanding (#MeToo promotion) 185
sexual harassment: ideas/definitions, transformation 188; legal definition 187
sexuality: concept, imposition 203; conceptualization 205; idea 187; Middle East studies, understanding 203–6; pondering 97; scholarship, epistemic violence 265; self-definition 181; socio-cultural categorisation 50–1; unidirectional travel, Massadian depiction 204–5
sexuality studies (Sexuality Studies): Queer Sexuality Studies 205; relevance 174–5; transnational Sexuality Studies 205; understanding 203–6
sexualization, explicit mention (absence) 210

sexualized racism, discourses 50
sexual justice: alternative sexual justice 259; scholarship, reconceptualization 265–8
sexual liberation, fast-track 147
sexual non-normativity: acceptance 205; navigation 204; story, emergence 211
sexual politics, analysis 211–12
sexual violence: experiences, shaping 188; exportation 261; narratives 29, 46; transnational online activism, critical reflections 181
sexual violence (South Africa) 47
sexual violence, shame (attachment) 54
sex worker, body (comparison) 149
Shaheen Bagh, criminalization 295
shapes, loss 97
shared destiny, choice 209
shared experience, perception 253
shared past, creation (question) 254–5
shared time 249; creation 252; possibility (investigation), edited fieldnote excerpts (usage) 249
sharing present time, sharing 247
Shefer, Tamara 173, 176, 181, 259
Shklovsky, Viktor 127
Simpson, Leanne Betasamosake 135–6
simultaneity 246–7
singularity 150–2, 187; existence 151; psychological effects 151
singularizing, event 151
Sister Ode (Naidoo) 1, 20
situated knowledge (knowledges) 132–3, 267; concepts 89–90; production, geopolitics (scrutiny) 173; reflection 6
situated narratives 62
slavery: history 275; narrative 64–5; pre-slavery, fantasy 114; ravages/history 274–5; Trans-Atlantic slavery, histories 297–8; trans-Atlantic slave trade, history (initiation) 114–15
SlutWalk 188
social circle, introduction 74–5
social context 90–4; importance 93
social inequalities 51; preventative healthcare, connection 240–2
social initiatives, instigation 165
social locations, existence 198–9
social movements/student movements, convergence (India) 295–6

social phenomena, analysis 207
social relationalities 166–9
societal inequalities, critique 135
socio-cultural categorisations, basis 50–1
soft socialism 139–40
solipsistic disciplines 132
soul, revitalization 107
South Africa: coloniality/apartheid, history
    282; contexts, research 259–60;
    global surveillance 260–2; HIV
    public education billboard *264*;
    post-Apartheid South Africa,
    happiness study (theoretical/
    methodological considerations)
    274; postcolonial South Africa,
    happiness study (theoretical/
    methodological considerations)
    274; postdoctoral stay, description
    289–91; "rape capital of the
    world," recognition 47; young
    people, alternative sexual justice
    engagements 259
South African Community Agency for
    Social Enquiry (CASE) study 66
South Africa, rape: academic articles,
    examination 48; research, ethical
    complexity 51–2; writing,
    discomfort 47–9
South Atlantic connections 196–7
Southern knowledge, representation 261
South-South connection 196
South-South relations 174
Soviet imperialism, spatiotemporalities 8
spaces, multiplicity 142
spatial margins 248
spatio-temporally located societal relations
    89
spirit, revitalization 107
spiritual activism 105–7; occurrence 107;
    usage 117
spiritual energies, disconnection 115
state-sponsored evolutionism 215
Stories of the Heart 60
strategic alliances, question 126
strategic gestures 99
stratum (strata) 95–8; link 96; research,
    relationship 98–9
structural/institutionalized racism 111
stuckness 84–6
student movements/social movements,
    convergence (India) 295–6
subjectivity (subjectivities) 89; affirmative
    subjectivity, empowerment

95; concept 91; contemplation
    95; definition 90; erasure 48;
    focus 90–1; living 94; political
    subjectivity 184–5; research,
    relationship 94–9
support session 84
sustainability, planetary ethics 122
sustainable healthcare systems, formation
    233
Sweden, Ugandans (arrival) 108–9
Swedish Foundation for International
    Cooperation in Research and
    Higher Education (STINT) project
    1, 19, 77; application 18–19;
    feminist perspectives, link 17;
    feminist scholars network, creation
    86–7; interest 82; international
    collaboration 30; students,
    workshop 84
Swedish white normativity 108–9
syncretic practices 143

Talpade Mohanty, Chandra 5
Tatar ethnicity 226
teaching, experience/reward 78
Temmes, Maria 175, 232
Tempest, The (Shakespeare) 134
temporal awareness: approach 255–6;
    discussion 252–4; meanings 176,
    246–9
temporal coordination, micropolitics 247,
    252–4
temporality 198; co-temporality 247;
    generalization 255; sense, creation/
    understanding 17, 189;
value-laden temporality 228
temporal othering: critique 246–7;
    ethnographic debates 176
territoriality/gatekeeping, rota 195
Thapar-Björkert, Suruchi 141
Theatre and Performance Studies,
    decentring (Manifesto) 290
theatre, transnational feminism
    (relationship) 287–90
theo-politics 141
therapeutic strategy, tailoring 233
third space 141
third world, women (heterogeneity) 275
This Bridge Called My Back (Moraga/
    Anzaldua) 18
thoughts, habitual processes (challenge)
    151
three-generations rule 220

320   *Index*

Thuthuzela Care Centre, visit (discomfort) 52
Tierra del Fuego 156; engagement 161–2; love 159; Selk'nam people 122, 155; *see also* Karokynka
Time and the Other (Fabian) 246, 254
time, politics 246
Times of Mobility (Lukić) 139
Tlostanova, Madina 7, 11, 125, 141; knowledge, geopolitics/body politics 106–7; project commitment 13
topoi (spaces/sites) 127–8
trans activism, struggle 186
Trans-Atlantic slavery, histories 297–8
trans-Atlantic slave trade, history (initiation) 114–15
trans collective (framing narrative) 181
transculturation 140, 143
transduction 150–2; concept 122, 150, 152; feminist tool 146–50; literary transduction, argument 122–3; literary transduction, concept 140, 146; literary transduction, feminist tool 139; process 150; prototype 146
transformation, occurrence 150
transformative tools, usage 144
translation: dialogue, comparison 287, 296–9; idea 297; question 299; trickster-like feminist practice 177–8
translator, role 156
translocal dimension, hemispherical policy 199199
translocal existence 222
translocalities/translocalidades 8
translocality 174, 196; analytical strategy 198–200; concept, appeal 199; conceptual field 198; cross-spatial framework 200; geopolitical tropos 198; notion 174
translocal lens 199–200
translocal South, troubles 178
translocal, term (usage) 8
trans* men/women, harassment 185
transnational activist feminism, uberization 173–4
transnational collaboration 115
transnational, concept (problems) 17
transnational digital feminist activism: featuring 190–1; uberization 186
transnational digital movements 173–4

transnational feminism (transnational feminisms) 8–10, 296–9; categories 196; concept 7, 17; defining 2; frameworks, approaches 14; imaginary 216; introduction 8–9; "New Tools in Transnational Feminisms" (working title) 2–4, 17; personalized medicine, transnational feminist engagement 232; pluriversal conversations 1, 6–8, 196; reliance 11–12; theatre/performance, relationship 287–90; theoretical framework 199; transversal transnational decolonial feminism, gender/sexual justice scholarship (reconceptualization) 265–8; writing, usage 83
transnational feminist analysis 235
transnational feminist knowledge, territoriality/gatekeeping (rota) 195
transnational feminist scholarship, politics (interrogation) 183
transnational intersectional feminist research 89, 91, 99–101
transnationalism: defining 2; opening 27
transnational literary texts, feminist interpretation 146
transnational literature 151–2
transnational online activism, critical reflections 181
transnational perspectives, COVID-19 pandemic (impact) 140
transnational project (Stint) (STINT) 1, 77; application 17–19; collaboration 30; feminist perspectives 17; feminist scholar network, creation 86–7; peer-to-peer learning 82; title, application 18; workshops 84, 87
transnational reading 139, 146–50
transnational relations, building 83
transnational research, vulnerability (method) 72
transnational scholarship, awareness 259
transnational solidarity (transnational solidarities) 178, 204, 287; argument 187
transnational studies 140–4
transnational turn 142
transnation, concept 143
transversal decolonial agendas 121–2
transversal dialogues 188
transversal politics 173, 296–9

Index 321

transversal transnational decolonial feminism, gender/sexual justice scholarship (reconceptualization) 265–8
trauma, idea 187
Truth and Method (Gadamer) 127
Tsing, Anna 72
Tucker, Heather 29, 72
Tuhiwai Smith, Linda 13, 125, 135
Tutu, Desmond 63
typological contemporaneity 246–7

uberization 173–4, 186
Ubuntu 106; concept, understanding 67; embodiment 67; practise 29, 68; relationship 31; selfless behaviour 67; *see also* Obuntu Bulamu
Ubuntu ngumtu ngabanye abantu 68
Undercommons, The (Harney/Moten) 294
universalizability 206
university, decolonization/transnational solidarities (relationship) 287
University of Cape Town 298
University of Chile, workshop event 158
University of Hyderabad 295
unnatural boundary, emotional residue 134
upper-class women: life satisfaction 280; sexual violence stories 185
US power (consolidation), area studies (intelligence-gathering force) 207–8
USSR, indigenization policies 215

value-laden temporality 228
Vemula, Rohith 285
victimization, descriptions 186–7
victims, sexual violence shame (attachment) 54
violence *see* sexual violence
viral hashtag, usage 173–4
visuality, mode (EOB production) 222
visual methodologies 217
volitional action, impact 93
vulnerability (vulnerabilities): identification 76; impact 74; prices 73; sharing 88; transnational research method 29, 72
vulnerability as method 72
Vulnerable Observer, The (Behar) 60

waiting 43; chronic waiting 254–5; existential waiting 254–5; notions 249; occurrence 253; pasts/futures,

unevenness 254–5; perception 253; prolongation 248–9; recalibration 252; situation 252; temporal architecture 253; time 253
Waiting for an Uncertain Future: The Temporalities of Irregular Migration (WAIT) 247–9
waiting together, ethnographic examples 252
Waldby, Catherine 238
Walk: South Africa (project) 299
war, geopolitics 144
War on Terror (US) 207–8
"We Are Scared" (queer stories) 73–4
Weinstein, Harvey 183–4
well-being 277
wellness: holistic approach 232; optimization 240
West Asia 174–5, 203; gender relations, analysis 211–12; LGBT organizations, creation 210; politics 203, 211; Queer politics 178; Queer Sexuality Studies 205; renaming 207–8; sexual politics, analysis 211–12; unfamiliarity/interruption 208; US interventions 209
Western-centric God tricks 12
Western heteronormativity/ homonormativity, perpetuation 204
"Western" life, replicas 148
Western/non-Western, term (usage) 235
Western/Northern feminism, hegemonic power (destabilization) 189
Western universalisms, unlearning 11
whanau (methodological tool) 135
WhatsApp message 157
white American obruni, relations 72
white colonization 114–15
whiteness 219; barrier 112; encounter 108–9; experience 112; fear, overcoming 112; feminist discourses, association 182; friction 29, 72; invisibility 41; location point 5; opposition 115; oppositional space 113; political focus 112; power, realization 112; privileging 175; racializations/ aspirations 216; reflections 82–3; Russianness, relationship 226; seminars 111; tricks 197; understanding 112, 226
white normativity, encounter 108
white (obruni) outsider, scepticism 73

322   Index

white party, attendance 74–5
white people: comfort 112; idolization 114; power 114
white privilege 44
white spaces, comfort 112
white upper-middle-class women, life satisfaction 280
white women, sexual violence stories 185
witnessing, experience 63
women: heterogeneity 275; positionalities, complexities 279–80
women of colour activism, struggle 186
women-of-colour multi-genre texts 18
"women of colour," racialized positionalities (connection) 216
womxn: intersecting social positionings 51; shaming process 52–3
Woolf, Virginia 95, 97, 289
words, colliding (askew arrivals) 2–5
workshop *see* writing workshops
world, ethnicized vision 215
World Values Survey 279
wounds, opening 63–4
Wretched of the Earth, The (Fanon) 296
writing: academic writing, orientation 81; affect, usage 31; Black South African participants 86–7; border-crossing feminist co-writing process, materialization 156–62; care 51–2; creative writing practices 162–6; discomfort 47–9; emotional aspects 77; Ensayos, usage 164; framing, relationship 85–6; LGBT activism story (re-writing), regional lens (usage) 210–11; one-liners, usage 84;

online class exercises 79; process, reflection 85; stuckness 85–6; talent 158; thinking tool 80–1; transnational commitments 177; work, break 165
Writing Academic Texts Differently (Lykke) 82, 85
writing workshops 30; Budapest writing workshop 83–4; emphasis 78; facilitation 78; facilitator-led writing workshops 87; hierarchies 86–7; hybridity 80–1; importance 77; intensity 84; organization 13, 20, 82; participation 82; space, impact 83; student participations 82

Xaba, Wanelisa A. 27–8, 33
xenophobia, manifestations 225
xenophobic Russian nationalism, manifestations 223

Yangeldina, Dinara 175, 215
"Yhuuu *Makukhanye*! Qamata Makude kukhanye" 36
young people: alternative sexual justice engagements (South Africa) 259; sexualities (South Africa) 176–8; sexualities (South Africa), research 261–5; sexual practices, research 259, 265
youth, theft 64–5

zero point, hubris 133
Zobova, Inna (interview) 226
zones of awkward engagement 72
Zuangh Xiao Qiao 146, 149, 150

Printed in the United States
by Baker & Taylor Publisher Services